MINORITY ACCOMMODATION
THROUGH TERRITORIAL
AND NON-TERRITORIAL AUTONOMY

Minority Accommodation through Territorial and Non-territorial Autonomy

Edited by
TOVE H. MALLOY
Director, European Centre for Minority Issues, Flensburg
and
FRANCESCO PALERMO
Director, Institute for Studies on Federalism and Regionalism, EURAC, Bolzano/Bozen

OXFORD
UNIVERSITY PRESS

OXFORD
UNIVERSITY PRESS

Great Clarendon Street, Oxford, OX2 6DP,
United Kingdom

Oxford University Press is a department of the University of Oxford.
It furthers the University's objective of excellence in research, scholarship,
and education by publishing worldwide. Oxford is a registered trade mark of
Oxford University Press in the UK and in certain other countries

First Edition published in 2015
Impression: 1

Published in the United States of America by Oxford University Press
198 Madison Avenue, New York, NY 10016, United States of America

British Library Cataloguing in Publication Data
Data available

Library of Congress Control Number: 2015945726

ISBN 978–0–19–874666–9

Printed and bound by
CPI Group (UK) Ltd, Croydon, CR0 4YY

Acknowledgements

This volume is the second in a series of books constituting the output of a major programme that the European Centre for Minority Issues (ECMI) has initiated with the aim of exploring, understanding, and developing the concept of non-territorial autonomy (NTA) together with a number of partners. The series is expected to consist of five volumes that will address the status quo, the tensions within the concept, alternative approaches, theoretical and conceptual challenges, and new modes of application. The series will be elaborated from the perspectives of law and political science; it will be policy-oriented, and it will be global in scope. Authors and partners are members of the ECMI's general network, and series editor is Tove H. Malloy. The ECMI would like to thank the Board of Oxford University Press for its interest in the topic and willingness to enter into this working relationship.

This volume incorporates papers presented during a workshop organized by the European Academy, Bolzano/Bozen, Institute for Studies on Federalism and Regionalism, in cooperation with the ECMI, in Bolzano/Bozen, November 2011. Particular thanks go to the directors of the two institutions—Francesco Palermo in Bolzano/Bozen and Tove H. Malloy in Flensburg—for their generous support in securing funding for the project. The editors are also thankful to the staff of the two institutions, who have contributed to making the workshop happen.

The editors are deeply grateful to the contributors to this volume. They were very patient with us both in the search for a publisher and in the editorial process. A special thanks to Karl Kössler for providing invaluable support during the review process. We are also thankful to Oana Buta for providing editorial and copy-editing support and preparing the index, and to Paulina Borowska for assisting in preparing the front matter. At Oxford University Press, the editors would like to thank Alex Flach for his support in bringing our work to the Board of the publisher, Cathy Keable-Elliott for excellent copy editing, Keerthana Christopher for patiently guiding us through the editing process, as well as Elinor Shields and Natasha Flemming for assisting with the paperwork.

Tove H. Malloy
Series Editor
Flensburg

Contents

III. TERRITORIAL AND NON-TERRITORIAL AUTONOMY IN A GLOBAL PERSPECTIVE

Table of Cases

INTERNATIONAL COURT CASES

PCIJ

HRC

IACtHR

ECtHR

ECJ

NATIONAL COURT CASES

Bosnia and Herzegovina

Canada

Colombia

Estonia

Finland

Former Yugoslav Republic of Macedonia (FYROM)

Spain

Switzerland

Table of International Treaties

Table of Documents

OAS

UN

CSCE/OSCE

COUNCIL OF EUROPE

EC/EU

EP

List of Abbreviations

AC	Advisory Committee
CA	Constituent Assembly
CCPR	International Covenant on Civil and Political Rights
CEE	Central and Eastern Europe
CERD	Committee on the Elimination of Racial Discrimination
CoE	Council of Europe
CONAMAQ	National Council of Ayllus and Markas of Qullasuyu
CSCE	Conference for Security and Co-operation in Europe
CSUTSB	Confederación Sindical Única de Trabajadores Campesinos de Bolivia
ECtHR	European Court of Human Rights
EIA	Environmental impact assessment
EPRDF	Ethiopian People's Revolutionary Democratic Front
EU	European Union
FCNM	Framework Convention for the Protection of National Minorities
FRELIMO	Mozambique Liberation Front
FPIC	Free, prior, and informed consent of indigenous peoples
HCNM	High Commissioner on National Minorities
IOs	International organizations
IRA	The Indian Reorganization Act
JBNQA	James Bay and Northern Quebec Agreement
LTTE	Liberation Tigers of Tamil Eelam
MAS	Movement for Socialism–Political Instrument for the Sovereignty of the Peoples
MK	Mi'kmaw Kina'matnewey
NCA	National cultural autonomy
NSD	National self-determination
NTA	Non-territorial autonomy
NWFP	North-West Frontier Province
OSCE	Organization for Security and Co-operation in Europe
PGW	People's War Group
PRI	Institutional Revolutionary Party, Partido Revolucionario Institucional
ROC	Rest of the country
RSFSR	Russian Soviet Federative Socialist Republic
SWRD	Solomon West Ridgeway Dias
TA	Territorial autonomy
TANTA	Territorial autonomy and non-territorial autonomy
UDMR	Democratic Union of Hungarians in Romania
UN	United Nations
UNDRIP	UN Declaration on the Rights of Indigenous Peoples
USSR	Union of Soviet Socialist Republics
Venice Commission	Commission for Democracy through Law

List of Contributors

Bill Bowring is a Professor of Law at Birkbeck College, University of London; a Barrister in Field Court Chambers, Gray's Inn; President of the European Lawyers for Democracy and Human Rights; Founder and Chair of the European Human Rights Advocacy Centre (EHRAC).

Joshua Castellino is Professor of Law and Dean of the School of Law at Middlesex University, London, and Adjunct Professor of Law at the Irish Centre for Human Rights, Galway, Ireland. He co-chairs the Thematic Group on Gender, Social Exclusion and Human Rights within the United Nations Sustainable Development Solutions Network.

Jan Erk teaches comparative politics at the University of Leiden in the Netherlands. His work has appeared in the journals *Comparative Politics, Comparative European Politics, Comparative Political Studies, Current History, European Political Science, Political Quarterly, Publius: The Journal of Federalism, Journal of Common Market Studies, Nations and Nationalism, West European Politics, Regional and Federal Studies, Canadian Journal of Political Science, Journal of Public Policy, Journal of Democracy, Public Administration, Nationalism and Ethnic Politics*, among others. Dr Erk is the co-editor of the journal *Regional and Federal Studies*.

Karl Kössler is Senior Researcher at the Institute for Studies on Federalism and Regionalism of the European Academy of Bolzano/Bozen. After degrees in law as well as in political science and the minor subjects sociology, history, and economics, he obtained a PhD in comparative public law and political science. His research focuses on comparative federalism and regionalism, as well as fundamental rights, participatory democracy, and policymaking in multilevel systems.

Tove H. Malloy is Director of the European Centre for Minority Issues in Flensburg, Germany, and Professor at the Europa-University, Flensburg.

Ephraim Nimni is a Reader (PhD Hull) in nationalism and conflict resolution at the School of Politics, International Studies, and Philosophy at Queen's University Belfast.

Geneviève Nootens has been Professor of Political Science at the Université du Québec à Chicoutimi since 1998. Her research is mainly concerned with the redeployment of democratic practices and the diffusion of sovereignty; majority and minority nationalism; and plurinational societies.

Alexander Osipov is a Senior Research Associate of the European Centre for Minority Issues in Flensburg, Germany, and the head of ECMI's Justice and Governance Cluster.

Francesco Palermo, PhD, is Professor of Comparative Constitutional Law, University of Verona, and Director of EURAC's Institute for Studies on Federalism and Regionalism. A former Senior Legal Adviser to the OSCE HCNM, he is currently the President of the Council of Europe's Advisory Committee on the Framework Convention for the Protection of National Minorities.

David J. Smith is Professor of Baltic History and Politics and Head of the Central and East European Studies Subject Group at the School of Social and Political Sciences, University of Glasgow. During 2012–14 he was also a Visiting Researcher at the Uppsala Centre for Russian and Eurasian Studies, Uppsala University.

Dr Markku Suksi is Professor of Public Law at Åbo Akademi University, Finland.

Alexandra Xanthaki is a Reader at the Brunel Law School at Brunel University, UK, where she teaches human rights. She has written extensively on minority and indigenous rights.

Introduction

Tove H. Malloy

Autonomy as a strategy for accommodation of ethno-cultural diversity in multicultural societies has been a policy tool for over six centuries. Yet, policymakers remain uncomfortable with it, and political scientists and legal scholars continue to relegate it to the list of ad hoc solutions. The latter may be explained by the individualistic approach to democratic franchise in liberal theory. But the former is due to the hegemonic position of territory in the modern paradigm of societal organization and state construction. Territory, or the need to hold power over territory, is a main reason for interstate as well as intra-state conflicts and disputes. The spell of territory on the individual's mind brings about feelings of homeland, nation, community, belonging, etc., and with it the need to delineate boundaries and exclusive possession. But also allegiance to extra-territorial homelands has caused tension in plural societies. Here the lack of loyalty to the territory of residence seems to cause tension. Either way, many of these disagreements have been settled through autonomy arrangements. Governments have, albeit reluctantly, implemented autonomy in various forms in response to diversity and pluralism with the ultimate goal of securing social and territorial cohesion. From the early notion of the *millet* system in the Ottoman Empire to the misconstrued notion of national cultural autonomy (NCA) applied in post-Soviet states, such as Estonia and Russia, autonomy arrangements have been adopted to abate separatism and dissent. Especially during the twentieth century, numerous models of autonomy have been implemented. Although autonomy has never attained the rank of an international standard,[1] it has achieved quite a good record at the state level. This book seeks to address this paradox.

Two autonomy models have dominated the tool-kit of state construction. Territorial autonomy (TA) has been applied in multiple cases; for instance, if sub-state territories inhabited by a majority of distinct ethno-cultural characteristic had been incorporated into a neighbouring state territory after settling territorial disputes,[2] or if a serious risk of assimilation of such distinct groups was

[1] See Zelim A. Skurbaty, 'Introduction', in *Beyond a One-Dimensional State: An Emerging Right to Autonomy?*, edited by Zelim A. Skurbaty (Leiden: Martinus Nijhoff Publishers, 2005), pp. xxxi–li.

[2] The Åland Islands.

present.[3] It has also been implemented as a devolution tool in regions where local identities are distinct from the national identity and there is a desire to preserve the distinct identity.[4] Non-territorial autonomy (NTA) has also been applied after conflicts, but is seen mainly in cases where smaller ethno-cultural groups, without claims to territory and living dispersed among the majority, are at risk of assimilation, especially in the area of culture.[5] Dispersed minority groups may demonstrate allegiance to another nation and territory, including the language and culture of that nation and territory. Analytically, the two concepts are separated in the academic literature. Whereas TA is defined as a group concept and on a territorial basis, NTA is assigned to the individual based on the personality principle.[6] However, this distinction is perhaps a bit simple. Members of minorities living in sub-state autonomous territories may also experience assimilation tactics similar to members of dispersed minorities, while dispersed minorities may mobilize collectively and politically in order to achieve autonomy based on homeland arguments. Likewise, the negation of territory in NTA proves problematic precisely because minority groups may implicitly make references to territory in their cultural and linguistic identities. Finally, autonomy policies are complicated by the fact that minorities are notoriously difficult to define. Even designated beneficiaries of autonomy policies, usually specific minorities, may elude a succinct description and definition. In other words, the nexus between minority-territory-autonomy is more complex than often assumed. This leads to a muddled conceptualization of the two different but closely related concepts and eventually to bad policymaking.

1. A Complicated Nexus

The notion of a triadic nexus in minority studies is not new. But whereas the agents and the variables in Rogers Brubaker's nexus on nationalizing states and national minorities were cognitive,[7] the main variable in the understanding of our nexus is neither cognitive nor rational. While territory might be seen as a fixed or dependent variable, it also functions as 'agent'—an unpredictable one when it comes to its influence on the human mind and the formation of identity. William E. Connolly has described the function of territory as twofold.[8] On the one hand, territory, deriving from the Latin *terre*, means land, earth, soil as well

[3] Vojvodina, Serbia, and South Tyrol, Italy.

[4] Scotland and Wales, United Kingdom; Greenland and the Faroe Islands, Denmark; Corsica, France.

[5] Estonia, Hungary, Slovenia.

[6] See discussions of Karl Renner and Otto Bauer's theory of the principle in this volume by Ephraim Nimni (Chapter 3) and Jan Erk (Chapter 6).

[7] See Rogers Brubaker, *Nationalism Reframed: Nationhood and the National Question in the New Europe* (New York: Cambridge University Press, 1996).

[8] William E. Connolly, *The Ethos of Pluralism* (Minneapolis: University of Minnesota Press, 1995), p. xxii and Ch 5.

as nourishment and sustenance. The effect is that it can play a positive role in people's self-identification with belonging to a certain place. On the other hand, territory may also derive from the Latin *terrere*, which means to frighten, to terrorize, and to exclude. From *terrere* comes the notion *territorium*, which implies borders and exclusion. This puts the two in tension. While *terre* provides sustenance, *territorium* implies repression. Connolly connects these interpretations to the modern organization of territory and the state and argues that 'to occupy territory, then, is both to receive sustenance and to exercise violence. To become territorialized is to be occupied by a particular identity.'[9] And he summarizes, 'territory is sustaining land occupied and bounded by violence.'[10] On the basis of this, Connolly concludes that territorialization is part of identity, not only national identity but also religion, class, race, gender, sexuality, and other ascriptions, where one does not exclude the other—thus allowing for multiple or hybrid identities. Rejecting the traditional view of territorialization as one state—one nation, he calls for a new democratic ethos that incorporates the divisiveness of territory.

The inability to see territory in its true sense means, according to Connolly, that the modern territorial system of states and international relations is nostalgic, anachronistic, and does not reflect reality. This is because, the system actually accepts 'disalignment'[11] and 'impurities'[12] in both state and nation formation. Competing demands for nationhood within the same territory exist as well as contestations to the state's monopoly over citizens' allegiances and identifications. There is no longer one corresponding place of collective political power, and there is 'no a priori reason why deep differences with respect to…state priorities must be expressed only within the parameters of state politics'.[13] In short, the spatialization of democratic politics must be pluralized and democracy must be disaggregated. Otherwise, the territorial state will stifle democratic energies or translate them into national chauvinist sentiments. Connolly does not explicitly discuss autonomy or policymaking; his argument is theoretical. However, following his line of thought, one might see autonomy as an abnormality in state construction and international relations. To be more precise, TA would represent the 'disalignment' of the boundaries of the sovereign state, and NTA may be seen as accommodating the 'impurity' of society. As such, both may be seen as a threat to social cohesion and the unity of the state. Nevertheless, states have acknowledged and accepted, albeit under pressure, these faults. In this volume, we seek to demonstrate that the presumption of alignment and unity is a myth because autonomy is applied prolifically around the globe.

The other variable in the nexus is the ethno-cultural group, usually a minority in a non-dominant position. Again, one could argue that the variable is an 'agent' of some unpredictability. The issue of definition impacts on this variable.

[9] Connolly, *The Ethos of Pluralism*, p. xxii.
[10] Connolly, *The Ethos of Pluralism*, p. xxii.
[11] Connolly, *The Ethos of Pluralism*, p. 136.
[12] Connolly, *The Ethos of Pluralism*, p. 138.
[13] Connolly, *The Ethos of Pluralism*, p. 159.

The concept minority has defied definition both in the literature and in law for decades. This is to the consternation of many international lawyers because it is difficult to litigate on someone's behalf without knowing whom the defendant is. The UN Sub-Committee on the Prevention of Discrimination and Protection of Minorities has grappled with the issue almost since its establishment, and a number of prominent experts have been asked to seek a solution to the problem.[14] Basically, the problem of a legal definition in international law is a question of whether a universal definition of minorities can be properly articulated. Inasmuch as international law instruments must apply to a wide range of states, a definition would by necessity have to be broad and general. That is near impossible in contemporary circumstances where minorities self-identify according to particular characteristics and a hybrid of diverse affiliations. It is for the same reason that Brubaker warns against 'groupism,' that is, the tendency to take bounded groups as fundamental units of analysis and basic constituents of the social world.[15] This is why scholars prefer to argue that the question of a definition is unique to each case.

Seeking a definition, furthermore, runs into the dilemma of whether to use objective or subjective criteria.[16] Objective criteria may result in discrimination; subjective criteria could lead to segregation. This is why in the legal context experts will have to work with the premise that a minority is a matter of fact, not law. It has also been suggested that minorities are voluntary associations,[17] and most human rights instruments aimed at protecting minorities provide that belonging to a minority is a free choice.[18] This does not, however, allow for the innate bonds that many cultures foster. Notwithstanding this dilemma, there are scholars outside the realm of law who have volunteered definitions over the years; they have usually combined objective and subjective criteria.[19] The problem of

[14] Francesco Capotorti, 'Study on the Rights of Persons Belonging to Ethnic, Religious and Linguistic Minorities', UN Doc. E/CN.4/Sub.2/384/Rev.1; Jules Dechênes, 'Proposal Concerning a Definition of the Term "Minority"', UN Doc. E/CN.4/Sub.2/1985/31. See also Tove H. Malloy, *National Minority Rights in Europe* (Oxford: Oxford University Press, 2005), Ch 7.

[15] Rogers Brubaker, *Ethnicity without Groups* (Cambridge, MA: Harvard University Press, 2004), p. 2.

[16] For a good discussion, see Gaetano Pentassuglia, *Minorities in International Law* (Strasbourg/Flensburg: Council of Europe and ECMI, 2002), Ch 3.

[17] John Packer, 'On the Definition of Minorities', in *The Protection of Ethnic and Linguistic Minorities in Europe*, edited by John Packer and Kristian Myntti (Åbo: Institute for Human Rights, 1995), pp. 23–65, as well as John Packer, 'Problems in Defining Minorities', in *Minority and Group Rights in the New Millennium*, edited by Deirdre Fottrell and Bill Bowring (The Hague: Kluwer International Law, 1999), p. 49.

[18] See, for instance, the UN Declaration on the Rights of Persons Belonging to National or Ethnic, Religious and Linguistic Minorities (adopted 19 December 1992), art 3(2), and the European Framework Convention for the Protection of National Minorities (adopted 1 February 1995), art 3(1).

[19] Inis L. Claude, *National Minorities: An International Problem* (Cambridge: Harvard University Press, 1955), p. 2; J. A. Laponce, *The Protection of Minorities* (Berkeley: University of California Press, 1960), p. 6. See also in general, Carlile Aylmer Macartney, *National States and National Minorities* (London: Oxford University Press, 1934) and Tore Modeen, *The International Protection of Minorities in Europe* (Åbo: Åbo Akademi, 1969).

the objective and/or subjective views is related to the issue of predetermination versus self-determination.[20] Where self-determination allows minorities to manifest themselves, predetermination requires advanced decisions on the identity of minorities. A combination of the two may, therefore, be the best solution.

Finally, the third component of the nexus, autonomy, is by no means a clear concept. The notion of autonomy has been extensively explored in moral and political philosophy and has become a cornerstone of our understanding of liberal theories of justice and democracy. But between Emanuel Kant's early account of autonomy as the ability of the individual to discern, write, and enact her own moral laws[21] to the late modern view in education that autonomy is the individual's authenticity in terms of total sovereignty and right to make choices about moral values and self-construction,[22] there is an ocean of scholarship with little relevance for our discussion. The notion of autonomy in focus in this volume is rather more derived from justice and the idea that a person has the freedom and the right to be in control of her own life within reasonable parameters. Self-determination is at the centre of this argument, but it is qualified by the need to mediate between demands. Thus, an autonomous person is able to see the reasonableness of making choices between first- and second-order desires and is willing to compromise when needed.[23] When speaking of collective autonomy, as we do in this volume, the notion becomes somewhat complicated in that it has to build on an assumption of collective agency if autonomy is to have any value. While personal or individual agency is not usually problematic in individual autonomy, collective agency is controversial precisely because of the issue of individual choice. Collective agency is thus wrought with controversies that are beyond the scope of this book.[24] Suffice it to note that the collective agency presupposed in collective autonomy involves making compromises between the individual members for the purpose of preserving the collective unity. For this reason, a just framework of individual rights within the collective realm must be a basic requirement. The concept of autonomy in focus is, therefore, a political as well as a legal notion.

[20] Arend Lijphart, 'Self-Determination versus Pre-Determination of Ethnic Minorities', in *Power-Sharing Systems*, edited by Will Kymlicka (Oxford: Oxford University Press, 1995), p. 275.

[21] Emanuel Kant, *Groundwork of the Metaphysics of Morals*, translated by Mary Gregor (Cambridge: Cambridge University Press, 1997).

[22] See, for instance, Edward L. Deci and Richard M. Ryan, *Intrinsic Motivation of Self-Determination in Human Behaviour* (New York: Plenum, 1985) and Christopher P. Niemiec and Richard M. Ryan, 'Autonomy, Competence, and Relatedness in the Classroom. Applying Self-Determination Theory to Educational Practice', *Theory and Research in Education*, vol. 7, no. 2 (2009): pp. 133–44.

[23] Gerald Dworkin, *The Theory and Practice of Autonomy* (Cambridge: Cambridge University Press, 1988), p. 20. See also John Rawls, *A Theory of Justice* (Oxford: Oxford University Press, 1971/1973).

[24] Collective agency is a core issue rendering the discussion on collective rights controversial. See Tove H. Malloy, *National Minority Rights in Europe*, Ch 3. See also David Gauthier, *Morals by Agreement* (Oxford: Clarendon Press, 1986).

However, insofar that it is both a political and legal notion, autonomy as strategy has taken two distinct directions in history. On the one hand, there has been the security approach, which has been the most dominant. It aims to control non-dominant groups through some sort of accommodation. This aim is instrumental; it is a means to secure the territorial integrity of the state first and foremost, and as a secondary aim, to maintain the status quo for cohesion and unity. In contrast, there has been the normative approach. The aim here is to accommodate non-dominant groups based on good faith rather than control. While this aim is also instrumental, it has the purpose of implementing some positive measures for non-dominant groups because they are seen as representing an intrinsic cultural value, be it a culture, a nation, a religion, or other. The latter is based in liberal democratic theory and the idea that individuals, as well as individuals jointly, are free self-determining agents insofar that this freedom is exercised within reasonable bounds. Marc Weller and Stefan Wolff have linked the two, arguing that 'to endow an ethnic group with legislative, executive and judicial powers to address these concerns effectively will contribute to individual, group and state security and thus to preventing the disruption of the territorial and/or social integrity of a given country.'[25] In other words, normative frameworks and security are inter-dependent when strategizing autonomy as a diversity management tool.

2. The Aim of the Book

Interdependence is the theme of this book. Interdependence of law and politics, of frameworks and security, as well as in the triadic nexus, has not been clearly examined in the academic literature. Analyses of the political and legal concept of autonomy have focused primarily on justification and much less on institutionalization. While the justification debate has sought to explain why or why not collective autonomy is a good strategy for resolution of tension or conflict in diverse and divided societies, the institutional debate has focused on implementation and outcome. Again, one cannot fully comprehend the concept of autonomy without examining both. However, whereas justification has drawn quite some attention in the literature,[26] the institutional frameworks required to design

[25] Marc Weller and Stefan Wolff, eds, *Autonomy, Self-Governance and Conflict Resolution. Innovative Approaches to Institutional Design in Divided Societies* (London: Routledge, 2005), p. 13.

[26] See, for instance, Arend Lijphart, *The Politics of Accommodation: Pluralism and Democracy in the Netherlands* (Berkeley: University of California Press, 1968); Arend Lijphart, *Democracy in Plural Societies* (New Haven, CT: Yale University Press, 1977); Hurst Hannum, *Autonomy, Sovereignty, and Self-Determination. The Accommodation of Conflicting Rights* (Philadelphia: University of Pennsylvania Press, 1990); John McGarry and Brendan O'Leary, eds, *The Politics of Ethnic Conflict Resolution* (London: Routledge, 1993); Ted Robert Gurr, *Minorities at Risk* (Washington, D.C.: United States Institute of Peace Press, 1993); Ruth Lapidoth, *Autonomy. Flexible Solutions to Ethnic Conflicts* (Washington, D.C : United States Institute of Peace, 1996); Yash Ghai, ed., *Autonomy and Ethnicity* (Cambridge: Cambridge University Press, 2000); Michael Hechter, *Containing Nationalism* (Oxford: Oxford University Press, 2000); Otto Bauer, *The Question of Nationalities and Social Democracy* [Nationalitätenfrage und die Sozialdemokratie] with an Introduction by Ephraim Nimni and Preface by Heinz Fischer (Minneapolis: University of

and implement good autonomy arrangements have received far less attention,[27] especially with regard to NTA.[28] For this reason, this volume explores the nexus minority-territory-autonomy through a debate between theory and practice. While the strategy is to speak truth to the hegemonic view of the modern territorial system of state construction and international relations, the goal is to further the good application of autonomy as a strategy for managing diversity. As a part of this goal, we hope to inform both design and decision-making on autonomy arrangements by contributing to a better understanding of legal frameworks and security as part of both TA and NTA, two distinct but related models within the nexus. We will do this through a theoretical discussion that exposes the tensions and dialectics of the nexus as well as through a presentation of the practical implementation of the two models in a number of countries covering three continents.

3. The Plan of the Book

The argument proceeds in three steps. In Part I, we begin by juxtaposing the two models, TA and NTA, in a theoretical discussion aiming at excavating the tensions and dialectics of the nexus minority-territory-autonomy. As already noted, each of the components of the nexus is complex, difficult to define, unpredictable as 'agent', and variable as well as intrinsically intertwined. Francesco Palermo starts out in Chapter 1 by asking some of the very hard questions in this debate: who 'owns' a territory and how should the implicit paradigm of ownership be dealt with in the debate on autonomy and good governance? He focuses on TA and distinguishes between autonomy *for* a group versus autonomy *of* a territory. By the first he means that ethno-cultural groups, who have devolved powers in terms of autonomy, by implication hold ownership of the territory in question, whereas on the second notion, he argues that the right to autonomy belongs to the territory, thus the governance of that territory may be governed autonomously by one or often several groups. The latter notion, according to Palermo, is taking hold in the

Minnesota Press, 2000); Tim Poitier, *Conflict in Nagorno-Karabakh, Abkhazia and South Ossetia. A Legal Appraisal* (The Hague: Kluwer International Law, 2001); Zelim A. Skurbaty, ed., *Beyond a One-Dimensional State: An Emerging Right to Autonomy?* (Leiden/Boston: Martinus Nijhoff Publishers, 2005); and Ephraim Nimni, Alexander Osipov, and David J Smith, eds, *The Challenge of Non-Territorial Autonomy. Theory and Practice* (Oxford: Peter Lang, 2013).

[27] Good examples include: Markuu Suksi, ed., *Autonomy, Applications and Implications* (The Hague: Kluwer Law International, 1998); Weller and Wolff, *Autonomy, Self-Governance and Conflict Resolution*; Andre Legare and Markku Suksi, 'Rethinking the Forms of Autonomy at the Dawn of the 21st Century', *International Journal on Minority and Group Rights*, vol. 15, nos 2–3 (2008): pp. 143–55, and Jens Woelk, Francesco Palermo, and Joseph Marko, eds, *Tolerance through Law: Self-Governance and Group Rights in South Tyrol* (Leiden: Martinus Nijhoff Publishers, 2008). The seminal text on NTA is, of course, Karl Renner's *Das Selbstbestimmungsrecht der Nationen in besonderer Anwendung aug Österreich* [The Right of Nations to Self-Determination especially in Austria] (Leipzig/Vienna: Franz Deuticke, 1918).

[28] We do this in a previous volume; see Tove H. Malloy, Alexander Osipov, and Balázs Vizi, eds, *Managing Diversity Through Non-Territorial Autonomy: Accessing Advantages, Deficiencies, and Risks* (Oxford: Oxford University Press, 2015).

autonomy discourse due to the increasing diversity of societies. He calls, therefore, for a new semantic that rejects the Westphalian hegemony and welcomes the reality of diversity in territories seeking autonomy. Essentially, Palermo is pointing out the difference between TA and consociationalism (or NTA) while also showing that they overlap. The rest of Part I aims, therefore, to excavate this tension with specific focus on NTA.

In Chapter 2, Geneviève Nootens speaks to the strategic debate on autonomy by unpacking the concept of NTA in two theoretical steps. First, she questions the ambivalence among states in accepting NTA as a governance tool, suggesting that the hegemony of state sovereignty prevents governments from seeing the issues rationally. Next, she questions whether NTA, or what she terms de-territorialization of self-government, does in fact contribute to state security and unity. The aim of her discussion is to ascertain whether NTA is an added value to liberal democracy. On this, she remains sceptical. Unlike Nootens, Ephraim Nimni is entirely convinced about the value of NTA to liberal democracy in Chapter 3. He explains how NTA is, in theory and in fact, a democratic alternative to traditional models of diversity management in liberal democracy, especially models based on the centralist atomist principle. Drawing on a number of existing models of application, Nimni argues for a transformation of democratic theory toward seeing multicultural societies as a commonwealth of demoi. Markku Suksi follows this line of argument to some extent in Chapter 4, arguing that NTA may have the potential for breaking the strict territoriality of the sovereign state in so far that NTA arrangements allow for cross-border and international relations between beneficiaries of NTA and their kin abroad. He also mentions specific provisions in international law that may be seen as sources of an emerging right to autonomy. Nevertheless, Suksi remains somewhat sceptical, mainly due to the lack of operationalization of NTA. Drawing on the constitutional frameworks of Estonia, Finland, and Serbia, he offers a comparative and institutional discussion of NTA based on non-territoriality in terms of powers, membership, and representation. Because institutionalization and public policy design for NTA is weak or missing in many cases, Suksi is reluctant to endorse a paradigm shift.

Part II moves to history and law exemplified by a discussion of historical legacies and the issue of universal application. Not surprisingly, the historical legacy of autonomy has its roots in the statecraft of empires, multicultural empires in need of securing unity and avoiding territorial break-up. Jan Erk starts the discussion in Chapter 5 with an analysis of the *millet* system of the Ottoman Empire. Like Nootens and Nimni, he faults the Westphalian nation state system for the pains that modern societies experience in terms of accommodating ethno-cultural diversity under the yoke of a dated, inflexible, and exclusionary ethos. Thus, he sees the pre-modern *millet* system as an NTA model, albeit not perfect, for preserving ethnic, religious, and linguistic diversity in large territorial states. In Chapter 6, Bill Bowring examines autonomy in the Russian Empire in a discussion of the evolution from empire to federal state, and thus from TA to NCA. Although the current version of NCA, as applied in the Russian Federation, is discredited by most experts today, Bowring argues that autonomy has deep roots in the region and in Europe.

In Part III, we turn to the global perspective in a discussion involving three continents. In Chapter 7, David Smith begins with an analysis of NTA as a political strategy in Eastern Europe. He examines successes and failures in four countries, Estonia, Hungary, Romania, and Russia, all of which represent the legacy of communism in their choice of strategy. Smith seeks to place strategizing in two current debates: the political management of ethnic diversity, on the one hand, and democratization and participation, on the other. Both agendas have come in contact with NTA as a viable tool for achieving results. Alexander Osipov takes the analysis on Russia a step further in Chapter 8 through a very detailed examination of the way in which NTA has been adopted by the Russian regime as a strategy for diversity management. Drawing on a theoretical approach seeing NTA arrangements as discursive frames for symbolic accommodation, Osipov seeks to show that a false consciousness has allowed symbolic NTA arrangements to be seen as sincere accommodation.

In Chapter 9, Alexandra Xanthaki takes the discussion to the western hemisphere and the application of indigenous TA in North and Latin America. Highlighting the different approaches to colonization between the rulers of the two continents as well as different state formations, Xanthaki explains how this resulted in diverse approaches to and different histories of TA. In addition, she examines two aspects of NTA, the right to participation in central politics of the state with regard to issues pertaining to indigenous matters and to legal pluralism. The latter Xanthaki considers among the main challenges in the implementation of autonomy for indigenous peoples in the hemisphere.

From the Americas, the focus moves to South Asia. In Chapter 10, Joshua Castellino examines regional autonomy, meaning TA, in India, Pakistan, Sri Lanka, and Nepal. The four cases are selected as examples of states with live conflict-laden autonomy questions but also as significant evidence of autonomy arrangements as a regional custom in the area. Given the interplay of existing arrangements and unsettled situations, Castellino questions whether South Asia may not, in fact, be the most dynamic region in implementing autonomy as diversity management in the next decades.

In the Conclusions, Karl Kössler reiterates the argument against the hegemony of territory in interstate relations while at the same time recognizing that autonomy will not change this system. He sees, however, the fact of diversity as the major challenger to the 'chimera' of homogeneity. In this sense, he sees NTA as an emerging function that may well gain greater importance in state formation of non-homogenous culturally diverse societies. This is not at the price of TA but rather in complementarity to TA. As such, he sees a burgeoning redefinition of democracy in search for new narratives of diversity. This will be the focus of volume three.

I

AUTONOMY AND TERRITORY

1

Owned or Shared? Territorial Autonomy in the Minority Discourse

Francesco Palermo

1.1 Introduction

The link between ethnicity and territory is one of the most explored in literature, although significantly more from a minority rights perspective than in comparative federal studies.[1] Such a link has an institutional, a discursive,[2] but also an implicit dimension that is too often simplistically underpinned: the question of the understanding of a territory predominantly inhabited by a minority group. This raises a wide range of questions that are often not explicitly addressed, as the answers by different actors involved might be diametrically opposite, thus jeopardizing precarious conflict settlements based on territorial autonomy. While the settlement of conflicts might, in fact, require solutions that precisely avoid making incompatible views explicit, when the delicate balance between unexpressed underpinnings is upset, the lack of clarity as to how the link between (minority) ethnicity and territory is understood by the different parties involved might turn into the most explosive root for conflicts.

It is therefore essential to cast some light on basic questions related to (and far too often implicitly assumed by) the debate on (territorial) autonomy. To what extent does minority protection require territorial arrangements for self-government? Is minority self-government necessarily a threat to the state's unity? What are the consequences of territorial arrangements on minorities within the autonomous territory? Above all, who 'owns' a territory and how should the implicit paradigm of ownership be dealt with in the autonomy discourse?

This chapter explores from a comparative perspective the territorial responses to questions regarding the accommodation of diversities. The focus will be on contemporary challenges posed to territorial solutions as instruments for the accommodation of minority issues, including the evolving concept of territory (section 1.2).

[1] But see inter alia Robert Agranoff, ed., *Accommodating Diversity: Asymmetry in Federal States* (Baden-Baden: Nomos, 1999) and Alan Tarr, Robert Williams, and Joseph Marko, eds, *Federalism, Sub-National Constitutions and Minority Rights* (Westport: Praeger, 2004). On the reasons, see below.

[2] See the chapter by Alexander Osipov in this volume.

Against this background, the different understandings of the link and the recent practice of selected international bodies will be analysed (section 1.3), leading to some concluding remarks (section 1.4). It will be argued that territorial solutions are indeed necessary devices to address minority issues, although in the present context several new elements must be carefully considered, such as the issue of the addressees of such arrangements, the evolution that minority-related concepts (including territory) are facing in the present era, marked by the challenge of diversity, and the overall understanding of territorial arrangements, still hostage to an outdated logic of ownership, which limits the potential of autonomy as an overall instrument of good governance.

Prior to any further consideration, however, a preliminary, fundamental remark is necessary to clarify the close relationship between minorities and territories. It has been rightly pointed out that

> minorities as such do not exist. Rather, there exist large and small, numerous and otherwise, social groups. In abstract, all groups, each endowed with its own identity, equally represent the natural and cultural diversity of the human species. A social group may be seen as transformed into a minority when, on the basis of a shared and single feature of reference, it establishes relations with another group which, by virtue of a largely (but not solely) quantitative criterion comes to constitute the majority.[3]

Quantitative and qualitative elements to determine a minority status have thus to be referred to a given territory in which specific numerical and power relations exist. In principle, the whole world is a territory, and thus, even a 'universal' approach to minorities is in the end territorial. Legally, a minority can only be identified in relation to the scope of application of a law, which is necessarily territorial. This to a large extent also applies to non-territorial (personal or cultural) forms of autonomy for minorities and groups: these forms of autonomy also have a territorial scope of application, and are often established only as a secondary alternative when territorial arrangements are not available.[4]

It is thus fair to say that territory is the fundamental, unavoidable reference and context for the application of minority rights. The relationship between groups and territories, however, is far from being uniform.

1.2 Links between Ethnicity and Territory: Different Approaches

Having clarified that territory is a necessary and logical precondition for the very identification of a minority and thus for the protection of minority rights, a variety

[3] Roberto Toniatti, 'Minorities and Protected Minorities: Constitutional Models Compared', in *Citizenship and Rights in Multicultural Societies*, edited by Tiziano Bonazzi and Michael Dunne (Keele: Keele University Press, 1995), pp. 45–81.

[4] See Karl Renner, *Das Selbstbestimmungsrecht der Nationen in besonderer Anwendung auf Österreich* [The Right of Nations to Self-Determination] (Leipzig/Wien: Deuticke, 1918). The concept of personal autonomy goes back to the so-called Austro-Marxists, who elaborated it between the end of the nineteenth and the beginning of the twentieth centuries. On non-territorial autonomy, see the respective chapters in this volume.

of approaches can be observed as to the relationship that the legal system imposes between minorities and territories.[5] Simplifying, three main abstract approaches can be identified for our purposes, on a scale ranging from the maximal emphasis on the ethno-cultural dimension to the strongest accentuation of the territorial one—something that social scientists would call a scale ranging from ethnic to civic nationalism,[6] although in this context the scope is slightly different and therefore it is preferable not to rely on the nationalism terminology.[7]

A first model vests territories with the exclusive task of being the framework for the self-government of specific minority groups. Because of geographic or historical reasons, territorial autonomy is conceived in these cases as the exclusive instrument for group protection, representation, and participation within a broader national framework. Typical examples are islands on which a population different from the rest of the state is settled, which belong to a nation state because of peculiar historical events, such as in the case of the Åland islands (vis-à-vis Finland), of Greenland or the Faroe islands (vis-à-vis Denmark), of New Caledonia (vis-à-vis France), and the like. In such cases, where the population is homogeneous by fact or by law,[8] territorial autonomy fully overlaps with self-government of the concerned groups. However, while such overlap might be necessary in the case of remote islands for obvious geographic reasons, the coincidence *ope legis* between a territory and a group is often pursued also in much less homogeneous areas, with many more problems attached. Beside controversial, violent, and not yet fully settled contexts,[9] a paramount example in this regard can be observed

[5] European Commission for Democracy through Law (Venice Commission), 'Opinion on the Interpretation of Article 11 of the Draft Protocol to the European Convention on Human Rights appended to Recommendation 1201 of the Parliamentary Assembly', (adopted 1993), CDL–INF (1996), para 3c. As the Venice Commission pointed out, there is 'no common practice in the matter of territorial autonomy, even in general terms'.

[6] See, among many others the classic work by Michael Ignatieff, *Blood and Belonging: Journeys into the New Nationalism* (Toronto: Penguin, 1994).

[7] Frederic W. Maitland, *Township and Borough: The Ford Lectures 1897* (Cambridge: Cambridge University Press, 1964), pp. 6–29. While the phenomenon is pretty much the same, the scope of this analysis is broader and narrower at the same time. It is broader, because not all links between ethnicity and territory can be framed in national terms, as some identities are really territorial rather than national and do not aspire to own nationhood. It is narrower, since the territorial dimension only refers here to sub-national entities and only to those inhabited (predominantly) by (national) minorities, plus it is not necessarily based on citizenship but rather on residence. Furthermore, lawyers might be more at ease with the old concept of *legal geography* developed by Frederic Maitland, who used this term to identify the relationship between a community and its territory. Irrespective of definition issues, the question here is about the relation between organized communities and territorial space in sub-national areas whose autonomy was established with a view to accommodating ethnic claims. For these reasons, the nationalism discourse and terminology does not entirely fit here, and a territorial (ethnic or civic) discourse is preferable.

[8] The legal system presupposes and imposes that these territories be considered uniform in terms of elements defining the traditional groups inhabiting the territory and of their representation in the state structure. On the case of the Åland islands, where more than 100 groups are settled, see Bogdan State, 'Immigrant Integration on Åland—An Exploratory Study', *Åland Peace Institute Report*, no. 2 (2007), accessed February 2015, http://www.peace.ax/en/publications/report-series.

[9] Such as in several Eastern and south-eastern European states, as well as in the Iraqi autonomous region of Kurdistan according to the 2005 constitution, etc.

in Québec, whose identity is framed in ethnic/language terms even though several other French speakers are settled outside the province and, conversely, many non-French speakers live in Québec (English speakers and natives). A few years ago, the Canadian Parliament adopted a motion recognizing that Québécois 'form a nation within a united Canada',[10] and several legal rules attribute to Québec the exclusive role of representing 'French Canada' on the federal scene.[11] Such an approach is the simplest from a legal point of view, because it only requires dealing with one side of the problem—autonomy—which is supposed to cover any other diversity issue.

A second type of relationship between ethnicity and territory is to be observed when ethnic and territorial elements do coexist and interplay with each other, with the consequence that a broad leverage is left in determining which one should prevail in the single case, depending on the subjects at stake as well as on variable political priorities. Unlike in the previous category, in these cases, autonomy arrangements do take into account the heterogeneity of the population settled in a territory, although territorial self-government is in the first place conceived for the protection of one (or more) specific (minority) groups. Several examples fall into this category. Some countries rely on the principle of territoriality, such as, for example, in Belgium,[12] in Switzerland,[13]

[10] Canadian Parliament, Motion of 27 November 2006. Though non-legally binding, the motion aims at resolving the long-lasting and still open wound of the role of Québec within Canada. It culminates a process marked by the failure of two proposed constitutional amendments (1987 and 1991), by two provincial referenda on the proposal of unilateral secession (1992 and 1995) and by a fundamental opinion issued by the Canadian Supreme Court (*Reference re. Secession of Québec* [1998] 2 S.C.R. 217). One of the open issues regards the concept of 'Quebecker', and whether this should be intended in territorial or in ethnic terms. It is worth noting that the English term 'Quebecker' or 'Quebecer' is normally used to refer to any resident of the province, regardless of his/her language, whereas in French the word 'Québécois' is used both in the civic (i.e., all residents) and in the ethnic sense (i.e., only French-speaking inhabitants or even only those of French descent). See also the entry 'Québécois' in the *Oxford English Dictionary*. Not by chance, even the English text of the motion uses the French term Québécois.

[11] An interesting example is art 6 of the Canadian Supreme Court Act 1985, according to which three justices out of nine must come from Québec. This provision conventionally excludes non-French speakers from Québec from the chance of being appointed.

[12] The evolution of the Belgian system after the constitutional transformation that culminated in the new constitution of 1993 (and its later amendments) shows some tendency towards the first model. Significant in this respect is the institutional merging that took place in Flanders between regional and community institutions in which the latter basically 'absorbed' the first. See Wilfried Swenden, 'Personality versus Territoriality: Belgium and the Framework Convention for the Protection of National Minorities', in *European Yearbook for Minority Issues* (Leiden/Boston: Martinus Nijhoff Publishers, 2002/2003), pp. 331–56; Roland Vogt, 'Belgium: A Nation State without a National Identity?', in *European National Identities: Elements, Transitions, Conflicts*, edited by Roland Vogt, Wayne Cristaudo, and Andreas Leutzsch (New Brunswick, New Jersey: Transaction Publishers, 2014), pp. 13–29; Michael Keating, 'So Many Nations, So Few States: Territory and Nationalism in the Global Era', in *Multinational Democracies*, edited by Alain-G. Gagnon and James Tully (Cambridge: Cambridge University Press, 2001).

[13] The principle of territoriality in Switzerland was firstly elaborated as an unwritten constitutional corrective to the freedom of language by the federal court (see judgment *Association de l'Ecole française* [1965] BGE 91, I, 480, and judgment *Brunner* [1980] BGE 106, Ia, 299) and was subsequently formalized in the (Con-)federal constitution (art 70 of the Swiss Constitution 1874, in the text after total revision 1999). See Keith Davidson, 'Language and Identity in Switzerland', *English Today*, no. 26 (2010): pp.15–17; Seraina Pedrini, Andre Bächtiger, and Marco R. Steenbergen, 'Deliberative Inclusion of Minorities: Patterns of Reciprocity among Linguistic Groups in Switzerland', *European Political Science Review*, no. 5 (2013): pp. 483–512.

and to some extent also in the European Union (EU).[14] This principle means that a territory is identified by law with a language and a culture, which are the sole official ones of that territory. Within the framework of a multinational polity, this means that the territories are somewhat frozen in their cultural identity, because this is guaranteed by the central constitution, which therefore provides for the stabilization of groups but also for the guarantee of forced cooperation among them. Other, and no less numerous, examples are those countries in which self-government for groups was the driving force for territorial autonomy, but self-government developed also beyond the original scope, *quasi* becoming a priority per se and (gradually) attenuating the 'original intent' of 'mere' minority protection, moving towards a territory-centred system in which ethnicity becomes recessive to autonomy as such. Examples of this kind of evolution are to be found, among others, in New Brunswick in Canada,[15] in Macedonia,[16] and in South Tyrol in Italy.[17]

[14] Unlike any other international organization, the EU recognizes the official status of all languages that are official at national level in the various member states (since January 2007, when Irish was accorded the status of a full official language of the EU, the sole exception is represented by Letzeburgesch, which is official in Luxemburg but not in the EU)—see art 342, Treaty on the Functioning of the European Union (ex art 290, TEC) and Council Regulation (EEC) No 1 determining the languages to be used by the European Economic Community [1958] OJ 017. See further Francesco Palermo, 'Linguistic Diversity within the Integrated Constitutional Space', *European Diversity and Autonomy Papers*, no. 2 (2006), accessed February 2015, http://www.eurac.edu/documents/edap/2006_edap02.pdf.

[15] In the province of New Brunswick, the French- and English-speaking populations are by and large equal in size. The powers of that province, however, are largely made up the same as any other Canadian province except Québec. See André Magord, *The Quest for Autonomy in Acadia* (Brussels: Peter Lang, Editiones Scientifiques Internationales, 2008); Matthew Hayday, *Bilingual Today, United Tomorrow* (Montreal/Kingston: McGill-Queen's University Press, 2005); William Paul Cross, ed., *Democratic Reform in New Brunswick* (Toronto: Canadian Scholars' Press, 2007); James Bickerton, 'Seeking New Autonomies: State Rescaling, Reterritorialization and Minority Identities in Atlantic Canada', in *Political Autonomy and Divided Societies: Imagining Democratic Alternatives in Complex Settings*, edited by Alain-G. Gagnon and Michael Keating (Basingstoke: Palgrave Macmillan, 2012), pp. 98–117.

[16] After the Ohrid agreement of 2001 and the subsequent constitutional amendments, Macedonia has established a strongly promotional minority protection system, which nevertheless basically only regards the Albanian community. Beside the rules adopted at the state level for the representation of the Albanian minority, in 2002 a law on local self-government was adopted, whose aim was to maximize the number of municipalities in which Albanians make up 20% of the population (and thereby make Albanian an official language at the local level). The subsequent referendum held in 2004 failed because of insufficient participation in the ballot, and the law was therefore confirmed: accordingly, a much higher number of municipalities than before became bilingual. See further Joseph Marko, 'The Referendum on Decentralization in Macedonia in 2004: A Litmus Test for Macedonia's Interethnic Relations', in *European Yearbook for Minority Issues* (Leiden/Boston: Martinus Nijhoff Publishers, 2004/2005), pp. 695–721. The territorial dimension of minority protection (in spite of the fact that the Ohrid agreement states that 'there are no territorial solutions to ethnic claims') has been confirmed by the Macedonian Constitutional Court in a ruling of October 2007, when the court stroke down parts of the law on the use of flags of the communities—see Macedonian Constitutional Court No. U.br.133/2005-0-1, Official Gazette 134, 6-11-2007. See Ivana Tomovska, 'Post-Conflict Developments and Decentralization in Macedonia', *European Yearbook for Minority Issues* (Leiden/Boston: Martinus Nijhoff Publishers, 2008), pp. 146–7; Marina Andeva, 'The NTA Model in Development or in Revision? The Case of the Republic of Macedonia', accessed June 2015, http://ecpr.eu/Filestore/PaperProposal/2508d467-48d2-48f9-ae89-57bf8d6f4d28.pdf; Zhidas Daskalovski, 'Macedonia', in *Nations in Transit 2007: Democratization from Central Europe to Eurasia*, edited by Jeannette Goehring (New York: Rowman & Littlefield, 2007).

[17] Autonomy for South Tyrol was conceived as an instrument for the protection of the German-speaking minority, as explicitly stated in its international foundation, the Gruber-Degasperi

A third linkage between territorial autonomy and group protection is represented by the contexts in which ethnicity was instrumental in determining the reasons for the development of territorial autonomy, but the legal design of the autonomy regime emphasizes the territorial dimension more than the ethnic one. One could think of the Spanish autonomous communities where the historic nationalities are settled:[18] beside the clear attempts to identify the autonomous territory with one nation (or nationality),[19] this concept is inclusive in terms of belonging to the group,[20] which is normally defined by a free choice of individuals who commit themselves to a culture and a language.[21] The same is true for Scotland, which has developed a civic, territorial identity protected through self-government and where the very referendum on independence in September 2014 was open to all residents, irrespective of ethnicity, origin, or language.[22] Similarly, one can think

Agreement of 1946. However, the process of reconciliation and normalization that has been taking place in that area in the last thirty years has gradually emphasized the territorial elements of the autonomy regime vis-à-vis the ethnic ones. For further analysis, see Jens Woelk, Francesco Palermo, and Joseph Marko, eds, *Tolerance through Law: Self Governance and Group Rights in South Tyrol* (Leiden/Boston: Martinus Njihoff Publishers, 2008).

[18] According to Spanish constitutional terminology, this pre-legal element as a precondition for autonomy is called 'differential factor' (*hecho differencial*). Art 151 of the Spanish constitution of 1978 provides for the 'fast track to autonomy' for the pre-existing nationalities, even though this term never appears in the constitution. As a matter of fact, the communities that achieved autonomy this way were those in which the national character is most developed (Basque Country, Catalonia, Galicia) plus Andalusia. On origin and development see, inter alia, Esteban Arlucea Ruiz, 'The Qualitative Development of the Spanish System of Autonomous Communities: Changes to the Statutes of Autonomy', in *The Ways of Federalism in Western Countries and the Horizons of Territorial Autonomy in Spain*, edited by Alberto López Basaguren and Leire Escajedo San Epifanio (Berlin: Springer, 2014), pp. 575–86.

[19] The terminological issue ('nation' vs 'nationality') strongly re-emerged during the process of adoption of the new autonomy statute for Catalonia in 2006. The issue was resolved with a compromise: the (legally non-binding) preamble affirms that 'in reflection of the feelings and the wishes of the citizens of Catalonia, the Parliament of Catalonia has defined Catalonia as a nation by an ample majority', whereas the (legally binding) text of the statute only contains the word 'nationality'. This, however, was held unconstitutional by the Constitutional Tribunal in its seminal ruling on the Catalan statute no. 31/2010. See X. Arbos Marin, 'The Federal Option and Constitutional Management of Diversity in Spain', in *The Ways of Federalism in Western Countries and the Horizons of Territorial Autonomy in Spain*, edited by Alberto López-Basaguren and Leire Escajedo San Epifanio (Berlin: Springer, 2014), pp. 375–99; Giacomo Delledonne, 'Speaking in Name of the Constituent Power: The Spanish Constitutional Court and the New Catalan *Estatut*', *Perspectives on Federalism*, no. 3 (2011), accessed June 2015, http://www.academia.edu/523782/Speaking_in_Name_of_the_Constituent_Power_the_Spanish_Constitutional_Court_and_the_New_Catalan_Estatut.

[20] See Markku Suski, *Sub-State Governance through Territorial Autonomy: A Comparative Study in Constitutional Law of Powers, Procedures and Institutions* (Berlin/Heidelberg: Springer, 2011), p. 111; Frans Schrijver, *Regionalism After Regionalisation: Spain, France and the United Kingdom* (Amsterdam: Amsterdam University Press, 2006), p. 97.

[21] See again the new autonomy statute for Catalonia. Art 1 states that 'Catalonia, as a nationality, exercises its self-government constituted as an autonomous community'. Moreover, the preamble affirms that 'the contribution of [Catalan] citizens has shaped an integrating society'. Also the Basque identity is, by and large, defined in cultural and linguistic (thus basically voluntary) terms, rather than in ethnic terms. See, for an historical perspective, Coro Rubio Pobes, *La identidad vasca en el siglo XIX* [The Basque Identity in XIXth Century] (Madrid: Biblioteca nueva, 2003).

[22] Anthony P. Cohen, 'Nationalism and Social Identity: Who Owns the Interest of Scotland?', *Scottish Affairs*, no. 18 (1997): pp. 95–107; Iain McLean, Guy Lodge, and Jim Gallagher, *Scotland's Choices: The Referendum and What Happens Afterwards* (Edinburgh: Edinburgh

of the Croatian region of Istria,[23] as well as of the Serbian Autonomous Province of Vojvodina:[24] in both of these cases, regional autonomy has a clear territorial emphasis, because the national minorities are numerically inferior to the national population even at the regional level. Similarly, other examples of ethnic-originated, but substantially territorially managed self-government can be observed in all cases in which forms of autonomy (additional competences, etc.) for territories in which minorities are settled are subject to numerical clauses; in these cases, it is up to the same minority groups to set self-government in motion.[25]

1.3 Autonomy *for* or Autonomy *of*? Territoriality and its Limits

In the end, all forms of minority self-government including, to some extent, those normally labelled as non-territorial autonomy, have a territorial dimension. The overlap between territory and its 'ownership' by a national, ethnic, or linguistic group can be more or less intense, but the legal instruments to address minority issues are by and large all territorial, both because they are applicable only to a specific territory and because they confer to minority groups certain self-government powers within that territory.[26]

University Press, 2013); *The Agreement on a Referendum on Independence for Scotland 7th Report* (Session 2012–13); *Scottish Independence: Constitutional Implications of the Referendum 8th Report* (Session 2013–14), http://www.publications.parliament.uk/pa/ld201314/ldselect/ldconst/188/188.pdf.

[23] See John Ashbrook, *Buying and Selling the Istrian Goat: Istrian Regionalism, Croatian Nationalism, and EU Enlargement* (Bruxelles: Peter Lang, 2008); Dejan Stjepanovic, 'Regions and Territorial Autonomy in Southeastern Europe', in *Political Autonomy and Divided Societies: Imagining Democratic Alternatives in Complex Settings*, edited by Alain-G. Gagnon and Michael Keating (London: Palgrave and Macmillan, 2012).

[24] Serbian Constitution of 2006, Art(s) 182–7. See Science and Technique of Democracy, 'The Participation of Minorities in Public Life' (Strasbourg: Council of Europe, 2011); see also the Statute of Autonomous Province of Vojvodina (Law on Establishing the Competences of the Autonomous Province of Vojvodina, no. 99/09); Chiara Guglielmetti and Sonja Avlijaš, 'Regionalization and Regional Development in Serbia', in *Regional Dynamics in Central and Eastern Europe: New Approaches to Decentralization*, edited by Francesco Palermo and Sara Parolari (Leiden: Martinus Nijhoff Publishers, 2013), p. 204; Marijana Pajvančić, 'The Basic Principle of the Constitutional State. The Constitution of Serbia', *Facta Universitatis. Law and Politics Series*, no. 8 (2010): pp. 43–64.

[25] The examples range from the Finnish 'prototype' (at local level, only municipalities inhabited by more than 8% of Swedish speakers can be officially bilingual—see Language Act of 1922 as recently replaced by Language Act no. 423/2003) to more recent cases making use of the same principle. See, e.g., the Italian law no. 482/1999 (which provides for the establishment of forms of municipal self-government upon request of one third of the members of the municipal council) and the Czech law on Regions no. 129/2000, para 78, providing that minority self-governments can be set up in the regions in which at least 5% of the people belongs to a recognized minority.

[26] For non-territorial arrangements, this link is attenuated and partial, as it is not designed in terms of ownership of a whole territory. The scope of application of the personal/cultural rights is however still territorial, as mentioned above: only members of one particular group are entitled to specific rights in a given territory. As for territorial arrangements, non-territorial ones also

The overlap between one group and one territory reveals an interiorized ownership-relation that goes back even to the very names of groups and territories: territories have usually been named after the populations residing in them, and vice versa, to an extent that makes it almost impossible, in most cases, to determine which name has been developed first.[27] Our own minds are shaped taking implicitly for granted that territories are the property of groups, and the whole history of mankind is marked by wars and conflicts for the ownership of territories. When autonomy is granted, this addresses a population by conferring control over a territory, now limited by constitutional rules, but still essentially framed as exclusive sovereignty, following the same abstract pattern of statehood (people, territory, control). In other words, it seems that the implicit paradigm of the link between ethnicity and territory is always an ethnic and not a civic one: when linked with minority groups, territorial autonomy is generally framed as autonomy *for* that particular group,[28] even in cases where the approach is more civic than ethnic.

The conferment of a territorial self-government *for* minority groups,[29] however, does not address the whole matter of autonomy[30] and might even be detrimental to the overall management of complexity, because it risks replicating the state pattern at a lower level. Territoriality alone—in terms of (absolute or partial) control of a territory by a group—is thus a far too simple solution for a far too complex problem.

In fact, the ultimate rationale of territorial solutions based on autonomy *for* groups, is to transform minority issues into deliberative processes based on the majority rule. Playing with the territorial scope of legal norms, minority issues

succeed in their purpose of being exclusive and addressing only members of minority groups, as demonstrated by several examples of legal impossibility to pre-determine who belongs to groups and to exclude those not pertinent to them. See, inter alia, the issue of registration as members of the minority groups that arose with regard to the Minority Self-Governments in Hungary in 2005 and for Minority Councils in Serbia in 2009. See European Commission for Democracy through Law (Venice Commission), 'Opinion on the New Constitution of Hungary adopted by the Venice Commission at its 87th Plenary Session' (adopted 17–18 June 2011), CDL-AD(2011)016; European Parliament Resolution, 'On the Recent Political Developments in Hungary' (adopted 16 February 2012) 2012/2511(RSP). Here, ethnic nationalism is referred to as a characteristic of the general ideological environment. Practical applications of nationalist doctrines differ significantly. For instance, Hungarian nationalism targets predominantly kin minorities outside the country while the Slovakian one concerns primarily domestic policy.

[27] For some hints on such a complex and not fully explored area, see Walker Connor, 'Homelands in a World of States', in *Understanding Nationalism*, edited by Montserrat Guibernau and John Hutchinson (Oxford: Blackwell, 2001), pp. 53–73.

[28] See Marc Weller, 'Introduction', in *Asymmetric Autonomy and the Settlement of Ethnic Conflicts*, edited by Marc Weller and Katherine Nobbs (Philadelphia: University of Pennsylvania Press, 2010), pp. 2–7.

[29] See (also on some contradictions of non-territorial autonomy arrangements) Rainer Bauböck, 'Territorial or Cultural Autonomy for National Minorities?', in *The Politcs of Belonging: Nationalism, Liberalism and Pluralism*, edited by Alain Dieckhoff (Lanham: Lexington Books, 2004), pp. 221–58.

[30] This is why it is a relatively marginal aspect in the comparative federalism literature, while it is of primary importance in a minority rights perspective, as stated above.

are addressed through the classical logic of majority-based democracy, turning (national) minorities into (sub-national, territorial) majorities, or at least into much more consistent minorities. Accordingly, the will of the autonomous body is (forcibly) coincident with that of the (territorial) majority of the (national) minority.

Overall, territorial self-government has proved to work well.[31] Its immense strength lies not only in its being a viable alternative to external self-determination (thus preventing possible conflicts), but also, and even more so, in its ability to not derogate from the fundamental element of Western constitutionalism (majority rule) in addressing minority issues. By doing so, minority issues do not jeopardize the democratic foundations of the legal systems and can be pragmatically accommodated (although with some difficulties and compromises) within the classical—majority-based—deliberative procedures. Like a wizard, the legal system transforms minorities into majorities and incorporates them into a majority-based decision-making process. It could provocatively be said that territoriality changes, or at least aims to change, the very nature of minority groups, because it turns them into (potential) majorities. Such an approach, while efficient in many cases, might turn majority–minority relations upside down, but it cannot completely resolve them, for the simple reason that it is still based on a principle that is ultimately at odds with minority rights: majority rule.

However, there are several clear signs that such an approach to autonomy based on ownership (and, when referred to minority groups, conceived as autonomy *for* such groups only) is getting outdated. Instead, a more comprehensive and sophisticated view of autonomy is emerging, focusing on territories rather than on groups 'owing' them and including minority rights in a wider perspective, which can be called autonomy *of*; of territories as such, rather than just for one group thereby settled.

1.3.1 Beyond ownership: trends in theory and practice

In recent times, at least three factors have contributed to making minority issues much more complex than a purely territorial approach suggests: the emergence of power-sharing as a counter-majority mechanism; the increasing attention to the rights of the groups sharing a territory, irrespective of their status of formally recognized minority; the decreasing importance of the state as the exclusive point of reference for determining minority positions.

[31] See Marc Weller, ed., *Asymmetric Autonomy as a Tool of Ethnic Conflict Settlement* (Philadelphia: University of Pennsylvania Press, 2009). See also Alan Tarr, Robert Williams, and Josef Marko, eds, *Federalism, Sub-National Constitutions and Minority Rights*; Yash Ghai, ed., *Autonomy and Ethnicity* (Cambridge: Cambridge University Press, 2000); Ruth Lapidoth, *Autonomy: Flexible Solutions to Ethnic Conflicts* (Washington, D.C.: United States Institute of Peace Press, 1996). For interesting reflections, see Susannna Mancini, 'Rethinking the Boundaries of Democratic Secession: Liberalism, Nationalism and the Right of Minorities to Self-Determination', *International Journal of Constitutional Law*, vol. 6, nos. 3–4 (2008): pp. 553–84, esp. 562–6.

Power-sharing or ethnic consociational democracy is a governmental technique that aims at overcoming the majority–minority spill over by obliging all involved groups through institutional cooperation beyond their numerical ratio.[32] It can be paritarian (i.e., the groups have the same number of representatives in the power-sharing institutions)[33] or proportional (i.e., the groups' representation is proportional to their numerical consistency, but nonetheless guaranteed irrespective of their numerical strength).[34] Power-sharing follows a different pattern than does territorial autonomy. Although of course applied to a territory, it does not try to turn minorities into majorities; rather, it develops a form of government that is based on a different rationale than is majoritarian democracy. Power-sharing is an instrument that makes it possible to go beyond the classical democratic paradigm (based on the rule of majorities) by enforcing a more sophisticated decision-making (based on the rule of law) in a way that none of the groups may be outnumbered (at least not without having been effectively involved) within the institutions of the state or sub-national unit. The recent proliferation of power-sharing agreements[35] testifies to the insufficiency of a 'pure' territorial model to exclusively address minority issues by simply 'majoritarizing' them.

The second critical element that shows the limits of territorial solutions in terms of explicit or implicit ownership clearly emerges from the above considerations. Territories are (and will more and more be) all but homogeneous in ethnic terms. Aiming to transform national minorities into regional majorities (or at least into more consistent minorities), territorial autonomy does not address the fundamental issue of the rights of regional minorities or majorities within minorities, that is, of persons belonging to the national majorities, which are numerically inferior

[32] For a comprehensive analysis and a detailed illustration of several case studies, see Marc Weller and Stefan Wolff, eds, *Autonomy, Self-Governance and Conflict Resolution: Innovative Approaches to Institutional Design in Divided Societies* (London: Routledge, 2005). See also John McGarry and Brendan O'Leary, 'Must Pluri-National Federations Fail?', *Ethnopolitics* (March 2009): pp. 5–25; Brendan O'Leary and Joanne McEvoy, eds, *Power-Sharing in Deeply Divided Places* (Philadelphia: University of Pennsylvania Press, 2013); Brendan O'Leary and John McGarry, 'Territorial Pluralism: Its Forms, Flaws and Virtues', in *Federalism, Plurinationality and Democratic Constitutionalism: Theory and Cases*, edited by Ferran Requejo and Miquel Caminal (New York: Routledge, 2012), pp. 17–50.

[33] Such as, e.g., in the case of the Government and of the Constitutional Court in Belgium, of the Presidency, the Council of Ministers and the House of Peoples in Bosnia and Herzegovina (see however ECHR, *Sejdić and Finci v. Bosnia and Herzegovina* [2009], appl. 27996/06 and 34836/06), etc.

[34] Such as, e.g., in South Tyrol for the composition of the provincial and regional governments, in Canada for the composition of the Supreme Court, in Belgium for the Senate, in Switzerland for the Federal Council as well as for the Federal Tribunal, etc.

[35] From Northern Ireland to Macedonia, from Mindanao to Bougainville, from Bosnia and Herzegovina to Kosovo, just to quote examples from the last decade. Scott Gates and Kaare Strøm, 'Power-Sharing, Agency and Civil Conflict—Power-Sharing Agreements, Negotiations and Peace Processes', *CSCW Policy Brief*, no.1 (2007): pp. 1–15; Bumba Mukherjee, 'Why Political Power-Sharing Agreements Lead to Enduring Peaceful Resolution of Some Civil Wars, but not Others?', *International Studies Quarterly*, no. 50 (2006): pp. 479–504; Brendan O'Leary, 'The Limits to Coercive Consociationalism in Northern Ireland', *Political Studies*, no. 37 (1989): pp. 562–87; Sasho Ripiloski and Stevo Pendarovski, 'Macedonia and the Ohrid Framework Agreement: Framed Past, Elusive Future', *Perceptions*, vol. 18, no. 2 (2013), pp. 135–61; Shane Kelleher, 'Minority Veto Rights in Power Sharing Systems: Lessons from Macedonia, Northern Ireland and Belgium',

in the autonomous territory, nor of smaller minorities within that same territory (so-called minorities within minorities), nor of the overall integration of ever-more plural societies. Scholars[36] and international organizations[37] have recently paid increasing attention to this phenomenon, starting from a substantive approach to rights: according to this approach, minorities are not a stable artefact, but rather a dynamic, relational factor whose very nature as minority groups largely depends on the applicable law.[38] In sum, belonging to majorities and minorities resembles a revolving door rather than being a permanent factor. So, for example, vegetarians might not be a minority in general, because they are not recognized as such by the law, but they can become a minority vested with enforceable rights in some context, in which specific regulations apply (e.g., in prison, if the menu is not differentiated). Similarly, English speakers in Québec cannot be considered a national or ethnic minority in the traditional sense,[39] nor are they with respect

Adalah's Newsletter, May 2005; Brendan O'Leary, 'Debating Consociational Politics: Normative and Explanatory Arguments', in *From Power Sharing to Democracy Post-Conflict Institutions in Ethnically Divided Societies*, edited by Sid Noel (Montreal/Kingston: McGill-Queen's University Press, 2005), pp. 3–43; Stefan Wolff, 'Between Stability and Collapse: Internal and External Dynamics of Post-Agreement Institution Building in Northern Ireland', in *From Power Sharing to Democracy Post-Conflict Institutions in Ethnically Divided Societies*, edited by Sid Noel (Montreal/Kingston: McGill-Queen's University Press, 2005), pp. 44–66; Florian Bieber, 'Power Sharing after Yugoslavia: Functionality and Dysfunctionality of Power-Sharing Institutions in Post-War Bosnia, Macedonia, and Kosovo', in *From Power Sharing to Democracy Post-Conflict Institutions in Ethnically Divided Societies*, edited by Sid Noel (Montreal/Kingston: McGill-Queen's University Press, 2005), pp. 85–103; Patrick J. O'Halloran, 'Post-Conflict Reconstruction: Constitutional and Transitional Power-Sharing Arrangements in Bosnia and Kosovo', in *From Power Sharing to Democracy Post-Conflict Institutions in Ethnically Divided Societies*, edited by Sid Noel (Montreal/Kingston: McGill-Queen's University Press, 2005), pp. 104–19; Gordon Peake, 'Power Sharing in a Police Car: The Intractable Difficulty of Police Reform in Kosovo and Macedonia', in *From Power Sharing to Democracy Post-Conflict Institutions in Ethnically Divided Societies*, edited by Sid Noel (Montreal/Kingston: McGill-Queen's University Press, 2005), pp. 120–214; Tozun Bahcheli and Sid Noel, 'Power Sharing for Cyprus (Again)? European Union Accession and the Prospects for Reunification', in *From Power Sharing to Democracy Post-Conflict Institutions in Ethnically Divided Societies*, edited by Sid Noel (Montreal/Kingston: McGill-Queen's University Press, 2005), pp. 215–38; Steven I. Wilkinson, 'Conditionality, Consociationalism, and the European Union', in *From Power Sharing to Democracy Post-Conflict Institutions in Ethnically Divided Societies*, edited by Sid Noel (Montreal/Kingston: McGill-Queen's University Press, 2005), pp. 239–63; John McGarry and Brendan O'Leary, 'Federation as a Method of Ethnic Conflict Regulation', in *From Power Sharing to Democracy Post-Conflict Institutions in Ethnically Divided Societies*, edited by Sid Noel (Montreal/Kingston: McGill-Queen's University Press, 2005), pp. 263–96.

36 See on the various meanings of the concept, Avigail Eisenberg and Jeff Spinner-Halev, eds, *Minorities within Minorities: Equality, Rights and Diversity* (Cambridge: Cambridge University Press, 2005).

37 See section 1.3.2.

38 Sebastian Poulter, 'Limits of Pluralism', in *Discrimination: the Limits of Law*, edited by Bob Hepple and Erika M. Szyszczak (London: Mansell, 1992), pp. 183–215.

39 See expressly in this sense the UN Human Rights' Committee decision in the case of *Ballantyne et al. v. Canada*, Communications Nos. 359/1989 and 385/1989, *Ballantyne/Davidson v. Canada* and *McIntyre v. Canada*, in UN doc. GAOR, A/48/40 (II), p. 103, para 11.5, when the Committee refused to view English speakers in Québec as a minority, because they are part of the national majority in Canada even though they are a minority in Québec. See further Dominic McGoldrick, 'Canadian Indians, Cultural Rights and the Human Rights Committee', *The International and Comparative Law Quarterly*, vol. 40, no. 3 (1991): pp. 658–69.

to subject matters decided by the federal government, but they are a functional minority when it comes to subjects decided at the provincial level, in which they are minoritized in the decision-making process.

Increasing attention is paid in literature and in law to groups labelled as 'regionally, non-dominant titular peoples'.[40] This term describes groups that are part of the (local) population and, although locally inferior, who constitute the 'majority' group at the national level. Such a concept reveals well the deficits arising from the combination of territoriality and majority rule and forces the development of more accurate devices to deal with ethnic complexity as such, regardless of the specific territorial dimension in which it might be observed. In simple words, at least where the basic conditions of survival for groups are given,[41] a qualitative leap is required where the instruments of diversity management are concerned. In these contexts, today's complexity requires instruments that are able to protect groups that can be occasionally in a minority position, that are dynamic and not static. Modern instruments for diversity management should address diversity issues in general and should not only focus on the protection of predefined minority groups. A more comprehensive approach to group rights and to the integration of complex multi-ethnic societies is thus required.

The third critical element is the increasing awareness of the fact that the state cannot any longer be the exclusive level of reference for the identification of minority positions.[42] Although it is true that beginning in the Westphalian age the state has been the sole master of minority definition and rights,[43] and although it is not contestable that the state still plays the main role in this respect, it cannot be denied that considering as minorities only the groups that are numerically inferior to the population of the state and fulfilling the other criteria elaborated by Capotorti in the 1970s would be a formalistic exercise that neglects the reality. The limit of a purely territorial approach to minority issues emerges as a consequence of numerous phenomena impacting on the very rationale of territories, including cross-border cooperation also as a means to enhance minority protection[44]

[40] Tim Potier, 'Regionally Non-Dominant Titular Peoples: The Next Phase in Minority Rights?', *JEMIE*, no. 2 (2001): 3, accessed June 2015, http://www.ecmi.de/fileadmin/downloads/publications/JEMIE/JEMIE06Potier11-07-01.pdf.

[41] Unfortunately, for many minority groups in Europe and in the world, the fundamental question is still their own survival as a group. In these situations it does not seem possible to move beyond the dimension of 'mere' legal protection and, from the perspective of the majority, legal recognition of the minority. In many cases, the explicit recognition of basic rights of protection (in the fields of language, culture, participation, etc.) would already be a major step forward.

[42] As it still was in the well-known attempt for a definition by Francesco Capotorti, 'Study on the Rights of Persons Belonging to Ethnic, Religious and Linguistic Minorities', UN Doc E/CN.4/Sub.2/384/Add. 1–7 and Francesco Capotorti, 'The Protection of Minorities under Multilateral Agreements on Human Rights', *The Italian Yearbook of International Law*, vol. 2 (1976): p. 14.

[43] On the historical developments, see Eduardo Ruiz-Vieytez, *The History of Legal Protection of Minorities in Europe (XIIth–XXth Centuries)* (Derby: University of Derby, 1999).

[44] See arts 17 and 18 of the Framework Convention on National Minorities and, more broadly on the role of cross-border cooperation in ethnic sensitive areas; Francesco Palermo, 'The "New Nomos" of Cross-Border Cooperation', in *Globalization, Technologies and Legal Revolution. The Impact of Global Changes on Territorial and Cultural Diversities, on Supranational Integration*

and more generally globalization,[45] that overall changed the most rooted attitude towards autonomy.[46] More specifically, recent and significant examples of a new and more substantial approach to the link between minorities and territories beyond the state and the national dimension are provided by several international and supranational organizations such as the Council of Europe (CoE), the EU, and the Organization for Security and Cooperation in Europe (OSCE).

1.3.2 Beyond territory: the contribution of international (soft) law

At least two important bodies of the CoE have started to pave the way to a new understanding of territory with regard to minority issues.[47] The Commission for Democracy through Law (Venice Commission) has convincingly pointed out that the territorial reference for determining the existence of a minority does not necessarily coincide with the state,[48] nor is the concept of minority necessarily dependent on the requirement of citizenship. In a fundamental report, the Commission stated that citizenship (i.e., the formal relationship with a state and thus a territory) can no longer be considered the only criterion for the recognition of minority rights and that non-citizens should also benefit from specific minority protection.[49] The Commission's definition of a minority 'does not limit the protection of the rights of minorities only to persons belonging to minorities who are citizens' of the state they live in.[50] Instead, 'a new, more dynamic tendency to extend minority protection to non-citizens has developed over the recent past'.[51]

Similarly, the Advisory Committee on the Council of Europe's Framework Convention for the Protection of National Minorities requires an inclusive approach to minority rights that goes beyond the formal requirement of citizenship, this being sometimes, as a matter of fact, a tool for excluding titular groups

and Constitutional Theory. Liber Amicorum in Memory of Sergio Ortino, edited by Francesco Palermo, Giovanni Poggeschi, Günther Rautz, and Jens Woelk (Baden-Baden: Nomos, 2012), pp. 71–90.

45 Fernand de Varennes, 'The Challenges of Globalization for State Sovereignty: International Law, Autonomy and Minority Rights', in *Globalization, Technologies and Legal Revolution*, edited by Francesco Palermo, Giovanni Poggeschi, Günther Rautz, and Jens Woelk (Baden-Baden: Nomos, 2012), pp. 113–37.

46 Zelim A. Skurbaty, ed., *Beyond a One-Dimensional State: An Emerging Right to Autonomy?* (Leiden/Boston: Martinus Nijhoff Publishers, 2005).

47 Other CoE bodies have also played a role in such a process. Suffice here to mention the Congress of Local and Regional Authorities and its role in monitoring the implementation of the Charter of Local Self-Government.

48 Venice Commission, 'Opinion on Possible Groups of Persons to which the Framework Convention for the Protection of National Minorities Could Be Applied in Belgium' (adopted 12 March 2002) CDL-AD(2002)1.

49 See Venice Commission, 'Report on Non-Citizens and Minority Rights' (adopted 15–16 December 2006) Study no. 294/2004, CDL-AD(2007)001.

50 Venice Commission, 'Opinion on the Draft Law on Amendments to the Law on National Minorities in Lithuania', CDL-AD (2003)013, para 5.

51 Venice Commission, 'Opinion on Two Draft Laws Amending the Law on National Minorities in Ukraine', CDL-AD (2004)013, para 18.

from the benefit of fundamental rights.[52] Therefore, the Advisory Committee also encourages an extensive interpretation of the Framework Convention with a view to extending its application to non-citizens where appropriate,[53] and calls for a substantive rather than formalistic approach to the issue of titular groups.[54] Even more significant for our purposes are the achievements of the Committee's Third Thematic Commentary on Linguistic Rights of Persons Belonging to National Minorities (2012).[55] Acknowledging that identity is not static but evolving throughout a person's life[56] and that multiple affiliation is in fact quite common and thus identity can change 'depending on the relevance of identification for him or for her in a particular situation',[57] the Committee admits that what really matters is integration of diverse societies.[58] This can also be pursued by autonomy arrangements, which 'can be beneficial to persons belonging to minorities',[59] but the real challenge for such arrangements is not to isolate titular groups but rather to make autonomous territories more suitable than (nation) states for developing integration and coexistence among different groups.

Such an approach is promoted even more explicitly by the most recent set of recommendations issued by the OSCE High Commissioner on National Minorities (HCNM), the Ljubljana Guidelines on Integration of Diverse Societies (2012).[60] Taking further the achievements of the previous Lund Recommendations on the Effective Participation of National Minorities in Public Life (1999),[61] the Guidelines state that

> in certain circumstances, territorial self-governance arrangements, such as territorial devolution of powers, may also facilitate the representation of individual minority groups. Regardless of form, institutions of self-governance must be based on democratic principles and processes

[52] See, e.g., Advisory Committee on the Framework Convention for the Protection of National Minorities, 'First opinion on Estonia' (adopted 14 September 2001), ACFC/INF/OP/I(2002)005, para 17.

[53] See, e.g., Advisory Committee on the Framework Convention for the Protection of National Minorities, 'First opinion on Lithuania' (adopted 21 February 2003), ACFC/INF/OP/I(2003)008, para 90.

[54] See further Swenden, 'Personality versus Territoriality', pp. 331–56; and Annelies Verstichel, André Alen, Bruno de Witte, and Paul Lemmens, eds, *The Framework Convention for the Protection of National Minorities: A Useful Pan-European Instrument?* (Antwerp: Intersentia, 2008).

[55] Advisory Committee on the Framework Convention for the Protection of National Minorities, 'Thematic Commentary No. 3—The Language Rights of Persons Belonging to National Minorities under The Framework Convention' (adopted 24 May 2012), ACFC/44DOC(2012)001 rev, on which Francesco Palermo, 'Addressing Contemporary Stalemate in the Advancement of Minority Rights: The Commentary on Language Rights of Persons Belonging to National Minorities', in *Minorities, their Rights, and the Monitoring of the European Framework Convention for the Protection of National Minorities. Essays in Honour of Rainer Hofmann*, edited by Tove H. Malloy and Ugo Caruso (Leiden/Boston: Martinus Nijhoff Publishers, 2013), pp. 121–40.

[56] Thematic Commentary no. 3, para 13.

[57] Thematic Commentary no. 3, para 18.

[58] Thematic Commentary no. 3, para 12.

[59] Thematic Commentary no. 3, para 90.

[60] Tove H. Malloy, ed., *Minority Issues in Europe: Rights, Concepts, Policy* (Berlin: Frank & Timme GmbH, 2013), p. 146; Josef Marko, 'Five Years After: Continuing Reflections on the Thematic Commentary on Effective Participation. The Interplay between Equality and Participation', in *Minorities, their Rights, and the Monitoring of the European Framework Convention for the Protection of National Minorities: Essays in Honour of Rainer Hofmann*, edited by Tove H. Malloy and Ugo Caruso (Leiden/Boston: Martinus Nijhoff Publishers, 2013), p. 98.

[61] In the Lund Recommendations the HCNM affirmed the fundamental democratic role of territorial arrangements for minority self-governance (paras 19 and 20), and also called for a possible

to ensure that they can legitimately claim to reflect the views of all the communities settled in the concerned territory and that they fully respect the human rights of all persons, including of minorities, within their jurisdictions. In this context, power-sharing arrangements, where in place, should not be constructed in a manner that excludes any communities from representation.[62]

Such an integration-oriented approach to autonomy is perhaps so far the most advanced statement on territorial autonomy issues contained in an international document, as international law is notoriously hesitant to take any position on territorial organization of states.

Also in the EU, despite the absence of a direct power to regulate minority issues,[63] a number of decisions of the European Court of Justice are quite relevant in supporting a view of territory in terms of provider of services (which can include minority-relevant issues) rather than in terms of ownership. The rulings are formally grounded on subject matters not prima facie relevant to specific minority issues, such as the free movement of people and the principle of non-discrimination on the ground of nationality, but they have de facto introduced an EU system of minority protection[64] that has also had important consequences in terms of European legislation and ramifications in various areas, including the right to vote, adopting a more 'civic' criterion of residence vis-à-vis the state-centred criterion of citizenship.[65] The essence of these rulings is that rights established for specific minority groups in a particular territory, such as the right to use a minority language with administrations and in court, must be available to all who happen to be in that territory, irrespective of their nationality, ethnic belonging, and even residence.

All this leads one to believe that although territory is still (and will always be) an unavoidable term of reference for the very recognition of minority positions, its practical meaning and its scope are largely variable from case to case and in

combination of territorial and non-territorial arrangements for a successful minority participation. See further the special issue of the *International Journal on Minority and Group Rights*, vol. 16, no. 4 (2009): pp. 511–700, entirely devoted to the Lund Recommendations on their tenth anniversary.

[62] Ljubljana Guidelines on Integration of Diverse Societies (adopted November 2012), no. 39.

[63] The reference to rights of 'peoples belonging to a minority' added to the values on which the EU is grounded (art 2, TEU as amended by the Treaty of Lisbon in 2009) does not seem to provide any specific power in this field. See more extensively Gabriel N. Toggenburg, 'The Dark and the Bright Side of the Moon: Looking at Linguistic Diversity through the Telescope of the Common Market', in *Globalization, Technologies and Legal Revolution*, edited by Francesco Palermo, Giovanni Poggeschi, Günther Rautz, and Jens Woelk (Baden-Baden: Nomos, 2012), pp. 275–315.

[64] Inter alia cases Mutsch (*Ministere Public v. Robert Heinrich Maria Mutsch* [1985] C-137/84), Bickel and Franz (*Criminal proceedings against Horst Otto Bickel and Ulrich Franz*, C-274/96), Angonese (*Roman Angonese v. Cassa di Risparmio di Bolzano SpA*, C-281/98), Kamberaj (*Servet Kamberaj v. Istituto per l'Edilizia sociale della Provincia autonoma di Bolzano and Others*, C-571/10). See further Francesco Palermo, 'The Use of Minority Languages: Recent Developments in EC Law and Judgments of the ECJ', *Maastricht Journal of European and Comparative Law*, vol. 8, no. 3 (2001): pp. 299–318 and Toggenburg, 'The Dark and the Bright Side of the Moon'.

[65] See, inter alia, case *Spain v. UK*, C-145-04, on the right to vote for the European Parliament for non-citizens (following the seminal ruling of the European Court of Human Rights on *Matthews v. United Kingdom* [1999], case no. 24833/94,) and case *Eman and Sevinger v. College van Burgemeester*, C-300/04, where the Court held that the opposite situation is also admissible, i.e. to deny the right to vote to some category of European citizens based on their residence (in this case, Dutch citizens of the Antilles). See also ECtHR, *Melnitchenko v. Ukraine* [2004].

general are changing because of the evolution of the overall legal environment. Like all other concepts and instruments that can be used for minority protection, the meaning of territory and autonomy also needs to be profoundly updated in the light of the present challenges. A territorial dimension is inherent to minority rights, provided, however, that territory is seen in a more inclusive and flexible way.

Parallel to the evolution of ethnic conflicts, in a first phase separation and strong legal safeguards are required to re-establish mutual confidence, whereas more flexible and integrative instruments become necessary in a subsequent and more mature stage of conflict settlement.[66] Similarly, the concept and the functions of territory are also deemed to change alongside the evolution of majority–minority relations, at least in situations of consolidated protection in which the minority is recognized and accepted and its survival no longer a matter of discussion—in short, where a sufficient level of protection, and consequently of trust, has been reached. In these contexts, the most radical instruments for 'rebalancing' past injustice gradually lose their (necessity and) legitimacy in favour of mechanisms that allow for greater cooperation in the management of the 'question of diversity'. In these situations one can no longer automatically count on the presumption that the interests of the minority (i.e. of the majority of the minority, with all the potential problems attached to the issue of representation)[67] must by default prevail over other constitutional objectives. Therefore, the differentiating norms have now to be justified more punctually and specifically. The legal instruments, subject to the stricter scrutiny of proportionality, reasonableness, and adequacy, thus become necessarily more sophisticated. In the end, in these situations mere 'protection' might even risk becoming counterproductive for the same minority that may find itself in a rather isolated position (in an extreme hypothesis, confined to a sort of humiliating 'reservation') instead of fully participating in the development of its own group, as well as of mainstream society as a whole. This is by no means an easy task: because of the permanent change in the external context and because of the internal dynamics of the respective groups, all normative solutions and legal instruments need constant rebalancing, adaptation, and reconsideration. This makes 'one size fits all' and 'once and for all' solutions—including with regard to territorial arrangements—nearly impossible and counterproductive.

In other words, in a more advanced stage of diversity management such as we are increasingly experiencing in several parts of the world, territory maintains its central role if its understanding moves away from an old-fashioned design as something simple, static, hard-law-based, and exclusive, toward a more modern factor that is necessarily complex, variable, inclusive, and also based on several

[66] On the time dimension of conflict settlement, see further Jens Woelk, 'Südtirol: Ein Lehrbeispiel für Konfliktlösung' [South Tyrol: An Example of Conflict Resolution], *Die Friedens-Warte—Journal of International Peace and Organization*, no. 1 (2001): pp. 101–24.

[67] See Francesco Palermo, 'At the Heart of Participation and of its Dilemmas. Minorities in the Executive Structures', in *Political Participation of Minorities. A Commentary on International Standards and Practice*, edited by Marc Weller (Oxford: Oxford University Press, 2010), pp. 434–52.

soft-law instruments. Complexity, variability, non-exclusivity, soft persuasion instead of hard imposition are key elements of the modern law of minorities.[68]

1.4 Concluding Remarks: Ownership vs Governance? For a New Semantic of Autonomy

Despite all such theoretical and practical developments towards a more sophisticated and inclusive approach to territorial autonomy and to the very understanding of territory, much of the autonomy debate is still—often involuntarily—trapped in the Westphalian nation state discourse, both in the prevailing practice of international organizations (which in general shy away from engaging in autonomy issues)[69] and in the dominant minority rights literature. Autonomy is still seen in terms of something 'belonging' to groups competing for the ownership of a territory, as one (majority) group accommodating another (minority), thus as an instrument to mitigate the deficits of minority participation by replicating the nation state on a smaller scale.

Such an approach (autonomy *for*) quite effectively makes it possible for territorially compact minorities to manage their own affairs by simply controlling (or having a greater influence on) the devolved institutions. This view, however, reveals the same flaws as the nation state approach, which pretended that territories be homogeneous and dominated by one titular group (the nation), in some case granting some rights (up to a certain degree of control to 'their own' territory) to other recognized groups. Not only is such a view far too narrow and simplistic in today's world, but it is often the reason why fragile democracies reject it and why vocal (or even secessionist) minorities invoke it. The fear of autonomy on the side of the states and its frequent overestimation on the side of some minority groups are inversely proportional to the stability of democracies: a strong democracy is not afraid of autonomy, and a democratic minority usually does not see it as the first step towards independence. But the more autonomy is presented as an instrument for ethnic self-governance, the more it becomes a threat.

This paradox is particularly evident in the post-communist world. To a large extent, the ethnicization of autonomy in post-communist countries is the main legacy of the communist past. This is still the case in China, where the law on 'national regional autonomies' equals autonomy with ethnic self-government,[70]

[68] Francesco Palermo and Jens Woelk, 'From Minority Protection to a Law of Diversity? Reflections on the Evolution of Minority Rights', in *European Yearbook of Minority Issues* (Leiden/Boston: Martinus Nijhoff Publishers, 2005), pp. 5–13 and the following remarks by Tove H. Malloy, 'Towards a New Paradigm of Minority Law-Making: A Rejoinder to Palermo and Woelk's Law of Diversity', *European Yearbook of Minority Issues*, vol. 4 (Leiden/Boston: Martinus Nijhoff Publishers, 2006), pp. 5–27.

[69] For critical remarks see Alain-G. Gagnon, *L'âge des incertitudes. Essais sur le fédéralisme et la diversité nationale* [The Age of Uncertainty: Essays on Federalism and National Diversity] (Québec: Presses de l'Université Laval, 2012).

[70] Yash Ghai and Sophia Woodman, 'Unused Powers: Autonomy Legislation in the PRC', *Pacific Affairs*, no. 2 (2009): pp. 29–46; Michael C. Davis, 'Establishing a Workable Autonomy in Tibet', *Human Rights Quarterly*, no. 30 (2008): pp. 227–58.

but also in Russia, where the very names of the sub-state entities depend on whether or not their territorial basis corresponds to the ethnic divisions of the populations.[71] This is also the reason why hardly any territorial autonomy regime has been established in former communist countries.[72] In fact, not unlike during communism, ethnic autonomy is still in practice accepted only if it is limited to folklore and has no political significance. Substantive autonomy, instead, is immediately linked to (threats of) secession because a different concept of autonomy is simply not imaginable.[73] The paradoxical outcome is that the predominant understanding of autonomy in post-communist countries still does not differ substantially from that of the former Soviet Union, which was, effectively, 'a pseudo-federation of (on paper) ethnoterritorial republics'.[74] And the international community, albeit involuntarily, endorses this view of autonomy by default, refusing to openly engage in the development of a more territorial and less ethnic approach to autonomy.

Autonomy has, however, also an indirect and perhaps even more important meaning for minorities: what I suggest calling autonomy *of*. Although it is not at all a recipe for success,[75] autonomy is in fact first and foremost an instrument of good governance, which implies targeting a territory as a whole and not only the dominant group (i.e. its majority) within it. Autonomy was actually devised for governance purposes and this function becomes even more relevant the more complex the society and thus the more complex the administration. This is the main reason why the number of federal or quasi-federal countries has more than tripled in the course of the twentieth century, and at present the majority of the world's

[71] According to art 65 of the Russian Constitution of 1993, the Russian Federation is composed of 89 constituent entities (21 republics, 1 autonomous region, 46 regions (*oblast*), 9 territories (*krai*), 10 autonomous areas (*okrug*) and two federal cities). Republics, autonomous regions, and the autonomous *oblast* have an ethnic connotation, whereas other sub-national entities have not (*oblast*, *krai*, federal cities). See G. Alan Tarr, 'Creating Federalism in Russia', *South Texas Law Review*, no. 40 (1999): p. 689; Giovanni Poggeschi, 'Federalism in Russia: Ethnic and Asymmetrical', in *Asymmetries in Constitutional Law. Recent Developments in Federal and Regional Systems*, edited by Francesco Palermo, Carolin Zwilling, and Karl Kössler (Bolzano/Bozen: Quaderni dell'Accademia Europea di Bolzano, 2009), pp. 97–116.

[72] The only relevant case has been Crimea, which recent annexation by Russia represents a self-realizing prophecy. See Doris Wydra, 'The Crimea Conundrum: The Tug of War between Russia and Ukraine on the Questions of Autonomy and Self-Determination', *International Journal on Minority and Group Rights*, vol. 10, no. 2 (2004): pp. 111–30.

[73] Robert Brubaker, *Nationalism Reframed: Nationhood and the National Question in the New Europe* (Cambridge: Cambridge University Press, 1996), pp. 30–1.

[74] Anatoly M. Khazanov, 'Ethnic Nationalism in the Russian Federation', *Daedelus*, 1/1997, p. 126.

[75] Comparative practice shows examples of both successful and failed territorial arrangements. See for illustration and examples, *Ethnopolitics*, vol. 1, no. 8 (March 2009), with papers by Graham K. Brown, 'Federalism, Regional Autonomy and Conflict: Introduction and Overview', *Ethnopolitics*, vol. 1, no. 8 (March 2009): pp. 1–4; McGarry and O'Leary, 'Must Pluri-National Federations Fail?'; and Stefan Wolff, 'Complex Power-Sharing and the Centrality of Territorial Self-Governance in Contemporary Conflict Settlements', *Ethnopolitics*, vol. 1, no. 8 (March 2009): pp. 27–45.

population lives under federal or quasi-federal rule.[76] In other words, autonomy is an instrument for the management of complexity. And as all countries are increasingly diverse and increasingly complex with respect to the governance functions to be performed, autonomy has benefits that go beyond minority self-government or the protection of ethnocultural differences. If a territory, irrespective of its ethnic composition, can autonomously decide on a number of issues (alone or in cooperation with other territories, belonging to the same or to a different country, sharing the same problems),[77] it is likely that the decisions will be qualitatively better and the territory will develop more harmoniously with benefits extending to all communities settled there.

Furthermore, autonomy is a mechanism for enhancing democracy; it is about shared and thus de-concentrated powers.[78] Therefore, it could prove particularly helpful in contexts in democratic transition but also in more consolidated areas in order to prevent drawbacks in conflict settlements based on territorial autonomy. While there is no right to autonomy for persons belonging to national minorities, there is a right to democratic governance, which autonomy might help to establish.[79]

Minority issues are embedded in larger contexts and cannot be disconnected from them. Thus, the more efficient overall governance is, the less likely it is that minority rights will be neglected and even less likely that minority issues will develop into conflicts. In fact, the bigger the problems are in terms of territorial, democratic, and economic development, the more likely ethnic conflicts will be. In turn, the efficiency of the state structure—to which autonomy can effectively contribute if properly used and understood—is a powerful tool for providing the appropriate conditions for minority rights to be respected and for accommodating diversity issues. Admittedly, in some cases the opposite is also true: ethnic self-government can ease tensions and, if this is the case, may contribute to the overall development of a territory. But this depends on a number of circumstances, including the consent of the state to ethnic autonomy, which is not explicitly given in most contexts, or just reluctantly acknowledged following a violent conflict.[80] Thus, a territorial approach to autonomy is more likely to benefit ethnic groups than an ethnic approach would tend to benefit a territory as a whole.

[76] See Thomas O. Hueglin and Alan Fenna, *Comparative Federalism: A Systematic Inquiry* (Toronto: Broadview Press, 2006), p. 3.

[77] See Francesco Palermo, '"Bridges" in Self-Determination Disputes? External Relations of Sub-National Entities and Minority Groups', in *Settling Self-Determination Disputes. Complex Power-Sharing in Theory and Practice*, edited by Marc Weller and Barbara Metzger (Leiden/Boston: Martinus Nijhoff Publishers, 2008), pp. 667–88.

[78] See Weller and Wolff, eds, *Autonomy, Self-Governance and Conflict Resolution*.

[79] Jens Woelk, 'Minderheitenschutz durch territoriale Autonomie: "Reservate" oder nachhaltige Intergrationsprozesse?' [Minority Protection through Territorial Autonomy: 'Reserved' or Sustainable Integration Processes?], in *Jahrbuch des Föderalismus 2002. Föderalismus, Subsidiarität und Regionen in Europa*, edited by Europäisches Zentrum für Föderalismusforschung (Baden-Baden: Nomos, 2002), pp. 117–37.

[80] Yoram Dinstein, 'Autonomy', in *Models of Autonomy*, edited by Yoram Dinstein (Tel Aviv: Tel Aviv University Press, 1981), p. 302. According to Dinstein, 'autonomy is most often only reluctantly granted, and usually ungratefully received'.

For these reasons, the mainstream discourse around autonomy needs a new semantic. At present, it is still far too static and self-referential, both in terms of conceptual over-simplification and in terms of scarce exchange among the scholars who look at this issue from different and separated perspectives. The Westphalian semantic which affects not only the nation state but very often also the 'nation-region' (autonomy *for*) limits the potential of autonomy as an instrument for territorial development (autonomy *of*) and has to be overcome by looking more closely at the territories rather than at groups. If this is going to happen, territorial autonomy can be key to the future of minority rights. While the 1990s and (to a much lesser extent) the first decade of this century have been the golden age of minority rights, the future belongs rather to autonomy: it will be a lot about the capacity of territories to build their own future and to accommodate diversities by developing territories as a shared common good rather than as private property of one or more groups. Territorial governance will include minority governance rather than the other way around.

2

Can Non-Territorial Autonomy Bring an Added Value to Theoretic and Policy-Oriented Analysis of Ethnic Politics?

Geneviève Nootens

2.1 Introduction

It is no easy thing to define non-territorial autonomy (NTA). Part of the problem is that the notion is built upon a paradox: it depends upon a model that recognizes the intractability of state sovereignty, in which minorities are asked to renounce any substantial territorial power. Moreover, there are different views of NTA: although there seems to be a consensus on the types of claims that are deemed relevant for NTA arrangements, it is not clear to what kind of groups those may apply. There is even disagreement as to whether NTA actually is non-territorial at all. And, moreover, practitioners and scholars do not seem to agree on a shared meaning of autonomy.

Answering the question of whether NTA can bring any added value to theoretic and/or policy-oriented analysis of ethnic politics requires clarifying those issues. This chapter aims at contributing to a systematization of different views of NTA and its contextualization among other notions pertaining to autonomy and the territorialization of ethnicity. The first part will be devoted to a clarification of what NTA is as a device of self-governance. This requires a clarification of what is meant by autonomy, as well as specifying the types of groups that could claim and/or benefit from NTA arrangements. As to autonomy, notwithstanding possible disagreement as to meaning and content, there seems to be a trend toward a consistent use of autonomy to designate *internal self-determination*. As to groups that could benefit from NTA, there is no consensus on the naming (designation) of the groups that are to be empowered through NTA arrangements, nor on the claims or characteristics that are deemed relevant for justifying and designing such arrangements. A significant problem here rests with the possible confusion between ethnic groups and nations. I stress that nationalist claims are not simply claims to the protection of specific features deemed to be unique to a group's identity: they are related to the issue of self-determination, which is a basic challenge to state sovereignty.[1] I suggest that from this point of view, characterizing national groups as primarily cultural-linguistic may be a powerful political move, helping in downgrading the type of claims that national groups can legitimately make when challenging state power. I then conclude the first section by presenting different views of the kinds of claims related to NTA.

Having provided a systematization of NTA and of 'definitional' matters, I then turn to the issue of whether it can bring any added value to theoretic or policy-oriented analysis of ethnic politics. As I explain in the second part of this chapter, any answer to this question depends upon a careful characterization of the groups whose members may benefit from such arrangements and of the contexts in which they are to apply, and on the more general framework in which such arrangements are to be embedded. Actually, although NTA is not necessarily appropriate for, nor sought by, significant, territorially concentrated (substate) nations, it may be a valuable and useful device in some other cases. In such cases, the added value of NTA depends upon three main issues: whether it lowers the stakes related to territorial conflicts and contributes to 'desecuritize' minority issues; whether it actually does empower minorities while strengthening their capacity to participate as equals in the public life of the state; and whether in the long run it can contribute to the building of more inclusive democratic policies. I conclude by stressing that it is still very far from clear that whatever its virtues, the deterritorialization of self-government should be promoted.

2.2 What is NTA?

Both territorial autonomy (TA) and NTA are devices of self-governance intended to allow some groups who differ from the majority population in a state to enjoy partial independence in decision-making in some fields. Before explaining what NTA is, however, we must first try to clarify what is meant by autonomy and what types of groups could claim/benefit from NTA arrangements. We can then try to sketch a more systematic view of NTA.

2.2.1 About autonomy

The right to autonomy has been increasingly discussed in international organizations (IOs) and the literature, but 'there is no internationally recognised right to autonomy for minorities'.[2] Indeed, there is no consensus, in the literature, on

[1] On the contradistinction between ethnies and nations, see section 2.2.2.

[2] Francesco Palermo, 'When the Lund Recommendations are Ignored. Effective Participation of National Minorities through Territorial Autonomy', *International Journal of Minority and Group Rights*, vol. 16, no. 4 (2009): p. 657. On autonomy, see amongst others, Markku Suksi, ed., *Autonomy: Applications and Implications* (The Hague: Kluwer Law International, 1998), pp. 7–32; Zelim A. Skubarty, ed., *Beyond a One-Dimensional State: An Emerging Right to Autonomy?* (Leiden/Boston: Martinus Nijhoff Publishers, 2005); Alain G. Gagnon and Michael Keating, eds,

the precise meaning, object, and structures characteristic of autonomy, and there seems to be a great deal of confusion when it comes to explaining precisely what it is. While some define it as self-government/self-rule, others argue it should not be equated with self-government.[3] Some consider that decentralization processes can be appropriately described as autonomous arrangements, whereas others take autonomy to differ from decentralization in being more than a mere delegation of powers; and some scholars use it to describe the status of federated entities as well, while others consider autonomy to describe the status of entities that are less empowered than the ones that are members in a federation.

Basically, the concept of autonomy points to the idea of self-legislation. In the context of a discussion of TA and NTA arrangements, it is related to the issue of dealing with a diversity due to the presence of minority groups (ethnic, religious, linguistic, or national), and to some idea either of subsidiarity (a 'weaker' sense of autonomy, closer to what local and self-government can achieve) or of self-government (a 'stronger' sense, closer to what the status of federated entities entails).[4] McGarry and Moore stress that in modern political usage, autonomy 'refers to a form of self-rule that gives ethnic and national minorities substantial powers to govern their own affairs but falls short of independence'.[5] Ghai defines it as 'a device to allow minorities claiming a distinct identity to exercise control

Political Autonomy and Divided Societies: Imagining Democratic Alternatives in Complex Settings (London: Palgrave Macmillan, 2012).

[3] Skubarty, *Beyond a One-Dimensional State*; Ruth Lapidoth, *Autonomy. Flexible Solutions to Ethnic Conflicts* (Washington, D.C.: US Institute of Peace Press, 1997), p. 54. Skubarty, e.g., argues that *autonomous* entities are *self-governing* entities, whereas Lapidoth stresses that *self-government* implies a 'considerable degree of *self-rule*' and usually applies to a specific region, whereas *autonomy* is a flexible concept, the substance of which ranges from limited powers to very broad ones and is not necessarily territorial. See also Javaid Rehman, 'The Concept of Autonomy and Minority Rights in Europe', in *Minority Rights in the 'New Europe'*, edited by Peter Cumper and Steven Wheatley (The Hague: Martinus Nihjoff Publishers, 1999), p. 218: 'in the context of minority rights, lawyers and jurists disagree as to the precise content of autonomy; its relationship with federalism, regionalism, devolution, and wider concepts such as self-government and self-determination'.

[4] Kristin Henrard, 'Minorities and Socio-Economic Participation: The Two Pillars of Minority Protection Revisited', *International Journal on Minority and Group Rights*, vol. 16, no. 4 (2009): p. 550. Minority groups are defined both by their different ethnic, religious, and/or linguistic characteristics and by the fact that they are in a non-dominant position: a minority is 'a population with ethnic, religious and/or linguistic characteristics differing from the rest of the population, a numerical minority and non-dominant position and the wish to hold on to that separate identity'. See also Capotorti's and Deschêne's definitions quoted in Georg Brunner and Herbert Küpper, 'European Options of Autonomy: A Typology of Autonomy Models of Minority Self-Governance', in *Minority Governance in Europe*, edited by Kinga Gál (Budapest: Local Government and Public Service Reform Initiative of the Open Society Institute, 2002), p. 15.

[5] John McGarry and Margaret Moore, 'Karl Renner, Power Sharing and Non-Territorial Autonomy', in *National Cultural Autonomy and its Contemporary Critics*, edited by Ephraim Nimni (London: Routledge, 2005), p. 79; McGarry and Moore, 'Karl Renner', p. 90: 'Autonomy should be distinguished from mere regional self-administration (where regions implement policies decided by central governments) and from local-municipal government (where there is only a capacity to pass minor regulations or by-laws). It should also be distinguished from sham varieties of "autonomy" associated with control strategies, such as when a state devolves power to co-opted and unrepresentative elites, concedes the form of autonomy without substance, or imposes autonomy on groups which do not want it'.

over affairs of special concern to them while allowing the larger entity to exercise those powers which cover common interests'.[6] Lapidoth argues that it is 'a means for diffusion of powers in order to preserve the unity of a state while respecting the diversity of its population'.[7] In a closely similar way, Wolff and Weller suggest viewing it as an element of state construction addressing the needs of diverse communities; according to them, the various definitions of autonomy have in common the notion of the *transfer* (rather than delegation) of some powers from a central government to the 'autonomous' entity. Autonomy, then, is 'the legally entrenched power of ethnic and territorial communities to exercise public policy functions (legislative, executive, and adjudicative) independently of other sources of authority, but subject to the overall legal order of the state'.[8] Heintze stresses that it is to be regarded 'as the granting of internal self-government to a region or group of persons, thus recognizing partial independence from the influence of the national or central government. This independence can be determined primarily by the degree of actual as well as formal independence enjoyed by the autonomous entity in its political decision-making process'; the essential element of autonomy is the granting of certain rights to a specific part of the state population, 'in view of its characteristics which differ from the majority of the population'.[9] Henrard stresses that autonomy—which she equates with self-governance—is one of the two fundamental dimensions of the participation of minorities (the other one being representation, namely, 'having a say' in state institutions).[10] In a similar way, Skubarty sees autonomy as being 'congenial to integration which presupposes the recognition of distinctive identities and cultures and participation of the members of distinctive groups in political, economic and cultural structures of the state'.[11]

Notwithstanding possible disagreement as to meaning and content, there seems to be a trend toward a consistent use of autonomy to designate *internal self-determination*. Henrard explicitly relates the two dimensions of the participation of minorities—namely, representation and autonomy—to the right of

[6] Yash Ghai, 'Autonomy as a Participatory Right in the Modern Democratic State. Public Participation, Autonomy and Minorities', in *Beyond a One-Dimensional State: An Emerging Right to Autonomy?*, edited by Zelim A. Skubarty (Leiden/Boston: Martinus Nijhoff Publishers, 2005), p. 38.

[7] Lapidoth, *Autonomy*, p. 3.

[8] Stefan Wolff and Marc Weller, 'Self-Determination and Autonomy: A Conceptual Introduction', in *Autonomy, Self-Governance, and Conflict Resolution: Innovative Approaches to Institutional Design in Divided Societies*, edited by Marc Weller and Stefan Wolff (London: Routledge, 2005), p. 13.

[9] Hans Joachim Heintze, 'On the Legal Understanding of Autonomy', in *Autonomy: Applications and Implications*, edited by Markku Suksi (The Hague: Kluwer Law International, 1998), pp. 7, 9. See also Steven Roach, 'Minority Rights and an Emergent International Right to Autonomy: A Historical and Normative Assessment', *International Journal on Minority and Group Rights*, vol. 11 (2004): p. 411. Autonomy is a right to local self-rule.

[10] Kristin Henrard, '"Participation", "Representation" and "Autonomy" in the Lund Recommendations and their Reflections in the Supervision of the FCNM and Several Human Rights Conventions', *International Journal on Minority and Group Rights*, vol. 12 (2005): p. 141.

[11] Zelim A. Skubarty, 'Introduction', in *Beyond a One-Dimensional State: An Emerging Right to Autonomy?*, edited by Zelim A. Skubarty (Leiden/Boston: Martinus Nijhoff Publishers, 2005), p. xxxiv.

internal self-determination;[12] Wolff and Weller argue that it is indeed a substitute for self-determination discourses within states;[13] Heintze stresses that it 'may serve to realize the right to self-determination or the rights of minorities'.[14] Yet, when it comes to TA, states may well be reluctant to enter into autonomy arrangements for more or less the same reasons they are unwilling to recognize nations' right to self-determination, namely, the fear of secession and the threat it poses to the territorial integrity of the state. Indeed, Kymlicka has argued that European organizations nowadays see NTA arrangements as worth considering precisely because they enable them to avoid the highly charged issue of TA, in a context in which many post-communist states in Central and Eastern Europe (CEE) are opposed to TA and some actors are convinced that the idea that a territory belongs to a particular ethnic group should be challenged in order to break the link that nationalist ideas establish between ethnic identities and territory.[15] I will come back on this issue in the second part of this chapter.

2.2.2 Who could claim/benefit from NTA arrangements?

There is also no consensus on the naming (designation) of the groups that are to be empowered through NTA arrangements, nor on the claims or characteristics that are deemed relevant for justifying and designing such arrangements. A significant problem rests with a possible confusion/equation of nations with ethnic groups. Those phenomena are related but they are not the same thing. Ethnic groups are, according to Smith, 'named human populations with shared ancestry, myths, histories and cultures, having an association with a specific territory and a sense of solidarity'.[16] Nations, by contradistinction, are 'socio-political entities with a wide range of social institutions and a shared political identity'.[17] Keating rightly stresses that 'Most ethnic groups do not identify themselves as nations or make claims for territorial self-government. Most nations, in turn, comprise several different ethnic groups'.[18] Modern nations may have ethnic origins, and may still depend upon an ethnic core; but they are much more inclusive and heterogeneous

[12] Henrard, '"Participation", "Representation" and "Autonomy"', p. 135.

[13] Wolff and Weller, 'Self-Determination and Autonomy'.

[14] Heintze, 'On the Legal Understanding of Autonomy', p. 28; but see Roach, 'Minority Rights', p. 425, on the problems raised by the promotion of the freedom of peoples in the context of an internal (democratic) right to self-determination.

[15] Will Kymlicka, 'National Cultural Autonomy and International Minority Rights Norms', *Ethnopolitics*, vol. 6, no. 3 (2007): p. 387.

[16] Anthony D. Smith, *The Ethnic Origins of Nations* (New York: Blackwell, 1986), p. 32. See also Anthony D. Smith, *Nationalism and Modernism. A Critical Survey of Recent Theories of Nations and Nationalism* (London/New York: Routledge, 1998), p. 29. Ghai takes ethnicity to be a broad concept covering a variety of factors (language, race, religion, colour) that distinguish one group of people from others. But this seems too large a definition for it to be analytically useful.

[17] Michael Keating, *Plurinational Democracy. Stateless Nations in a Post-Sovereignty Era* (Oxford: Oxford University Press, 2001), p. 5.

[18] Keating, *Plurinational Democracy*, p. 5.

than earlier ethnic groups.[19] In other words, 'Nations...are distinguished from ethnic groups in being, or aspiring to be, global societies, containing within them the full range of social institutions and mechanisms for social regulation...Ethnic groups, by contrast, are partial societies, advancing the claims of one group within a broader context'.[20] Hence, nationalism (that makes the nation a political subject and claims for it some degree of self-determination) is not necessarily ethno-nationalism, and ethnicity is not necessarily politicized.[21] In the West, indeed, there has been a clear trend towards the de-ethnicization of nationalist movements.[22] Nor can nations be appropriately conceived of merely as 'cultural communities'. Culture is of course a significant component of modern nationalism, but it is so through its combination with wider claims to self-government. Culture, in nationalism, is a political 'resource' used either to legitimize/consolidate the established order (majority nationalism) or to challenge it (minority nationalism).[23]

Nationalist claims, then, are not simply claims to the protection of specific features deemed to be unique to a group's identity. Claims to nationhood are basically related to the issue of self-determination,[24] hence to broad political claims. Claims to nationhood are related to the claim that the nation has been historically constituted as a self-governing community, and that 'its people see themselves as a nation and wish to determine their future as a collectivity'.[25] Therefore, whereas ethnicity does not necessarily challenge state sovereignty, nationalities do, since minority nationalism 'challenges the assumed coincidence between politically significant identities and political boundaries. Since the eighteenth century, when conceptions of democracy and self-determination first entered the public realm, it was widely assumed that these identities and boundaries would coincide so that states would be nation-states', namely, that their territory would coincide with a political identity of the people as constituting a single, sovereign nation.[26] Nationalities

can reasonably claim that the current state system is unfair. Like majority nations, they are politically mobilised; they have a history and homeland; they seek to exercise political

[19] Smith, *Nationalism and Modernism*; Eric Kaufman, 'Dominant Ethnicity and Dominant Nationhood. Empirical and Normative Aspects', in *Dominant Nationalism, Dominant Ethnicity. Identity, Federalism and Democracy*, edited by Andre Lecours and Geneviève Nootens (Brussels: PIE/ Peter Lang, 2009), pp. 35–56. Kaufman argues that nations are actually hybrids from ethnies (communities of shared ancestry, real or imagined) and the modern state.

[20] Keating, *Plurinational Democracy*, p. 7.

[21] Andre Lecours and Geneviève Nootens, 'Understanding Majority Nationalism', in *Contemporary Majority Nationalism*, edited by Alain G. Gagnon, Andre Lecours, and Geneviève Nootens (Montreal: McGill-Queen's University Press, 2011). Even when nations are built around an ethnic core, their nationalism is not necessarily a mere extension of such a core; and dominant nationalism is not necessarily a mere reflection of dominant ethnocultural features.

[22] Michael Keating, 'Europe, the State and the Nation', in *European Integration and the Nationalities Question*, edited by John McGarry and Michael Keating (London: Routledge, 2006), pp. 23–34.

[23] Lecours and Nootens, 'Understanding Majority Nationalism'.

[24] Keating, *Plurinational Democracy*, p. 3.

[25] Keating, *Plurinational Democracy*, p. 3. Self-determination 'is part of the normative content of nationality itself'.

[26] John McGarry, Michael Keating, and Margaret Moore, 'Introduction: European Integration and the Nationalities Question', in *European Integration and the Nationalities Question*, edited by John McGarry and Michael Keating (London: Routledge, 2006), p. 7.

self-government. Increasingly, their demands have been framed in exactly the same language and with the same normative underpinnings as the claims to self-determination made by states themselves, moving from an ethnic particularism to a broader civic nationalism invoking liberal democratic norms and often embracing the new international order.[27]

It is not surprising, then, that states prefer to have the issue of nationalities' rights rephrased in the more general language of human rights or in the more restricted one of cultural rights. Jackson Preece has rightly stressed that recognizing individual rights of citizenship alongside state rights is no threat to any existing nation state's sovereignty, whereas an international system of minority rights would not only limit states' sovereignty but would also 'grant international status of some kind... to national units that could come to rival the power or authority of the nation states affected'.[28] Malloy stresses that indeed, international law sees national minorities as cultural groups, and that national minorities' rights have been categorized mainly as cultural, rather than political, ones—a move that renders national minorities ineligible for self-determination.[29]

The issue of the types of groups[30] that are to be empowered through autonomy arrangements and the one of the claims that are deemed relevant are closely related: for example, if nations are considered as endowed with an original, primary right to self-determination that contradistinguishes them from other types of groups, then they are to be recognized a right to autonomy arrangements of a scope much wider than the ones granted to groups whose claims relate to more specific issues such as religion or the use of patronyms; actually, they shall be recognized as having a right to co-determine the terms of association within the larger polity. We shall come back on this issue in the second part of this chapter, since the most discussed model of NTA—namely, national cultural autonomy (NCA)—actually makes nations primarily cultural-linguistic groups, concerned with cultural and linguistic issues,[31] whereas some sub-state nations seek power not only over these issues, but also over economy, policing, and broad social domains.

[27] McGarry, Keating, and Moore, 'Introduction', p. 7.

[28] Jennifer Jackson Preece, *National Minorities and the European Nation-States System* (Oxford/New York: Clarendon Press, 1998), p. 43.

[29] Tove Malloy, *National Minority Rights in Europe* (Oxford: Oxford University Press, 2005), p. 17. Cultural rights are inadequate to protect 'co-nations', since those are groups with strong political identities.

[30] I use this expression for matters of simplicity, not in order to essentialize groups. People's attachments to, e.g., a nation rest on representations of themselves and others, feelings of belonging, and participation in some institutions, language, and culture (see, e.g., Michel Seymour, *De la tolerance à la reconnaissance* [From Tolerance to Recognition] (Montreal: Boréal, 2008)), not on some 'essential' characteristics, by virtue of which individuals making up them would be all alike and would automatically identify with it.

[31] Renner attaches autonomy to the nation, for sure, but 'he defines nations as primarily cultural-linguistic groups'; McGarry and Moore, 'Karl Renner', p. 79.

Actually, one should be careful when states (or IOs) characterize nationalist claims as ethnic or cultural ones. This may be a useful way either to stigmatize minority nationalism for being illiberal or non-modern (such a strategy has been used in the West), and/or to downplay the significance of minority nations' claims to self-determination. Hence, it seems to me that, for example, Wolff and Weller's claim that most self-determination conflicts 'are, in one way or another, conflicts between communities that distinguish themselves from one another by "ethnic" criteria, such as language, religion, culture, etc'[32] needs to be nuanced: ethnic criteria do not necessarily sustain claims to self-determination; and excluded ethnic groups can rather claim distinct treatment that would allow them to participate fully in the state, rather than to preserve some distinct characteristics.[33]

One last remark about nationalities and minority nationalism. A national minority is

> a group numerically inferior to the rest of the population of a state, in a non-dominant position, well-defined and historically established on the territory of the state, whose members—being nationals [citizens] of the state—possess ethnic, religious, linguistic or cultural characteristics differing from those of the rest of the population and show, if only implicitly, a sense of solidarity, directed towards preserving their culture, traditions, religion, or language.[34]

In Europe, 'national minorities' has typically referred 'to "old" minorities or historically settled groups, living on or near what they view as their national homeland, who find themselves in a minority in a larger state'.[35] But there are different 'varieties' of nationalities. A nationality

> may exist as a minority that is wholly contained within a 'host' state, such as the Scots within the UK. It may also be a minority in one state (the 'host' state), but have ethnic kin

[32] Wolff and Weller, 'Self-Determination and Autonomy', p. 4.

[33] Keating, *Plurinational Democracy*, p. 5, Language does not necessarily allow for demarcating ethnic groups, moreover.

[34] Jackson Preece, *National Minorities*, p. 28.

[35] Will Kymlicka, 'National Cultural Autonomy and International Minority Rights Norms', in *Cultural Autonomy in Contemporary Europe*, edited by David J. Smith and Karl Cordell (London: Routledge, 2008), p. 48; Rainer Bauböck, 'Autonomy, Power-Sharing and Common Citizenship: Principles for Accommodating National Minorities in Europe', in *European Integration and the Nationalities Question*, edited by John McGarry and Michael Keating (London: Routledge, 2006), p. 87; Will Kymlicka, 'National Cultural Autonomy and International Minority Rights Norms', *Ethnopolitics*, vol. 6, no. 3 (2007): p. 384: 'Generally speaking, they are groups that have lost out in the rough and tumble of European state formation over the past five centuries and whose homelands ended up being incorporated (in whole or in part) into larger states dominated by a neighbouring people. National minorities were active players in the process by which the early-modern welter of empires, kingdoms and principalities in Europe was turned into the modern system of nation states, but they either ended up without a state of their own ("stateless nations", such as the Catalans and Chechens) or ended up on the wrong side of the border, cut off from their co-ethnics in a neighbouring kin state ("kin state minorities", such as the ethnic German in Denmark and Italy or ethnic Hungarians in Romania and Slovakia).' See also Malloy, *National Minority Rights*, p. 21: national minorities are 'the groups that have inadvertently found themselves "on the wrong side of the border"'. Let me stress that Bauböck argues that a national group ceases to be a minority when it forms a demographic

who dominate another state (the 'kin' state). This is a classical configuration throughout Central and Eastern Europe, and examples include the Hungarians of Slovakia, Romania and Serbia; the Serbs and Croats of Bosnia-Herzegovina...; and the Turks of Bulgaria.... Nationalities may also be minorities in more than one state, and majorities in none, such as the Basques in Spain and France.[36]

Nations of the first kind are what Seymour calls 'minority nations'; the second and third ones are national minorities, properly speaking.

2.2.3 Claims related to NTA

NTA implies the organization of minority groups that are not geographically concentrated in specific regions of a state and the granting of some rights to its members wherever they live on the territory of the state. In non-territorial forms of autonomy, competences are transferred not in relation to a certain specific territory but in relation to a certain community, 'irrespective of size and place of residence in the State'.[37]

According to Coakley, approaches of (national)/ethnic conflict resolution that do not have a territorial basis originate in certain characteristics of the traditional state, which recognized as its component elements not politically mobilized individuals, 'but discrete and clearly defined groups, each consisting of a set of individuals, families or other low-level units linked...to their group in terms of ascriptive characteristics'.[38] Some traditional states offer examples of early forms of non-territorial ethnic autonomy: the Polish–Lithuanian Commonwealth until 1764 as to the Jewish community; the *millet* system of the Ottoman Empire; the Austro-Hungarian Empire.[39] With the growth of the modern state, though, the thrust of political development moved away from the group, in the direction of the individual, and the principle of equality before the law was seen as being incompatible with the idea of granting privileges to groups. However, groups soon began to demand autonomy in the name of the principle of national self-determination.[40] It is not surprising that in the Austro-Hungarian Empire, where the problem was particularly acute, proposals for non-territorial solutions

majority in a state of its own, or 'when it is no longer subordinate but fully recognized as a constituent people in a multinational state'.

36 McGarry, Keating, and Moore, 'Introduction', p. 1.

37 Henrard, '"Participation", "Representation" and "Autonomy"', p. 141.

38 John Coakley, 'Approaches to the Resolution of Ethnic Conflict: The Strategy of Non-Territorial Autonomy', *International Political Science Review*, vol. 15, no. 3 (1994): p. 298: 'For this system to move in a direction that could be labelled "non-territorial ethnic autonomy", two changes were required. First, the state would have to give recognition to non-territorial groups that were not merely clearly definable but, rather, definable in ethnic terms. Second, a minimum degree of autonomy would have to be conceded to these groups. These conditions were not really met by arrangements that simply gave de facto representation in central institutions to ethnic groups'.

39 Coakley, 'Approaches to the Resolution of Ethnic Conflict', p. 299.

40 Coakley, 'Approaches to the Resolution of Ethnic Conflict', p. 299.

to the issue of national groups' autonomy dated back to the middle of the nineteenth century.[41] There is no need here to come back on the model developed by Renner and Bauer (NCA) to address the issue of the intermingling of nationalities in the Empire, since it has already been largely debated.[42] Let me recall, though, that models of NCA were initially proposed for 'old minorities' in CEE, including both stateless nations and kin state minorities, and that 'The groups targeted by post-1990 European norms of minority rights substantially coincide with the groups targeted by the original theories of NCA in the late nineteenth and early twentieth centuries'.[43]

As Osipov has stressed, though, 'Terms related to NTA are different and include such notions as "cultural", "personal", "exterritorial", "corporate", "segmental", and "autonomy"; meanwhile, "autonomy" might be interchangeable with "self-government". Each term has certain implications and nuances'.[44] As a first tentative move to clarify issues related to NTA, let us look briefly at how a number of scholars have described forms of autonomy that are not territorial. Their main characterizations and delineations of NTA compared to TA are summarized in Table 2.1. Most of them converge on a definition of NTA as being either *personal* or *cultural*, and as being used to address religious, ethnic, cultural, and/or linguistic issues. However, for some of the scholars included in the table, 'cultural autonomy' is the generic expression encompassing all forms of NTA.[45] Others prefer to have 'personal autonomy' as the generic expression,[46] but sometimes equate it with cultural autonomy.[47] Finally, some of them specify subspecies of non-territorial (cultural or personal) autonomy. Hence, Ghai argues that cultural autonomy can be personal, cultural (sic?), or political; Heintze argues that NTA can be of three types (cultural, personal, and functional);[48]

[41] Coakley, 'Approaches to the Resolution of Ethnic Conflict', p. 299. See also Wolff and Weller, 'Self-Determination and Autonomy', pp. 1–25: the concept of NTA has been developed systematically in political theory since the mid–nineteenth century, and has played a significant role in consociational theory after World War II.

[42] Ephraim Nimni, ed., *National Cultural Autonomy and its Contemporary Critics* (London: Routledge, 2005); David J. Smith and Karl Cordell, eds, *Cultural Autonomy in Contemporary Europe* (London: Routledge, 2008).

[43] Will Kymlicka, 'National Cultural Autonomy and International Minority Rights Norms', in *Cultural Autonomy in Contemporary Europe*, edited by David J. Smith and Karl Cordell (London: Routledge, 2008), p. 49.

[44] Alexander Osipov, 'National Cultural Autonomy in Russia: A Case of Symbolic Law', *Review of Central and East European Law*, vol. 35 (2010): p. 32. See also Henrard, '"Participation", "Representation" and "Autonomy"', p. 141.

[45] Roach, 'Minority Rights'; Ghai, 'Autonomy as a Participatory Right in the Modern Democratic State', pp. 3–45; Asbjørn Eide et al., 'Cultural Autonomy: Concept, Content, History and Role in the World Order', in *Autonomy: Applications and Implications*, edited by Markku Suksi (The Hague: Kluwer Law International, 1998), pp. 251–76; Rainer Bauböck, 'Territorial or Cultural Autonomy for National Minorities?', *IWE-Working Paper Series*, no. 22 (2011).

[46] Lapidoth, *Autonomy*; Skubarty, *Beyond a One-Dimensional State*; Wolff and Weller, 'Self-Determination and Autonomy'.

[47] Lapidoth, *Autonomy*.

[48] But he also presents cultural autonomy as a kind of personal autonomy, and both seem to cover the very same issues.

Table 2.1 NTA regimes (broad delineation)

	TA regimes	NTA regimes of autonomy	Specific components of NTA regimes
Skubarty	Autonomy regime with a specific territorial organization	– personal autonomy regime that does not require compact settlement of a religious or ethnic minority – power-sharing autonomy regime (particular form of participation in decision-making processes of the government)	Neither require the group to be concentrated in one specific region
Ghai	Minority concentrated in one region, and constitutes the majority in that region	Cultural autonomy: the minority is not geographically concentrated, and can be granted autonomy over specific matters such as culture, language, religion, and personal law	Cultural autonomy can be personal, cultural, or political
Lapidoth	The minority constitutes the majority in a specific region	Personal (cultural) autonomy: a community whose members are connected by individual characteristics such as ethnic consciousness or language, irrespective of the location in the state	
Wolff and Weller	Autonomous entity defined in territorial terms, regardless of whether the individuals living on the territory belong to one ethnic group or another	Autonomous entity defined in personal terms: an ethnic group is granted autonomy rights, and all its members can enjoy these rights regardless of where they live on the territory of the host state	
Roach	Right to exercise limited sovereignty over provincial territorial borders	Cultural autonomy: non-territorial and self-administered form of local governance for matters affecting the maintenance and reproduction of a group's culture	
Heintze	Regions given a special status comprising the competence of self-government organs to regulate certain matters Group lives in a well-defined area and constitutes the majority in this area	Aimed at ethnic groups not territorially concentrated	Can be – personal: based on the personality principle; primary field of application are cases in which there are no separate areas of group settlement; a public corporate body represents the

(*Continued*)

Table 2.1 *Continued*

	TA regimes	NTA regimes of autonomy	Specific components of NTA regimes
			minority in relation to the state and has the competence to govern specific minority affairs, particularly culture, language, and education; its subjects are the members of ethnic groups – cultural: a personal autonomy limited to identity issues such as language, education, etc. – functional: selected state functions are transferred to private minority group organizations with respect to culture, media, education, and religion
Eide		Cultural autonomy: the right to self-rule in regard to matters affecting the maintenance and reproduction of culture, by a culturally defined group	
Henrard	Self-government for a group territorially concentrated within a defined area in which it constitutes the majority	Competences transferred irrespective of size and place of residence in the state, in relation to a certain community	
McGarry and Moore		Self-rule of a group of people over all members of the group but not over a geographical area	Implies state-created/ official institutions Goes beyond 'associational autonomy' allowed in all liberal regimes Involves some degree of institutional separation and collective self-government
Malloy		Non-territorial arrangements and non-territorial collective autonomy	NTA does not necessarily imply collective autonomy Not confined to cultural arrangements

	TA regimes	NTA regimes of autonomy	Specific components of NTA regimes
			Covers all types of self-management that national minorities can handle, including: – collective autonomy rights, usually granted in the area of culture (e.g., education and religion) (but may be granted in other areas) – individual rights to personal cultural autonomy (de facto cultural autonomy through individual human and minority rights) – functional collective autonomy
Kymlicka		National cultural autonomy	
Bauböck		Cultural autonomy: devolution of political powers to nationalities formed on a non-territorial basis and through voluntary individual affiliation	Cultural autonomy is said to be personal when membership is determined by individuals themselves rather than by state authorities or by the representatives of the community

Bauböck considers personal autonomy as a subspecies of cultural autonomy. Let me stress that Kymlicka and Bauböck are the only ones to specifically relate NTA to some kind of nationality claims—actually, to NCA. Let us also recall that in the *Explanatory Note to the Lund Recommendations*, non-territorial arrangements

> are further explained as self-governance in terms of exclusive jurisdiction, administrative authority and management as well as specified legislative and judicial jurisdiction. These functions may be achieved through delegation, devolution or division of constitutional powers, such as through federalism... The Explanatory Note implies that ethnic criteria may function as basis for NTA whereas this is not the case with territorial autonomy.[49]

[49] Tove H. Malloy, 'The Lund Recommendations and Non-Territorial Arrangements: Progressive De-territorialization of Minority Politics', *International Journal on Minority and Group Rights*, vol. 16, no. 4 (2009): p. 666.

2.3 Can NTA Bring any Added Value to Theoretic or Policy-Oriented Analysis of Ethnic Politics?

Any answer to this question depends upon a careful characterization of the groups whose members may benefit from such types of arrangements and of the contexts in which such arrangements are to apply, and on the more general framework (state, regional, international) in which NTA arrangements are/would be embedded. As a preliminary remark, let us stress that if NTA is intended to address religious, ethnic, cultural, and linguistic issues, then it is not necessarily appropriate for, nor sought by, nations as 'socio-political entities with a wide range of social institutions and a shared political identity'.[50] NTA is not usually claimed by 'developed nationalist movements',[51] 'significant and territorially concentrated minorities',[52] 'sizeable and territorially concentrated sub-state nationalist movements'.[53] Why is this so? Because nations usually seek self-government, and self-government is about large scope public authority, not merely cultural self-expression.[54] As McGarry and Moore stress,

> The types of power that such [significant and territorially concentrated] minorities seek, including power over the economy, policing, control over population influxes, which language is dominant, require control over territory. This is connected with the territorial nature of the modern state, and the fact that the exercise of its most important functions tends to be on a territorial basis.[55]

Actually, 'little more than control over education, cultural affairs and relatively unimportant matters can be devolved to a body lacking a defined territorial jurisdiction and therefore unable to develop coercive powers to secure compliance with its directive'.[56] In other words, a mechanism addressing cultural issues depending upon some individual characteristics, and lacking wide-scope territorial jurisdiction, cannot meet most of the claims of minority nations. Let us think, for example, of Québec and Catalonia: those nations have developed, wide-scope state institutions that can perform exactly the same functions as the Canadian/Spanish states; they rule over a specific territory; their claims do not bear only on cultural issues, even if culture and language are significant dimensions of conceptions of the nations in both cases; and they conceive of themselves as liberal

[50] Keating, *Plurinational Democracy*, p. 5.

[51] Coakley, 'Approaches to the Resolution of Ethnic Conflict'.

[52] McGarry and Moore, 'Karl Renner'.

[53] Will Kymlicka, 'Western Political Theory and Ethnic Relations in Eastern Europe', in *Can Liberal Pluralism be Exported? Western Political Theory and Ethnic Relations in Eastern Europe*, edited by Will Kymlicka and Magda Opalski (Oxford: Oxford University Press, 2001), pp. 13–106.

[54] Keating, 'Europe, the State and the Nation', p. 28.

[55] McGarry and Moore, 'Karl Renner', pp. 82–3.

[56] John Coakley, 'National Territories and Cultural Frontiers: Conflicts of Principle in the Formation of States in Europe', *West European Politics*, vol. 5, no. 4 (1982): p. 36.

democratic and pluralist nations, dedicated to the protection of basic liberal rights and to the inclusion of every citizen in the public sphere.

But that does not mean NTA can't be a valuable and useful device in some other cases, depending upon the situation of the members of the group and the claims they make. It is largely agreed that NTA arrangements may be useful in cases of dispersed and intermixed populations, who claim either limited autonomy upon specific matters, or cannot realistically hope to achieve anything other than such limited autonomy, at least in the short run. Actually, I would like to propose that the added value of NTA as to the analysis of ethnic politics depends upon three main issues: whether it lowers the stakes related to territorial conflicts and contributes to 'desecuritizing' minority issues; whether it actually does empower minorities while strengthening their capacity to participate as equals in the public life of their 'host' state; whether in the long run it can contribute to the building of more inclusive democratic polities.

2.3.1 Territory, sovereignty, minorities

NTA devices have been widely, though not exclusively, debated in the context of CEE, where TA arrangements seem hard to achieve because populations are interspersed; past attempts to delineate boundaries according to ethnic criteria have often have deplorable consequences (such as ethnic cleansing); and there has been a 'securitization' of the state–minority relationship.[57] A number of other factors (amongst which, the presence of kin states)

> have encouraged three interrelated assumptions which are now widely accepted by ECE countries: (a) that minorities are disloyal, not just in the sense that they lack loyalty to the state...but in the stronger sense that they collaborated with former oppressors, and continue to collaborate with current enemies or potential enemies; (b) that a strong and stable state requires weak and disempowered minorities—put another way, ethnic relations are seen as a zero-sum game...; and (c) that the treatment of minorities is above all a question of national security.[58]

Kymlicka stresses that under conditions of geopolitical insecurity and incomplete democratic conditions, there are genuine difficulties with negotiating/adopting TA.[59] This is why NTA may appear promising, as it seems to contribute to 'deterritorialize security concerns'.[60] In Europe, NTA arrangements—mostly embodied

[57] Kymlicka, 'Western Political Theory', p. 62. On the resurgence of the popularity of NTA in Eastern Europe, see also McGarry and Moore, 'Karl Renner'. Kymlicka recalls that there has been enormous resistance in CEE countries towards the idea of TA for national minorities, and that the only cases in CEE (outside Russia) where TA has been accepted are those where the national minority grabbed political power and established de facto autonomy without the consent of the central government.

[58] Kymlicka, 'Western Political Theory', p. 67.

[59] Even when this is not the case, states tend to resist TA because of the spectre of secession, and even in the West, where TA arrangements are nowadays more generally accepted, the pursuit of TA by minority nations has been controversial and fiercely resisted for a while.

[60] Malloy, 'The Lund Recommendations', p. 666.

in the NCA model—have been put forward precisely because territory is a highly symbolic and material stake. Recall, for example, that Renner built his model of the multinational state upon the critique of the 'territorial' principle. He held the nation state model as largely responsible for the persistent struggles between national groups and for the assimilation of minorities. According to him, 'the logic of territorial autonomy, which involves creating homogeneous units, cannot be achieved, and…will always leave some minorities. The personal principle is preferred because the rule applies only to people who have accepted that they are members of the group in question'.[61] In other words, NCA was put forward as a way of lowering the stakes related to the issue of the possession of territory as a zero-sum game.[62]

Are NTA arrangements actually helpful in achieving this task? They probably are in some cases. But they succeed in doing so partly because they downplay the significance of the attachment of national minorities to their 'homeland' or 'historic territory'. The minority is endowed with arrangements that require it to renounce TA and hence, control over social power of a wider scope (i). In turn, this points to the fact that (paradoxically?) NTA arrangements—at least as they have been devised up to now—actually depend upon a territorialist viewpoint (ii).

(i) As Kymlicka explains, NTA is nowadays seen as worth considering because it enables IOs to avoid the 'highly charged issue' of TA.[63] On this view, the central virtue of NTA is that it challenges the tendency of national minorities to assert nationalist political claims over territory.[64] For some actors, this is part of a long-term strategy aimed at improving the prospects of adopting a more adequate model that would combine TA and NTA. But for others, it is grounded in a principled moral commitment against nationalist ideas and their role in violent ethnic conflicts; from this point of view, the underlying cause of ethnic conflict in post-communist Europe is the very fact that ethnic identities are linked to territory through national ideas of a group's homeland. Hence, NTA is to be seen as a tool for *deterritorializing* the identities and claims of those sub-state national groups;[65] 'According to this line of argument, the central virtue of NCA is that it accommodates ethnocultural diversity while resisting any concessions to territorialized nationalist claims'.[66] In other words, NTA arrangements (including NCA) fit tightly with the search for arrangements and rights that are least threatening to states: IOs 'have appeared interested in supporting less threatening forms of NTA rather than TA'.[67]

61 McGarry and Moore, 'Karl Renner', p. 81.

62 From this point of view, the 'logic' of NCA differs from the one of the Ottoman *millet* system.

63 See also Malloy, 'The Lund Recommendations', p. 677: 'The aim of the NTA provisions of the Lund Recommendations was to lead governments away from fearing territorial autonomy claims towards contemplating NTA as alternatives'.

64 Kymlicka, 'National Cultural Autonomy', p. 388.

65 In a context where there is a confusion between nations and ethnic groups and where the ethnic criterion of boundary delimitation has recreated tense inter-ethnic relations.

66 Kymlicka, 'National Cultural Autonomy', p. 387.

67 McGarry, Keating, and Moore, 'Introduction', p. 17.

Yet, sub-state national groups are most often deeply attached to what they consider to be their 'homeland' or 'historic territory'. And TA still remains one of the central aspirations of nationalities.[68] Actually,

> The problem of ethnic violence and potentially destabilising ethnic conflict in post-communist Europe is almost exclusively confined to groups that are capable of exercising self-government and of sustaining their own public institutions, and which therefore contest with the state for control over public institutions. And for these groups, the FCNM and OSCE norms are largely irrelevant.[69]

The point is that at the end of the day, the idea that NTA will suffice as a way to manage the concerns of national minorities downplays both their claims to self-rule and their attachment to a territory, and in turn benefits/supports the state's territorial integrity and stability.[70] This rests both on the characterization of minorities' claims as being mainly 'cultural' and on a relativization of their attachment to territory—a move not required from the majority. Yet, if NTA arrangements are really to contribute to lowering the stakes related to territory in a way that helps to achieve equality in the state—equality between people belonging to different national groups—they must promote the sharing of territory, rather than the deterritorialization of some claims. Of course, in a context where minority issues and their relationships with states are highly sensitive and securitized, NTA arrangements may appear as a wise appeasement policy. It may confine minority claims to relatively benign issues such as the choice of language in schools, or the management of museums; or encourage private sector associations that do not necessarily intrude into public policy issues related to nationality issues. But it should be very clear that doing so expresses a *parti pris* for the majority and the state's territorial sovereignty. It alleviates security concerns by reinforcing the ascendency of the majority upon public policy.

[68] McGarry, Keating, and Moore, 'Introduction', p. 17.

[69] Will Kymlicka, 'The Evolving Basis of European Norms of Minority Rights: Rights to Culture, Participation and Autonomy', in *European Integration and the Nationalities Question*, edited by John McGarry and Michael Keating (London: Routledge, 2006), p. 44.

[70] I do not wish to suggest that these are not important concerns, only that the logic of NTA does benefit the dominant majority and its conception of the state and citizenship (which may be more or less inclusive, of course). As McGarry and Moore, ('Karl Renner'), have stressed, the normative argument mostly employed by state elites to justify NTA arrangements is 'of the peace-and-stability sort', and involves a negative judgement about the secessionist dangers of TA. They also recall that 'Western states have also expressed a preference for NTA in Eastern Europe because of concern about stability or because they fear that, as in France and Greece, accommodation through territorial autonomy will give rise to similar demands from their own minorities. Since the Copenhagen Document of 1990 suggested TA as an option for the accommodation of minorities there has been a steady retreat in support for it in international documents, in part as a result of the conflicts arising from the break-up of Yugoslavia and the Soviet Union. These documents are not more likely to stress NT methods of accommodation than the territorial sort' (McGarry and Moore, 'Karl Renner'). IOs have endorsed autonomy for nationalities in areas where minorities have been able to win autonomy through military rebellion (Bosnia-Herzegovina, Kosovo, Macedonia, etc.); yet, 'Support for autonomy in these cases, then, is not a result of some pan-European norm, but a reaction to *realpolitik*, and the threat to regional stability' (McGarry, Keating, and Moore, 'Introduction', p. 13).

(ii) These considerations in turn raise the issue of whether NTA arrangements actually are non-territorial. In fact, they entail a territorial dimension since they are intended—at least in European models aimed at dealing with ethnocultural diversity—to deal with minorities that can claim a 'historic' relationship with a given territory but are included in a 'host' state. Kymlicka has argued that it is not clear how one can endorse NCA[71] as being targeted at traditional national minorities without accepting the legitimacy of claims based on historic settlement and traditional territory.[72] Moreover, the territorial units in which the personality principle will apply must be defined: the principle can operate 'only within a particular set of territorial boundaries'.[73] Hence, NTA arrangements always are supplementary to TA.[74] So, paradoxically, NTA arrangements implicitly depend upon the recognition of territorial attachments of minorities, but once again subordinate them to 'peace-and-stability' arguments that benefit the majority nation.

2.3.2 Autonomy and participation

IOs and scholars have paid more and more attention to the twofold issue of autonomy and participation of minorities. The effective participation of minorities—which has emerged as a recurrent theme for the Organization for Security and Co-operation in Europe (OSCE) and the High Commissioner on National Minorities (HCNM) in the 1990s—entails two dimensions: participation in decision-making (representation) and autonomy; the latter is related to the fact that minorities have certain concerns that are related only to themselves, the former to the fact that they have views and interests that are related to the polity as a whole.[75] According to Henrard, both dimensions are related to the right of internal self-determination.[76] I have already stressed that NTA arrangements downplay the significance of minorities' potential claims to self-rule, and are hence less threatening to state's integrity and stability. A further issue is whether they provide for autonomy in any significant way—which would in a strong sense involve internal self-determination. As Coakley stresses,

[71] NCA is the model he discusses.

[72] Kymlicka, 'National Cultural Autonomy', p. 309.

[73] Will Kymlicka, 'Renner and the Accommodation of Sub-State Nationalisms', in *National Cultural Autonomy and its Contemporary Critics*, edited by Ephraim Nimni (London: Routledge, 2005), p. 142.

[74] Will Kymlicka, 'Renner and the Accommodation of Sub-State Nationalisms', p. 141. Kymlicka stresses that NCA was proposed by Renner as a supplement to TA, at least tacitly, since he tacitly conceded that NCA was not an alternative to TA for the Hungarians. He adds that 'once Renner concedes this, the whole argument against TA for the Czechs, Poles, Croats and Slovenes disappears. For precisely the same argument can be advanced for viewing NCA as a supplement, rather than alternative, to TA for these groups. That is to say, one could support the further division of the Habsburg empire into, say, ten self-governing regions, instead of just two, each with its own parliament and public administration and each adopting NCA with its own territory for its own internal minorities'.

[75] Henrard, '"Participation", "Representation" and "Autonomy"', p. 134.

[76] Henrard, '"Participation", "Representation" and "Autonomy"', p. 135. On the idea of a right to effective participation, see also Keating, 'Europe, the State and the Nation', pp. 23–34.

Mere provision of separate electoral registers for two or more groups, or even concession of limited group control over schooling, do not constitute autonomy. Indeed, one of the characteristics that has made the non-territorial principle attractive (or at least acceptable) to many states is the fact that there are real, practical limits to the amount of power that may be devolved in a community that does not have a territory of its own.[77]

Keating also stresses that to provide common services to non-territorial groups is not the same thing as group self-government.[78] Rehman argues that autonomy bears a relationship to ethnic, linguistic, and religious minorities only when considered in a narrow, more restrictive sense.[79] Kymlicka suggests that the norms put forward by the FCNM and OSCE 'will work well in those countries which are essentially ethnically homogenous—where the dominant group forms 90–95 per cent of the population—and where the remaining ethnic groups are small, dispersed and already on the road to assimilation'.[80] He stresses that the FCNM and OSCE norms/recommendations 'remain essentially versions of the idea of a "right to enjoy one's culture". As such, they do not address the distinctive characteristics and aspirations of national minorities.'[81] So one can hardly argue that NTA arrangements really empower minorities, other than in a weak sense of autonomy—closer to subsidiarity than to self-rule.

Nonetheless, it may be the case that, as McGarry and Moore have argued, one cannot assess the potentialities of the model starting from existing arrangements. They rightly stress that Renner's scheme, for example, is more extensive than any current NTA regimes, and that 'Nowhere in Eastern Europe do minorities possess the wide-ranging control over cultural matters that was envisaged by Renner'.[82] Wolff and Weller have argued that in the post-Cold War era, the concept of NTA was actually narrowed to the cultural dimensions of ethnic conflict (education, language, religion), but that 'there is no need to conceive of it as being in principle confined to cultural and educational matters only'.[83] Malloy makes

[77] Coakley, 'Approaches to the Resolution of Ethnic Conflict', p. 311.

[78] Michael Keating, 'Territory, State and Nation in the European Union. How Relevant is Renner?', in *National Cultural Autonomy and its Contemporary Critics*, edited by Ephraim Nimni (London: Routledge, 2005), p. 184.

[79] Rehman, 'The Concept of Autonomy and Minority Rights in Europe', p. 218. Roach, 'Minority Rights', p. 426. Roach takes cultural autonomy to be a 'second-level' right to autonomy, and although he suggests that such a right may enhance 'the pliability of the concept of sovereignty', he does not explain how cultural autonomy can help in achieving such an aim.

[80] Kymlicka, 'The Evolving Basis of European Norms of Minority Rights', p. 44.

[81] Kymlicka, 'The Evolving Basis of European Norms of Minority Rights', p. 43. 'The FCNM and OSCE recommendations are strangely silent on all of the central claims at stake in the post-communist ethnic conflicts. They do not discuss how to resolve (often competing) claims relating to territory and self-government, or how to assign official language status. Nor do they provide any guarantee that minorities can pursue higher-level education or professional accomplishment in their own language…The resulting framework of minority-rights norms is both ineffective and unstable'.

[82] McGarry and Moore, 'Karl Renner', p. 84.

[83] Wolff and Weller, 'Self-Determination and Autonomy', p. 15.

a similar comment on the options offered in the NTA provisions of the Lund Recommendations.[84]

Yet, Renner's model clearly restricts the scope of nationalities' claims to cultural-linguistic issues, whereas when deprived of large scope social powers, minorities cannot hope to achieve significant forms of autonomy. This is why for many of them, particularly those that are large and territorially concentrated, NTA arrangements are a second-best option, even if in some cases, 'large minorities that are territorially concentrated will find non-territorial autonomy better than the alternatives on offer'.[85]

States do not willingly enter into autonomy arrangements, unless they are of a benign nature, because of the perception that such arrangements threaten their unity and stability. Yet, the less threatening nature of NTA arrangements is double-edged for minorities, since they actually allow for 'weak' forms of autonomy which are not necessarily really empowering. Bauböck, for example, has stressed that cultural autonomy reproduce inequalities of resources between national groups, leave minorities exposed to cultural assimilation resulting from territorial mobility, and leave the majority in control of territorial political power. It seems to be wishful thinking to believe that conflicts will vanish if minorities are allowed to use their own language in schools, manage their own libraries and museums, and use their patronyms. In the case of the most intractable conflicts, especially when national minorities may have a significant case for TA, it is doubtful that such a strategy of 'containment' will be successful in the long run.[86]

2.3.3 Democratic autonomy

Bauböck has argued that cultural autonomy creates incentives for illiberal government, and that TA should generally be preferred, although one may think of contextual justifications for introducing some elements of cultural autonomy either as residual, supplementary, or transitional.[87] He believes that contrary to TA, cultural autonomy does not have overall integrative effects.[88] He also stresses that minorities are likely to receive a better treatment under TA arrangements, since

[84] Malloy, 'The Lund Recommendations', p. 675. She argues that the options are confined 'to a narrow understanding of cultural autonomy. While the Explanatory Note explains that cultural autonomy may also involve certain social functions, it does not provide suggestions as to the other sides of culture, such as the role of economic functions of culture.... Arguably culture in the 21st century is more than education, language, religion and recognition of names and symbols as suggested in the Lund Recommendations'.

[85] McGarry and Moore, 'Karl Renner', p. 84. According to them, the Kurds in Turkey, e.g., would see NTA arrangements as a considerable advance over their current situation.

[86] A further issue would be to consider whether they contribute to sustain trust between members of minorities, on the one hand, and the state and/or members of the majority nation, on the other.

[87] Bauböck, 'Territorial or Cultural Autonomy'. Since it is mainly to the non-territorial dimension of cultural autonomy that Bauböck relates the issue of incentives for illiberal government, his argument can be taken to be a more general one against NTA, not only against cultural autonomy (although he focuses on cultural autonomy).

[88] Bauböck, 'Territorial or Cultural Autonomy', p. 19.

the latter compels the majority to consider members of the minority as equal citizens of the autonomous polity, whereas in cultural autonomy 'the local national majority has its own separate cultural institutions and need not accommodate the minority'.[89] He is concerned with the possibility that cultural autonomy would segregate civil society into different national compartments, whereas TA 'makes it more likely that pluralism in civil society will also be reflected within established national cultures', at least in conditions of territorial stability.[90]

The answer to the question of whether NTA arrangements can contribute to the building of more inclusive democratic polities depends partly upon how one conceives of inclusion, and on the interlocking of NTA arrangements with significant mechanisms ensuring the participation of the members of minorities *as members of minority groups* in the state. In Renner's view for example, NCA is embedded in a global conception in which the state is responsible for the political domain (in a tradition of administrative, rather than legislative, federalism), and it is coupled with a significant concern for minorities' participation within central government institutions.[91] This very same concern for participation and integration is central in the Lund Recommendations. If we are interested in people having and displaying significant attachments for/identification with ethnocultural/national groups, the participative dimension must include the recognition of those 'attachments' and hence, a commitment to integration rather than assimilation. Skubarty, for example, stresses that

> the solutions to the inter-group conundrums should be sought in the accommodation of heterogeneity by politics of comprehensive inclusion of the disenfranchised groups and a diffusion of powers—all of which could be summed up by the notion of autonomy. Autonomy from this perspective is antithetical to assimilation, which involves the elimination of separate identities constituting diversity, and congenial to integration which presupposes the recognition of distinctive identities and cultures and participation of the members of distinctive groups in political, economic and cultural structures of the state.[92]

But this gets us back to the issue of the nature of the state: as Kymlicka has stressed, different conceptions of the nature of the state ground different positions as to what is required for effective participation in it:

> From the point of view of most post-communist states, the members of national minorities should be able to effectively participate in the institutions of a unitary nation-state with a single official language. From the point of view of many minority organisations, the members of national minorities should be able to effectively participate in the institutions of a multilingual, multination federal state.[93]

[89] Bauböck, 'Territorial or Cultural Autonomy', p. 14.

[90] Bauböck, 'Territorial or Cultural Autonomy', p. 19.

[91] McGarry and Moore, 'Karl Renner', pp. 85, 88. According to them, Renner has anticipated consociational theory, although his commitment to NTA requires corporatist principles— it privileges national identities over non-national ones—hence making his form of power-sharing 'less liberal than it might otherwise have been'.

[92] Skubarty, 'Introduction', p. xxxiv. See also Henrard, '"Participation", "Representation" and "Autonomy"'.

[93] Kymlicka, 'The Evolving Basis of European Norms of Minority Rights', p. 59.

He stresses that up to now, such a conflict has been mostly resolved, in post-communist Europe, by force, rather than principles, and that the idea of effective participation presupposes that the issue of the nature of the state has been resolved.[94]

2.4 Conclusion

Of course, context should be taken into account. The specific situation of minorities, the prevailing of mistrust, the impact of adopting measures of autonomy on the treatment of minorities by the majority, possible manipulations of arrangements by group elites, etc., should be properly assessed. NTA arrangements may be the best European organizations have to offer to minorities. Yet, they run contrary to what now appears as a significant trend in the West: the twofold trend toward the de-ethnicization and territorialization of nations.[95] Although the territorial solution may be difficult to apply in CEE, 'where the nationalities have not undergone the same process of territorial consolidation',[96] de-ethnicization seems to depend upon the adoption of territory as a more inclusive criterion. Moreover, it should be recalled that in the West, TA arrangements have not led to secession.

The main problem here, of course, is that claims of minorities to self-government (significant, large scope autonomy empowerment) run contrary to state sovereignty and states' interests. It seems, indeed, that sustainable solutions to the issues of the state–minority relationship rather depend upon a 'relativization' of statist assumptions such as the intractability of sovereignty and in a way contribute to reinforce statist assumptions.[97] This clearly is, paradoxically, the outer limit of NTA: at the end of the day, they are part of a model that recognizes the intractability of state sovereignty. In such a logic, territory remains the issue of a zero-sum game. This is precisely what must be challenged, if more equal relationships and sustainable solutions to the issue of national minorities are to be designed. Support for NTA arrangements, as long as they embody a reluctance to support TA in cases where TA arrangements would be more appropriate, shows that organizations are not yet ready to really challenge state sovereignty and to deal with the central aspirations

[94] Kymlicka, 'The Evolving Basis of European Norms of Minority Rights', p. 59.

[95] Joseph Marko, 'Effective Participation of National Minorities in Public Affairs in Light of National Case Law', *International Journal on Minority and Group Rights*, vol. 16, no. 4 (2009): p. 642; McGarry, Keating, and Moore, 'Introduction', p. 17: 'the HCNM's recommendations in this respect goes against what Keating describes as a growing norm in Western Europe, the "de-ethnicisation" of nationality movements, and an associated increased emphasis on territory as the criterion of inclusion'. France is a significant exception, due to a strong unitary state tradition. Marko has argued that in countries with a long historic record of the unitary state doctrine, whether in the West or in South and Eastern Europe (SEE) there are more significant difficulties in adopting an approach promoting the effective participation of minorities and their integration into society and political decision-making processes.

[96] Keating, 'Europe, the State and the Nation', p. 29.

[97] Malloy, 'The Lund Recommendations', p. 677. According to Malloy, the Lund Recommendations contain such statist assumptions.

of nationalities ,[98] unless minorities seize power by force. In other words, it is still very far from clear that whatever its virtues, NTA actually 'subverts territorially based nationalism' and that indeed, the deterritorialization of self-government should be promoted.[99] The main issue may not be to 'personalize' the right to self-determination, but rather to look for autonomy arrangements that allow for both shared rule and self-rule, as expressed by the ideal of federalism.

98 McGarry, Keating, and Moore, 'Introduction'; Keating, 'Europe, the State and the Nation', p. 24. The 'post-sovereignty' argument 'sees sovereignty not as a claim to the monopole of authority, but rather as a claim to an element of original authority (that is not derived from a higher authority), but which recognizes the existence of other sources of original authority which necessarily and inherently limit each other'. Keating recognizes, however, that it is often heard at a rhetorical level, rather than as a concrete policy proposal (Keating, 'Europe, the State and the Nation', p. 24).

99 Stéphane Pierré-Caps, 'The Principle of Personal Autonomy: A Solution for the Future?', in *The Politics of Belonging. Nationalism, Liberalism, and Pluralism*, edited by Alain Dieckhoff (Lanham: Lexington Books, 2004), pp. 259–82.

3

Minorities and the Limits of Liberal Democracy

Demoicracy and Non-Territorial Autonomy

Ephraim Nimni

3.1 Introduction

The liberal democratic nation state is generally understood to have an abundance of beneficial features.[1] People that live in liberal democracies are generally satisfied with the regime, and most people who do not live in a liberal democracy yearn to live under it. This is an extraordinary development; never before in the history of humanity was a culturally circumscribed form of governance met with such hegemonic approval across vastly diverse societies. Notions of civic national identities and liberal democracy have grown hand in hand with the nation state in the genesis of the 'Occident'.[2] However, in whatever way it is construed, the idea of national identity contains a particularistic element which is strangely at odds with assertions of universality cherished by liberals. The convergence in the nation state between a particular national tradition, with a specific sense of history, with a Universalist liberal world view which aims to realize universal individual values, remains one of the unexplained oddities of modernity.[3]

Following the above, there is a widespread tendency to take the nation state for granted as the only form of fair governance, and worse, to see nation and state as synonymous, considering the world as a collection of perennial nation states. This does not take into account the parochial origins of the nation state, and, how the nation state was historically created to satisfy the particular historical needs

[1] This article was made possible by the support and patience of Tove Malloy; I am enormously grateful.

[2] I use the term in the sense given by Edward Said: the Orient is, as much as the Occident, an 'idea that has a history and a tradition of thought, imagery and vocabulary that has given it reality and presence for the West'. Edward Said, *Orientalism* (London: Penguin Books, 1978), pp. 4–5. See also Diana Lary, 'Orientalism and Occidentalism', *Journal of the Canadian Historical Association*, vol. 17, no. 2 (2006): pp. 8–9.

[3] John Schwarzmantel, *Citizenship and Identity: Towards a New Republic* (London: Routledge, 2003), p. 28.

of state formation in Europe. Last but not least, it does not take into account the significance of this particular form of political organization for societies that have not had historical roots in Western European political traditions. This results in an utterly confusing and misleading analytical criterion that defines political phenomena as located either as 'below the nation state'—'sub-national' (sic); or above it—'international' (sic).[4]

There are countless debates and discussions on what is nation. Across profound intellectual and ideological divides, it emerges that a nation is a cultural artefact and as such very different from a state, which is a territorial institution of governance. It is well documented that the conflation between nation and state resulted from series of parochial events in late medieval Europe at the onset of modernity. The genesis of the nation state is widely associated with the rise of the European system of states, which international relations theorists call the 'Westphalian system'. This is the emergence in Europe of well-demarcated states which recognize each other's unqualified control over territory (sovereignty). Vivid evidence of the development of the modern state is shown by the fact that Europe in the fifteenth century was composed of some 500 political units and by the nineteenth century the number was twenty-five.[5]

There is a debate in international relations as to how this was achieved, but the outcome is that the nation became the powerful cultural glue that kept these states unified, giving sovereign legitimation to the state in eyes of the majority nation.[6] When these majority nations did not exist, the state constructed them by coercion and fiat.[7] The example of revolutionary France will be shown (see n. 30). This specific event in European history determined the way the international arena was constituted for centuries to come.

The term liberal democracy has different and contrasting meanings, and for this reason no consensual definition is possible. However, perhaps a common denominator could be extracted from contrasting definitions. Liberal democracy is a political system based on egalitarian rule and political liberties.[8] Here 'democracy' is only understood as a form of government that is accountable to the electorate, and one in which each citizen has a say on how the government is elected in periodical elections. Citizens are entitled and protected in expressing political views. While accepting that simplifications often occur in the expression of

[4] Bettina Engels, 'Contentious Politics of Scale: The Global Food Price Crisis and Local Protest in Burkina Faso', *Social Movement Studies*, vol. 14, no. 2 (2015): p. 181.

[5] Michael Hechter and William Brustein, 'Regional Modes of Production and Patterns of State Formation in Western Europe', *American Journal of Sociology*, vol. 85, no. 5 (1980): p. 1062; Pierre Bourdieu, Loic J. Wacquant, and Samar Farage, 'Rethinking the State: Genesis and Structure of the Bureaucratic Field', *Sociological Theory*, vol. 12, no. 1 (1994): pp. 4–5.

[6] Benno Teschke, 'Theorizing the Westphalian System of States: International Relations from Absolutism to Capitalism', *European Journal of International Relations*, vol. 8, no. 1 (2002): pp. 5–48.

[7] George W. White, *Nation, State, and Territory: Origins, Evolutions, and Relationships* (Lanham, Md: Rowman & Littlefield, 2007), p. 66; Andreas Wimmer and Yuval Feinstein, 'The Rise of the Nation-State across the World, 1816 to 2001', *American Sociological Review*, vol. 75, no. 5 (2010): p. 785.

[8] Kenneth A. Bollen and Pamela Paxton, 'Subjective Measures of Liberal Democracy', *Comparative Political Studies*, vol. 33, no. 1 (2000): p. 59.

political discourses, this common denominator raises questions and some important contradictions, which are at the heart of its democratic deficit discussed here.[9] The most basic of them is that liberalism in its many shapes and forms is individualistically oriented and democracy is a collective phenomenon. This potential contradiction creates for liberals a number of dilemmas, in which those normally at the more conservative side of liberalism emphasize individuality while those in the opposing faction emphasize democratic values and pluralism.

3.2 The Liberal Democratic Nation State and its Minorities

As the younger sister of the nation state, liberal democracy inherited from its elder sister a peculiar type of insensitivity towards the collective representation of cultural minorities. Minorities is a relational term and only exists in relation to dominant majorities (mostly titular nations). While minorities of different kinds and sorts have existed since the genesis of the nation state, and while the European Court of Human Rights has consistently protected minorities against discrimination, there are very few (if any) examples of sanctions when these rights are violated. In the case of the European Union (EU), while there are mechanisms in place to protect minorities these demand 'respect' and 'protection', but are no sanctions for a failure to protect.[10] Bührmann argues that it was only in 1978 in a lawsuit in California that the term 'diversity' was explicitly used to compensate minorities that suffered racial discrimination.[11] While this inattention might sound surprising, it is directly related to liberal democracy's aim to consolidate homogeneous demos through which the key principle of individual rights reigns supreme. In this way, liberal democracy can sustain its goal of an unrestricted equality between citizens while achieving a plurality of different and contrasting goals. This is what Charles Taylor calls 'procedural liberalism', a meticulously egalitarian procedure that provides the space for achieving a plurality of goals.[12] But for this egalitarian procedure, political inequality is the dangerous enemy. In the discouraging conflation of equality with sameness, not only, as Charles Taylor argues, is there more than a touch of ethnocentrism, but more ominously, difference is besmirched as inequality, and individual equality is elevated into the cornerstone of the collective identity of all citizens.[13] The ensuing minority alienation has a long history that goes back to the origins of the liberal democratic nation state, to the French Revolution and to the origins of English liberalism. It is one that

[9] Michael Farrelly, *Discourse and Democracy: Critical Analysis of the Language of Government* (Abingdon: Routledge, 2014), p. 16.

[10] Ahmed Tawhida, 'A Critical Appraisal of EU Governance for the Protection of Minority Rights', *International Journal on Minority and Group Rights*, vol. 17 (2010): p. 281.

[11] Andrea Bührmann, 'Gender—A Central Dimension of Diversity', in *Routledge Handbook of Diversity Studies*, edited by Steven Vertovec (Abingdon: Routledge, 2014), p. 23.

[12] Charles Taylor, 'Cross-purposes: the Liberal–Communitarian Debate', in *Debates in Contemporary Political Philosophy*, edited by Derek Matravers and Jon Pike (London: Routledge, 2003): p. 198.

[13] Taylor, 'Cross-purposes'; Tzvetan Todorov, *The Conquest of America and the Question of the Other* (Norman, OK: University of Oklahoma Press, 1999), p. 46.

until recently remained hidden under the seductive rhetoric of nation-building and of liberal modernization.

In the last few decades, some branches of feminism and multiculturalism began to problematize the liberal ideal of a procedural egalitarian citizenship, mounting in this way a challenge to the universal abstractions of liberal democracy. A feminism that is nurtured in a one liberal democratic national sovereignty could be oppressive to other women that are not part of it. Here, liberal democracy stands accused of decontextualizing gender oppression by focusing on abstract choices and possibilities that misrecognize the specificity of gender positions.[14] Carole Pateman's seminal work on the gendered character of liberal contractarian theory was followed by a concerted feminist questioning of the essence of the individual at the centre of liberal democratic theory.[15] The individual constructed by liberal democracy pretends to be universal: nationless, sexless, classless, disembodied, and is taken to represent an abstract, generalized model of humanity. But feminists began to argue that the liberal individual is derived from a precise cultural model, becoming a gendered, culturally particular, historically embodied person.[16] This idea influences well beyond feminism to constitute an important source of inspiration for contemporary multiculturalism.

Likewise, egalitarian, liberal democratic national sovereignty began to some extent to be considered as oppressive to outsiders of the dominant national community, or, what I prefer to call the 'titular nation'.[17] The original cultural specificity of liberal equality and individual equality of opportunity is hidden behind a veil of universalism, and as such it misrecognizes cultural diversity. The idea of a 'benign neglect' of minority cultures is far from benign; it ignores that minorities in liberal nation states often face disadvantages that majorities do not face.[18] Liberal democratic neutrality is therefore considered false.[19] Malik in a suggestive article proposes Minority Legal Orders to remedy the inequalities of liberal democracies.[20] For many feminists and multiculturalists, the egalitarian

[14] Daiva Stansiulis, 'Relational Positionalities of Nationalisms, Racisms, and Feminisms', in *Between Woman and Nation: Nationalisms, Transnational Feminisms, and the State*, edited by Caren Kaplan, Norma Alarcon, and Minoo Moallem (Durham NC: Duke University Press, 1999): p. 183; Mary Evans, 'Getting Real: Contextualising Gender', in *Sage Handbook of Gender and Women's Studies*, edited by Kathy Davis, Mary Evans, and Judith Lorber (London: Sage, 2006), pp. 475–6.

[15] Carole Pateman, *The Sexual Contract* (Stanford: Stanford University Press, 1988).

[16] Celeste Friend, 'Social Contract Theory', in *Internet Encyclopaedia of Philosophy*, 2004, accessed 2 February 2015, http://www.iep.utm.edu/soc-cont/.

[17] The term 'titular nation' is taken from the terminology of the former Soviet Union, but it is applicable to most liberal democratic nation states. It refers to the governing ethno-national community, usually the majority of the population, typically after which the state is named. The term is used in this way in Juan Linz and Alfred Stepan, 'Toward Consolidated Democracies', *Journal of Democracy*, vol. 7, no. 2 (1996): p. 25.

[18] Will Kymlicka, *Multicultural Citizenship* (Oxford: Oxford University Press, 1995), p. 110.

[19] Bhikhu Parekh, 'The Cultural Particularity of Liberal Democracy', in *Prospects for Democracy*, edited by David Held (Cambridge: Polity Press, 1993), pp. 156–75; Taylor, 'Cross-purposes'; James Tully, *Strange Multiplicity: Constitutionalism in the Age of Diversity* (Cambridge: Cambridge University Press, 1995).

[20] Maleiha Malik, 'Minorities and Law: Past and Present', *Current Legal Problems*, vol. 67, no. 1 (2014): pp. 67–98.

universalizing abstractions of liberal democracy are intolerant. Kymlicka argues that minority demands raise a deep challenge to the architecture of the liberal democratic nation state.[21] The accusation is of an arbitrary equality and of institutional and representative misrecognition of diversity. In a more radical fashion, Leslie G. Carr published 'Colour-Blind Racism', a polemical and influential attack on colour-blind notions of equality prevailing among liberals in the US.[22] Differences that affect women and to a lesser extent, minority communities, require that egalitarian liberal citizenship be alleviated with some remedial group rights, such as differential rights for women, and to a lesser extent, some group rights to minority communities.[23] Here we begin to find how the normative ideal of democratic inclusion begins to challenge and bring to the open the blind spots of liberal democracy. Non-territorial autonomy (NTA) is one of a variety of expressions of this democratic challenge. It will be discussed here because it offers an alternative in the form of minority representation, one that challenges the tyranny of the majority reflected in the liberal ideal of sole individual representation or one person one vote, to enhance the democratic representation of dispersed minorities.

However these challenges face considerable difficulties. In the contemporary world, there are very few, if any, who dare to criticize such an overriding political system, which in the most powerful states has become both hegemonic and synonymous with fair governance. With some very few exceptions, liberal democracy is exercised in the context of most 'Western' nation states, and these states uncritically submit to the limitations of the liberal modality of governance. Historically, liberal democracy and the nation state are intimately related even if they are not identical.[24] While accepting the important progressive and egalitarian achievements of liberal democracy, this chapter will argue that this regime hides behind its bonhomie and desire for real fairness a recurrent form of democratic deficit that enshrines under the guise of majority rule the collective autocracy of the titular nation. This takes the form of a disguised and sweet dictatorship of the majority that endorses the celebration of individual rights, freedom of expression and individualism, and even the relative protection of minorities, but that at the same time, imposes severe limits on the possibilities of minority community representation.[25] Instead, liberal democracy prefers the assimilation of cultural minorities into forms of governance based upon majority rule, which offers minority members participation as individual citizens, that is, assimilation with democracy as compensation. But this leads to an apparent contradiction of liberal

[21] Kymlicka, *Multicultural Citizenship*, p. 150.

[22] Leslie G. Carr, *'Colour-Blind' Racism* (Thousand Oaks, CA: Sage, 1997).

[23] Roland Axtmann, *Liberal Democracy into the Twenty-First Century: Globalization, Integration and the Nation-State* (Manchester University Press, 1996), p. 115.

[24] Axtmann, *Liberal Democracy into the Twenty-First Century.*

[25] Will Kymlicka and Christine Straehle, 'Cosmopolitanism, Nation-States, and Minority Nationalism: A Critical Review of Recent Literature', *European Journal of Philosophy*, vol. 7, no. 1 (1999): p. 75.

democracy: the advocacy of individual equality and representation while negating the collective representation of its minority communities.

As a consequence of the democratic deficit that results from the liberal antipathy to collective minority representation, the democratic ideal acts as a subversive catalyst for change. Among others, unrelated demands for NTA emerge among territorially dispersed minority communities in an attempt to supersede the democratic deficit of individually oriented liberal democracies. Conversely, when non-territorial collective representation of dispersed minority communities is incorporated into liberal democratic forms of governance, it expands the democratic value of the model, providing for a more plural, inclusive, stable, and representative modality of governance.

3.3 The Securitization of Minorities in Liberal Democratic Nation States

'The national state claims to treat all citizens as equal members of the nation; this fair principle only serves to disguise the tyranny of one group over another. The nation must be, all its citizens must be, animated with the same spirit. Differences are divisive and therefore treasonable.'[26] Nation state liberal democracies have a tendency to conflate territorial-NSD with popular sovereignty in the guise of majority rule.[27] The ultimate authority, the sovereign, is the body of citizens incarnated in the collective identity of the titular nation. However, this incarnation is mediated by a particular hegemonic discursive interpretation. To make this clear, the titular nation, while crammed with cultural baggage, is empty on political content, becoming in this way an arena for struggle between opposing ideological interpretations that aim to build hegemonic blocs as 'true' representatives of the nation. This is why generic forms of nationalism are neither 'left' nor 'right'. In contrast, concrete forms of nationalism are interpretations of the above-mentioned cultural baggage through an ideological lens that could be classified, among other things, as 'left' or 'right'. In either way, this characteristic of the sovereign nation compromises democratic representation because of its propensity to conflate ethnos with demos. Sériot uncovers an important point.[28] The contradictory conflation of ethnos with demos is not a circumstantial occurrence, but occurs in the peculiar characteristic of the term 'the people', which is from the start engraved with the apparently inconsistent duality ethnos–demos:

> We can then propose a classification scale with a bi-polar opposition between two extreme points, from a strong unanimity (on the basis of language, ethnicity or religion, that is

[26] Elie Kedourie, *Nationalism* (London: Hutchinson, 1960), p. 127.

[27] Lea Brilmayer, 'Secession and Self-Determination: A Territorial Interpretation', *Yale Journal of International Law*, vol. 16 (1991): pp. 179–80.

[28] Patrick Sériot, 'Ethnos et demos: la construction discursive de l'identité collective' [Ethnos and Demos: the Discursive Construction of Collective Identity], *Langage et société*, no. 9 (1997): pp. 39–51.

to say a hypertrophy principle of ethnos) to a broader consideration of the social division (the principle of demos). But this opposition is neither cultural nor ontological: the term the people points to the same referent, but built through a space of different features (my own translation).[29]

In other words, 'the sovereign people' is neither a civic nor an ethnic concept, but a mixed construction of both elements that creates a monistic identity from which ethnic and civic dimensions cannot be easily disentangled. If liberal democratic nation states were culturally homogeneous this will not be a problem. But there is almost always more than one nation or ethnic group in a sovereign territorial space, and minority ethnic groups and nations find it difficult to be collectively represented through the monist nationalism of the liberal democratic nation state's titular nation. In the manner above, the liberal democratic nation state has a democratic deficit in its failure to allow for the symbolic and political collective representation of minority communities that are part of the body of citizens.

National Self-Determination (NSD), as recorded in international law and enshrined in UN resolutions, and as argued in many liberal democratic theories, is the principle that nations have the right to freely choose their sovereign international political status with no external compulsion or external interference. In this doctrine, nationhood and territorial sovereignty are linked, for nations are a constitutive element of the configuration of nation states. It need not be so, and it was not so before modernity. The above is not the only way to understand NSD, and only one peculiar way to understand democracy. However, by virtue of being hegemonic, this interpretation is the most common and the most dangerous for minorities. It has the proclivity to sacrifice cultural minorities on the high altar of nation-building, to securitize cultural communities though the conflation of ethnos with demos. This is by no means a recent development, but one that goes back to earliest modern expressions of republican egalitarianism, and is in more ways than one, a constitutive failure of the modern liberal democratic nation state. Consider the statements of radical Jacobins:

The language of a free people (or sovereign people) must be one and the same for all.... Federalism and superstition speak low Breton, emigration and hatred of the Republic speaks German, the counter-revolution speaks Italian and fanaticism speaks Basque. Let's break these unfortunate and mistaken instruments...

Among the ancient languages, Welsh [*sic*] (Cymraeg), Gascon, Celtic, Visigoths, Phoenicians or Oriental that provide certain subtleties for communicating with various

[29] 'On peut alors proposer une échelle de classification avec une opposition bi-polaire entre deux points extrêmes, depuis un fort unanimisme (sur la base de la langue, de l'ethnicité ou de la religion, c'est-à-dire une hypertrophie du principe de ethnos) jusqu'à une large prise en compte de la division sociale (le principe du demos). Mais cette opposition n'est ni ontologique ni culturelle: si dans les deux cas le mot peuple désigne symboliquement le même référent, il le construit dans un espace de propriétés distinct.' Sériot, 'Ethnos et demos', p. 49.

citizens and countries that make up the territory of the Republic, we have observed (and reports from representatives that are in line with those of various agents sent to departments) that the said Breton, Basque language, German and Italian languages have perpetuated the reign of fanaticism and superstition, ensured the domination of priests, nobles and practitioners, prevented the revolution from reaching nine major departments, and may be to the advantage of the enemies of France (my own translation).[30]

Here you have a splendid *avant la lettre* example of securitization of minorities, 210 years before the term was coined! Securitization is not a contemporary innovation as many international relations users of securitization argue, but a by-product of the historical conflation of nations, popular sovereignty, and territorial states. In whatever way one defines national-popular sovereignty, it is a concept dependent upon the definition of cultural-territorial boundaries, which inexorably creates outsiders and cultural insiders.

To be sure, this argument is not a peculiarity of French republicanism, far from it. It is also present in the works of the founding father of English liberalism. Consider John Stuart Mill's well-known assertion that:

Free institutions are next to impossible in a country made up of different nationalities.... Among people without fellow-feeling, especially if they speak different languages, the united public opinion, necessary to the working of representative government cannot exist.[31]

For this reason, the securitization of minorities is not a contemporary situation brought about by the so-called war on terror but a constitutive deficiency of the nation state, particularly in its liberal democratic variance. This deficiency generated what Michael Mann calls in an important work, 'The Dark Side of Democracy'; its propensity for ethnic cleansing.[32] I will here immediately qualify Mann's generalization of the process he so eloquently and incisively describes with one important consideration. Ethnic cleansing is not the dark side of democracy, for the latter has forms that roundly escape this cruel imposition—democracy

[30] Bertrand Barère de Vieuzac, 'Rapport du Comité de salut public sur les idiomes', *Report of the Committee of Public Health on Languages* (1794), accessed 12 December 2014, http://www.tlfq.ulaval.ca/axl/francophonie/barere-rapport.htm. 'La langue d'un peuple libre doit être une et la même pour tous....Le fédéralisme et la superstition parlent bas-breton; l'émigration et la haine de la république parlent allemand; la contre-révolution parle italien et le fanatisme parle basque. Brisons ces instruments de dommage et d'erreur...Parmi les idiomes anciens, welches, gascons, celtiques, wisigoths, phocéens ou orientaux, qui forment quelques nuances dans les communications des divers citoyens et des pays formant le territoire de la République, nous avons observé (et les rapports des représentants se réunissent sur ce point avec ceux des divers agents envoyés dans les départements) que l'idiome appelé bas-breton, l'idiome basque, les langues allemande et italienne ont perpétué le règne du fanatisme et de la superstition, assuré la domination des prêtres, des nobles et des praticiens, empêché la révolution de pénétrer dans neuf départements importants, et peuvent favoriser les ennemis de la France.'

[31] John Stuart Mill, 'Considerations of Representative Government', in *Utilitarism, On Liberty and Considerations on Representative Government*, edited by H. B. Acton (London: J. M. Dent & Sons, 1862/1976): pp. 187–428.

[32] Michael Mann, *The Dark Side of Democracy: Explaining Ethnic Cleansing* (Cambridge: Cambridge University Press, 2005).

must *not* be exclusively conflated with popular sovereignty and liberal democratic representative democracy in nation states. What Mann refers to is the dark side of the sovereign, popular democratic nation state, and the likely by-product of the exercise of national (territorial) self-determination in areas of mixed populations. In these cases, when two or more national communities reside in the same territorial space, when it is not possible to territorially disentangle one from the other, popular national sovereignty and territorial national self-determination become a zero-sum game. The gain of one is unavoidably the loss of the other. For this reason, ethno-national conflicts in mixed areas are bloody, extremely violent, and protracted, for full victory and nation state for one means the expulsion or destruction of the other.

From here, and fortunately in a much less extreme fashion, resemblances notwithstanding, out of the concurrence of French republicanism and English liberalism, the model of a democratically sovereign monocultural state over which one (titular) nation exercises its right to self-determination, became the imprint of the modern process of liberal democratic national emancipation. It was used in the colonial settler states of the Americas and Oceania to politically preserve and protect the newly created colonial settler nations in lands illegitimately taken from indigenous peoples, who were then subjected to ethnic cleansing and genocide. Whatever other reasons are invoked, most of the European-inspired nation states of the Americas and Oceania were born under the original sin of genocide and ethnic cleansing. When the equality of all citizens is conflated with equality for all members of the nation under the guise of an egalitarian liberal democracy in nascent colonial settler societies, these societies are, as Michael Mann argues, at their most murderous, for they create a community of insiders that must destroy their local outsiders (which often outnumber the new nation), if the new-born liberal nation state is to expand and survive.

In whatever way one understands liberal democratic national-popular sovereignty, the demos is always entangled with residues of the ethnos, and as such defines mechanisms of inclusion and exclusion, mechanisms that by virtue of their inescapable national dimension, are to some extent cultural. Sovereignty is thus the prerogative of a titular nation, and this sits uncomfortably with normative claims of democracy and liberalism. This is convincingly shown in an example by Paul Stratham in relation to the debate over asylum seekers: he claims that the issue of asylum:

> Opens up a particular contradiction within liberal nation-states: it puts the universal principle that they should respect and protect human rights by offering asylum to aliens fleeing persecution in direct competition with the principle that they should primarily serve the interests of the national community of people from whom sovereignty derives—a group with a self-image of common descent and ethnicity enshrined in a shared nationhood.[33]

[33] Paul Stratham, 'Understanding Anti-Asylum Rhetoric: Restrictive Politics or Racist Publics?', *The Political Quarterly*, vol. 74, Supplement s1 (2003): p. 165.

When understood in the manner above, the doctrines of popular nation state sovereignty and NSD are monistic, and are neither pluralist nor inclusive. It is important to note here that the conflation of ethnos with demos might not be in some circumstances dangerous: in the form of collective rights and community representation, for example. Like in many deadly explosives, in isolation the ingredients are harmless; it could even be argued that in the case of collective rights, the conflation of ethnos with demos might offer a positive contribution to the expansion of democracy to alienated or subordinated communities. The argument here is that the formula becomes unstable and dynamite-like when it incorporates ethnos as the foundation for the *single demos*, and as an equivalent to popular territorial sovereignty in a single monist mixture. In this explosive mix, NSD and territorial sovereignty legitimize the governance of only a minority of nations, the titular ones. It threatens others with disappearance in most cases through forceful assimilation, or thankfully in a small number of cases, through ethnic cleansing and genocide. In this way, this type of sovereign self-determination contradicts liberal democratic, universally egalitarian values that laid the original foundation of its principles. Fortunately, this established doctrine of NSD is being frontally challenged by the demands of territorial minorities, first and foremost indigenous peoples, both territorially scattered and concentrated, and in this way, they (the territorial minorities) act as facilitators for a historical paradigm shift taking place on the meaning of NSD, and whose importance goes well beyond self-determination demands and revises well established notions in democratic theory.

3.4 The Centralist Atomist Principle and the Limits of Liberal Democracies

Otto Bauer argues that the liberal democratic state is an imperfect democracy because it is organized according to the 'centralist-atomist' principle.[34] In the genesis of the modern nation state, Bauer argues, one of its most important characteristics, its centralization of power, was initially developed by absolutism. This centralization was completed in a democratic manner, through the abolition of guilds, estates, and other segmental organizations. This had the effect of reducing recognized political players to their smallest parts (which Bauer calls 'atoms'), that is, to single individual citizens. For Otto Bauer and Karl Renner, a constitutional jurist, the legal representative order in liberal democracies knows only two units: on the one hand, the sovereignty of the state and on the other, the sovereignty of the individual citizen.

[34] Otto Bauer, *The Question of Nationalities and Social Democracy* [Nationalitätenfrage und die Sozialdemokratie], with an Introduction by Ephraim Nimni, Preface by Heinz Fischer (Minneapolis: University of Minnesota Press, 2000), pp. xv–xlviii.

Constitutionally, in nation state liberal democracies, there are two recognized sovereign politico-juridical entities, the atomized citizen and the collective totality. This logic is also applicable to federal territorial states with some adjustments to cater for the division of competences between the central state and the provinces. In both cases, the juridical political entities are atomized individuals and the sovereign will of the undivided collective. This is what Bauer calls the centralist-atomist structure of modern liberal democratic nation states. This organizational characteristic expels all intermediate communitarian players from the arena of representative politics.

There can be no doubt in Bauer's mind that in some important cases this led to the expansion of democracy through the irrevocable abolition of sectarian political privilege, in the form of castes, feudal guilds, landlords, etc. It simultaneously threw the new-born democratic baby out with the bath water, for it impoverished the quality of the nascent democracy. This is because it also abolished and made impossible mechanisms of representation of different, territorially scattered national and ethnic minorities which are left at the mercy of governmental bureaucracies and worse, of the tyranny of the majority; a less than adequate form of democracy.

The citizens of the modern state are nationally identified with the state through residence and citizenship, irrespectively of ethnic and national affiliations.[35] Most states represented in the UN are thus seen as nation states whether or not they are ethnically or nationally homogeneous. In the liberal democratic nation state the cultural practice of the dominant nation (the titular nation or if you prefer, the official ethnicity of the state) is disguised by a procedural practice that claims neutrality but is derived from the cultural and historical experiences of the dominant national community.

Following the logic of this argument, atomistic states, however much consideration they might show for individual and democratic rights, and however egalitarian their practices, are averse to recognizing collective representation mechanisms for their cultural minorities. These demands are effectively suppressed with what are apparently 'democratic instruments', via the tyranny of the majority. In a paradoxical way, this situation puts de facto, but not d*e jure* multination states in a position of instability, for there are no actionable legal mechanisms to represent national minorities. Both majorities and minorities are faced with an increasingly difficult dilemma: to coercively assimilate cultural minorities through the lure of democratization, or alternatively to split the de facto multination state along national lines. Both strategies have been tried with calamitous results.

[35] Uri Ra'anan, Maria Mesner, Keith Armes, and Kate Martin, eds, *State and Nation in Multi-Ethnic Societies: The Breakup of the Multinational State* (Manchester and New York: Manchester University Press, 1991).

3.5 NTA as a Democratic Alternative

NTA is not a specific model for the incorporation of minorities or dispersed communities, nor does it have a common prescription or line of action. It is a generic form of collective rights and collective representation, which aims to share sovereignty between different communities. The modality develops forms of community representation across non-territorial lines, allowing for minority communities to be collectively represented in governance, while sharing a territorial space with other communities that are equally represented. The idea emerges to remedy the limitations of the atomist-centralist characteristic of liberal democracies by which modalities of representation are only individually based. It expands democracy and enhances pluralism through the participation of hitherto estranged minorities and cultural groups. The principal advantage of NTA models is that they incorporate modalities of governance that can take place while the self-determining communities reside in shared territorial spaces, obviating in this way what is often a lethal competition for exclusive territorial sovereignty. I have developed this argument in detail elsewhere, so I will only present the argument here schematically.[36]

NTA includes an mixture of different arrangements such as consociationalism and national cultural autonomy (NCA), but also forms of representation that de-territorialize self-determination, as in the case of indigenous communities, the juridical autonomy of religious communities, or in the practice of many forms of religious and/or multicultural forms of representation, as in the recognition of the Jewish Beth Din in the United Kingdom and the proposal from the former Archbishop of Canterbury, Dr Rowan Williams[37] to incorporate aspects of sharia law into British law.[38] Models of NTA are incessantly evolving into different forms and shapes, becoming an important tool for the effective participation of minorities in public life, as advocated by the 'The Lund Recommendations on the Effective Participation of National Minorities in Public Life'.[39]

The difficulty in comprehending the characteristics of NTA results from the fact that it seems counter-intuitive to understand mechanisms of community representation outside the framework of the accepted universal vision of one citizen one vote modality of liberal democratic nation states. This state-centric view recognizes national communities only as a collection of imagined communities inherently

[36] Ephraim Nimni, 'Democratic Theory and the Autonomy of Non-Christian Religious Courts in the UK', in *New Multicultural Identities in Europe*, edited by Erkan Toğuşlu, Johan Leman, and İsmail Sezgin (Leuven: University of Leuven Press, 2014), pp. 195–211.

[37] Rowan Williams, 'Civil and Religious Law in England: A Religious Perspective', *Ecclesiastical Law Journal*, vol. 10 (2008): pp. 262–82.

[38] Nimni, 'Democratic Theory and the Autonomy of Non-Christian Religious Courts in the UK'.

[39] Ephraim Nimni, 'Cultural Minority Self Governance', in *Political Participation of Minorities: A Commentary on International Standards and Practice*, edited by Marc Weller and Katherine Nobbs (New York: Oxford University Press, 2010), pp. 634–60.

limited and sovereign, which are furthermore legitimized by territorial states.[40] In view of this hegemonic manner of thinking, to understand non-territorial minority governance requires a leap of imagination, to be counter-intuitive and challenge the supremacy of the state-centric paradigm. For minority nationalisms to remain viable in a world overcrowded by nation states, they have to be oriented to forms of NSD that can provide satisfaction to their representation needs, without dismembering existing states.

Furthermore, the cultural configuration of nation states in the contemporary world severely tests the eighteenth-century template of cultural unity as a tool for state centralization. It is not cultural unity that is the distinguishing mark of most contemporary nation states, but the opposite, a de facto cultural and religious diversity that challenges the *de jure* model of the cultural unity of the liberal democratic nation state. Liberal theorists assume that the protection of the rights of individuals is sufficient to protect minority rights and ensure justice in culturally diverse societies. As argued above, traditional liberal thinking supports the ideal that a set of neutral political and social rights, based purely on individual needs, is sufficient to guarantee equality.

Unfortunately, this is not the case. A majority in a liberal democratic state can block the inclusion or influence of a cultural minority without abandoning the individual civil and political rights of minority members. The majority can monopolize important powers, even those affecting the cultural survival of the minority community such as language, education, and development. This intrusion is an injustice, but if individual members of the minority community are recognized the right to free speech, to campaign for their point of view, and to petition the government, the rights of these individuals are not considered violated.[41] Likewise, in a one person one vote system, cultural minorities by virtue of numbers do not have electorally much influence. Consider, for example, indigenous peoples. They have in most cases been the victims of colonization by settler liberal democracies. The victims of conquest and destruction of ancestral lands by settler colonialism and those who have been made marginal minorities in their homelands have a unique claim for self-governance, community rights, and the recognition of their cultural heritage.[42] Yet many colonial settler societies are established liberal democracies (US, Canada, Australia, and Argentina, to cite a few); the principles of individual human rights are not sufficient to recognize the need for collective enfranchisement of indigenous peoples. To prevent these injustices, traditional human rights principles need to be supplemented with communal minority rights, which in the majority of cases require forms

[40] Benedict Anderson, *Imagined Communities: Reflections on the Origin and Spread of Nationalism* (London: Verso, 1991), p. 6.

[41] Kymlicka and Straehle, 'Cosmopolitanism, Nation-States, and Minority Nationalism: A Critical Review of Recent Literature', p. 75.

[42] Leanne Simpson, 'Anticolonial Strategies for the Recovery and Maintenance of Indigenous Knowledge', *American Indian Quarterly*, vol. 283, no. 4 (2004): pp. 373–84.

of non-territorial autonomous representation for indigenous and other dispersed minority communities.[43]

3.6 NTA and its Multiplicity of Forms

NTA operates in different and varied forms. The common denominator is the challenge to the hegemony of territorial sovereignty and the creation of modalities of community political representation for minority and territorially scattered communities. As the democratic deficits of the liberal democratic nation state model are slowly uncovered, NTA models emerge independently in different parts of the world, triggered by similar problems, but without necessarily being aware of each other, and without cross-referencing experiences. In this way, modalities of NTA acquire slowly but surely the form of a bottom-up incremental paradigm shift in areas of minority representation, NSD, and democratic governance. In what follows, a few old and new examples of NTA models will be schematically presented.

3.6.1 NCA

The NCA model is often presented as the symbol of NTA, but this is only partially correct. It is one important model in the trajectory of NTA, but it is not the only one, nor does it exhaust all aspects of NTA. NCA has its origins in the final days of the Habsburg Empire. It was an ingenious attempt by the intellectual elite of the Austrian Socialist Party to convert the Austrian side of the Habsburg Empire from a disorderly union of different nationalities brought together by coercion into a democratic federation of nationalities, in which all nationalities felt adequately represented. Austria was at that time an advanced industrial parliamentary dual monarchy, operating in accordance with the standards of representative democracies of the day.[44] The NCA model was bold and innovative for its time. In sharp contrast to prevailing forms of national autonomy through territorial governance, the NCA model attempted to protect the Austrian part of the empire from disintegration into nation states. The central idea was that autonomous cultural communities could create mechanisms of political representation on a non-territorial basis, as most of them shared their residential areas with others. The idea was to create a democratic multination state in which the political representation of the national communities inhabiting the Austrian Empire is exercised by national corporations on a non-territorial basis. In this context, the idea of majorities and

[43] Michelle Bonner and Matt James, 'The Three R's of Seeking Transitional Justice: Reparation, Responsibility, and Reframing in Canada and Argentina', *The International Indigenous Policy Journal*, vol. 2, no. 3 (2011), retrieved from: http://ir.lib.uwo.ca/iipj/vol2/iss3/3.

[44] Ephraim Nimni, 'Nationalist Multiculturalism in Late Imperial Austria as a Critique of Contemporary Liberalism: The Case of Bauer and Renner', *Journal of Political Ideologies*, vol. 4 (1999), pp. 289–314.

minorities ceases to have its explosive meaning, for even if there were only a small number of members of a national community in a particular region, the numerical relation was not important because they were collectively represented across the territory of the multination state. It was above all an attempt to bring fresh solutions to the nationalities problem that dogged central Europe.[45]

In contemporary terms, a model that has some similarities to NCA was introduced in the Brussels-Capital region[46] because of the impossibility of separating two national communities in an urban environment.[47] But except for Van Parijs, the similarities with NCA are hardly mentioned. In sharp contrast; the Russian State Duma also adopted a Russian federal law on NCA in 1996, explicitly referring to the Austrian model and to Karl Renner. But unfortunately, the resulting Russian model has little resemblance to Bauer and Renner's original NCA model.[48]

The NCA model suggests that the multination state be managed in a parallel, two-tier system, with participating national communities endowed with a collective persona, in the form of legally guaranteed autonomous corporations. The idea is that members of each national body, whatever their area of residence, form a single public body or association endowed with legal personality and collective rights.[49] The model was never implemented in Austria, but it was for a time implemented in the Baltic states during the interwar period.[50]

3.6.2 Consociationalism

Consociationalism is, for better or worse, the best known of the NTA modalities. It presents a clear alternative to the tyranny of the majority provoked by the liberal democratic one person one vote system, and it has been used with some success to manage conflict. The term was popularized by Arend Lijphart,[51] but was significantly enhanced by John McGarry and Brendan O'Leary in a series of seminal works on conflict resolution in Northern Ireland[52] and recently on human rights

[45] John Hiden and David Smith, 'Looking beyond the Nation State: A Baltic Vision for National Minorities between the Wars', *Journal of Contemporary History*, vol. 41 (2006): p. 387.

[46] Philippe Van Parijs, 'Must Europe Be Belgian? On Democratic Citizenship in Multilingual Polities', in *The Demands of Citizenship*, edited by Catriona McKinnon and Iain Hampsher-Monk (London/New York: Continuum, Bloomsbury Publishing, 2000): p. 246.

[47] Dirk Jacobs and Marc Swyngedouw, 'Territorial and Non-Territorial Federalism in Belgium: Reform of the Brussels Capital Region, 2001', *Regional and Federal Studies*, vol. 13, no. 2 (2003): pp.127–30.

[48] Bill Bowring, 'Burial and Resurrection, Karl Renner's Controversial Influence on the "National Question" in Russia', in *National Cultural Autonomy and its Contemporary Critics*, edited by Ephraim Nimni (London: Routledge, 2005), pp. 191–206.

[49] Nimni, 'Nationalist Multiculturalism in Late Imperial Austria as a Critique of Contemporary Liberalism', pp. 296–7.

[50] For a detailed recent discussion, see Hiden and Smith, 'Looking beyond the Nation State'.

[51] Arend Lijphart, *Democracy in Plural Societies: A Comparative Exploration* (New Haven, CT: Yale University Press, 1977).

[52] Rupert Taylor, ed., *Consociational Theory, McGarry and O'Leary and the Northern Ireland Conflict* (London: Routledge, 2009); Brendan O'Leary, 'Debating Consociational Politics: Normative and Explanatory Arguments', in *From Power Sharing to Democracy: Post-Conflict Institutions in*

and power-sharing.[53] Consociationalism is a more centralized, elite-based model than NCA, and it is structured around the principles of a grand coalition across conflicting cultural divides, mutual veto on matters vital for the continuity of the minority communities, proportionality in representation, and the segmental autonomy of each community. In Northern Ireland the representation is electoral in accordance with the one person one vote system, in line with the D'Hondt method, but government coalitions require separate community support. In fact each of the two blocs has veto powers. As with NCA, the aim is to engage in a process of power-sharing in which all participant communities feel as represented partners. The idea is to make government more responsive to the participation of minorities and to offer alternative outcomes to territorial nationalism and secession. The model has been applied with success in Northern Ireland, leading to the pacification of the country and showing the way towards the long-term resolution of what was an intractable conflict. In this regard, it has served as an example for many similar conflicts elsewhere.

3.6.3 The Ottoman *millet* system

The *millet* system was an autocratic regime of minority community governance which bore similarities to the previous two models, but with the crucial difference that the *millet* system until the 1860s was not organized according to democratic principles, but instead vested all power and authority in the religious leader of the minority community. The Ottoman *millet* system nevertheless exhibited remarkable tolerance and recognition of the autonomy of minority communities and their way of life. In a paradoxical way, because the Ottoman Empire was an autocratic system, it did not require assimilation to create a community of equals, but required instead loyalty and submission to the authority of the Sublime Porte (*Bab-ı Ali*), the Ottoman site of government. Once submission and loyalty were assured, the minorities were left to manage their own affairs with minimal interference from the Ottoman authorities. The model in its original, pre-1860s, Ottoman form is not suitable for democratic societies. Yet, if it could be democratized and run in accordance with established principles of human rights, it could be a very valuable addition to the contemporary expansion of models of NTA, particularly in Islamic societies. In a recent thought-provoking article Tas argues for the democratization of the model together with the incorporation of modalities of territorial autonomy

Ethnically Divided Societies, edited by Sid Noel (Montreal: McGill-Queen's Press, 2005): pp. 3–43; John McGarry and Brendan O'Leary, 'Consociational Theory, Northern Ireland's Conflict, and its Agreement: What Critics of Consociation Can Learn from Northern Ireland', *Government and Opposition*, vol. 41 (2006): pp. 249–77.

[53] Christopher McCrudden and Brendan O'Leary, *Courts and Consociations: Human Rights versus Power Sharing* (Oxford: Oxford University Press, 2013).

into a hybrid system which he calls TANTA (Territorial Autonomy and Non Territorial Autonomy).[54]

Interestingly, and showing the lack of European alternatives to non-territorial minority autonomy, the *millet* system has caught the imagination of many contemporary political theorists concerned with minority rights and the recognition of difference. Nuri Yurdusev argues that the Ottoman Empire granted more minority autonomy than many of the known empires.[55] It recognized forms of institutional diversity and created a political and social environment for the reproduction of diverse cultures. It allowed for forms of limited diversity and stability in ways that are rarely combined in contemporary societies. Bhikhu Parekh argues that despite its important shortcomings, the *millet* system had great virtues including 'a remarkable record of religious toleration that puts Western Europe to shame'.[56] Several authors, including Sarah Abrevaya Stern, argue that the Ottoman Jewish community thrived under the *millet* system, enjoying forms of protection not extended to minorities under Christian rule.[57] Non-Muslims were allowed to maintain their own courts and institutions and evolved into corporate structures as a result. Stern further argues that as far as Jews were concerned, the success of the *millet* system was reflected in the 'virtual absence of anti-Semitism from the Ottoman landscape', something that cannot be said of Christian Europe.[58] The noted political philosopher Michael Walzer considers that the autonomous arrangements of the *millet* system represent the most stable regime of toleration known in world history. Walzer claims that 'the rulers recognised the value of group autonomy, and this recognition has worked effectively for group survival'.[59] However, Will Kymlicka argues that while the *millet* system was generally tolerant of group differences, it was not a liberal society, for it did not tolerate individual dissent within its constituent communities.[60]

As said, the Ottoman *millet* was undemocratic and authoritarian as it vested power on religious authorities. But at the same time, it did not demand assimilation to the titular nation and afforded more tolerance and protection to minorities than current republican and majoritarian democracies. Unlike the nation state, the logic of ethnic assimilation was not the dominant logic of Ottoman politics.[61]

[54] Latif Tas, 'The Myth of the Ottoman Millet System: Its Treatment of Kurds and a Discussion of Territorial and Non-Territorial Autonomy', *International Journal on Minority and Group Rights*, vol. 21, no. 4 (2014): p. 523.

[55] Nuri A. Yurdusev, *Ottoman Diplomacy, Conventional or Unconventional?* (Basingstoke: Palgrave Macmillan, 2004), p. 20.

[56] Parekh, 'The Cultural Particularity of Liberal Democracy', p. 205.

[57] Sarah A. Stern, 'The Permeable Boundaries of Ottoman Jewry', in *Boundaries and Belonging: States and Societies in the Struggle to Shape Identities and Local Practices*, edited by Joel Migdal (Cambridge: Cambridge University Press, 2004), pp. 49–70.

[58] Stern, 'The Permeable Boundaries of Ottoman Jewry', p. 55.

[59] Michael Walzer, *Arguing about War* (New Haven, CT: Yale University Press, 2004), p. 177.

[60] Will Kymlicka, 'Two Models of Pluralism and Tolerance', *Analyse & Kritik*, vol. 14 (1992): p. 36.

[61] Mesut Yeğen, 'The Kurdish Question in Turkish State Discourse', *Journal of Contemporary History*, vol. 34 (2009): p. 557.

3.6.4 The plurinational state of Bolivia

A recent promising example of NTA is the constitutional order in the plurinational state of Bolivia. Here indigenous groups and intellectuals created a plurinational state project to support indigenous non-territorial self-determination. This is now inscribed in the Bolivian constitution of 2009.[62] Latin American indigenous movements, and in particular, the new constitutional arrangements in Bolivia, refer to 'plurinationalism' in formulating demands for indigenous communities' rights, and for the transformation of what thus far is a nation state into a plurinational state, granting collective rights to the commonwealth of indigenous communities that inhabit it.[63]

The Bolivian constitution defines the state as 'plurinational and communitarian' as it recognizes the collective rights of its indigenous nations. The definition of the plurinational state implies the recognition of a 'commonwealth of demoi' and the meaning of this will be discussed in section 3.8 in the European context. This recognition grants indigenous communities collective rights and the status of collective personae. In this regard, Article 2 of the constitution states that 'Given the existence of pre-colonial indigenous nations and peoples and their ancestral connection over its territories, the self-determination of these communities is hereby recognized in the framework of the unity of the state.'[64] Article 11 of the constitution states that its aim is to establish a 'participative, representative and communitarian' democracy'.[65] The constitution also defines the people of Bolivia as: 'the totality of Bolivians, the indigenous nations and peoples, the intercultural and afro-Bolivian communities which constitute together the Bolivian people'. Here we have a definition of the people which is markedly different from the homogenizing view of the traditional nation state. It presents the plurality of rural communities and mixed race urban groups (mestizos), as well as the afro-Bolivian communities. The emphasis is then in the unity of the Bolivian people in the plurality of community representation.[66] The linguistic diversity of the plurinational state of Bolivia is also an important marker of both unity and diversity. While

[62] Isabella Radhuber, 'Indigenous Struggles for a Plurinational State: An Analysis of Indigenous Rights and Competences in Bolivia', *Journal of Latin American Geography*, vol. 11, no. 2 (2012): p. 167.

[63] Bret Gustafson, 'Manipulating Cartographies: Plurinationalism, Autonomy, and Indigenous Resurgence in Bolivia', *Anthropological Quarterly*, vol. 82 (2009): p. 987.

[64] Carlos Romero Bonifaz, 'Los Ejes de la Constitución Política del Estado Plurinacional de Bolivia' [The Axes of the Political Constitution of the Plurinational State of Bolivia], in *Miradas. Nuevo Texto Constitucional*, edited by Vicepresidencia del Estado Plurinacional, Universidad Mayor de San Andrés e Instituto Internacional para la Democracia y la Asistencia Electoral (La Paz: Instituto Internacional de Integración del Convenio Andrés Bello, 2010), p. 22, http://vicepresidencia.gob.bo/IMG/pdf/texto_miradas_ncpe.pdf.

[65] Almut Schilling-Vacaflor, 'Bolivia's New Constitution: Towards Participatory Democracy and Political Pluralism?', *European Review of Latin American and Caribbean Studies*, vol. 90 (2011): p. 4.

[66] Ximena Soruco Sologuren, 'Estado plurinacional-pueblo, una construcción inédita en Bolivia' [The People's Plurinational State, an Unprecedented Construction in Bolivia], *OSAL*, Año X, no. 26 (2009), accessed 3 June 2015, http://bibliotecavirtual.clacso.org.ar/clacso/revista/20100316123037/04sologu.pdf.

the language of the colonizers (Castilian-Spanish with the incorporation of words and grammatical constructions from other vernacular languages) remains both the lingua franca and the language of sections of the elite, Quechua, Aymara, and Guarani and other minor indigenous languages remain spoken languages, creating circumstances in which individuals are bilingual and even trilingual. The constitution guarantees in Article 5 the rights of all citizens to address the government in their vernacular languages.

The result of this creative modality of NTA is that indigenous self-determination is not building separate entities set apart from the rest of society; rather, the call is for multilevel governance, allowing for a degree of indigenous self-determination but also participation in state-sanctioned systems of governance. In other words, the indigenous movements seek not just separation but also inclusion.[67]

3.6.5 La Paix des Braves

An example of NTA as an agreement between two stateless nations sharing the same territorial space is the 2001 agreement between the nation of Québec (la nation québécoise) and the Cree indigenous nation or *La Paix des Braves* ('The Peace of the Braves', reminiscent of the 1701 peace treaty between the French settlers and the indigenous Iroquois). After much bickering and disagreement between settlers and indigenous people (First Nations), the formal agreement between the Cree and Québécois nations was signed between the government of Québec and the Grand Council of the Crees. The agreement was negotiated by the Premier of Québéc Bernard Landry and Grand Chief of the Crees Ted Moses. The agreement provided for the sharing of revenues and joint management by the Cree and the Québécois of mining, forestry, and hydroelectric resources on traditional Cree lands in Québec. It aimed at developing more equitable Cree participation in employment, forestry, and revenue in natural resource industries in northern Québéc. The preamble of the agreement recognizes the treaty as a symbolic 'nation to nation' agreement between the Cree and the Québécois, two stateless nations.

La Paix des Braves recognized the ancestral rights of indigenous peoples to their lands, and, subject to Cree agreement, allowed Hydro-Québec to exploit hydroelectric resources in exchange for a financial settlement to be given collectively to the indigenous Cree nation. The agreement from the point of view of the government of Québec brought considerable advantages to the Cree nation in the fields of development of education, social and sanitary issues, and tourism. The benefits are nevertheless debated in the literature. Sceptics argue that while the agreement brought significant benefits to some sections of the Cree nation, it

[67] Tom Perreault and Barbara Green, 'Reworking the Spaces of Indigeneity: The Bolivian Ayllu and Lowland Autonomy Movements Compared', *Environment & Planning D: Society and Space*, vol. 31 (2013): p. 53.

could not transcend entirely the colonial relations between the two peoples.[68] The agreement is important because it shows the possibilities of cooperation between stateless nations inhabiting the same territory, and allowed for what Nootens calls the 'unnailing of democracy' from the tyranny of the nation state and its inflexible frontiers, allowing the formation of a constitutional legal and democratic multinational association between stateless nations that share the same territory.[69]

3.7 The Transformation of Democratic Theory— From the Nation State Demos to a Commonwealth of Demoi

Since their development in the eighteenth to the early twentieth century, democratic theories took for granted the insertion of political democracy within the institution of the nation state. More often than not, they took this assertion at face value without explanation or justification. Recently, and as a result of the newly recognized democratic shortcomings in the practice of democracy, important arguments and objections are beginning to emerge in the area of international political theory, questioning if the nation state can be the exclusive locus of democratic activity. In what I have described elsewhere as a Kuhnian Paradigm shift,[70] the emerging approaches are ambitiously addressing long-neglected issues, such as whether it is possible to realize democracy beyond the skeleton of the nation state and in particular, if NSD should only mean the creation of separate states. Further important questions emerging are what kind of democracy could exist outside the domain of the nation state, and how different might its foundations be, and what institutions and practices will reform or replace the regime of the contemporary nation state.

Initially, contemporary advocates of cosmopolitanism began to challenge the insertion of democratic theory within the framework of the nation state. David Held, for example, advocates in a number of important works a model of cosmopolitan democracy that transcends the borders of the nation state, and that assumes the entrenchment of a cluster of rights and obligations enshrined within

[68] Ephraim Nimni, 'Nationalism, Ethnicity and Self-Determination: A Paradigm Shift?', *Studies in Ethnicity and Nationalism*, vol. 9, no. 2 (2009): pp. 319–32; Harvey Feit, 'Governmental Rationalities and Indigenous Co-Governance: James Bay Cree Co-Existence, from Mercantilist Partnerships to Neoliberal Mechanisms', in *Unsettled Legitimacy: Political Community, Power, and Authority in a Global Era*, edited by Steven Berstein and William D. Coleman (Vancouver: UBC Press, 2010), pp. 97–128. See also Ephraim Nimni, 'Nationalism, Ethnicity and Self-Determination: A Paradigm Shift?', *Studies in Ethnicity and Nationalism* (2009): pp. 319–32; also in Keith Breen and Shane O'Neill, eds, *After the Nation? Critical Reflections on Post-Nationalism* (London: Palgrave Macmillan, 2010), pp. 21–37.

[69] Geneviève Nootens, *Désenclaver la démocratie, Des Huguenot à la paix des braves* (Montréal : Québec Amérique, 2004). The examples above are just a small sample. The Sami parliaments in Scandinavian countries, the modalities for minority autonomy in Hungary and Serbia, as well as the myriad different forms of indigenous autonomy in different parts of the world are also pertinent examples.

[70] Nimni, 'Nationalism, Ethnicity and Self-Determination: A Paradigm Shift?', pp. 319–32.

the constitutions of parliaments and assemblies, as well as various regional bodies such as the EU, with a global parliament and an interconnected legal system.[71] The argument in Held's work is for broad conception pluralism within a single fully inclusive demos.

While this approach can be commended for its departure from the domination of the nation state formation, it leaves intact the problem of community representation and the recognition of collective democratic subjects, the core of democratic demands of indigenous peoples and scattered minority communities. Taking the argument on an important and decisive step further, James Bohman argues that a form of radical plural democracy requires deeper transformations of democracy away from the morphology of the nation state.[72] He further argues that conditions exist for democratization beyond the limits of the nation state, and that this expansion is not only possible, but necessary for the renewal of democratic theory. Bohman argues that democracy must function across rather than simply beyond borders. The renewed democratic theory must not demolish cultural differences, as in the early republican model of the nation state, which was not only one of nation building, but simultaneously one of nation destroying.[73] This means that democracy must now become a democracy of the demoi, a plural and diverse conglomerate of democratic communities and constituencies. This is not only a change to the institutional structure of the nation state, but also a change in the political subject that sustains the democratic formation, from a unified constituency to a plurality of diverse constituencies, from 'a people' to 'peoples'. In other words, Bohman brings the debate about the expansion of democracy to the recognition of the collective rights and collective personae of the constituent communities or demoi.[74]

Bohman's argument speaks to the needs and demands of indigenous peoples and territorial minorities, in that it eliminates the key stumbling block for the communitarian political participation of these communities: territorial sovereignty as a condition for collective community participation. This argument is crucially important for the emancipation of territorial minorities because it distinguishes this approach to democracy from cosmopolitan arguments that imagine a single institutional skeleton of authority, a kind of a global state. Even more so, its comprehensive understanding of democratic values is sharply different from those who link global democracy to what could be defined as a minimalist approach, a kind of compelling human rights legal apparatus existing above the nation state, only limiting its sovereignty when it transgresses the agreed framework of human rights. This last approach is of no use to minority communities, for as argued

[71] David Held, *Models of Democracy* (Cambridge: Polity Press, 2006), pp. 307–9.

[72] James Bohman, 'From Demos to Demoi: Democracy across Borders', *Ratio Juris*, vol. 18, no. 3 (2005): pp. 297–8.

[73] Walker Connor, 'Nation-Building or Nation-Destroying?', *World Politics*, vol. 24, no. 3 (1972): pp. 319–55.

[74] James Bohman, *Democracy across Borders: From Demos to Demoi* (Cambridge, MA: The MIT Press, 2007), p. 13.

earlier, majoritarian democracies can transgress the rights of cultural minorities without violating an individualist definition of democratic rights.

To develop democracy beyond the borders of the nation state is important but it is not sufficient to overcome the pluralist deficit of the modern nation state. It is self-defeating to maintain the faulty configuration of the nation state, only to expand it to a gigantic world cosmopolitan constituency. Instead of perceiving democracy as cosmopolitan (non-national and cultural), democracy as the domain of single demos, democratic theory must break with this residue of the nation state and understand democracy not as a single body but as a plurality of constituent democracies. In this way, it becomes international and intercultural, operating not beyond borders but across borders. This is not negating but affirming the democratic value of the collective governance of nations and cultural communities, and creating democratic models that incorporate self-determining constituent autonomous communities with recognized rights for effective collective representation.

Democracy must be organized in more than one unit in order to satisfy demands for recognition that result from the logic of pluralist democratic governance. In this, global democracy cannot be some analogical world of individuals enjoying equal rights, which inevitably leads to the misrecognition of minorities and the corresponding tyranny of the majority. Instead global democracy must be seen as a plurality of demos (demoi) within a federal arrangement instead of a state-inspired conception of single demos.[75] In other words, democracy must be implemented in a commonwealth of demoi, understanding by that a highly interconnected world, where territories are shared between differing demoi and territorial polities cannot be the basis for exclusive sovereignties.

3.8 The EU as a Commonwealth of Demoicracies

Whether cosmopolitan or national, many democratic theories suffer nowadays from a territorial bias that prevents them from accounting properly for the new democratic reality in Europe.[76] The growth of governance beyond nation states is arguably an important political development. Transnational organizations have in recent years been challenged on normative grounds for their lack of democracy in the form of various democratic deficits.[77] This criticism is particularly salient with regards to the EU, with the infamous 'democratic deficit supported by friends and

[75] Ferran Requejo, 'Value Pluralism and Multinational Federalism', in *The Conditions of Diversity in Multinational Democracies*, edited by Alain-G. Gagnon, Montserrat Guibernau, and Francois Rocher (Montréal, Québec: The Institute for Research on Public Policy, 2004), p. 26.

[76] Samantha Besson, 'Deliberative Demoi-cracy in the European Union: Towards the Deterritorialisation of Democracy', in *Deliberative Democracy and its Discontents*, edited by Samantha Besson and Jose Luis Marti (Aldershot: Ashgate, 2006), p. 182.

[77] Magdalena Bexell, Jonas Tallberg, and Anders Uhlin, 'Democracy in Global Governance: The Promises and Pitfalls of Transnational Actors', *Global Governance*, vol. 16 (2010): pp. 81–2.

foes of European integration'. This requires an urgent reconceptualization of the modus operandi of the EU away from comparisons with the nation state. Here the recent writings of Francis Cheneval and Kalypso Nicolaïdis are leading the way for a conceptualization of the EU away from analogies of the nation state.

Cheneval and Schimmelfennig argue that it is mistaken to discuss the EU and its democratic deficit with democratic analogies from the nation state (they use the term states-people).[78] To replace analogies with the nation state, they use the term 'demoicracy', following Bohman, to signify a polity of multiple demoi as the appropriate characterization of the EU. Following this argument, any normative evaluation of democracy in the EU must start from the premise that it is an institution with many demoi and not a nation state, in other words a demoicracy. This argument is important and constructive, for it helps to establish the foundational differences between the EU and nation states. We can then move away from the architecture of the nation state, and since the democratic terminology associated with the nation state has become so hegemonic, it is imperative, as Cheneval and Schimmelfennig do, to borrow Bohman's argument to break out of analogies with the nation state. For these authors, demoicracy represents an intermediary level between nation state and international politics. This is a key first step to move away from the architecture of the nation state while discussing European democracy.

Yet the EU demoicracy cannot be composed exclusively of states-people as its collective constituents, for European states have different cultural minorities and nations whose identity is different from the titular nation of the state. Consider, for example, the Turkish permanent residents in Germany. They are culturally different from the titular nation of the Federal Republic of Germany, as explicitly defined in ethnic terms in the German constitution, and in terms of their numbers, they are more numerous than the citizens of several EU states. In democratic terms, the case for their collective representation in the EU demoicracy is compelling.

Nicolaïdis follows a similar line of argument.[79] She defines 'demoicracy' as 'a Union of peoples, understood both as states and as citizens, who govern together but not as one'. However, there are in Europe many that are neither states nor citizens who, nevertheless, are peoples. At the same time, there is promise and innovation in the argument for, like Cheneval, she argues that demoicracy as a normative concept is best understood distinct from both national and supranational versions of single demos polities. She further argues that the concept of 'demoicracy' can serve both as an analytical lens for the EU and as a normative benchmark. Consequently, the normative discussion must follow different lines of argumentation from the ones utilized to evaluate democracy in nation states. Here also, the union of states and citizens has not yet entirely escaped the

[78] Francis Cheneval and Frank Schimmelfennig, 'The Case for Demoicracy in the European Union', *Journal of Common Market Studies*, vol. 51, no. 2 (2013): pp. 334–50.

[79] Kalypso Nicolaïdis, 'European Demoicracy and its Crisis', *Journal of Common Market Studies*, vol. 51, no. 2 (2013): p. 352.

morphology of the nation state. For that it is necessary to include, as components of the community of demoi, intermediate categories such as ethnic and national minorities, and dispersed communities that are culturally different from their respective titular nations in the context of the nation state.

The discussion of demoicracy in the EU is in its infancy and carries promise. It opens the way for a long overdue disentangling of democracy from the strait-jacket of the nation state. It is refreshing and thought provoking, but it has to be considered an initial step, as a first attempt to conceptualize the term. To solidify the concept of demoicracy, it becomes imperative to understand more precisely the characteristics of the participant demoi, and to enhance democratic mechanisms of international and intercultural representation. Here demoicracy and modalities of NTA are following converging paths. We might reach the moment when European institutions learn from the practices of indigenous peoples and other territorially scattered minorities. A commonwealth of demoi holds the promise of expanding democracy through the incorporation of territorial and non-territorial representation of minority communities, something that the ideals of popular sovereignty and NSD have failed to do for the liberal democratic nation state model. In the meantime the democratic deficit of the nation state continues to hold up democratic values, forcing democrats into unpalatable contradictions.

3.9 Conclusion

Liberal democracies were designed to function and sustain the environment of nation states. They remain the most desirable political systems because they privilege individual rights and protect the freedoms they grant to individual citizens. Yet, as this chapter shows, liberal democracies have not done well in protecting and representing the growing number of minority communities that live in their midst. At the same time, they protect and nourish the dominant culture of the state. This is unquestionably a democratic deficit. If the world had been neatly divided into monocultural nation states, then nation state liberal democracy would have been the near-perfect system of governance. Yet, not only this is *not* the case, but to sustain this delusion is a dangerous fantasy. Particularly if nation states where born out the idea that that they will assimilate minorities with democracy as compensation, then self-governance is granted to some and not to others, all of whom are, ostensibly, equal citizens. Here we have a neat violation of the egalitarian principles that sustain liberal democracy. In a world that clamours for the recognition of difference this is, to say the least, unfair. Rather than a perfect match between the state and the titular nation of the state, the contemporary reality of liberal democratic nation states is of diversity and cultural pluralism and not cultural monism. While *de jure* nation states, liberal democratic nation states are de facto plurinational and pluri-ethnic, debunking the normative ideal of one nation in one state and exercising without wanting to, a sweet tyranny of the majority over their minority communities.

As shown above the atomist centralist system of governance, while eliminating privilege, also eliminated the possibility of the political representation of minority communities under the universalization of one person one vote. Individuals that adhere to the cultural mores of the titular nation do well under these circumstances. But those loyal citizens that feel that their personal identity is manifested in adherence to minority communities could feel alienated. Their communities cannot find a way to be represented simply because they are numerical minorities, thus the tyranny of the majority rules.

It is here that the democratic credentials of nation state liberal democracies are incomplete. Following this failure, different mechanisms of community incorporation begin to emerge. First was the wave of early feminism that argued that the contractarian characteristics of liberal democracy undermine the full incorporation of women because these contractarian characteristics were designed to fulfil the life cycle of men. Remedial mechanisms to incorporate women as equals were suggested. In an incremental move, multiculturalism followed similar lines of argumentation by arguing that minority cultures also require some form of recognition of their *differentia specifica,* arguing that the liberal democratic nation state levels all citizens into equal and homologous quantities in a domain where citizens are neither equal nor homologous. Here, to restore the equality of minorities, patterns of recognition of difference are required.

Feminism and multiculturalism embraced the idea that the recognition of difference is a mechanism to expand democracy; as an important device to ensure equality of opportunities between citizens of liberal democracies. Following this, dispersed minorities within nation states began to take the argument one step further and demand not only recognition, but representation, an essential ingredient of democratic governance. In particular, indigenous peoples displaced by colonial settler societies began to demand NSD that did entail territorial sovereignty because they were made into minorities in their own ancestral lands. Even if these demands were strongly connected to their ancestral lands, ethnoscapes central to their identity, indigenous demands were not for absolute control over their ancestral lands. Here different types and forms of NTA began to emerge, in different places and times, unconnected and often even not aware of each other. Others, such as dispersed national communities in monistic states, began to expand democratic principles by demanding forms of representation in existing structures of governance. NTA becomes then a modality for multi-community governance, and not a specific model for the incorporation of minorities or dispersed communities. It is rather a mechanism for the allocation of collective rights and representation to territorially dispersed minorities that find it impossible to build autonomous territorial regions of their own. This is also why NTA does not provide a prescription or a common line of action. It is a demand for the expansion of the key democratic value of community representation to overcome the monistic limitations of the nation state. It includes NCA and consociationalism, as well as incipient forms of dispersed community representation. NTA is thus a generic form of collective rights and collective representation, which aims to expand democracy by sharing sovereignty between different communities.

Demoicracy emerges as a contemporary neologism that demands deeper transformations of democracy away from the morphology of the nation state. It further argues that there is a need for democratization beyond the limits of the nation state, and that this expansion is necessary for the renewal of democratic theory. This renewed democratic theory must not demolish cultural differences, as in the early liberal democratic model of the nation state, but crucially, democracy must now also become a democracy of the demoi, a plural and diverse conglomerate of democratic communities and constituencies.

This argument is then applied to the evaluation of the EU. Any evaluation of democracy in the EU must start from the premise that it is an institution with many demoi and not a nation state. Therefore its democratic deficit is not commensurable with the democratic deficit of the nation state.

Here, demoicracy and NTA are fellow travellers, travelling along converging paths, aiming at the expansion of democratic values beyond the architecture of the nation state and the limitations of an individualistically oriented liberal democracy.

4

Non-Territorial Autonomy

The Meaning of '(Non-)Territoriality'

Markku Suksi

4.1 Introduction

During the past few decades, a notion of non-territorial forms of autonomy has started to develop in doctrine and also in at least so-called soft-law sources of international law.[1] In Paragraph 35 of the final document of the so-called Copenhagen Meeting in 1990 of the Conference on Security and Co-operation in Europe (CSCE), the participating states noted, within the frame of participation, the efforts undertaken in some states to protect and create conditions for the promotion of the ethnic, cultural, linguistic, and religious identity of certain national minorities by establishing, as one of the possible means to achieve these aims, appropriate local or autonomous administrations corresponding to the specific historical and territorial circumstances of such minorities and in accordance with the policies of the state concerned.[2] The situation of dispersed minorities may be such that other than territorially circumscribed solutions become necessary. Therefore, in Paragraph 17 of the so-called Lund Recommendations of the High Commissioner on National Minorities of the Organization for Security and Co-operation in Europe (OSCE), it is pointed out that '[n]on-territorial forms of governance are useful for the maintenance and development of the identity and culture of national minorities'.

While the exercise of public authority in a territorial jurisdiction is normally limited to the territory in question for the benefit of a concentrated group of persons (such as the Åland Islands, Scotland, Puerto Rico, Hong Kong, Aceh,

[1] I wish to express my gratitude to professor Mikko Lagerspetz, Ms Jana Stahl, Dr Kristian Myntti, Mr Chema Arraiza, and Ms Heidi Öst for comments and materials received.

[2] Alexander Osipov, 'Non-Territorial Autonomy and International Law', *International Community Law Review* 13 (2011): pp. 398–400. He points out that already in the CSCE Meeting of Experts on National Minorities in Geneva in 1991, reference was made to domestic solutions of minority protection, such as 'self-administration by a national minority of aspects concerning its identity in situations where autonomy on a territorial basis does not apply' and that the Advisory Committee on the Framework Convention for National Minorities (FCNM) has commented on the matter of non-territorial autonomy.

Zanzibar, and the Memel Territory[3]), non-territorial forms of autonomy make it possible to detach the exercise of public authority from jurisdictional boundaries at the sub-state or local government level. This would facilitate the extension of a particular material jurisdiction to, for example, such minorities which are not living in a certain part of the country, but are dispersed amongst the majority population.[4] The needs of such dispersed minorities may be addressed by means of, inter alia, non-territorial forms of autonomy that can be based on, for instance, a so-called personality principle.

Non-territorial autonomy (NTA) as a general concept lacks certainty, while its components may be easier to pinpoint. Whether NTA is perceived as a specific form of ethnicity-based organization or as a general principle of group agency, the meaning and contexts of its detachment from territory are far from being clear and require examination. Alexander Osipov has dissected the general notion of NTA from a critical and even a nihilistic point of view, but seems nonetheless to arrive at conclusions that at least from a more legal point of view seem relatively optimistic, provided that the muddled concept of NTA is dismantled into its relevant parts.[5] It is therefore easy to agree with Osipov: a mere reference to non-territorial autonomy is insufficient, and what is needed is an examination of various elements related to non-territorial forms of autonomy. It is submitted here that the main issues in this respect are institutional design, the powers of the institutions, the determination of membership in the group for which the NTA has been created, and the mechanisms of participation of the members of the group. Because the use of private entities for the provision of public services and the exercise of public powers does not create the same territorial-jurisdictional issues as the creation, under the legislation of the state, of particular statutory institutions that are charged with public tasks in relation to a minority, the focus of this chapter is on such public institutions that are specifically designed for such purposes through statutory measures of the state.

Public international law does not contain any solid provisions that establish NTA. As concluded by Osipov, the provisions concerning NTA found in some sources of international law are, in general, declaratory and thus not directly implementable or enforceable.[6] Therefore, the normative expressions of NTA have to be found at the national level. In Europe, arrangements involving NTA exist,

[3] Markku Suksi, *Sub-State Governance through Territorial Autonomy* (Berlin/Heidelberg: Springer-Verlag, 2011); Markku Suksi, 'Territorial Autonomy: the Åland Islands in Comparison with Other Sub-State Entities', in *Autonomies in Europe: Solutions and Challenges*, edited by Zoltán Kantór (Budapest: L'Harmattan, 2014), pp. 37–58.

[4] David J. Smith, 'Minority Territorial and Non-Territorial Autonomy in Europe: Theoretical Perspectives and Practical Challenges', in *Autonomies in Europe: Solutions and Challenges*, edited by Zoltán Kantór (Budapest: L'Harmattan, 2014), p. 18.

[5] Alexander Osipov, 'Changing the Angle: Does the Notion of Non-Territorial Autonomy Stand on Solid Ground?', *ECMI Issue Brief*, no. 29 (2013).

[6] Osipov, 'Non-Territorial Autonomy', p. 409.

according to Osipov[7] and Eide,[8] in a number of countries, such as Croatia, Estonia, Hungary, Russia, and Slovenia.[9] In addition, Serbia can be mentioned in this context.

What is the relationship between the above-mentioned issues, on the one hand, and the question of territoriality, on the other, on the basis of examples found mainly in the legal orders of Estonia, Sweden, Finland, and Serbia?

The methodological point of departure is mainly that of comparative law, but we are not aiming at a comprehensive analysis of all the varying situations. Instead, instances of NTA on which much work has already been done, such as the above-mentioned Hungary, Russia, and Slovenia, are left aside. This inquiry does not touch upon how identities of minorities are socially constructed, nor upon political claims that minorities may have for the creation of different forms of NTA.[10]

4.2 Institutions

4.2.1 Different institutional forms of non-territorial autonomy

The academic and also practical interest in trying to resolve the complicated issue of NTA emerged with the attempts of Bauer and Renner to provide a theory for the organization of various nationalities within the Austro-Hungarian space.[11] According to Ephraim Nimni, the model of Bauer and Renner opposed the concept of the nation state and proposed the organization of 'nations into nonterritorial public corporations with comprehensive autonomous rights, operating within de-nationalised territorial states'.[12] He characterizes the work of Renner by saying that it and his concept of personal autonomy is a deviation from

> 'earlier socialist attempts to grant autonomy to the various national groups within their territorial units' by introducing the idea that 'the citizen should become a member of the

[7] Alexander Osipov, 'National Cultural Autonomy in Russia: A Case of Symbolic Law', *Review of Central and East European Law* 35 (2010): pp. 27–57.

[8] Asbjørn Eide et al., 'Cultural Autonomy: Concept, Content, History and Role in the World Order', in *Autonomy: Applications and Implications*, edited by Markku Suksi (The Hague: Kluwer Law, 1998), pp. 251–76.

[9] Ferenc Eiler and Nóra Kovács, 'Minority Self-Governments in Hungary', in *Minority Governance in Europe*, edited by Kinga Gál (Budapest: Local Government and Public Service Reform Initiative of the Open Society Institute, 2002), pp. 173–97; Niamh Walsh, 'Minority Self-Government in Hungary: Legislation and Practice', *Journal on Ethnopolitics and Minority Issues in Europe* (2000), accessed 21 November 2013, http://www.ecmi.de/fileadmin/doc/JEMIE04Walsh30-07-01.pdf.

[10] Osipov, 'Changing the Angle'; Mabel Wong, 'Reclaiming Identity: Rethinking Non-Territorial Autonomy', *Journal on Ethnopolitics and Minority Issues in Europe*, vol. 12, no. 1 (2013): pp. 56–75.

[11] Otto Bauer, *The Question of Nationalities and Social Democracy* [Nationalitätenfrage und die Sozialdemokratie], with an introduction by Ephraim Nimni and preface by Heinz Fischer (Minneapolis: University of Minnesota Press, 2000), pp. 266, 270, 281–3; Karl Renner, 'State and Nation', in *National Cultural Autonomy and its Contemporary Critics*, edited by Ephraim Nimni (London/New York: Routledge, 2005), pp. 15–47.

[12] Ephraim Nimni, 'Nationalist Multiculturalism in Late Imperial Austria as a Critique of Contemporary Liberalism: The Case of Bauer and Renner', *Journal of Political Ideologies*, vol. 4,

autonomous national association of his co-nationals, irrespective of his domicile. These autonomous national organizations ought to have their agencies all over the empire.... The citizen, even though he may live within a territory where the majority belongs to a different national group, in questions of genuine national interest should not be subject to its laws but to those of his own supra-territorial national organization.'[13]

As pointed out by Svante Cornell, '[c]ultural autonomy does not carry the far-reaching consequences implicit in territorial autonomy: territory and ethnicity are not linked',[14] and therefore, it can be said that the (assumed) threat that territorial autonomy poses to the territorial unity of the state is alleviated.[15] However, he continues by stating that 'there is no creation of statelike institutions',[16] which would be true if the private law form were used exclusively,[17] but cultural autonomy seems to presume statelike institutions of a public law nature. However, contributions in literature have also mentioned concepts such as personal autonomy and functional autonomy.[18]

It seems clear that associations created under the private law of a state by persons belonging to minorities may do a great deal for the advancement of the position of the minority and the promotion of the cultural interests of the minority. This means that the concept of national cultural autonomy (NCA) that Bauer and Renner put forward at the end of the nineteenth century and during the first decades of the twentieth century is not necessarily the only way in which NTA could be organized. However, an exemption from the application of the laws or policies of the country would normally require legislative action from the lawmaker of the state, and so, too, would the delegation of public powers, authority, and tasks to an entity that presents itself as an autonomy arrangement for a minority. Using the pure private law form for the implementation of such aims is probably not possible. Therefore, certain terminological specifications are necessary in order to distinguish between personal autonomy, functional autonomy, and cultural autonomy.

no. 3 (1999): p. 4. According to Nimni, '[t]he model of national autonomy requires that all citizens declare their nationality when they reach voting age. Members of each national community, whatever their territory of residence, would form a single public body or association endowed with legal personality and sovereignty and competent to deal with all national-cultural affairs. These corporations would organize the educational system of their members, the legal system, and all other issues that are national in character.'

[13] Robert A. Kann, 'Karl Renner (December 14, 1870–December 31, 1950)', *Journal of Modern History*, vol. 23, no. 3 (1951): p. 244.

[14] Svante E. Cornell, 'Autonomy as a Source of Conflict: Caucasian Conflicts in Theoretical Perspective', *World Politics*, vol. 54 (2002): p. 249.

[15] Aleksandr Aidarov and Wolfgang Drechsler, 'The Law and Economics of the Estonian Law on Cultural Autonomy for National Minorities and of Russian National Cultural Autonomy in Estonia', *Halduskultuur—Administrative Culture*, vol. 12, no. 1 (2011): p. 50.

[16] Cornell, 'Autonomy as a Source of Conflict', p. 249.

[17] Osipov, 'National Cultural Autonomy in Russia', pp. 27, 36–7. According to Osipov, the Russian national cultural autonomies are NGOs. It seems they could be understood as entities of private law if a clear distinction between public law and private law existed in the Russian Federation.

[18] Kinga Gál, ed., *Minority Governance in Europe* (Budapest: Local Government and Public Service Reform Initiative of the Open Society Institute, 2002), p. 8; Georg Brunner and Herbert

4.2.2 Institutional forms of civil law turning into functional autonomy

Personal autonomy as institutional form would have to be distinguished from material personal autonomy, which implies a choice for a person as concerns different legal regimes (e.g., choice of whether or not to use a system created for the provision of services in minority languages, the choice of moving from a territorial autonomy or jurisdiction to other parts of the state or to another state). The institutional implications of personal autonomy are indicated by Article 27 of the UN Covenant on Civil and Political Rights (CCPR) in combination with Article 22 of the same Covenant. According to these provisions, persons belonging to minorities have the right to use the horizontal relations in the realm of civil law to create platforms for such activities that may give expression to the linguistic, ethnic, or religious particularities of the group. What is clear on the basis of a number of interpretations concerning the European Convention on Human Rights is that associations that wish to provide a platform for the exercise of some facet of the group identity of a minority, however political it may be, have the right to be registered as legal persons, if such a requirement exists in the legal order of the state for legal personality to take effect.[19] At the same time, a minority does not generally have the right to claim a certain official position for the governance of a matter,[20] except within the area of education, where it is well established under public international law that a minority population would have the right to set up its own private schools, under certain conditions established under the 1960 UNESCO Convention against Discrimination in Education and in a number of other international instruments adopted after that.[21]

The area of education is illustrative of how the civil law form created by persons who belong to a minority might be furnished with public powers: a private school that operates in a minority language and is maintained by an association with members from amongst that minority would, for the purposes of the formal

Küpper, 'European Options of Autonomy: A Typology of Autonomy Models of Minority Self-Governance', in *Minority Governance in Europe*, edited by Kinga Gál (Budapest: Local Government and Public Service Reform Initiative of the Open Society Institute, 2002), pp. 27, 29.

[19] *Sidiropoulos and Others v. Greece* [1998)], ECtHR, no. 26695/95, *Reports of Judgments and Decisions* 1998–IV; *Stankov and the United Macedonian Organisation Ilinden v. Bulgaria* [2001], ECtHR, nos. 29221/95 and 29225/95, *Reports of Judgments and Decisions* 2001-IX; *Metropolitan Church of Bessarabia and Others v. Moldova* [2001], ECtHR, no. 45701/99, *Reports of Judgments and Decisions* 2001-XII.

[20] *Gorzelik and Others v. Poland* [2004)], ECtHR, no. 44158/98, *Reports of Judgments and Decisions* 2004-I.

[21] UNESCO Convention against Discrimination in Education (adopted 14 December 1960, entered into force 22 May 1962). See also the case of *Minority Schools in Albania*, Advisory Opinion, 1935 PCIJ (ser. A/B) No. 64 (Apr. 6), para 79: 'The Court therefore finds that paragraph 1 of Article 5 of the Declaration of October 2nd, 1921, ensures for Albanian nationals belonging to racial, linguistic or religious minorities the right to maintain, manage and control at their own expense or to establish in the future charitable, religious and social institutions, schools and other educational establishments, with the right to use their own language and to exercise their religion freely therein.'

recognition of diplomas, often be required to have an operating licence granted under the education legislation of the state to the association or school. Through the licence, public authority to issue diplomas, to grade students, and perhaps even to exercise disciplinary powers over the students is delegated to such a minority association or school.

The delegation of public powers to the private entity means that the private entity is made part of the public administration of the state. For instance, a school of that kind would normally, after the delegation of powers, belong to the indirect public administration or *mittelbare Staatsverwaltung* of the state.[22] In such a situation, the minority association or minority school is tasked with the public function of education. This is a situation which already could belong to functional autonomy, because representatives of the minority are in charge of managing a certain public function under the laws of the state, probably more or less in the same way as the regular schools and under the supervision of the education authorities of the state. For the minority, the use of the private school as the institutional form would provide the flexibility of organizing the school where the children are and to enroll students irrespective of, for instance, municipal borders. Similar flexibility through the use of private entities for the provision of public services may exist in other substantive areas.

Examples of such incorporation of minority organizations are, for instance, the private schools operating in the German language in southern Denmark, ultimately based on the 1955 Copenhagen Declaration on the general rights of the German minority. According to Part II, Paragraph 3, the German minority is recognized the possibility of setting up kindergartens, schools for general education, and community colleges, as provided by law. The German-language schools in southern Denmark operate under the Act on Free Schools,[23] which, inter alia, requires that such schools are set up as foundations,[24] exempts teachers at these German-language schools from the requirement of proficiency in Danish, and gives certain powers in the area of allocation of resources to the *Deutscher Schul- und Sprachverein für Nordschleswig*, that is, the German Association of School and Language for Northern Schleswig. In this way, civil law institutions are used in the provision of public services and exercise of public authority for the minority and by the minority. Similar arrangements, allowing flexibility also in relation to jurisdictional borders within the state, can be found in most other countries. As explained above, this form of functional autonomy is not the focal point of our interest in this chapter, although such forms of organization may be non-territorial in nature.

[22] Modeen Tore and Allan Rosas, eds, *Indirect Public Administration in the Fields of Education and Pensions* (Åbo: Åbo Academy Press, 1990), pp. 15–18, 27–40, 97–122, 146–56, 203–18, 220–68.

[23] Bekendtgørelse af lov om friskoler og private grundskoler m.v. 2011 [Act on Independent Schools and Private Schools].

[24] There is no formal requirement of an operating licence in Danish law, but if the school receives public funding, it is obliged under the law to comply with rules issued by the Danish Ministry of Education.

4.2.3 Functional autonomy within line administration

An even clearer case of functional autonomy as an exponent of institutional form would be present when the regular administrative agencies are organized so as to contain separate branches for the majority and the minority. In such a case, the line administration of the state (or a municipality) is created both in the majority and the minority language so that they function parallel to each other in dealing with the same issues, but in two different languages. A definition of functional autonomy of a linguistic minority thus organized could hold that '[f]unctional autonomy aims at providing adequate linguistic services to a minority population in respect of a certain public function...by means of creating special linguistically identified units at different administrative levels inside the general line-organization charged with the national or local administration of the public function'.[25]

This is an approach that produces a relatively integrated administrative structure for the minority, but requires that it is created through public law rules of the state in question (as is the case with some aspects of administration in, for instance, Finland, Sweden, Malaysia, South Tyrol, and Hong Kong, as well as Macedonia.[26] In such situations, the languages are not separated into different legal persons, but instead dealt with, for instance, within the legal person of the state and the legal person of the municipality. Insofar as the system of functional autonomy involves the appointment of civil servants and the nomination of members of statutory boards from among the members of the minority, the arrangement may support the implementation of Article 25(c) of the CCPR, according to which every citizen 'shall have the right and the opportunity... [t]o have access, on general terms of equality, to public service in his country'.[27] Arrangements of this kind would probably enhance the opportunity of members of the minority population to have access to the public service of the country.

For instance, in the field of education in Finland, the line administration of the state is linguistically diversified, and so, too, is the administration of education at the level of local government. The National Board of Education shall, according to the act regulating its activities, have a unit for tasks concerning instruction in

[25] Markku Suksi, 'Functional Autonomy', *International Journal on Minority and Group Rights*, vol. 15 (2008): p. 199.

[26] Castellino Joshua and Elvira Domínguez Redondo, *Minority Rights in Asia: A Comparative Legal Analysis* (Oxford: Oxford University Press, 2006), pp. 165–71; Suksi, *Sub-State Governance through Territorial Autonomy*. It seems that in Macedonia, the implementation of the 2001 Ohrid Framework Agreement of Macedonia has led to functional autonomy at least at the level of local government within the field of education.

[27] Art 25(a) of the International Covenant on Civil and Political Rights (adopted 16 December 1966, entered into force 23 March 1976) 99 UNTS 171 (ICCPR) may also be of relevance insofar as it refers to direct participation, which has been interpreted so as to include memberships, inter alia, of popular assemblies which have the power to make decisions about local issues or about the affairs of a particular community and in bodies established to represent citizens in consultation with government. See General Comment No. 25: The right to participate in public affairs, voting rights and the right of equal access to public service (art 25), 12/07/1996. CCPR/C/21/Rev.1/Add.7, para 6.

the Swedish language,[28] and at the regional level, there is a joint service unit for Swedish-speaking instruction, with the entire country as its operational area,[29] although the Swedish-speakers mainly live in the western and southern coastal areas of Finland. The regional level oversees the administration of education in municipalities, where bilingual municipalities have, according to the Local Government Act, the obligation to have a separate school committee for the Finnish-speaking and the Swedish-speaking linguistic groups, with committee members drawn from these groups or similar language-based sections of a joint school committee.[30] The task of either the committee or the section in a bilingual municipality is to manage the schools of the municipality operating in that particular language, either Finnish or Swedish. The teachers of the Finnish-speaking schools are required to have excellent proficiency in the Finnish language, and the teachers of the Swedish-speaking schools are required to have excellent proficiency in the Swedish language.[31] In operating this linguistically diversified educational administration, the two linguistic groups of course implement the same education legislation, but each in its own language.

A similar organizational solution is applied in Sweden in relation to the Sami schools.[32] The Sami Education Board is the state administrative authority for the six Sami primary schools (grades 1–6). According to the Swedish School Act, municipalities have the responsibility to organize the provision of educational services throughout the country.[33] Hence the municipality is the territorial entity within which the jurisdiction under the School Act is created. However, the Sami may, under the School Act, complete their duty to attend school in separate state-owned Sami schools, at which (more or less) the same curriculum,[34] established by the government of Sweden, is followed as in the regular public schools. Hence, Sami children may attend regular public schools,[35] but the expectation and hope is that they will attend one of the Sami schools.[36] The Sami schools are

[28] Lag om utbildningsstyrelsen [Law on Education Board] 182/1991, para 4.

[29] Statsrådets förordning om regionförvaltningsverken 906/2009 [Government Decree on the Regional State Administrative Agencies], para 6.

[30] Kommunallag 365/1995 [Local Government Act], para 16.

[31] Markku Suksi, 'Två språk i kommunalförvaltningen—möjligheter enligt kommunallagstiftningen' [Two Languages in Local Government—Opportunities under Municipal Legislation], *Tidskrift, utgiven av Juridiska Föreningen i Finland*, no. 5 (2012): pp. 518–21; Förordning om behörighetsvillkoren för personal inom undervisningsväsendet 986/1998 [Ordinance on the Qualification Requirements for Staff in the Education Sector], para 9.

[32] Suksi, 'Functional Autonomy', p. 217.

[33] Swedish School Act 1985, no. 1100.

[34] According to the School Act, s 1(7), the state is the 'owner' of the Sami schools. Because the Sami schools operate in municipalities where there is also a municipally owned school, it is possible to conclude that the Sami schools and the regular public schools have overlapping jurisdictions.

[35] Sami children who attend regular public schools in grades 1 to 6 are entitled to an integrated curriculum that also contains instruction in the Sami language and other relevant topics. Sami children in secondary schools are entitled to an integrated curriculum that contains instruction in the Sami language and other relevant topics.

[36] Under the Decree on Sami Schools 1995, no. 205, s 6(6), the Sami Educational Board may prescribe that knowledge of the Sami language gives preference to a person seeking appointment as teacher at a Sami school.

maintained by the Sami Educational Board, which is a public authority under the Swedish Ministry of Education. In spite of the fact that the members of the Board are appointed by the Sami Assembly (or Sami Parliament, as the body is often termed), the Sami schools are state schools.[37] On the basis of the fact that the management of these state-owned Sami schools is in the hands of the Sami themselves through the Sami Educational Board, which is a public authority of the Swedish state, the administration of education of the Sami in Sweden could well be identified as a case of functional autonomy.

4.2.4 National cultural autonomy

A third mode for the organization of NTA would be NCA. It has been provisionally referred to by Asbjörn Eide as the 'right to self-rule, by a culturally identified group, in regard to matters which affect the maintenance and reproduction of its culture', a situation in which the state undertakes not to impose its own regulations in the field covered by cultural autonomy, but leaves a reserved domain for the internal management by the group to which cultural autonomy has been granted.[38] Cornell presents similar thoughts when denoting cultural autonomy as a 'scheme whereby members of particular ethnic communities are endowed with specific rights and duties in relation to the government'.[39] He points out that this is used in certain countries for religious communities, as in Israel for Muslims and Christians and in India for Muslims.[40] Within a scheme of cultural autonomy, '[m]embers of particular groups may also be given special rights to preserve their culture and language, often through the institution of native language schools for minorities. Cultural autonomy is not territorially based; it may still, nevertheless, be either individually or group based and either voluntary or compulsory.'[41] Like territorial autonomy, cultural autonomy, too, 'must be grounded in the legal system of the particular country and as such form a part of that state's system of government'.[42]

[37] Ulla Aikio-Puoskari, *Rapport om den samiska undervisningen i grundskolorna i Norden: En nordisk jämförelse med utgångspunkt i undervisningens grundförutsättningar* [Report on the Sami Teaching in Primary Schools in the Nordic Countries: a Nordic Comparison based on the Fundamental Conditions of Instruction] (Enare: Samiskt Parlamentariskt Råd/Sametinget, 2011), pp. 40–41, 50, 83, 86–7, 98–9, 101, 119. Under the Act on the Sami Parliament 1992, no. 1433, s 1(1), the Sami Parliament of Sweden is a state authority with the function of overseeing issues that concern Sami culture in Sweden. Under s 2(1) of the same Act, the Sami Parliament has the authority to appoint the members of the Board for Sami schools as referred to in the Swedish School Act, s 8(6).

[38] Eide, 'Cultural Autonomy', p. 252.

[39] Cornell, 'Autonomy as a Source of Conflict', p. 249.

[40] Eide, 'Cultural Autonomy', pp. 261–2; Giovanni M. Quer, 'De-Territorializing Minority Rights in Europe: A Look Eastward', *Journal on Ethnopolitics and Minority Issues in Europe*, vol. 12, no. 1 (2013): pp. 76–98.

[41] Cornell, 'Autonomy as a Source of Conflict', p. 249.

[42] Cornell, 'Autonomy as a Source of Conflict', p. 249.

Approaches of this kind to NTA seem to produce the best overlap with the conceptualization of Bauer and Renner. The creation of cultural autonomy would require that the lawmaker of the state elaborates special legislation that singles out the group that is to be exempted from the regular application of law (which exemption could, in itself, be very problematic) and creates a special jurisdiction that is under the self-management of this group. In contrast to functional autonomy, which may be integrative in nature, NCA could produce outcomes that separate the minority group from at least some of the public services that are provided for the general population. Aidarov and Drechsler summarize the characteristics of NCA in its Estonian variant by saying that 1) it seems rational in that both the majority and the minority accept NCA as the most rational alternative to territorial autonomy and to the politicization of culture; 2) a 'win–win-situation is created because NCA makes all national groups better off by ensuring power and resources to all of them and the majority is spared ethnic strife and conflict without having to give up its dominating role within the state; and 3) there is individual choice of group adherence.[43] However, at the same time, they identify certain weak points of NCA in a modern state: 1) 'the majority holding the state power actually has no rational incentives to welcome NCA if the chance for genuine conflict is low enough'; 2) the 'NCA has a normative background and objectives that can be understood to challenge the idea of the nation state'; and 3) 'the imagined communities themselves, with a possible lack of inner solidarity, connectedness, and cooperation, may not be able or willing to create or exploit NCA to begin with'. Institutional solutions that could be characterized as NCA are found in several countries, like Hungary, Latvia, and the Russian Federation, as well as Serbia, Estonia, and Finland.[44]

In Section 75(2) of the 2006 Constitution of Serbia, a right to collective self-government has been formulated: 'Persons belonging to national minorities may elect their national councils in order to exercise the right to self-governance in the field of culture, education, information and official use of their language and script, in accordance with the law'.[45] The provision is specified by the Act on the National Councils of National Minorities of 2009. It seems that the minority

[43] Aidarov and Drechsler, 'The Law and Economics of the Estonian Law', p. 51.

[44] Eiler and Kovács, 'Minority Self-Governments in Hungary', pp. 173–97; Markku Suksi, 'The Constitutional Development of the Baltic Countries', in *Human Rights in the Baltic States*, edited by Taina Dahlgren (Helsinki: The Finnish Helsinki Committee and the Ministry of Foreign Affairs, 1993), p. 34; Bill Bowring, 'Burial and Resurrection: Karl Renner's Controversial Influence on the "National Question" in Russia', in *National-Cultural Autonomy and its Contemporary Critics*, edited by Ephraim Nimni (London/New York: Routledge, 2005), pp. 191–206; Nicky Torode, 'National Cultural Autonomy in the Russian Federation: Implementation and Impact', *International Journal on Minority and Group Rights*, vol. 15 (2008): pp. 179–93; Osipov, 'National Cultural Autonomy in Russia', pp. 27–57. For Latvia, see the Act on the Unrestricted Development and Right to Cultural Autonomy of Latvia's Nationalities and Ethnic Groups, which in s 7 creates a Consultative Nationalities Council to function as a participant in the drafting of laws in Latvia's Supreme Council.

[45] Constitution of Serbia 2006, s 75(2).

self-governments are constituted as legal persons and given public powers that are exercised through elected bodies based on voluntary registration of persons.

The Constitution of Estonia contains in Section 50 a relevant point of departure for an analysis of this form of NTA. According to the provision, national minorities have the right, in the interests of national culture, to establish self-governing agencies under conditions and pursuant to procedure provided by the Act on Cultural Autonomy of National Minorities. According to Section 2 of the Act, the cultural autonomy of a national minority shall mean the right of persons belonging to a national minority to establish cultural autonomy bodies in order to perform culture-related rights (for instance, education and welfare services) granted to them by the Constitution. Persons belonging to the German, Russian, Swedish, and Jewish national minorities are identified as ones who may establish cultural autonomy bodies without any numeral requirements, while persons of other national minorities may do so if they amount to over 3,000 individuals. A NCA may, for instance, set up its own educational institutions that operate in the language of the minority.

Section 17(3) of the Constitution of Finland provides that the Sami as an indigenous people have the right to maintain and develop their own language and culture. This 'material' provision is supplemented by Section 122(4), according to which the Sami have linguistic and cultural self-government in their native region, as provided by an act. The act that creates the institution of linguistic and cultural self-government is the Sami Assembly Act (often denoted as the Sami Parliament Act). It organizes the Sami in Finland politically in the so-called Sami Assembly (often referred to as the Sami Parliament). Within this organization, the Sami promote the use of the three Sami languages spoken in Finland in, inter alia, schools and public administration, while also representing the Sami as the body that has to be officially heard when measures affecting the Sami are contemplated by public authorities. This non-territorial form of autonomy or administration does not seem to serve the purpose of separating the Sami from the rest of the society, but rather the purpose of providing some additional public services and avenues of influence.[46]

4.3 Territory vs Non-Territory

In Estonia, the juxtaposition of territoriality and non-territoriality is present in constitutional practice in a direct manner. The towns of Narva and Sillamäe in the north-eastern corner of Estonia have a predominantly Russian-speaking population, and relatively early on in the independence of Estonia, the city councils of the two towns decided to organize autonomy referendums at the municipal level. The question posed on 16 and 17 July 1993 in the town of Narva was the

[46] In Finland, another statutory body of an advisory nature exists for the Swedish-speaking Finns in the Assembly of the Swedish-speakers (Folktinget).

following: 'Do you want Narva to have a status of national-territorial autonomy within the Republic of Estonia?' The question put to the voters in Sillamäe on 17 July 1993 was the following: 'Do you want Sillamäe to have a status of national-territorial autonomy within the Republic of Estonia, where equal rights would be guaranteed to all citizens?'. The Legal Chancellor of Estonia initiated proceedings in the Supreme Court of Estonia in relation to both referendums. The Court issued decisions in which the two referendums were declared unconstitutional and the results, as well as subsequent measures on the basis of the referendums, null and void.[47]

These demands for territorial autonomy were connected to the unclear situation of the Russian-speaking non-citizens of Estonia. The Court found that the creation of national-territorial autonomous units is not a local, but a national issue. Such issues should be determined according to procedures of decision-making applicable at the national level, and therefore, the two referendums on national-territorial autonomy fell outside the jurisdiction of local government for reasons of violation of Section 154(1) of the Constitution of Estonia. The Court also held that Section 50 of the Constitution provides 'the opportunity for national minorities to establish, in the interests of their national culture, self-governing authorities under the conditions and procedures' set forth in the Act on Cultural Autonomy for National Minorities. Hence the Constitution presupposed the existence of such an act and gave the Court a legal basis for invalidating the referendums. However, the National Minorities Cultural Autonomy Act was enacted only on 26 October 1993, some two to three months after the two decisions by the Supreme Court that struck down referendums on territorial forms of autonomy, and the Act entered into force on 28 November 1993.[48] In both cases, the Court was of the opinion that '[t]he Constitution does not provide for a national-territorial autonomy. Lack of mention of such national-territorial autonomy in the Constitution means that such autonomy is contrary to the spirit of the Constitution.'

The right of self-determination was not directly an issue in the two referendums. However, it may be possible to propose that provisions on cultural autonomy for national minorities in the Constitution may exist for several reasons, the protection of minorities being one of them and the avoidance of secessionist challenges to the self-determination of the state another one.[49] By avoiding a territorial designation of autonomy arrangements, the state might feel less exposed to potential territorial problems that the presence of minorities in the state may give rise to.

[47] Markku Suksi, *On the Constitutional Features of Estonia* (Åbo: Åbo Akademi, 1999), pp. 45–6; Decision No. III-4/A-2 of the Constitutional Review Chamber of the Supreme Court of Estonia of 11 August 1993 and Decision No. III-4/A-3 of 6 September 1993 of the Constitutional Review Chamber of the Supreme Court of Estonia.

[48] National Minorities Cultural Autonomy Act 1993, passed by the Act of 26 October 1993 (RT I 1993, 71, 1001), entered into force 28 November 1993. Amended by the following Acts: 05.06.02 entered into force 01.07.02–RT I 2002, 53, 336; 19.06.02 entered into force 01.08.02–RT I 2002, 62, 376.

[49] Aidarov and Drechsler, 'The Law and Economics of the Estonian Law', p. 52.

The origins of the 1993 Act on Cultural Autonomy for National Minorities can be found in inter-war Estonia. The 1920 Constitution of Estonia contained in Sections 21–23 a set of important minority provisions. Of these, Section 21 provided that '[t]he members of minority nationalities within the confines of Estonia may form corresponding autonomous institutions for the promotion of the interests of their national culture and welfare in so far as these do not run contrary to the interests of the State'. In fact, this idea was explicitly present already in the 1918 Declaration of Independence of Estonia. In order to give a more concrete basis for the creation of autonomous institutions of national minorities, the Parliament of Estonia enacted in 1925 the Act on the Cultural Autonomy for National Minorities.[50] Of course, this Act was revoked at the same time as the entire legal order of Estonia was annihilated after World War II, when Estonia became part of the Soviet Union. However, the Soviet occupation ended with the re-introduction of Estonian independence in 1990–1. In addition, the idea of cultural autonomy was reintroduced, which took place in 1993 by means of the Act on the Cultural Autonomy for National Minorities. The contents of the 1993 Act were, at the time of the reintroduction, similar to those of the 1925 Act.[51] Presenting the 1993 Act from a law and economics point of view and arriving at a mixed evaluation about its effects, Aidarov and Drechsler have characterized the 1993 Act as a success from two points of view: the Act had a performative function, inter alia, in relation to a foreign audience at the same time as it supported the idea of state continuity of Estonia between the first era of independence during the interwar period and the period after independence from the Soviet Union.[52] However, their conclusion seems to be that the existence of the Act has not meant anything at all for the Russian-speaking population of Estonia.

In 2004, the Ingrian Finnish established their body of cultural autonomy in Estonia, and in 2007, the Swedish achieved the same status.[53] In 2006, the

[50] David J. Smith and John Hiden, *Ethnic Diversity and the Nation State—National Cultural Autonomy Revisited* (Oxford/New York: Routledge, 2012); Eide, 'Cultural Autonomy', pp. 253–5; on the 1925 law, Georg von Rauch, *Geschichte der baltischen Staaten* [History of the Baltic States] (München: Deutscher Taschenbuch Verlag, 1990), pp. 137–8). An English translation of the law available on: http://www.einst.ee/factsheets/cult_auton/.

[51] Eide, 'Cultural Autonomy', p. 257.

[52] Aidarov and Drechsler, 'The Law and Economics of the Estonian Law', pp. 46–8; See also Smith and Hiden, *Ethnic Diversity*, p. 111. Smith and Hiden make the point that the 'reinstatement of the interwar cultural autonomy was primarily a symbolic gesture. Its main aim was to counter international criticism of citizenship and other legislation and thus enhance Estonia's reputation in the eyes of its new Western partners, thereby improving the country's prospects for integration into international structures.'

[53] Mikko Lagerspetz, 'Cultural Autonomy of National Minorities in Estonia: The Erosion of a Promise', *Journal of Baltic Studies*, vol. 45, no. 4 (2014): pp. 457–75. See the Charter for the Swedish National Cultural Autonomy 2007, adopted in Tallinn on the basis of s 22 of the Act on Cultural Autonomy for National Minorities, accessed 3 April 2013, http://www.eestirootslane.ee/sv/stadgar. According to Lagerspetz, in 2012 there were 357 Ingrian Finns altogether and 375 Swedes, which means that the beneficiaries of the legislative framework are very few.

association 'Russian Cultural Autonomy' and some other organizations applied for cultural autonomy for the Russians, but the application was denied in 2009, whereupon the association took the matter to the courts.[54] The complaint was denied in June 2009 by the Administrative Court of Tallinn and in June 2010, the Appellate Court decided not to overturn the decision of the Administrative Court. Finally, in November 2010, the Supreme Court made a decision of inadmissibility, which meant that the decisions of the lower courts remained in force.[55] In 2009, the Legal Chancellor dealt with a case regarding how quickly the request for cultural autonomy should be processed by the state organs (this was also dealt with by the court). Apparently, no decision was made by the state regarding the application because there was an expectation that a new act on cultural autonomy would be adopted. The underlying idea seems to be that the existing law does not function properly, which has also been mentioned in the recommendations of the Committee of Ministers of the Council of Europe on the basis of the Framework Convention on National Minorities[56] and the opinions of the Advisory Committee on the Framework Convention,[57] as well as in the reports on Estonia by the European Commission against Racism and Intolerance.[58] Thus a new act

[54] Mikko Lagerspetz and Henri Vogt, 'Estonia', in *Handbook of Political Change in Eastern Europe*, edited by Sten Berglund et al. (Cheltenham, UK/Northampton, MA: Edward Elgar, 2013), pp. 51–84. Some further applications by the Russian minority were filed in 2009 and 2011.

[55] See the decision by the Appellate Court for Tallinn of 1 June 2010, No. 3-09-464. For an account of the process, see also Aidarov and Drechsler, 'The Law and Economics of the Estonian Law', pp. 45–6; Lagerspetz, 'Cultural Autonomy of National Minorities in Estonia'.

[56] See, e.g., Resolution ResCMN (2002)8 on the implementation of the Framework Convention for the Protection of National Minorities by Estonia: 'Some of the initiatives to protect national minorities, such as the National Minorities Cultural Autonomy Act, contain elements that are not particularly suited for the present situation of minorities in Estonia and need to be revised or replaced in order for them to be effective with respect to all minorities concerned.' See also Resolution ResCMN (2006)1, in which concern was expressed that '[t]he National Minority Cultural Autonomy Act remains unchanged despite the fact that it is generally considered to be ineffective', and where the Committee of Ministers recommended that authorities 'address shortcomings in the National Minority Cultural Autonomy Act by drawing up, in consultation with those concerned, legislation that is more inclusive and takes better into account the present-day concerns of persons belonging to national minorities'. In Resolution CM/ResCMN (2012)9, the Committee of Ministers notes that '[t]wo national minorities (the Ingrian-Finnish and the Swedish) receive baseline funding in line with the National Cultural Autonomy Act', but does not otherwise comment on the Act on National Cultural Autonomy.

[57] See Advisory Committee on the Framework Convention for the Protection of National Minorities, Opinions: ACFC/INF/OP/I (2002)005, ACFC/INF/OP/II (2005)001, and ACFC/OP/III(2011)004. In the opinion of 2011, there was much focus on the need to amend the Act on Cultural Autonomy for National Minorities.

[58] See European Commission against Racism and Intolerance, Second Report on Estonia (adopted 22 June 2001), CRI (2002) 1, para 16; European Commission against Racism and Intolerance, Third Report on Estonia (adopted 24 June 2005), CRI (2006) 1 (in which the ECRI concludes that 'the Law on Cultural Autonomy for National Minorities should be amended in order to reflect the current realities of Estonian society'); European Commission against Racism and Intolerance, Fourth Report on Estonia (adopted 15 December 2009), CRI (2010) 3 (in which it is recommended that Estonian authorities amend the Law on Cultural Autonomy for National Minorities as soon as possible and that representatives of minorities be involved and consulted in this process).

would resolve the problem of who is entitled to represent a minority group in Estonia for the purposes of applying for cultural autonomy. The government seems to have had plans to submit a draft bill concerning a new act on cultural autonomy to the Parliament in 2012, but by June 2015, this does not seem to have taken place.

Non-territorial autonomy is somewhat similarly organized in Serbia, where under Article 2 of the Act on National Councils of National Minorities of 2009 all fifteen minorities of Serbia had the possibility of setting up their respective national councils. The Act outlines the details of the powers of a national minority council and the manner in which the persons belonging to a minority may participate in the functioning of a council. Such national councils have been set up, inter alia, by the Roma and the Hungarians,[59] the latter being the largest minority group in Serbia. The Serbian Hungarian National Council represents altogether 250,000 Hungarian-speaking persons throughout the territory of Serbia (although living primarily in Vojvodina) with regard to their needs in such areas as culture, education, information, and the official use of language and script, as well as other issues that may be relevant for the national council.[60]

In Finland, the (non-)territoriality of the Sami Assembly (alias Sami Parliament) takes on another dimension. The Sami Assembly is tasked to function as the representative body of the Sami for the purposes of matters related to Sami languages and culture, and the cultural autonomy of the Sami is territorially delimited to the homeland of the Sami. This area is, according to Section 4 of the Act on the Sami Assembly, constituted by three and a half municipalities in the northernmost part of Finland, and a map of the territory is attached to the Decree on the Sami Assembly (1727/1995). Although the activities of the Sami Assembly take place, in principle, within that territory, the 'membership' of the Sami cultural autonomy is not limited to those Sami persons who live in the Sami homeland, but applies to all Sami throughout the territory of Finland (see section 4.5). This means that the cultural autonomy of the Sami in Finland is both territorial and non-territorial, at the same time.[61]

[59] Perhaps because of the relatively small size of the Jewish minority in Serbia, it is provided in the Serbian Act, s 134 that the Executive Board of the Union of Jewish Municipalities of Serbia shall function as a national council and the President of the Union of Jewish Municipalities of Serbia is a member of the Council of National Minorities of the Republic of Serbia.

[60] Tamás Korhecz, 'Non-Territorial Autonomy in Practice: The Hungarian National Council in Serbia', in *Autonomies in Europe: Solutions and Challenges*, edited by Zoltán Kantór (Budapest: L'Harmattan, 2014), pp. 151–63.

[61] Nimni, 'Nationalist Multiculturalism in Late Imperial Austria', p. 11; Eide, 'Cultural Autonomy', p. 252. The Government of Finland proposed to the Parliament that ILO Convention No. 169 be ratified, and if this happens, the rights of the Sami will be strengthened over the entire state of Finland, not only in the northernmost part. The matter is pending in the new Parliament elected in April 2015.

4.4 Powers

It has been suggested that persons belonging to a minority who are members of a NCA of a non-territorial kind would be exempted from application of general law or the law applicable on the other members of the society. It has been held that

> [i]n Bauer and Renner's model, even if the citizen lives in a territory where the majority belongs to a different national group, in questions of national and ethnic interest, citizens of different ethnies are not subject to the cultural practices of the majority, but can rely on their own, trans-territorial national organization, which has the status of a public corporation'.[62]

Within that form of organization, the minority communities would be able to levy taxes on the members of the community,[63] that is, the entities of cultural autonomy would have the power to compel their members to support financially the cultural and governing institutions of their group.[64]

In reality, however, this is often not the case. For instance, in Estonia, the national cultural autonomies do not, under the law, have any significant public powers that the state would have transferred to the NCA on the basis of the law, least of all a general power to collect taxes from the members. However, according to Section 27 of the Act on Cultural Autonomy, the funds of a cultural autonomy body and the bodies and institutions thereof are constituted of, inter alia, cultural self-administration contributions in a size determined by the cultural council, which could approximate tax powers, although they are probably better characterized as annual membership fees. The main source of funding seems to be appropriations from the state budget according to law and support designated for specific purposes as well as support for specific purposes allocated from the budget of the local government to the educational, cultural, and social welfare institutions of cultural self-administration.[65] National cultural autonomies may receive financial support, donations, and bequests. Under the Act, national cultural autonomies may also receive support from foreign organizations. This is a

62 Nimni, 'Nationalist Multiculturalism in Late Imperial Austria', p. 11.

63 Aidarov and Drechsler, 'The Law and Economics of the Estonian Law', p. 44. It has been maintained on the basis of the 1925 Act on National Cultural Autonomy of Estonia that the Russians in Estonia did not attempt to create an NCA for a number of reasons, one of which was that the 'Russians were generally poor and would not have wanted to pay any additional tax to maintain NCA, which the Russian NCA authority could indeed have levied'.

64 Geoffrey Brahm Levey, 'National Cultural Autonomy and Liberal Nationalism', in *National-Cultural Autonomy and its Contemporary Critics*, edited by Ephraim Nimni (London/New York: Routledge, 2005), pp. 162–3. However, under public international law, self-identification is the point of departure for association with a minority population, so ultimately, an obligation for a person to support an organization of NTA would have to be dependent on the free choice and will of the individual person.

65 A cultural autonomy body may use the assets allocated to it for specific purposes only pursuant to the prescribed procedure and for the intended purposes. Supervision over the use of the assets shall be exercised by duly authorized state supervisory bodies in adherence to the legislation in force.

generous concession in view of the possible suspicion amongst states regarding foreign involvement in their minorities by kin-states.

According to Section 4 of the Estonian Act, persons belonging to a national minority have the right, inter alia, to form and support national cultural and educational institutions and religious communities, establish national organizations, and perform national traditions and religious customs if this does not violate public order, damage health, or breach morality. In addition, such persons have the right to use their national tongue in public administration within the limits established by the Language Act, as well as to publish printed matter in their national languages and to carry out some other activities. At the same time, under Section 5 of the Act, the main objective of a cultural autonomy body is to organize studying in the mother tongue and supervise the use of the assets prescribed for such purpose, establish cultural institutions of national minorities and organize their activity, and to organize national cultural events. The body can also establish foundations, and grant stipends and awards for promoting the culture and education of national minorities.[66] In spite of the possibility of taking the legal actions that cultural autonomies of Estonia can undertake under the Act, doubts have been expressed concerning the legal personality of such bodies of cultural autonomy.[67]

The Act specifies that national minorities have the right to establish, in the interests of national culture, their own institutions of cultural self-administration which, in dealing with matters within their competence, shall adhere to Estonian legislation. According to Section 24 of the Estonian Act, the institutions of cultural self-administration are educational institutions where studies are conducted in the

[66] These aims are partly reproduced, partly developed for the Swedish cultural autonomy in s 5 of the Charter of the Swedish cultural autonomy.

[67] Lagerspetz, 'Cultural Autonomy of National Minorities in Estonia'. In spite of the provisions of the Act on National Cultural Autonomy 1993 and in spite of, e.g., the Charter of the Swedish cultural autonomy, it has been maintained that the cultural autonomies of Estonia continuously suffer from an unclear legal status that is supposed, at least partly, to be due to the fact that they would not be legal persons and that they would lack official legal status, which is surprising in view of what was said above about the powers of the entities (such as the power to create foundations; only legal persons can create new legal persons). The reason for this could potentially be found in the still somewhat fluid situation of the Estonian legal order by the time of the adoption of the Act, but more recently, other statutory associations and public institutions have been created so that they clearly fulfil the criteria for legal persons and can act directly on the basis of the relevant statute. Moreover, in its Third Report to the Advisory Committee of the Framework Convention, the Estonian Government explained that 'the current Act does not clearly stipulate that cultural autonomies constitute a legal person. This is a significant obstacle for the already established cultural councils of national minorities (Ingrian-Finnish, Swedish) in implementing the objectives of the Act. Currently under consideration are both the possibility of granting the cultural councils the status of a legal personality in public law or in private law (in the form of a nonprofit association).' See Third Report Submitted by Estonia Pursuant to Article 25, Paragraph 2, of the Framework Convention for the Protection of National Minorities (13 April 2010) 2010ACFC/SR/III (2010)006. They therefore use, for their daily activities, foundations set up by themselves for carrying out business expeditiously. See also Mikko Lagerspetz, 'When Formal and Informal Rules Meet: The Four Sets of Rules of the Estonian Language and Minority Regime', in *Sociologies of Formality and Informality*, edited by Adriana Mica, Jan Winczorek, and Rafał Wiśniewski (Frankfurt: Peter Lang, 2015), pp. 127–48.

national language or which offer intensive studies of national culture (pre-school child care institutions and schools), institutions of national culture, enterprises and publishing houses of national culture, and national social welfare institutions.

None of these functions established in the Estonian law indicate that the autonomous entity would have law-making powers of its own. There is also no talk about exemptions from national legislation, but instead explicit confirmations that the activities of national cultural autonomies have to take place within the provisions of national law. Moreover, Section 25 of the Act stipulates that schools (classes) of a national minority should be opened and their work should be organized pursuant to the procedure provided by the Private Schools Act. This means that the schools are in fact operated within the regular frame established by the legislator of the state, not on the basis of norms established by the minority group itself; such a school of the minority would, in the course of its activities, exercise public powers as specified in the Private Schools Act (such as grading, issuing certificates, disciplinary powers, etc.).

The situation in respect of powers and tasks is somewhat similar in Finland as concerns the Sami Assembly. The Sami Assembly is a legal person incorporated under the Sami Assembly Act, entitled to possess its own resources and property and to engage in economic transactions with other legal persons (and so would the cultural autonomies in Estonia seem to be, too, although as explained above, their status as legal persons has been doubted). According to Section 5 of the Sami Assembly Act, the general powers of the Assembly consist of the task of the Sami Assembly to look after the Sami language and culture, as well as to take care of matters relating to their status as an indigenous people and of the task, in these matters, to suggest initiatives and make proposals to the authorities, and to issue statements. In the pursuance of these matters the Sami Assembly shall furthermore use the powers prescribed in the Act or elsewhere in the law. However, the Sami Assembly Act or other pieces of law do not seem to contain, at least at the moment, any significant powers for the Sami Assembly. In particular, the Sami Assembly does not have any legislative powers, nor are the Sami persons who qualify as voters in the elections to the Sami Assembly exempted in any way from the application of national legislation.

From a more administrative point of view, under ss. 5–8 of the Act, the Sami Assembly shall adopt its own rules of procedure, and it shall draw up an annual report for the government of Finland enumerating events of importance in the development of matters of specific relevance to the Sami. The Assembly shall also decide how the funds designated over the state budget for the common use of the Sami shall be allocated. In addition, the obligation to negotiate, placed upon the public authorities of Finland in Section 9 of the Act,[68] seems to imply a task

[68] As provided in sub-section 2 of the provision, in order to fulfil its obligation to negotiate, the relevant authority shall provide the Sami Assembly with the opportunity to be heard and discuss matters. Failure to use this opportunity in no way prevents the authority from proceeding in the matter. This obligation includes, inter alia, land use, natural resources, social and health issues, and other matters that may affect the Sami.

for the Sami Assembly to engage in negotiations with authorities, whenever such become necessary on the basis of the list of items included in the Act. An important task for the Sami Assembly is to establish, through its election committee, who is and who is not qualified to vote in the elections to the Sami Assembly, that is, to decide who is entitled to participate in decision-making in Sami matters in the Assembly. This means that the Sami Assembly does not have complete discretion in determining the boundaries of its own electorate, but needs to make decisions on the right to vote on the basis of the Act (see section 4.5).

The Sami Assembly is not in charge of the general delivery of public services to the Sami population in the Sami homeland. Instead, those services are produced by the municipalities (e.g., education, social affairs and health, environment) or by state authorities (e.g., public order, justice) within their territorial and material jurisdictions in the Sami homeland. From the point of view of the principle of effective participation (see sections 4.5 and 4.6), it may be asked whether the participation of Sami through the Sami Assembly can be effective when they participate in something that does not entail any significant or relevant public powers.[69] Also, no powers of taxation or collecting annual membership fees are foreseen in the Act. Instead, under Section 2 of the Act, an appropriation shall be made in the state budget for the tasks established in the Sami Assembly Act. Hence it seems the Sami Assembly has even fewer formal powers than the Estonian national cultural autonomies (although the intention here is not to imply that the Estonian government has a duty to hear the Estonian cultural autonomies on decisions that the government is about to make). However, the Mining Act of Finland (621/2011) grants the Sami, as represented by the Sami Assembly, the possibility of making an input into decision-making when mining licences in the Sami homeland are prepared and decided by governmental authorities. The Mining Act also grants the Sami Assembly a formal position as a complainant in situations in which the possibility of this indigenous population of preserving and developing their culture and language could be circumscribed.[70]

In this respect, the situation is very different in Serbia, where the Act on National Councils of National Minorities, in fact, places relatively significant powers in the national council of each national minority so constituted so as to complement ordinary administrative decision-making.[71] According to Section 10 of the Act, the general competences of a national council encompass the independent power of, inter alia, adopting and amending the statute of the national council, managing its property and establishing proposals of national symbols, emblems, and holidays of national minorities, and deciding on the official use of

[69] It is an entirely different matter that the Sami participate in local government on a par with other inhabitants of the northernmost municipalities, and in that sense, it can be said that the municipal organization can offer an effective vehicle of participation for the Sami on a par with the avenues of participation of those inhabitants of the relevant municipalities who are not Sami.

[70] Giuseppe Amatulli, *The Legal Position of the Sami in the Exploitation of Mineral Resources in Finland, Norway and Sweden* (Åbo: Institute for Human Rights of Åbo Akademi University, 2015), accessed 21 May 2015, http://www.abo.fi/fakultet/en/onlinepublications.

[71] Korhecz, 'Non-Territorial Autonomy in Practice', p. 155.

language and script as well as other areas of importance for the preservation of a national minority's identity. A national council also has the power to initiate the adoption of and to monitor the implementation of law and other regulations in the field of culture, education, information, and official use of language and script and to participate in the preparation of regulations and submit motions for amendments and supplements to regulations prescribing national minority rights guaranteed by the Constitution in the field of culture, education, information, and official use of language and script. Such a council can also propose a representative of the national minority to the council for interethnic relations with a unit of local self-government as well as decide on the issues of the national minority and represent the minority.

In addition, a number of more specific competencies have been enumerated in various fields identified in the Serbian Act on National Councils, such as education, including the teaching syllabus, textbooks, and teaching aids, culture, media, and the official use of language and script. Within these areas, the national councils have the possibility of making decisions, but the Act also contains numerous provisions concerning the right of the minority to propose and initiate measures, and to give opinions on relevant matters. In fact, on the basis of Sections 25 and 26 of the Act, these rights often seem to entail the corresponding duty on the part of the state, an autonomous province, or local government to take up an issue for discussion or to hear the relevant national council.

More importantly, a national council is empowered under Section 11 of the Act to establish institutions, associations, funds, and business organizations in the field of culture, education, and information. This means that a national council can set up, for instance, schools and news media. In case such services are already provided by the state, an autonomous province, or a local government, it is possible for the national council under Section 24 of the Act to request that these public bodies transfer the right of establishment of educational, cultural, or broadcasting institutions either entirely or partially to the relevant national council under terms established in sub-sections 4 to 6 of the Section.[72] Such transfers of institutions from other public authorities to the national councils have taken place at a relatively fast pace at least as concerns the Hungarian-speaking minority, and where the public authorities have been unwilling to work in the direction established by the initiative of a national council, subsequent litigation before courts of law contains examples where the position of a national council has been confirmed and the institution transferred to the national council.[73] Such a national council does not, however, seem to have any powers of taxation. The financial resources for the national councils are provided under Section 114 of the Act over the budgets of the regular entities of public administration, that is, over

[72] The provision defines the various institutions as follows: 1) Educational institutions where classes are held exclusively in the language of a national minority; 2) Cultural institutions whose main activity is to preserve and develop the culture of a national minority; 3) Institutions broadcasting public information exclusively in the language of a national minority.

[73] Korhecz, 'Non-Territorial Autonomy in Practice', p. 159.

the budgets of the Republic of Serbia,[74] the Autonomous Province of Vojvodina and the local self-government units (municipalities). The national councils can also receive donations and have other sources of funding.[75]

The Serbian national councils also have explicit avenues for conducting cross-border and international affairs. According to Section 27 of the Act, a national council shall, in accordance with the law, co-operate with international and regional organizations, state bodies, organizations, and institutions in the native countries, as well as with national councils or similar bodies of national minorities in other countries. In addition, the representative of a national council shall participate in negotiations or be consulted in respect of negotiations on the conclusion of bilateral agreements with native countries in the part directly related to the rights of national minorities. It thus seems that the Serbian point of view is very inclusive and without negative attitudes concerning so-called kin-state cooperation. This dimension is also reflected in the same provision in another way: the representatives of a national council shall participate in the activities of mixed intergovernmental bodies, the aim of which is to supervise the implementation of bilateral intergovernmental agreements on the protection of rights of a national minority concerned. Section 28 of the Act is very progressive in comparison with, for instance, many territorial autonomies in different countries in establishing that the representatives of national minorities, through the Council of National Minorities of the Republic of Serbia, shall take part in the conclusion of international agreements, which in this context is specified to mean the process of accession to international or regional agreements related to the status of national minorities and protection of their rights.

Generally speaking, it seems that non-territorial cultural autonomies have not been vested with broad powers, except in the case of the Serbian national councils. In situations where public powers have been vested in separate institutions of a minority, the public functions are normally intended to be taken care of on the basis of self-government of the group.[76] In so far as public powers have been delegated under the law to such entities, issues of accountability arise and need to be addressed in the legislation. Areas where accountability issues would be relevant are, for example, hiring school teachers (where 'malpractice' could result in a need

[74] According to s 119, there exists a particular budgetary fund of national minorities, managed by the ministry in charge of minority and human rights issues. The fund finances projects and programmes in the field of culture, education, information, and official use of language and script of national minorities.

[75] Korhecz, 'Non-Territorial Autonomy in Practice', pp. 156, 160–2.

[76] It is, without doubt, possible to view even entities of cultural autonomy as expressions of functional autonomy delegated by the state to an entity outside the regular administrative structure: public functions are in such cases transferred to statutory entities incorporated under public law. See Osipov, 'Changing the Angle', p. 10: 'In this context, the adjective of "non-territorial:, like most other potential adjectives ("cultural" or "personal"), are to a certain degree problematic. Functional autonomy turns out to be more appropriate, however, "non-territorial" may also serve as a generic term if we are to give respect to the recently established tradition of naming ethnicity-based arrangements.' Osipov seems to be, quite correctly, focusing on the public powers and public functions that such statutory entities should or could have.

to terminate the employment of such a teacher) and management of property owned by the non-territorial autonomous entity. In addition, accountability raises questions of how the legal remedies and the right to complaint to judicial organs over decisions that the bodies exercising public powers within such non-territorial autonomy arrangements have been organized. If public powers have been vested in entities of a non-territorial nature, legal remedies must be available.

4.5 Determination of Membership

The personality principle can, in principle, constitute a dimension of non-territorial autonomy, but the application of the principle may be broad or more limited, depending on how freely an individual is allowed to choose membership in the relevant NTA. As pointed out by Nimni, 'Bauer starts from assuming individual choice in defining affiliation to organized national communities (the personality principle)', giving expression to the idea of individuals rationally and reasonably deciding their national identity (however complicated this might be from a theoretical point of view).[77] In addition, according to Nimni, '[t]he model of national autonomy proposed by Renner requires that all citizens declare their nationality when they reach voting age. Members of each national community, whatever their territory of residence, would form a single public body or association endowed with legal personality and sovereignty and competent to deal with all national-cultural affairs'.[78] Here, the theory of Bauer and Renner seems to envision a system of compulsory self-identification amongst all persons and their subsequent affiliation with a national community, which could be a problem against the background of, for instance, Article 3(1) of the European Framework Convention for the Protection of National Minorities.[79]

According to Section 2 of the Estonian Act on National Cultural Autonomy, the cultural autonomy of a national minority shall mean the right of persons belonging to a national minority to establish cultural autonomy bodies in order to perform culture-related rights granted to them by the Constitution. In principle, that right belongs to national minorities with a population exceeding 3,000 persons, but no such quantitative limit is set on the German, Russian, Swedish, or Jewish national minorities, which means that these explicitly mentioned minorities can also create a cultural autonomy with less members. So far, the Swedish of Estonia are the only 'mentioned minority' to have made use of this possibility. In

[77] Nimni, 'Nationalist Multiculturalism in Late Imperial Austria', p. 23.

[78] Nimni, 'Nationalist Multiculturalism in Late Imperial Austria', p. xxvii; Bauer, *Question of Nationalities and Social Democracy*. The concept of nationality is often utilized in the eastern part of Europe, while in the western part, reference is made to linguistic, cultural, or ethnic characteristics when minorities are described.

[79] According to the provision, '[e]very person belonging to a national minority shall have the right freely to choose to be treated or not to be treated as such and no disadvantage shall result from this choice or from the exercise of the rights which are connected to that choice'.

addition, Section 1 of the Act requires that the potential members of a cultural autonomy of a national minority are Estonian citizens who reside in the territory of Estonia, who have long-term, sound, and permanent ties with Estonia, who differ from Estonians by their ethnic belonging, cultural characteristics, religion, or language, and who are led by their wish to collectively maintain their cultural customs, religion, or language, which are the basis for their common identity. Once the body of NCA has been created for a minority population, non-citizens or aliens residing in Estonia may also, according to Section 6 of the Act, take part in the activities of cultural and educational institutions and religious communities. However, such aliens are not, according to the Act, entitled to participate in the elections of, or be elected or appointed to the directing bodies of institutions of cultural self-administration. In this respect, Section 3(1) of the Charter of the Swedish cultural autonomy in Estonia introduces a conflicting rule according to which the cultural council is elected by Swedes residing in Estonia and outside the territory of Estonia.[80]

The procedure for the establishment of a body of cultural autonomy is outlined in Section 7 of the Act and presupposes the creation of a nationality list of the national minority, that is, a list of persons who declare membership of the national minority.[81] According to Section 8(3), a person is entered on a nationality list based upon the person's application,[82] which means that self-identification is the point of departure for such a list,[83] prepared for the purposes of the creation of a body of cultural autonomy under Section 7(2), by national cultural associations or unions of such associations. The procedure for the maintenance and use of nationality lists shall be established by the government of the Republic. On the basis of Section 10 of the Act, an application to establish a cultural autonomy body shall be submitted through the corresponding national cultural association or a union of such associations to the government of Estonia, which shall deal with the application according to the Administrative Procedure Act. This means that NGOs or associations under civil law created for the promotion of

[80] However, at least for candidates in elections, the decree on election procedures to the cultural council, s 12(2), stipulates that a candidate in an electoral district shall be a permanent resident of that district, which effectively rules out out-of-country candidates.

[81] On the creation, maintenance, and use of the nationality lists of national minorities, see the decree of the Estonian government no. 238 of 1 October 1996, entitled 'Vähemusrahvuste rahvusnimekirjade pidamise ja kasutamise kord' [Order of Maintenance of Lists of Names of National Minorities].

[82] According to s 8 of the Act, the following information shall be registered concerning each person entered on the nationality list: 1) given name and surname; 2) the date and place of birth; 3) sex; 4) nationality and mother tongue; 5) personal identification code; 6) marital status; 7) data on minor children; 8) residence; 9) religion; 10) the signature of the applicant, and the date. According to sub-section 2, children under 15 years of age shall also be entered in the nationality list at the request of their parents.

[83] A person can also, under s 9, be deleted form a nationality list if the person requests it, i.e., if the self-chosen identification of the person changes, or if the person renounces Estonian citizenship or takes up permanent residence in a foreign country, which means that the person cuts ties with the public administration of Estonia. Of course, a person's membership of the cultural autonomy body also ceases upon the death of the person.

the position of minority populations are given an important position in initiating NCA in Estonia.[84] However, there seems to exist a distinction on the basis of citizenship between civil law organizations, on the one hand, and the institutions of the NCA, on the other: while aliens or non-citizens can be members of regular associations, they cannot be members of national cultural autonomies organized as statutory associations under public law.

Apart from the nationality list, a separate polling list shall be prepared for the elections of the cultural council of the national minority. According to Section 15 of the Act, the polling list shall be prepared on the basis of the nationality list of the relevant minority for the organization of direct and uniform elections by secret vote to the council every three years. The number of mandates in a cultural council can vary between twenty and sixty persons, as determined by the general election committee of the national minority. As established in Section 14 of the Act, the rules for the elections of a cultural council of a national minority shall be prepared and approved by the government.[85] However, under Section 16, elections shall not be organized if less than half of the persons entered on the nationality list have given consent for their entry on the polling list. Section 19 of the Act requires a quorum of more than 50 per cent of the persons entered on the polling list for the election of a cultural council to be valid.

The Sami Assembly of Finland is a statutory body established in the Act on the Sami Assembly (or the Sami Parliament Act, as the piece of law is often referred to). The Assembly is elected for a period of four years, but the constituency is not limited to the Sami living in the territory of the Sami homeland. Instead, according to Section 20(1) of the Act, the country is, for the purpose of elections to the Sami Assembly, one electoral district. The right to vote is determined in Section 21 of the Act so that the right to vote in elections to the Sami Assembly shall belong to every Sami, regardless of locality of residence, who reaches the age of 18 years no later than on the last election day, provided that he or she is a Finnish citizen, or that he or she is a foreign citizen domiciled in Finland in accordance with the Municipality of Residence Act (201/1994) on the last date when the request for inclusion in the electoral roll can be made. The right to vote is thus not limited to Sami who are citizens of Finland, but extends itself also to such citizens of Nordic countries (Sweden, Norway) who are resident in Finland and who qualify as Sami. This definition of the right to vote also means that the

[84] Aidarov and Drechsler, 'The Law and Economics of the Estonian Law', p. 45. Aidarov and Drechsler describe the process of setting up a body of national cultural autonomy. First relevant NGOs, i.e., a cultural society of a national minority or a union of such societies, have the right to compose a national register. The promoter(s) of the initiative 'should submit an application that it wants to do so to the Minister of Culture who refers the application to a committee composed of representatives of the Ministry, the Ministry of Internal Affairs and of cultural societies of national minorities, which then informs the Minister of the quality of the application.' The Ministry also publishes a general announcement of the application in order to inform other potential societies amongst the group of the procedure for setting up an NCA body.

[85] On the election procedures to the cultural council of a national minority cultural council, see the Decree of the Estonian government no. 137 of 6 May 2003 entitled 'Vähemusrahvuse kultuurinõukogu valimise eeskiri' [Electoral Rules of the Cultural Council of Minorities].

constituency of the Sami Assembly is to some extent disconnected from the territory within which the cultural autonomy functions. Taking into consideration the fact that around 60 per cent of the Sami of Finland live outside the Sami homeland, the non-territorialization of the constituency is a significant feature of their cultural autonomy.

Provided that every Sami has the right to vote, the definition of who is a Sami, included in Section 3 of the Act, becomes interesting. According to the provision, a Sami for the purposes of election to the Sami Assembly means a person who considers himself or herself a Sami, which means that there is an element of self-identification in the Sami definition (the subjective criterion). However, the person must, in addition, fulfil at least one of the three more 'objective' criteria, that is, 1) that he himself or at least one of his parents or grandparents has learnt Sami as his first language (the linguistic sub-criterion); 2) that he is a descendant of a person who has been entered in a land, taxation, or population register as a mountain, forest, or fishing Lapp (the registration sub-criterion); or 3) that at least one of his parents has or could have been registered as an elector for an election to the Sami Delegation or the Sami Parliament (the voter sub-criterion).[86] As explained above, the Sami Assembly is empowered to determine, when deciding on the list of voters before every election, who is and who is not a Sami for the purposes of the elections to the Sami Assembly (although once entered on the list of voters, the qualification is good for the future elections and is not tried for each individual before every election). The indigenous group is therefore primarily in charge of controlling of who is and who is not a Sami for the purposes of the Sami Assembly elections.

With a view to the fact that the Sami Assembly does not have any significant public powers, it should be somewhat of a surprise that the Supreme Administrative Court has been approached several times by persons who have applied for inclusion on the list of voters in the Sami Assembly elections. Since the end of the 1990s, the Court has reviewed more or less all of the criteria for becoming a voter in the Sami Assembly elections. The subjective criterion is present in all the cases, while the objective sub-criteria may surface in different ways. In the decision 19.09.2003/2223 of the Supreme Administrative Court, the matter proceeded actually from a person's father, who was enrolled as a voter for the election to the Sami Assembly in 1999 on the basis of his grandfather's skills in one of the Sami languages (the linguistic sub-criterion). However, the person had been denied enrolment although his father was a voter. The Court granted enrolment on the basis of the voter sub-criterion. In another case (SAC 1999:55), the ancestor of the applicant had last been registered in the property rolls amongst

[86] Kristian Myntti, *Minoriteters och urfolks politiska rättigheter* [Political Rights of Minorities and Indigenous Peoples] (Rovaniemi: Lapplands universitet, 1998), p. 330. It should be observed that unlike in Sweden and Norway, the definition of a Sami person in Finland is not tied to reindeer herding or to other traditional Sami livelihoods. Also, the government proposal to tighten the second criterion met with opposition in the Parliament of Finland, whereupon the government withdrew its amendment proposal during the spring of 2015.

the Sami in 1762, but the Court held that the applicant was to be regarded as a Sami not only on this basis for the purposes of cultural self-government. Instead, the cut-off point was to be around 1875, that is, four to five generations back in time, a point of time also mentioned in the *travaux preparatoires* of the Sami Assembly Act. He was therefore not entitled to the right to vote in the elections to the Sami Assembly in 1999 on the basis of the registration sub-criterion. In another case decided in 1999,[87] this definition of the cut-off point was sustained by the Supreme Administrative Court: the father of the grandfather of the applicant had been registered as a Sami in the roll of individuals of 1870, and therefore, the applicant was to be regarded as a Sami for the purposes of Section 3(2) of the Sami Assembly Act.

Finally, in a more recent case,[88] self-identification based on an 'all things considered' approach resulted in a holistic assessment. In this case, it was not enough for a person to be considered as a Sami according to Section 3 of the Sami Assembly Act because he himself considered himself a Sami, because he, according to a certificate of an archives authority, was a descendant to a person who had been registered as a mountain Lapp in the 1825 roll of deeds and taxes, or because he had, in addition, produced some evidence that his uncle had been proficient in a Sami language. This meant that none of the sub-criteria were satisfied. Instead, the Court undertook an evaluation which, in addition to the above-mentioned circumstances, took into account evidence that, taken together, indicated that this person, living in the municipality of Inari in the Sami homeland, identified himself with everything Sami and led a Sami lifestyle. On the basis of such a holistic assessment, the Court found that he should nonetheless be considered as a Sami, who should, upon request, be entered upon the list of voters of persons entitled to vote in elections to the Sami Assembly.

These cases decided by the Supreme Administrative Court of Finland show that the creation of a constituency for the purposes of election to a body that represents a certain ethnic or linguistic group may end up in considerable definitional problems. There are good grounds for letting the group itself manage the membership of the cultural autonomy institution and for controlling who is granted access to the group. Complete self-identification by any person who wishes to belong to the group could result in an inflation of membership by persons who show no organic affinity to the group for whom the institution has been set up, with the risk of assimilation with the majority looming at the end of the path.[89] At the same time, the creation of a separate, ethnically based constituency implies the creation of

[87] SAC 22.9.1999/3183. [88] SAC 2011:81.

[89] Myntti, *Minoriteters och urfolks politiska rättigheter*, p. 347; Cornell, 'Autonomy as a Source of Conflict', p. 249. For the Sami in Finland, the determination of the group is a value that is not only tied to language, but also to the prospective rights to land, traditional livelihoods, and other things of an indigenous nature that the Sami might expect to be re-arranged as a consequence of a possible ratification by Finland of ILO Convention No. 169. Therefore, in contrast to what has suggested ('[c]ultural autonomy does not carry the far-reaching consequences implicit in territorial autonomy: territory and ethnicity are not linked'), the case of the Sami in Finland would carry some far-reaching consequences because of the bond between the indigenous group and the territory.

distinctions that may be understood by persons who are left outside as overly exclusive and as mechanisms that might bar them from exercising influence on decisions that could affect them.[90] This, in particular, is a concern amongst the non-Sami living in the Sami homeland, who actually constitute a very clear majority in the area. In addition, the non-territorial nature of the constituency has resulted in a peculiar system of election, established in Section 38 of the Sami Assembly Act, which tries to combine the national interest with the local interest. The twenty-one members of the Sami Assembly are the candidates who got the most votes in the election, provided that the total group of candidates contains at least three candidates from each of the four municipalities in the Sami homeland. If any of these municipalities does not have three candidates among this group, then the three candidates from this municipality with the most votes shall have been elected. This means that altogether at least twelve members originate in the municipalities of the Sami homeland, while the other nine members may also originate in the rest of Finland, that is, outside the Sami homeland, depending on how strong a support they have in the elections. In practice, representatives from elsewhere in Finland have been very few.

According to Section 9 of the Serbian Act on National Councils of National Minorities, the number of members of a national council of a minority can range between fifteen and thirty-five members according to the numbers belonging to the relevant national minority, as established in the latest census. This means, for instance, that the Hungarian-speaking minority of 250,000 persons is entitled to a national council with thirty-five members. However, the actual number of persons actively identifying themselves as members of a national minority is defined in a different manner. As provided in Section 52 of the Act, the members of a national minority shall be entered in a special register of voters upon the fulfilment of the general conditions prescribed by the law, which apparently includes citizenship of Serbia. A separate register of voters shall be kept for each national minority. The members of national minorities shall be entered in the special register of voters on a voluntary basis, but a member of a national minority may be entered into only one special register of voters.[91] Hence the Serbian arrangement seems to reflect some of the most salient features of the theoretical construction of Bauer and Renner: individual choice to belong to the public corporation, albeit on a voluntary basis.[92]

[90] See also The Ljubljana Guidelines on Integration of Diverse Societies and Explanatory Note of November 2012 (adopted 7 November 2012), para 7, on a non-isolationist approach to minority issues: 'Since some minority rights are meaningful only when exercised in community with others, this may result in a degree of distinction from other groups in society in certain contexts. Nevertheless, isolation or excessive separation may weaken cross-community links and undermine the cohesiveness of society.'

[91] Korhecz, 'Non-Territorial Autonomy in Practice', p.154.

[92] See also The Ljubljana Guidelines on Integration of Diverse Societies and Explanatory Note of November 2012, para 6, on the primacy of voluntary self-identification: 'Identities are subject to the primacy of individual choice through the principle of voluntary self-identification. Minority rights include the right of individual members of minority communities to choose to be treated or not to be treated as such. No disadvantage shall result from such a choice or the refusal to choose. No restrictions should be placed on this freedom of choice. Assimilation against one's will by the

The cultural autonomy institutions in Estonia, Finland, and Serbia are designed so as to facilitate participation and, in particular, representation of national minorities. However, in the cases of Estonia and Finland, the citizenship requirement is partly relaxed, making it possible also for non-citizens to take part in the activities of these statutory bodies. In Estonia, this is done by allowing aliens residing in Estonia to take part in the activities of cultural and educational institutions and religious communities of national minorities, although they cannot participate in elections or be appointed to positions in the institutions; and in Finland, this is done by allowing non-citizens who qualify as Sami to register as voters in the elections to the Sami Assembly, provided that they are residents of Finland by the time of the request for enrolment on the list of voters. In Serbia, the requirement for the right to vote in the elections to a national council is the citizenship of Serbia. It seems that the fewer powers a cultural autonomy has, the more relaxed the citizenship requirements can be, while the reverse might be true with increasing powers of the cultural autonomies.

4.6 Representation of the Group

As concerns representation of the national minorities, including the Sami in Finland, in external forums, it seems that the normative frameworks are quite generous. The Estonian national cultural bodies may undertake activities abroad and represent the national minorities in relation to corresponding bodies in other countries. Section 2, Paragraph 6, of the Charter of the Swedish cultural autonomy declares that the aim of the cultural autonomy is, inter alia, to function as an interlocutor and cooperation partner with official bodies and scientific institutions in Estonia and with corresponding institutions in Nordic countries and elsewhere. In Section 10(6), the board of the Swedish cultural autonomy is given the task of representing the council in relation to governmental and non-governmental institutions and in relation to other legal persons and physical persons, both within Estonia and outside Estonia. Thus in spite of the fact that the cultural autonomy is tied to the national jurisdiction, the cultural autonomy of the Swedish in Estonia has, according to Section 2 of its Charter, inter alia, the aim of uniting Estonian Swedes in Estonia and in foreign countries.

According to Section 6 of the Act on the Sami Assembly, the Assembly shall represent the Sami in national and international connections. The latter is a clear authorization to cross the territorial boundaries of the state in the area of representation, but it would not indicate any possibility of exercising public powers outside the borders of Finland. As concerns the cross-border existence of all Sami, their statutory bodies in the three Nordic states (Finland, Sweden, and Norway)[93]

State or third parties is prohibited.' This guideline would seem to speak against such compulsory structures as required by the theory of Bauer and Renner.

[93] It should be noted that even if there is a Sami Assembly in Sweden, elected by the Sami in nationwide elections, the Swedish Sami Assembly is an organ of the state, not a separate legal

have created a joint Nordic forum for expressing themselves on behalf of the Sami at the international level, to which the Sami of the Russian Federation also are invited.[94] The Sami Parliamentary Council, in operation since 2000/2002, was created by means of a cooperation agreement signed by the then chairpersons of the three Nordic Sami Assemblies, complemented by the Rules of Procedure of the Parliamentary Council. Because the management of the joint Council alternates between the three Sami Assemblies (the Swedish one of which is a state agency), it seems that this Sami Parliamentary Council is not a legal person (such as an association), but instead another, more informal form of institutional cooperation.

The national councils in Serbia have the most advanced position in relation to the possibility of acting on behalf of the minority group. According to Section 5 of the Serbian Act, a national council may acquire and sell movable and immovable property, and it may also be a beneficiary of any public property. A national council constituted in the manner established in Section 3 of the Act is thus a legal person, as established in sub-section 3 of the provision: by registering itself with the register of national council, maintained by the Ministry in charge of human and minority rights, a national council acquires the status of a legal entity. As concluded above, the Serbian national councils also have explicit avenues for conducting cross-border and international affairs. They can cooperate with international and regional organizations, state bodies, organizations and institutions in the native countries, as well as with national councils or similar bodies of national minorities in other countries. They also participate in negotiations or are consulted in respect of negotiations on the conclusion of bilateral agreements with native countries concerning the part directly related to the rights of national minorities. Representatives of a national council shall also participate in the activities of mixed intergovernmental bodies, the aim of which is to supervise the implementation of bilateral intergovernmental agreements on the protection of rights of the national minority concerned. Finally, the representatives of national minorities shall take part, through the Council of National Minorities of the Republic of Serbia, in the conclusion of international agreements, which in this context is specified to mean the process of accession to international or regional agreements related to the status of national minorities and protection of their rights.

4.7 Conclusions

Non-territorial forms of autonomy potentially constitute a versatile form of public administration to the benefit of, for instance, a linguistic or ethnic minority. However, because territorial jurisdictions and territorial autonomy are clearly

person. Therefore, the Swedish Sami Assembly would not qualify as an NCA, at least under the definition of Bauer and Renner.

94 Kristian Myntti, 'The Sami Cultural Autonomies in the Nordic Countries', in *Minority Governance in Europe*, edited by Kinga Gál (Budapest: Local Government and Public Service Reform Initiative of the Open Society Institute, 2002), pp. 153–70.

more common as forms of organization, different non-territorial forms of autonomy (such as various institutional expressions of personal, functional, and cultural autonomy) have remained on the sidelines. One reason for this is that no comprehensive theory concerning non-territorial forms of autonomy exists. Instead, only for cultural autonomy, a theoretical foundation has been created through the work of Bauer and Renner. Therefore, and somewhat unjustifiably, the category of NTA is populated in the discussion mainly by examples of NCA.

Several institutional forms of autonomy exist outside the area of territorial autonomy, which means that several institutional forms of NTA can be identified, such as personal autonomy, functional autonomy, and cultural autonomy.

Personal autonomy, meaning individuals associating in a legal person under private law for maintaining a group's identity, may be connected with functional autonomy, if public authority is delegated to such a minority association, for example, through a licence to maintain a minority school. In such a case, the delegation of public authority creates indirect public administration that fulfils a certain public function. In the main, however, functional autonomy as institutional form can be understood so that the line administration of the state (or municipality) is established both in the majority and the minority language so that a division of the line administration into linguistically determined departments emerges. Such functional autonomy is created through public law rules of the state in question, but is normally not constituted as a distinct legal person. Therefore, functional autonomy would normally not fulfil the criteria for cultural autonomy as established by Bauer and Renner.

Cultural autonomy as institutional form is also normally created through public law rules of the state in question, but with a view to establishing legal persons, more specifically statutory associations under public law. Although they are based on the idea of self-government through elections amongst the relevant minority, such entities of cultural autonomy would deviate from the understanding of Bauer and Renner in that they would not be entitled to exercise legislative powers, nor would their membership be exempted from the application of general national legislation. What is typical for existing cultural autonomies, however, is that they are not necessarily created as territorial jurisdictions, but as public entities with jurisdictions that in principle encompass the territory of the entire state (in practice, however, the Sami Assembly of Finland is territorially delimited while at the same time national as concerns the constituency, and therefore, the cultural autonomy of the Sami may be a hybrid between territorial and non-territorial autonomy).

What would seem to be the reason for creating non-territorial autonomy, that is, what is the meaning of (non-)territoriality?

In general, territorial autonomy is created to make it possible to exercise public authority over a particular territory in a way which may even entail legislative powers. If the representative organ of the autonomous territory is empowered to pass legislative enactments proper and if the population of the territory can be qualified as a people, there is even a connection to the exercise of (internal) self-determination of that people, although the territory itself is a part of a state.

In this sense, territorial autonomy may go so far as to implement Articles 1 and 25 of the CCPR on self-determination and participation, and under such circumstances, territorial autonomy should operate under the requirement of free elections of Article 3 of the First Protocol to the European Convention on Human Rights. While it is fully possible to organize internal self-determination on a territorial basis without challenging the overall territorial integrity, self-determination, and sovereignty of the state within which such a territorial autonomy is located, many states seem to understand territorial autonomy as a challenge to the very existence of the state. Therefore, non-territorial forms of autonomy could be useful in states where territorial autonomy is perceived as a threat to the territorial integrity of the state (as is sometimes the case in Central and Eastern Europe).

Non-territorial autonomies normally do not entail the exercise of law-making powers, although at least some of them are clearly created for the exercise of public authority. In fact, an NTA arrangement can be qualified as an autonomy actually *only* if the state delegates public authority to the autonomous entity on the basis of law. On this basis, it can be said that there is normally no connection between the exercise of self-determination and non-territorial autonomy or a weak connection only, and because Article 3 of the First Protocol to the European Convention on Human Rights only applies to legislatures created under the constitution of the state, non-territorial autonomy would, as a rule, fall outside the application of Article 3. From that perspective, it can be maintained that NTA would not normally pose any threat to the sovereignty and territorial integrity of the state.

However, there seems to exist a participatory connection: non-territorial autonomy would be recognized as a participatory arrangement under Article 25 of the CCPR insofar as they have public functions and advisory tasks. Non-territorial autonomy makes it possible for the group to exercise some measure of public authority over its own members, but at the same time, individuals belonging to that collective are involved in the public administration of different matters. If a non-territorial form of autonomy has been delegated public authority that it can exercise in relation to the members of the relevant group by means of, for instance, binding decisions in individual matters (determine who is entitled to be enrolled as a voter, exercise disciplinary powers over pupils in a school, allocate social benefits, etc.), the participatory dimension could well amount to effective participation in the meaning of Article 15 of the Framework Convention on National Minorities. In this sense, NTA denotes self-control over certain matters important for the minority in question, but would not hold the potential of a challenge to the sovereignty and territorial integrity of the state. At the same time, the lawmaker of the state has a fundamental task with at least two options: to leave it to the personal autonomy of the individual to define her membership in a group or to draw up a definition on who is and who is not entitled to vote in the elections to the decision-making body of the cultural autonomy. However, as we have seen, the creation of separate jurisdictions for the purposes of internal elections to autonomy structures of the minority may create serious definitional problems around who is and who is not entitled to belong to the constituency.

Non-territorial autonomy is held to be suitable for dispersed minorities, because such autonomy can extend itself throughout the territory of the state and serve persons belonging to the relevant minority in the location where the person lives. In practice, however, minorities are often placed in some parts of the country and would not be evenly distributed throughout the territory of the state, and therefore, it appears that NTA is applied and provision of services through NTA takes place in areas where such minorities exist and where the need for minority services exists. An entire state is not necessarily the only territorial jurisdiction for the application of NTA, but it is also possible to design NTA that functions within territorial autonomies. In such situations, a territorial autonomy in which another minority or population group lives may be granted minority rights of its own, including, for instance, non-territorial forms of autonomy. Such is the case in South Tyrol, where the three linguistic groups (German, Italian, and Ladin) have schools in their own language administered on the basis of functional autonomy through school administrations that are linguistically organized. Such is also the case in Hong Kong with respect to the indigenous population in the so-called New Territories, which is represented in the electoral corporation Heung Yee Kuk and which has certain public functions in relation to its own membership.

What is striking in relation to the principles of self-determination and sovereignty of the state is that the non-territorial autonomies organized as cultural autonomies have several degrees of freedom as concerns cross-border and international activities in comparison with regular territorial autonomy. Estonia, Finland, and Serbia make international representation and activities explicitly possible, which is surprising and generous. The Estonian cultural autonomies are non-territorial also in the sense that they are explicitly allowed activities outside the borders of the state: the Estonian Swedes can cooperate with counterparts outside Estonia. The non-territorial cultural autonomies of the Nordic Sami (Finland, but also Sweden and Norway) can cooperate with each other over the borders of the three states. The Serbian provisions about the participation of cultural autonomies in the international activities of the state (treaty negotiations, funding, etc.) are the farthest reaching in this respect. This gives us reason to conclude that non-territorial forms of organization can perhaps break the strict territoriality that is normally attached to public administration, at least if no public authority is exercised in an extra-territorial fashion outside the borders of the state.

From a theoretical point of view, NTA holds a lot of promise as an alternative to territorial forms of autonomy. However, it is not possible to be very optimistic about the realization of that promise when looking at actual practice at the level of states. Instead, there appears to be reason to voice disappointment over the low level of public authority that entities belonging to the category of NTA generally can exercise, at least if cultural autonomies are considered. The legislature of a state may invest its time and resources on setting up institutions of cultural autonomy, but does not necessarily furnish those institutions with any significant powers and functions. It is, against this background, easy to agree with Osipov in his comment on legislation and institutions of NCA in the Russian Federation: 'In summary, national-cultural autonomy in Russia is a matter of symbolic, but not instrumental, law and policy. NCAs are highly valued but are ultimately useless, as ordinary NGOs can achieve all the goals and objectives that were intended for NCAs.'[95] There must be some value added when the statutory mechanisms are created and utilized.

Therefore, if NTA is set up, such institutions should not become vehicles of symbolism, but be tasked with realistic functions and the necessary public authority. One reason for the low level of use of NTA may be the need to tailor-make each solution: because such solutions fall outside any textbook example of 'rational' organization of public administration and require thinking outside the box, the setting up of non-territorial forms of autonomy are probably perceived as difficult, complex, and arduous. In addition, there does not exist enough general information on what the design of such administrative solutions entails. Serbia displays an interesting development in this respect with relatively recent legislation that implements the provision of public services and the exercise of public authority through statutory entities of cultural autonomy.

[95] Osipov, 'National Cultural Autonomy in Russia', p. 53.

II

AUTONOMY IN HISTORY AND LAW

5

Non-Territorial *Millets* in Ottoman History

Jan Erk

Until the lions have their own historians, the history of the hunt will always glorify the hunter.

African proverb

5.1 Introduction

The modern interstate system of sovereign states is generally assumed to have been established with the Treaties of Westphalia (in Münster and Osnabrück), which officially ended the Thirty Years War in 1648. Consequently, 'Westphalia…has become synonymous with the beginning as well as the end of what we understand as international relations'.[1] In addition to being credited with creating the modern interstate system of sovereign states, 1648 has also come to epitomize a world based on nation states—even if the idea of the 'nation' had to wait 150 years to be invented. Facing the monolithic Westphalian unitary state, scholars working on ethnic politics have recently tried to unshackle territory from the equation in order to help accommodate minority demands in a non-territorial way. But this presents a risk of reinventing the wheel.

Politically fragmented and legally differentiated territories, with overlapping and crosscutting jurisdictions marked by irregular and undefined borders, were more common historically than the reified notion of a territorial nation state. Territories were unmarked; borders were not only porous but the reach and range of state authority was very limited in its ability to enforce its rule throughout these territories. Furthermore, different laws were applicable to different individuals based on their legal status, adding further fluidity to the geography of political authority. Various forms of non-territorial autonomy (NTA) were common throughout the political landscape, but most of these have not yet been studied in depth. One big reason for this is that political systems defined by such

[1] Yongyin Zhang, 'System, Empire and State in Chinese International Relations', *Review of International Studies*, vol. 27, special issue (2001): p. 43.

heterogeneity first became endangered species following the spread of modern nationalism in the nineteenth century, and they eventually became extinct by the end of World War I.

The territorially compact, legally unified, and nationally uniform Westphalian nation state ideal played the key role in bringing an end to dynastic multi-ethnic empires, that is, the Habsburgs, Romanovs, and Ottomans, which rested on a collection of territorially mixed diverse populations. During the dismemberment of these empires, the principle of NTA for social groups (reflecting religious, ethnic, linguistic, racial cleavages) could not withstand the nineteenth-century onslaught of the nation state calling for territorial homogeneity. In due course, diverse peoples living side by side across diverse landscapes became an inconvenient hurdle to the new principles of national self-determination. The following sections aim to restore NTA to its proper historical context marked by jurisdictional heterogeneity.

5.2 Territorial Nation State and Westphalia

The Peace of Westphalia of 1648 settled the Thirty Years War which had divided much of central Europe. Initially sparked through the split the Reformation had brought to Christian unity, the conflict had drawn in France and Sweden in a war against the Habsburgs and their allies. The principle of *cuius regio, eius religio* (the ruler determines the religion of his realm) established at the end of the war came to be widely seen as the origin of our interstate system based on sovereign nation states. This is the moment when the dichotomy of internal hierarchy (within a sovereign state) and external anarchy (among sovereign states) was established, thereby setting the foundations of modern international relations. More recently however, some have voiced criticism of the frequent ahistoricism practised in the discussion of the 1648 settlement.[2] But there is a reason for the ahistoricism; or more precisely there *was*. The nineteenth-century literature on the Treaty of Westphalia, which initially begat most of the theorizing on the interstate system of sovereign states, was itself driven by a political agenda. For the champions of the nation state, who had taken on the declining multination empires, Westphalia was indeed a political goal, and the path to modern politics.

During the long nineteenth century, the nation state established itself at the heart of modern political system—both in terms of its position at the top of internal hierarchy and its external representation. Nation states pioneered a process whereby inhabitants, subjects, and ethnic kin transformed into citizens. It is imperative to note that historiography was not an impartial observer in all this; on the contrary, it played up the narratives of 'people's histories' in a way for them to

[2] Andreas Osiander, 'Sovereignty, International Relations, and the Westphalian Myth', *International Organization*, vol. 55, no. 2 (2001): pp. 251–87; Stephen D. Krasner, 'Rethinking the Sovereign State Model', *Review of International Studies*, vol. 27 (1996): p. 17.

qualify for the club of the Westphalia nation states. However, neither were nation states founded in Westphalia, nor was Westphalia the beginning of territorial exclusivity.[3]

Variations of the principle granting rulers exclusive jurisdiction in temporal matters had been established in various forms throughout medieval times, but it was almost a century before the 1648 Treaty of Westphalia that the principle of territorial exclusivity had come into being.[4] During the religious wars preceding the Thirty Years War, a principle giving the kings and princes of the Holy Roman Empire some exclusive jurisdiction had been put in place with the Peace of Augsburg in 1555. The peace treaty established the right to adopt the Reformation, *jus reformani*, which essentially allowed Protestant rulers the legitimacy to govern while within a nominally unified Holy Roman Empire. This was an important step in the territorialization of religion and politics.[5] But neither the Peace of Augsburg, nor the Treaty of Westphalia, granted the same rights granted to city-states, bishoprics, or directly ruled imperial territories within the Holy Roman Empire. The reach, range, and content of *cuius regio, eius religio* was thus not as extensive and principled as is often assumed.

Another important element often overlooked was that the Treaty of Westphalia established the principle of *cuius regio, eius religio* within the confines of the Holy Roman Empire. That is, above all the supposedly sovereign territorial states, an overarching imperial authority existed—albeit in rather weak form. As Gerald Strauss highlights there was a 'contradiction between the emperor's titular pretensions and actual helplessness'.[6] The Holy Roman Empire's constitution revised after 1648 further diluted the weak hold over the parts of the empire.[7] Nonetheless, this does not change the fact that most of the units signing the Treaty of Westphalia were indeed under the overarching imperial political authority. In sum, the political landscape before Westphalia, after Westphalia, and especially in the territories outside the Holy Roman Empire, was one of territorial and jurisdictional heterogeneity; and one where various forms of NTA were in place.[8]

[3] Jan Erk, 'The Risks of Scholarly Insulation: When Political Science Forgets Law and History', *Comparative European Politics*, vol. 11, no. 4 (2013): pp. 530–49; Krishan Kumar, 'Nation-States as Empires, Empires as Nation-States: Two Principles, One Practice?', *Theory and Society*, vol. 39 (2010): pp. 119–43.

[4] Gerard Leslie Harris, 'A Revolution in Tudor History?: Medieval Government and Statecraft', *Past and Present* (1963): p. 9; Walter Ulmann, 'This Realm of England is an Empire', *Journal of Ecclesiastical History*, vol. 30 (1971): pp. 175–203.

[5] Rogers Brubaker, 'Religion and Nationalism: Four Approaches', *Nations and Nationalism*, vol. 18, no. 1 (2012): p. 18.

[6] Gerald Strauss, 'Holy Roman Empire Revisited', *Central European History*, vol. 11, no. 3 (1978): pp. 290–301.

[7] Peter Schröder, 'The Constitution of the Holy Roman Empire after 1648: Samuel Pufendorf's Assessment in His Monzambano', *The Historical Journal*, vol. 42, no. 4 (1999): pp. 961–83.

[8] Donal A. Kerr, ed., *Religion, State, and Ethnic Groups* (Aldershot: Dartmouth, 1992); Hurst Hannum, *Autonomy, Sovereignty, and Self-Determination* (Revised Edition, Philadelphia: University of Pennsylvania Press, 1996).

5.3 Territorial Nation State, Multinational Empires, and Territory

The Thirty Years War preceding the peace had essentially been fought mostly within the German-speaking core of Europe. A multilevel and diverse amalgamation representing the unity of Christendom was no longer uniformly Roman Catholic due to the Reformation. Furthermore, most of the German-speaking territories where the war had been fought in central Europe were divided between city-states, bishoprics, dukedoms, principalities, kingdoms, republics, and empires—often with cross-cutting historical and royal ties and shared jurisdictions. Outside the Holy Roman Empire, the picture was even more diverse, and it would remain so until the unitary nation state brought in the dismemberment of the multi-ethnic Habsburgs and Ottomans.[9] The east of the continent was under the Habsburgs who ruled over a newly bifurcated empire divided between its Cisleithian and Transleithian halves with various affiliated and subject territories, while the Ottomans were overlords of yet another multi-ethnic and multi-religious empire with constituent units ranging from directly administered crown lands to vassal states.

But it was the Mediterranean basin that was a particularly strong contrast to the idea of an interstate system of sovereign states. The political landscape in the Mediterranean during the seventeenth and eighteenth centuries looked quite unlike the Westphalian world that was supposed to have come into being in 1648. Naval enclaves changed hands from the Ottomans to the Habsburgs and back, Venetians and Genovese held maritime colonies throughout, corsairs roamed under the vassalage of empires, territories were subject to overlapping jurisdictions. This was indeed not a world of compact, unified, and uniform sovereign states separated by clearly delineated borders. Territories and people were both subject to multiple legal statuses. Territorial jurisdictions (and claims) overlapped, while subjects carried the law with them across jurisdictions and territories. This heterogeneity was replicated throughout the Mediterranean basin with unclaimed territories interspersed with enclaves that fell under multiple jurisdictional claims. From Gibraltar to Beirut, colonies, protectorates, trading posts, and military bases peppered the shores of the Old World. The port of Tunis, La Goulette, for example, was under Spanish rule, but a little further east the Ottomans held the port of Djerba, and in between the Sultan of Tunis ruled. Such heterogeneity defined the Balkan territories between the Ottomans and the Habsburgs, but it also defined the other end of the Mediterranean basin. In his study of the Pyrenees region between France and Spain, Peter Sahlins documents how complicated and sometimes contradictory jurisdictional questions over ecclesiastical authority, commerce, and taxation defined *and* obscured territorial sovereignty. The idea

[9] Susan Reynolds, 'Empires: A Program of Comparative History', *Historical Research*, vol. 79, no. 204 (2006): pp. 151–65.

of territorial sovereignty following precise boundary lines is something we have imposed onto the past: 'The seventeenth century state was not, strictly speaking, a territorial state: it was structured instead around "jurisdictions" '.[10] Not only was there no clear internal hierarchy within the state, but there was also no simple international anarchy between these 'sovereign states'; quite simply 'jurisdictional conflicts at the borders and controversies about subjecthood or citizenship blurred distinctions between internal and external sovereignty'.[11]

Geography of course did not always allow for territorial compactness, for the territorial application of the law, and for jurisdictional exclusivity, but the state itself was not advanced enough to impose its rule in territories nominally under its jurisdiction in any case. Until modern communication and transportation allowed the growth in state capacity in the nineteenth century, state authority was limited in its reach and range. The imposition of political authority was at best partial throughout what was deemed to be state territory. Furthermore, borders were often unmarked and unenforceable. Until the nineteenth century, states were only able to impose real authority only in some areas under their formal authority; elsewhere (especially in the periphery and the colonies) state authority itself was irregular and haphazard—often characterized by enclaves linked up along corridors. Some of these enclaves were trading posts, some garrisons; some were proselytizing missions; some relics of dynastic inheritances from bygone years. These were often interconnected along rivers and valleys where the neighbouring areas either fell under vague overlapping and cross-cutting jurisdictions, or they were still uncharted for western political geography. Furthermore, the 'law' was carried by officials, merchants, sailors, soldiers, settlers, even pirates, rather than following territorial demarcations, adding further fluidity to the geography of political authority. Various forms of NTA for groups belonged to this patchwork of political, religious, and cultural representations of legal status. It is therefore important to avoid pasting a reductionist territorial vs NTA dichotomy onto the past. Adopting a *long durée* perspective on history will help minimize the risks of falling prey to the 'fallacy of presentism'.

5.4 The 'Fallacy of Presentism' and Historiography with an Agenda

Philippe Schmitter and Terry Lynn Karl call the imposition of present-day patterns and understanding of politics on to the past the 'fallacy of presentism'.[12] Those well

[10] Peter Sahlins, *Boundaries: The Making of France and Spain in the Pyrenees* (Berkeley/Los Angeles: University of California Press, 1989), p. 28.

[11] Lauren Benton, *A Search for Sovereignty: Law and Geography in European Empires 1400–1900* (New York: Cambridge University Press, 2010), p. 276.

[12] Philippe C. Schmitter and Terry Lyn Karl, 'Conceptual Travels of Transitologists and Consolidologists: How Far to the East Should they Attempt to Go?', *Slavic Review*, vol. 53, no. 1 (1994): p. 176.

immersed in the contours of European political history have always been aware that the notion of the Westphalian sovereign state emerged from a creative reading of history that helped bring legitimacy to the new nation states of the nineteenth century. The unitary nation state was not only a theoretical ideal-model for the social sciences, but it was also a political ideal-model for the late nineteenth/early twentieth centuries. The consequence of the Westphalia-centred world history has been an under-appreciation of how common various non-territorial arrangements had been.

The ideal of a territorially compact, legally unified, and nationally uniform nation state played the key role in the demise of dynastic multi-ethnic empires. And it was the Habsburgs and Ottomans, who, with their territorially, legally, and socially heterogeneous realms, became the first targets in the firing line. Nineteenth-century champions of the nation state had drawn a picture of self-governing nations fulfilling their historical destiny in standing up against reactionary dynastic empires. Their historiography was inseparable from the politics of the time. But the political use of Westphalia mattered more than historical accuracy of course. As Andreas Osiander puts it:

> [T]he habit of misunderstanding and largely ignoring the Holy Roman Empire in the last century and a half of its existence goes back to the nation-state oriented historiography of the nineteenth century. This habit was based on the notion that the unified, centralised, sovereign nation-state was the desirable endpoint of history...[13]

As the Habsburg and Ottoman multination empires started to dissolve under the pressures of nationalism in the nineteenth century, the emerging new states were in pursuit of the ideal of the compact, unified, and uniform nation state. The empires were undemocratic in many ways of course, but their replacements were not much of an improvement to the inhabitants of these territories. In a geography where ethnic/religious/linguistic groups had historically lived side by side, the nation state ideal meant someone had to be expelled to achieve the national homogeneity. The subsequent forced migrations in due course helped establish the nineteenth century Westphalian ideal in the former heterogeneous realms of multi-ethnic empires.

The culmination of this process was US President Wilson's 'Fourteen Points' outlining the new interstate system of nation states. The contents of that very document show how it was as much the specifics of dividing up the territories of the Habsburg and Ottoman empires as the principle of national self-determination that had helped delivered this result.[14] What Lauren Benton calls the 'imagined world of territorially homogenous and bounded states' played a key role in legitimizing the new states seceding from the multination empires.[15] However, from

[13] Osiander, 'Sovereignty, International Relations, and the Westphalian Myth', p. 269.

[14] Wilson Woodrow, 'Fourteen Points', 1918, accessed May 2012, http://avalon.law.yale.edu/20th_century/wilson14.asp.

[15] Benton, *A Search for Sovereignty*, pp. 276–7.

Macedonia to Kuwait, not all new states emerging from the dismemberment of the multi-ethnic empires neatly corresponded to the ideal of the nation state. The League of Nations conveniently found a way out of this problem by placing many of the new nation states under protectorates of new masters—this time the Western nation states who had defeated the Eastern empires. Since there were no empires left, there was no one to challenge the historiography which extols the inevitable progress brought by nation states.

Since the Habsburgs and Ottomans all collapsed by the end of World War I, by definition they were unable to write history through the perspective of the heterogeneous empire populated by diverse ethnic/religious/linguistic groups. Instead, what we had was the Austrian and Turkish nation states emerging from the ashes of the multination empires. The historiography of the Austrian and Turkish republics also become one of long-lived nations, and not of Habsburg and Ottoman multi-ethnic heterogeneity. These empires were not straightforward examples of ethno-linguistic accommodation in the modern sense, but they were built on an acknowledgement of ethnic/religious/linguistic diversity that for centuries had allowed coexistence. Their supposedly more progressive replacements in the late nineteenth and early twentieth centuries were built on a principled rejection of heterogeneity. What we have is a historiography dominated by the story of self-governing nations rebelling against imperialism. The history of the Balkans and the Middle East is written by the new states that emerged from the break-up of multi-ethnic empires.[16] And it is the homogenous nation state who plays the hero in this history.

5.5 Austro-Marxists Karl Renner and Otto Bauer

Around the turn of the nineteenth century, a number of Austrian intellectuals tried to devise mechanisms to keep the Austro-Hungarian Empire together. This heterogeneous empire comprising Czechs, Slovaks, Poles, Ukrainians, Slovenes, Croats, Serbs, Bosnians, Romanians, Italians, Hungarians, and of course, Germans, had come under strain in the face of increasing ethno-nationalism. Austro-Marxists like Karl Renner and Otto Bauer advocated a political system based on the 'principle of personality' and cultural sovereignty.[17] This was an attempt to surpass the problem of territoriality based on the notion of self-contained linguistic areas. Like the Ottomans, the Austro-Hungarian Empire lacked such a neat territorial division, so Renner and Bauer thought of nationality and national rights in

[16] See Harris Mylonas, *The Politics of Nation-Building: Making Co-Nationals, Refugees, and Minorities* (Cambridge: Cambridge University Press, 2012).

[17] Karl Renner (under the *nom de plume* Rudolf Springer), *Der Kampf der österreichischen Nationen um den Staat* [The Struggle of the Austrian Nations for the State] (Vienna/Leipzig: Deuticke, 1902); Otto Bauer, *Die Nationalitätenfrage und die Sozialdemokratie* [The Question of Nationalities and Social Democracy] (Vienna: Verlag der Wiener Volksbuchhandlung Ignaz Brand, 1907 (1924)).

non-territorial terms. Despite their radical epithet, Austro-Marxists were in fact a moderate offshoot of reformist social democracy. Karl Renner would later become the first President of the Austrian Republic formed after World War I.

According to Renner and Bauer, the answer was a system of cultural autonomy that would be based on the principle of personality. That is to say, individuals would declare their 'nationality' to relevant authorities and register with their national community of choice. As we have seen earlier, the legal principle and practice whereby people rather than territories fell under various jurisdictions was common throughout the world until the nineteenth-century advent of the unitary state. Renner and Bauer added new liberal democratic principles to the mix. The personality principle aimed to constitute nations on the basis of the free association of individuals regardless of where they lived.[18] The 'nations' would then be given exclusive powers in a number of policy areas (mostly education and culture) where they would have their own legislative, administrative, and executive institutions. This system was to be accompanied by proportional representation at the level of the empire through national lists, and proportionality in public administration.

Despite limited trials in the Moravian schools system, the Austro-Marxist proposals came a little too late and so we do not know whether the system of cultural autonomy could have saved the multi-ethnic empire. There is a rich literature put together by Austro-Marxists around the end of the nineteenth century dealing with the questions of non-territoriality and representation.[19] Yet, for centuries before that Ottomans and Habsburgs had interacted in the Balkans either as adversaries or allies. Of course, as Ephraim Nimni points out the 'crucial' difference Austro-Marxist proposals had from the *millet* system is that Renner and Bauer envisaged a democratic system of 'non-territorial national autonomy' based on internal democracy for the autonomous communities and individual consent.[20] But the 600-years-old *millet* system of NTA of the Habsburg's Balkan neighbour, the Ottomans, is conspicuous by its absence in the works of Austro-Marxists. In order to evaluate the promises and pitfalls of NTA, we have to see why the pre-modern Ottoman version lasted many centuries but the modern and democratic Austro-Marxist version remains a largely untested political design belonging to the last days of the Habsburgs.

[18] Alfred Pfabigan, 'The Political Feasibility of Austro-Marxist Proposals for the Solution of the Nationality Problem of the Danubian Monarchy', in *State and Nation in Multi-Ethnic Societies: The Breakup of the Multinational State*, edited by Uri Ra'anan, Maria Mesner, Keith Armes, and Kate Martin (Manchester/New York: Manchester University Press, 1991), p. 57.

[19] Theodor Hanf, 'Konfliktminderung durch Kulturautonomie. Karl Renners Beitrag zur Frage der Konfliktregelung in multi-ethnischen Staaten' [Conflict Mitigation through Cultural Autonomy. Karl Renner's Contribution to the Question of Conflict Management in Multi-ethnic States], in *Staat und Nation in multi-ethnischen Gesellschaften*, edited by Erich Fröschl, Maria Mesner and Uri Ra'anan (Vienna: Passagen Verlag, 1991), pp. 61–90.

[20] Ephraim Nimni, 'Nationalist Multiculturalism in Late Imperial Austria as a Critique of Contemporary Liberalism: The Case of Bauer and Renner', *Journal of Political Ideologies*, vol. 4, no. 3 (1999): p. 296.

5.6 The Ottoman *Millet* System

The Ottoman system of governance had both territorial and non-territorial components. Territorially, the Empire contained directly governed crown lands, indirectly governed vassal states, semi-autonomous cities, allied territories, tributary states, colonies, leased harbours, and fluid tributary arrangements with nomads, etc. There was a parallel system of non-territorial governance based on the coexistence of religious/cultural communities called the *millets*, literally 'nations', which were given religious and cultural autonomy.

During most of its history, the *millet* system had led to the peaceful but separate and parallel coexistence of diverse communities in the Ottoman Empire. In addition to running their own education systems and religious organizations, the *millets* administered civil law and adjudicated legal disagreements among their members as well. Religious leaders and clergy were thus functionaries of the Ottoman state. Issues like family law and inheritance were within the prerogatives of these communities. In principle, membership of the *millet* followed the personality principle and was not territorial.[21] But in practice, the territorial form of authority that prevailed in a region often played a big role in how the *millet* system functioned in practice. It should also be noted that the personality principle did not bring full equality to the various *millets*. Assimilation into the Turkish-speaking Sunni Muslim ruling class was encouraged, but reverse assimilation into Shi'a Islam, Christianity, and Judaism was not tolerated. There were certain restrictions on non-Muslims. Instead of the military service compulsory for Muslim men, Christians and Jews paid a poll tax, and they were also forbidden to carry weapons.[22]

An important characteristic of the *millet* system is that it was not a top-down coherent system designed by the Ottoman Turks but one that—despite the overwhelming military might of the imperial army—emerged from the limitations of central state power to exert direct and permanent control throughout the Empire's vast and distant territories ranging from Morocco to Aceh and from Somalia up to Crimea. In her 2008 book, *Empire of Differences*, Karen Barkey calls the Ottomans a 'negotiated empire': '[R]egardless of its strength an empire has to work with the peripheries in order to maintain a mix of compliance, tribute, and military cooperation, as well as to ensure political coherence and durability'.[23] Elsewhere, Barkey has unpacked what she means by a 'negotiated empire':

> The Ottomans' achievement at empire was based on their successful negotiating between contradictory, yet also complementary political structures, organisational forms and their

[21] Halil Inalcik, 'Centralisation and Decentralisation in Ottoman Administration', in *Studies in Eighteenth Century Islamic History*, edited by Thomas Naff and Roger Owen (Carbondale/Edwardsville: Southern Illinois University Press, 1977), pp. 27–52.

[22] Benjamin Braude and Bernard Lewis, *Christians and Jews in the Ottoman Empire: The Functioning of a Plural Society* (New York: Holmes and Meier, 1982), pp. 69–87.

[23] Karen Barkey, *Empire of Difference: The Ottomans in Comparative Perspective*, (Cambridge: Cambridge University Press, 2008), p. x.

cultural meanings. In their attempt to construct such rule and establish legitimacy, they had to balance ruling Christians and Jews, Slavs, Vlachs and Armenians, Muslims of Sunni, Shi'a and many Sufi beliefs, incorporate each and every one of their communities and their local traditions, but also collect taxes and administer the collectivities. This had to be done by allowing space for local autonomy, a requirement of negotiated rule. For exactly this reason, whatever religion would mean locally, it had to be about legitimacy and rule for the state.[24]

There was thus no coherent and consistent system of religious/cultural autonomy for the *millets* throughout the Empire. In addition to the rights and obligations of the *millets*, even the vocabulary changed throughout Ottoman territories, leading Benjanim Braude to conclude 'there was no overall administrative system, structure, or set of institutions'; the *millet* system 'was not an institution or even a group of institutions, but rather it was a set of arrangements, largely local, with considerable variation over time and place'.[25] In addition to the Christian *millets* of Jesusist (*iseviye*), Nazarene (*nasraniye*), Messianist (*mesihiye*), and Roman Catholic (*latin*), some of the other *millets* suggest ethnic/cultural rather than religious communities such as Greek (*rumi*) and Armenian (*ermeni*) while different terms seem to have been used for Jews (*yahudi* and *musevi*) in different times and places. Furthermore, the vassal and tributary states under Christian rulers in the Balkans and Eastern Europe such as Moldavia, Wallachia, Transylvania, and Crimea had 'softer' versions of the *millet* system where religious leaders and clergy were not formally functionaries of the Ottoman state. Smaller tributary states like Ragusa, Naxos, and Aceh were formally not imperial subjects, thus the *millet* system did not apply. It was the crown lands that constituted the bulk of Ottoman territories. And here the *millet* system—notwithstanding procedural heterogeneity—was the form of governance.

Besides, standardization in terminology and institutions in a multilingual and multi-ethnic pre-modern empire with far-flung territories is somewhat of an unrealistic expectation. What is important to stress here is that—despite variations in its application—religious/cultural communities provided the bottom-up legitimacy to the imperial system. Religious institutions ran education and cultural affairs, and their respective clergy applied civil law in the *millets* as imperial magistrates. Put simply, 'Religion functioned as an institution of the state and its practitioners emerged only as state officials'.[26] *Millets* were indeed the offices of the state; and by incorporating entire communities into its governance, the state established legitimacy.

In the context of the British Empire, John Darwin has identified similar limitations of central state power to exert direct and permanent control

[24] Karen Barkey, 'Islam and Toleration: Studying the Ottoman Imperial Model', *International Journal of Politics, Culture, and Society*, vol. 19 (2005): p. 10.

[25] Benjamin Braude, 'The Foundation Myths of the Millet System', in *Christians and Jews in the Ottoman Empire: The Functioning of a Plural* Society, edited by Benjamin Braude and Bernard Lewis (New York: Holmes and Meier, 1982), p. 74.

[26] Barkey, 'Islam and Toleration', p. 11.

throughout vast and distant territories: 'Emirs, sheikhs, pashas, chiefs, khans and zemindars could stay in their place and rule their own roost, so long as they offered (and sanctioned) no challenge to imperial authority'.[27] The difference between the 'indirect rule' of the British Empire and that of the Ottomans was that even in the distant provinces the main military force was the Ottoman professional army directly ruled from the centre. In order to prevent any potential territorial challenge to the might of the Empire, important military affairs were never outsourced to the local forces and the *millets* had no respective militia. But what worked for 600 years in keeping a multi-ethnic and multi-religious empire together could not withstand the onslaught of Westphalian nation state.

In the nineteenth century, the *millet* system came under strain as nationalist movements engulfed the diverse ethno-linguistic population of the Ottoman Empire. In order to reform the system and introduce civil equality, the Ottomans passed two major constitutional reforms in 1876 and 1908.[28] These reforms established a legal and administrative framework uniting the Empire, together with an updated model of the *millet* system in the form of cultural autonomy. Various ethnic groups—as religious communities started to break up along ethno-linguistic lines—were given proportional representation in the political and administrative structure of the Empire. Ideas of communitarian devolution and federalism became the key words for those who wanted to keep this heterogeneous union together. But the nationalism genie was out of the bottle. Especially for the *millets* with ethnic/cultural characteristics—rather than exclusively religious ones—the transition was relatively smooth. For example, the 'Rum' *millet* with relative ease turned into the Greek nation.[29] Other ethno-linguistic groups divided amongst different religious *millets* experienced a more convoluted path to national identity during these turbulent times. At the end, just like the Austro-Hungarian Habsburgs, neither the Ottoman reforms nor the Ottoman state itself survived World War I.

5.7 Conclusions

Notwithstanding its demise, the remarkable long life the *millet* system has had makes it imperative to carefully re-examine it in order to get a better sense of its workings over the *long durée*. Karl Renner and Otto Bauer had admirable liberal democratic goals for their system of NTA, but we do not have an extensive track

[27] John Darwin, 'Empire and Ethnicity', *Nations and Nationalism*, vol. 16, no. 3 (2010): p. 386.

[28] Cağlar Keyder, 'The Ottoman Empire', in *After Empire: Multiethnic Societies and Nation-Building. The Soviet Union and Russian, Ottoman and Habsburg Empires*, edited by Karen Barkey and Mark von Hagen (Boulder, Colorado: Westview, 1997), pp. 30–44.

[29] Viktor Roudometof, 'From Rum Millet to Greek Nation: Enlightenment, Secularization, and National Identity in Ottoman Balkan Society, 1453–1821', *Journal of Modern Greek Studies*, vol. 16, no. 1 (1998).

record that could help identify the patterns in its workings. Things never stay as they were intended on paper as they interact with the legal, political, cultural, religious, economic, demographic, and geographic context and evolve with time. The lessons from Ottoman history might appear uneven and imprecise, bound by time and place, and include failures as well as successes; but this is precisely why one has to seek to identify patterns and try to distil lessons. Political reforms have a tendency to have unintended and unanticipated consequences, so instead of focusing on the finer details of the institutional engineering in the abstract, one has to take stock of the big picture—and the complexity that inevitably comes with it. Ultimately such a holistic *long durée* perspective matters more to dealing with minority issues rather than facile institutional blueprints that have not seen much action in real life. As the German political scientist Theodor Eschenburg once put it 'something could be imperfect but work, the other could be perfect but not work'.[30]

One key lesson here is the need for more historical research on forms of NTA. Put simply, to credit Westphalia with the establishment of centralized and uniform territorial authority is historically incorrect. Forms of NTA were part of the heterogeneous patchwork of jurisdictions that defined the world until the nineteenth century. To reduce political history into a territorial vs non-territorial dichotomy would be both analytically and prescriptively misleading. The day-to-day working of the non-territorial *millet* system was inseparable from the particular type of territorial authority that it co-existed with. Whether the *millets* were within Ottoman crown lands or vassal territories mattered as well as the historical relationship between the religious leaders and clergy administrating the *millets* and their Ottoman overlords.

It is also important to note that not all of this jurisdictional heterogeneity was due to accidents of history, vagaries of geography, or the natural forces of circumstances. Lauren Benton's study of empires shows that precision in matters of jurisdiction was indeed deliberately avoided; indeterminacy of overlapping spheres of sovereignty and subsequent territorial anomalies were often systemic.[31] Without an examination of the legal, demographic, and political context, it is difficult to systematically map out the promises and pitfalls of the non-territorial *millet* system. There simply is not one single lesson, but a number of patterns do seem to characterize the *millet* system. The first one is the inevitable heterogeneity in its practice. What was originally a non-territorial system of religious autonomy acquired political, geographic, and cultural characteristics in time. Furthermore, it has to be noted that the *millets* held a comparatively low position in the hierarchy of political authorities; and there was very little room for horizontal *millet*-to-*millet* relations. Political loyalty to the crown and religious/cultural

[30] 'Das eine ist ungerecht, aber funktioniert, das andere ist gerecht, aber funktioniert nicht' [One is unfair, but it works, the other is just, but does not work], Theodor Eschenburg quoted in *die Zeit*, 21 October 1994, http://www.zeit.de/1994/43/die-lupenreine-demokratie-bringt-sich-um/seite-13.

[31] Benton, *A Search for Sovereignty*, p. 258.

autonomy for the *millet* made this a vertical relationship. However, endowed with corporate status and their own resources *millets* had relative financial autonomy, which underscored their autonomy in running schools and religious courts, as well as pre-modern welfare policies such as infirmaries and soup kitchens. This ensured the perpetuation of the *millets* regardless of who sat at the Sublime Porte in Istanbul. In comparative terms, the more ethno-linguistically unified a *millet*, the stronger were its chances of transforming itself into a modern nation. The *millet* system also effectively co-opted lay minority leaders into the establishment; it also robbed religions of a chance to become voices of grievance since religious leaders and clergy had become functionaries of the Ottoman state. Within the *millets* themselves elites often exercised near-monopoly of power with little room for internal dissent. All these shortcomings came with one big advantage: the principle of NTA inherent in the *millet* system helped preserve the ethnic/religious/linguistic diversity of former Ottoman territories.

6

From Empire to Multilateral Player

The Deep Roots of Autonomy in Russia

Bill Bowring

6.1 Introduction

This chapter focuses on Russia's unlikely experiment in national cultural autonomy (NCA). I start with Russia's accession to the Council of Europe (CoE) and the start of its experiment in NCA, both of which took place in 1996. I turn next to history: to the wide variety of forms of autonomy in the Russian Empire, which like other territorial empires, was rarely assimilationist as it expanded. I give an overview of a number of cases: Finland, the Baltics, Russian Germans, Ukraine, Georgia, Poland, Khiva and Bukhara, Tatars and Inorodtsy. Second, I turn to religious diversity in Russia, after Catherine II's reforms. Third, I look at the extensive scholarly literature on the constitutional role of autonomy in the latter years of the Russian Empire. Fourth, I examine Bolshevik nationalities policy before and after the 1917 Revolution, and the creation of the territorial autonomies in 1920–2. Fifth, I have a number of criticisms of Terry Martin's excellent *The Affirmative Action Empire*. Sixth, I return to the new Strategy, and to an apparent retreat from the NCA model. My conclusion emphasizes the deep roots of autonomy in Russia, and expresses concern for the future of non-territorial autonomy (NTA) in Russia.

This chapter seeks in particular to address the paradox identified by Aleksandr Osipov—why does the concept of NCA sound attractive to ethnic activists?[1] My aim is to show that autonomy has rather deeper roots in Russia than might at first be supposed.[2]

[1] Alexander Osipov, *Natsional'no-kul'turnaia avtonomiia: idei, resheniia, instituty* [National-Cultural Autonomy: Ideas, Decisions, Institutions] (St. Petersburg: Tsentr nezavisimykh sotsiologicheskikh issledovanii, 2004); Alexander Osipov, 'National Cultural Autonomy in Russia: A Case of Symbolic Law', *Review of Central and East European Law*, vol. 35, no. 1 (2010): pp. 27–57.

[2] I have been much assisted in this by the late Professor Oleg Kutafin's monumental work on Russian autonomy. Oleg Emelyanovich Kutafin, *Rossiyskaya avtonomiya* [Russian Autonomy] (Moscow: Prospekt, 2006).

The Russian Federation has recently grown. Since the illegal annexation of Crimea[3] in March 2014 there are now, according to the Russian government website,[4] eighty-five subjects of the Federation, the Republic of Crimea,[5] and its capital, the City of Sevastopol, which now have the status of a City of Federal Significance.[6] There are twenty-one ethnic republics, with the right to an official language in addition to Russian.[7]

Russia's ethnic and linguistic diversity is impressive if not unique. Russia's first Report, of 8 March 2000, to the Advisory Committee under the CoE's Framework Convention for the Protection of National Minorities (FCNM), stated that 'The Russian Federation is one of the largest multinational states in the world, inhabited by more than 170 peoples, the total population being about 140 million.'[8] Russia also reported that 'The education in Russia's schools is now available in thirty-eight languages.... As many as seventy-five national languages are a part (including languages of national minorities) of the secondary schools curricula.'[9] The annexation of Crimea means that there is one more 'people', the Crimean Tatars. On 1 October 2014 the CoE's Commissioner for Human Rights, Nils Muiznieks, told the Parliamentary Assembly of the CoE that his 'biggest concern' in Ukraine was the plight of Crimean Tatars who have remained in Crimea since it was annexed by Russia in March.[10]

6.1.1 How Does the Russian Federation Seek to Organize and Manage such Complexity?

Russia joined the CoE in 1996, signed the FCNM on 28 February 1996, ratified it on 21 August 1998 and it entered into force on 1 December 1998. The Report

[3] Crimea had the anomalous status of an autonomous republic in the unitary state of Ukraine. See Bill Bowring, 'The Crimean Autonomy: Innovation or Anomaly?', in *Autonomy, Self-Governance and Conflict Resolution: Innovative Approaches to Institutional Design in Divided Societies*, edited by Marc Weller and Stefan Wolff (Abingdon : Routledge, 2005), pp. 75–97.

[4] 'The Subjects of the Russian Federation in Internet', *The Website of the Government of Russia*, accessed 11 November 2014,

[5] State Council of Republic of Crimea Website, accessed 11 November 2014, http://crimea.gov.ru/.

[6] The Charter of the City of Sevastopol is dated 14 April 2014. It is said to be a City of Federal Significance, like Moscow and St Petersburg. See Official State of Government of Sevastopol, accessed 11 November 2014, http://sevastopol.gov.ru/1-3s-ustav-goroda-sevastopolya.html.

[7] See Bill Bowring, 'The Russian Constitutional System: Complexity and Asymmetry', in *Asymmetric Autonomy and the Settlement of Ethnic Conflicts*, edited by Marc Weller and Katherine Nobbs (Abingdon: University of Pennsylvania Press, 2010), pp. 48–74; Bill Bowring, 'Russian Legislation in the Area of Minority Rights', in *Managing Ethnic Diversity in Russia*, edited by Oleh Protsyk and Benedikt Harzl (Abingdon: Routledge, 2012), pp. 15–36.

[8] Report Submitted by the Russian Federation Pursuant to Article 25, Paragraph 1 of the Framework Convention for the Protection Of National Minorities (received on 8 March 2000), ACFC/SR(1999)015, accessed 11 November 2014, http://www.coe.int/t/dghl/monitoring/minorities/3_FCNMdocs/PDF_1st_SR_RussianFederation_en.pdf.

[9] Report Submitted by the Russian Federation Pursuant to Article 25, p. 27.

[10] See 'Europe's Human Rights Chief Concerned For Crimean Tatars', *Radio Free Europe Radio Liberty*, 1 October 2014, accessed 11 November 2014, http://www.rferl.org/content/ukraine-crimea-tatars-council-of-europe/26616091.html.

highlighted the experiment in non-territorial, personal autonomy initiated by the Federal Law 'On National-Cultural Autonomy'[11] of 17 June 1996.[12]

My own estimation in 2002 was that this adoption of the NCA form was a dramatic reversal of the Soviet hostility to NTA, dating back to the series of substantial polemics against this Austro-Marxist proposal, written by Lenin, Stalin, and Trotsky, to name but three.[13] At the same time it represented a significant victory on the part of Professor Valeriy Tishkov and his co-thinkers, including the politician Gavriil Popov, in their contemporaneous campaign against the very concept 'nation'.[14] For Tishkov and others, NCA was a viable alternative to the Soviet legacy of territorial autonomy (TA) and essentialized concepts of ethnicity and nationhood.

In 2004, Osipov provided the most cogent and searching critique to date of the NCA experiment since 1996 in Russia.[15] There is a paradox. Notwithstanding the evident weaknesses of the NCA form, it is surprisingly popular. In 2010 Osipov noted that:

> The concept of 'autonomy' still sounds attractive to ethnic activists. Despite legislative restrictions and bureaucratic burdens, the number of NCAs has grown over the years. By early 1999, 227 NCAs had been registered, of which 160 were local, 60 regional, and 7 federal. The respective figures for the beginning of 2005 were: 315, 173, and 16 (in total, 504). On 1 January 2009, there were 717 organizations, of which: 488 were local, 211 regional, and 18 federal.

[11] Federal Law on National-Cultural Autonomy 1996, accessed 11 November 2011, http://base.garant.ru/135765/.

[12] Report Submitted by the Russian Federation Pursuant to Article 25, p. 12 and elsewhere; Bill Bowring, 'Austro-Marxism's Last Laugh?: The Struggle for Recognition of National-Cultural Autonomy for Rossians and Russians', *Europe-Asia Studies*, vol. 54, no. 2 (2002): pp. 229–50; Bill Bowring, 'Burial and Resurrection: Karl Renner's Controversial Influence on the "National Question" in Russia', in *National-Cultural Autonomy and its Contemporary Critics*, edited by Ephraim Nimni (Abingdon: Routledge, 2005), pp. 191–206; Bill Bowring, 'The Tatars of the Russian Federation and National-Cultural Autonomy: A Contradiction in Terms?', *Ethnopolitics: Formerly Global Review of Ethnopolitics*, vol. 6, no. 3 (2007): pp. 417–35. Since Russia's first Report in 2000, I have published the two journal articles and the book chapter mentioned on the question of the Russian experiment in NTA. My particular focus has been the history of the hotly contested struggle in the late nineteenth and early twentieth centuries between the Austro-Marxist conception of non-territorial personal cultural autonomy, taken up with enthusiasm by the Jewish Bund and by Muslim activists; and the Social-Democratic and Bolshevik orthodoxy of TA under Lenin's banner of the Right of Nations to Self-Determination. See the text with that title, written in February–May 1914, and published in April–June 1914 in the journal *Prosveshcheniye* Nos. 4, 5, and 6. Signed: V. Ilyin. V. I. Lenin, *Collected Works* (Moscow: Progress Publishers, 1972), Volume 20, pp. 393–454, and http://www.marxists.org/archive/lenin/works/1914/self-det/. I have traced this contest through to the present day, with particular reference to the Tatars.

[13] Bowring, 'Austro-Marxism's Last Laugh', pp. 229–50.

[14] Valery Tishkov, 'O natsii i natsionalisme' [On the Nation and Nationalism], *Svobodnaya Mysl*, no. 3 (1996); Valery Tishkov, *Ethnicity, Nationalism and Conflict in and after the Soviet Union. The Mind Aflame* (London: Sage, 1997); Valery Tishkov, 'Zabyt o natsii. Post-natsionalisticheskoye ponimaniye natsionalism' [Forget about the Nation. A Post-Nationalist Understanding of Nationalism], *Voprosii Philosophii* (1998): pp. 3–26.

[15] See, e.g., Osipov, *Natsional'no-kul'turnaia avtonomiia*; Osipov, 'National Cultural Autonomy in Russia', pp. 27–57.

NCAs represent more than 60 ethnicities—in particular, federal NCAs have been established on behalf of Armenians, Assyrians, Azeris, Belarusians, Chuvash, Germans, Jews, Karachais, Kazakhs, Koreans, Kurds, Lezghins, Lithuanians, Poles, Roma, Serbs, Tatars, and Ukrainians. Regional and local NCAs have been set up in 72 of 83 constituent units (subjects) of the Russian Federation. Several NCAs represent ethnic groups officially acknowledged as small indigenous peoples of Russia.[16]

It is, however, necessary to return first to the history of autonomy in the Russian Empire.[17]

6.2 Autonomy in Tsarist Russia

The roots of Russian conceptions of autonomy extend back into the sixteenth century. In an authoritative overview, Robert Suny pointed out that

With Ivan IV's conquests of Kazan and Astrakhan in the mid-sixteenth century, the Muscovite state incorporated ethnically compact non-Russian territories, indeed an alien polity, and transformed a relatively homogenized Russia into a multinational empire...when the problem of security was settled, Moscow allowed local elites, though no longer sovereign, to rule and traditional customs and laws to continue in force. As these frontier regions became integrated in some ways into the empire as borderlands, many of them remained distinct administratively, though always subordinate to the center.[18]

Kutafin also made the point that as it expanded the Russian Empire often preserved in the territories it incorporated their local laws and institutions, and accorded them more or less broad autonomy.[19] He reminded his readers that the legal status of Russian regions changed continually over time.[20]

In the next sections I explore the wide variety of experiences of autonomy in the Russian Empire.

The most famous example of autonomy in the Russian Empire was Finland, about which Russian scholars have conflicting views. Some consider Finland to have been an independent state in de facto union with Russia. Others see it as a province with a high degree of autonomy. A third camp sees Finland as a non-sovereign state united

[16] Osipov, 'National Cultural Autonomy in Russia', pp. 42–3.

[17] In what follows I have revisited the research which I carried out for my chapter: Bill Bowring, 'Minorities Protection in Russia: Is There a 'Communist Legacy'?', in *Institutional Legacies of Communism: Change and Continuities in Minority Protection*, edited by Karl Cordell, Timofey Agarin, and Alexander Osipov (Abingdon: Routledge 2013), pp. 45–58, and Bill Bowring, *Law, Rights and Ideology in Russia: Landmarks in the Destiny of a Great Power* (Abingdon: Routledge, 2013), pp. 120–39.

[18] Ronald Grigor Suny, 'The Empire Strikes Out: Imperial Russia, "National" Identity, and Theories of Empire', in *A State of Nations: Empire and Nation-Making in the Soviet Union, 1917–1953* (Oxford: Oxford University Press, 2001), first delivered as a paper for the University of Chicago Conference, *Empire and Nations: The Soviet Union and the Non-Russian Peoples*, 24–26 October 1997, pp. 21–2, accessed 1 June 2014, http://www.dartmouth.edu/~crn/crn_papers/Suny4.pdf.

[19] Kutafin, *Rossiyskaya avtonomiya*, p. 41.

[20] Kutafin, *Rossiyskaya avtonomiya*, p. 42.

with Russia on the basis of subordination. N. M. Korkunov considered these distinctions to have enormous practical significance.[21] Thus, the Grand Duchy of Finland was considered to be a special independent state united with Russia only through the Romanov dynasty.

Finland was incorporated into the Empire in three stages. With the Treaty of Nystad, on 30 August 1721, at the end of the Great Northern War against Sweden, Estonia, Livonia, Ingria, and Southeast Finland (Kexholmslän and part of Karelia) were transferred to Russia. The Peace Treaty of 1743 transferred more territory; and on 5 September 1809 by the Treaty of Fredrikshamn, the remainder of Finland was annexed to Russia. During 1808–9 Aleksandr I gradually recognized Finnish autonomy, and on 16 March 1809 the Emperor opened the four-chamber *Seim*, or legislature, which had been elected according to Swedish electoral law.

The linguistic situation which resulted is of great interest.[22] On 25 October 1858 the Finnish language was allowed to be used in legal disputes and dissertations; on 1 August 1863 the Finnish language received equal status with Swedish for all purposes; and on 9 February 1863 the Russian language ceased to be a compulsory subject in primary schools. On 20 February 1865 the Finnish language became the working language in judicial and administrative institutions along with Swedish, and on 30 November 1871 the Finnish Senate was given the right to determine the language of secondary education.

Thus from 1863 it could be said that Finland was part of the Russian Empire, but with its own laws and judicial and administrative institutions. On 3 September 1863 Aleksandr II opened the *Seim* with the words that he preserved the basis of a constitutional monarchy reflecting the spirit of the Finnish people. From that date the *Seim* was elected every five years.

Other territories and subjects of the Empire, although not autonomous in the sense that Finland enjoyed, nevertheless had administrative or legal arrangements, which could give the impression that they were on the way to some kind of autonomous status.

The closest example to the experience of Finland is that of the Baltic territories. These were incorporated into Russia in the eighteenth century. Ingeborg Fleischhauerhas related that the Peace of Nystadt in 1721 reconfirmed the Baltic Germans' freedom of religion and *cultus*, which they had enjoyed under Swedish rule, that is, Protestantism including a Protestant University at Dorpat, German administration in town and country, and German law.[23] The Baltic territories were divided into the Estlyandskiy, Liflyandskiy, and Kurlyandskiy governorates, as part of one general-governorate with Ostzeiskiy Krai. The inhabitants of these *krais* maintained their own religious observance, as well as their own laws—the German, Swedish, Polish laws in operation before Russian rule.

[21] Nikolai Mikhailovich Korkunov (1853–1904), leading scholar at St Petersburg University; Nikolai Mikhailovich Korkunov, *Russkiye gosudarstvennoye pravo* [Russian State Law] (St Petersburg: Typography of Russian Association, 1892), p. 134; Kutafin, *Rossiyskaya avtonomiya*, p. 46.

[22] Kutafin, *Rossiyskaya avtonomiya*, p. 55.

[23] Ingeborg Fleischhauer, 'The Nationalities Policy of the Tsars Reconsidered—The Case of the Russian Germans', *The Journal of Modern History*, vol. 53, no. 1 (1981): pp. D1065–90.

With the great judicial reforms of Aleksandr II in 1864, the Baltics obtained their own judicial organs. They had their own system of local government. The Baltic nobility provided the Empire with soldiers, diplomats, senior civil servants, and members of the court.

The Russian Germans were not mentioned at all by Kutafin in his book on Russian autonomy. However, Fleischhauer has pointed out that the Russian Empire's attitude to non-Russians was 'based on pragmatic and not on racial grounds.'[24] National groups considered useful for imperial purposes were to be attracted and favoured by the state. The Russian Germans comprised three groups: the Baltic Germans, often called *ostseizskiye nemtsy*; the urban population; and the colonists.

According to the 1897 census the three groups together numbered about two million, with 1.3 million colonists; half a million urban dwellers: 375,000 in industry, 100,000 in trade and commerce, 50,000 in academic professions, and 35,000 in the civil service and army, as well as more than 50,000 belonging to the hereditary or personal nobility, or honorary citizens.[25] By the outbreak of World War I the German population was much larger and very wealthy.

According to Fleischhauer, this success was in part the result of the Germans' legally privileged situation. I have already mentioned the privileges of the Baltic Germans. The urban Germans in the Empire enjoyed ten years' exemption from taxes outside the cities and five years' within them; free movement in Russia and the right to leave when they wished; large state loans for new factories; tax-free imports and exports in the first years; use of local Russian labour including serfs; and membership of the Russian guilds with all their privileges.[26]

German peasants settling in Russia had the following privileges. According to the 'call' of 1763, every male farmer was given 30 to 60 *desyatiny* of arable land, granted by the Crown as community property belonging to the colony in which the farmer settled; thirty years' exemption from taxes; exemption from all forms of military service for ever; freedom of movement; the right to acquire goods, chattels, and land in the whole Empire; freedom to leave and to export all legally acquired property; free transition to another social estate, state loans; etc.[27]

The oldest German colonies were those on the Volga, with about 30,000 settlers after the first two decades of settlement. Colonies were established in other parts of Russia. And at the beginning of the twentieth century colonies were established in Siberia. There were some 300 colonies in all.

Ukraine, by contrast, lost all of its initial autonomy by degrees. Thus, the *Pereyaslavska Rada* (Pereyaslavskaya Council) of 8 January 1654 decided upon the union of the Ukrainian-Cossack formation of Bogdan Khmelnitskiy and Russia (in 1954 Khrushchev celebrated its anniversary by transferring Crimea from the

[24] Fleischhauer, 'The Nationalities Policy of the Tsars Reconsidered', p. D1066.
[25] Fleischhauer, 'The Nationalities Policy of the Tsars Reconsidered', pp. D1072–3.
[26] Fleischhauer, 'The Nationalities Policy of the Tsars Reconsidered', p. D1078.
[27] Fleischhauer, 'The Nationalities Policy of the Tsars Reconsidered', pp. D1082–3.

Russian SFSR to the Ukrainian SSR).[28] Also known as the *Martovskiy Stati*, this created the autonomous status of Ukraine within Russia, together with the rights and privileges of the Cossack elders, and Ukrainian institutions and clerics. The territory of Ukraine was divided into three parts: Left Bank Ukraine, divided into *polka*; Slobodskiy Ukraine, also divided into five *polka*; and the Zaporozhskiy Sech, the most autonomous part of Ukraine. *Polki* and 'hundreds' (*sotni*) were the territorial administrative units of Ukraine. Power was concentrated in the hands of the *hetman*, who commanded military forces and made and administered the laws. Control over the activities of the Ukrainian authorities was instituted in 1663 by the *Malorossiiskaya Prikaz*, replaced in 1722 by the *Malorossiiskaya Kollegiya*.

In 1734 the power of the *hetman* was abolished, and the Cossack forces came under Russian command. However, in 1747 the *hetman* institution was revived, with control over the *Zaporozhskiy Sech*.

In 1764 the *hetman* was again abolished, and the *Malorossiiskaya Kollegiya* was once more put in charge of Ukraine, with a presidency of four Russians and four Ukrainians. However, Ukrainians were not able to participate, and the General Governorate of *Malaya Rossiya* was created. The laws effective in Ukraine were the second and third Lithuanian Statutes, and Magdeburg (town) law. In 1728 a commission was established for the codification of Ukrainian law, which in 1743 completed preparation of the *Svod* 'Law by which the *Malaya Rossiiskaya* people are to be judged.' It had three books: Lithuanian Statute, Saxon *Zertsala*, and the book 'Order'. Courts were established in 1763 on the basis of the Lithuanian Statutes. In 1796 Left Bank Ukraine became the Malorossiiskaya *Guberniya* (governorate); and Slobodskaya Ukraine became the Slobodsko-Ukrainsko *Guberniya*. Right Bank Ukraine was divided into the Kiev, Volynsk, and Podolsk governorates, in 1832 re-named the Kiev General Governorate.

In this way Ukraine lost all of its autonomy, and re-emerged as an independent state only after World War I, as a Soviet Union republic after World War II, and as an independent state after 1991.

Georgia has a very long history of independence, and was for long, in opposition to the Ottoman Empire, seen as a state under Russia's protection. Closer ties were instituted by the Treaty of 1783, according to which Tsar Irakliy of the Kingdom of Kartli-Kakheti[29] recognized no authority higher than himself save the Russian Empress, who for her part undertook to protect him from external foes.[30] The final unification of Russia and Georgia took place in 1801 at the request in 1800 of Tsar Georgiy to Paul I. On 12 January 1801 Aleksandr

[28] N. N. Soleinik, 'Pereyaslavskaya Rada 1654 goda: Sovremennoye politico-pravovoye issledovaniye' [The Pereyaslavakaya Rada of 1654: Contemporary Political and Legal Research], *Vedomosti of Belgorod State University*, vol. 28, no. 22 (165) (2013): pp. 207–10.

[29] Created in 1762 by the unification of two eastern Georgian kingdoms, which had existed independently since the disintegration of the united Georgian Kingdom in the fifteenth century.

[30] Ronald Grigor Suny, *The Making of the Georgian Nation* (Bloomington/Indianapolis: Indiana University Press, 1994), pp. 57–9.

I explained to the Georgian people in a Manifesto that although he desired to preserve the independence of Georgia, he was obliged by force of circumstances to preserve the Tsardom of Georgia for Russia. The *Ulozheniye* of Tsar Vakhtang was preserved as the law of Georgia.

Much blood was shed subsequently for Georgia's independence: as Moshe Lewin has shown, Lenin's last struggle was against Stalin, on the question of independence for Georgia, which Lenin supported despite the fact that Mensheviks would be in power.[31]

Even more tragically than Ukraine and Georgia, Poland continuously lost its autonomy, largely through the actions of the Russian Empire, and in the end disappeared completely.

As a result of the three Partitions of the eighteenth century and the decision of the Congress of Vienna in 1814, Russia gained part of the territory of Poland, on which the Polish Tsardom (kingdom) was organized. In 1815 Poland within the Empire received a constitutional charter and the status of a kingdom. The Russian emperor became also the king of Poland. Its legislature was the *Seim*, with elections in 1820 and 1825. The *Seim* contained a senate, composed of the Polish nobility, and the *Posolskiy Izby*, elected in the localities. The *Seim* had full legislative competence, including fiscal. The official state language was Polish.

However, after the Polish uprising of 1830, the Organic Status was published, amending the Polish constitution, and making Poland an inseparable part of the Empire. The customs border between Russia and Poland was abolished in 1850.[32]

After the further uprisings of 1863–4 the last traces of autonomy were extinguished. Nevertheless, even after the end of autonomy the *Code Civil* of Napoleon I and other French legislation were preserved, with obligatory force in the Duchy of Poland from 1 May 1808, and extended in 1810 to the governorates taken from Austria.

As Kutafin points out, not all the states incorporated into Russia lost their autonomy. For example, Khiva, now in Uzbekistan, was to a large extent independent even though de facto fully subordinated to Russia.[33] According to the Treaty of 12 August 1873 Said-Mukhamed Rakhim-Bogodur Khan maintained executive power. Bukhara, also now in Uzbekistan, had even higher autonomy. Its status was defined in a Treaty of 28 September 1873. The emir of Bukhara exercised power from Tashkent, and from 1893 Russia maintained an ambassador. Of course, neither Khiva nor Bukhara were formally part of the Russian Empire. They were considered to be states under Russia's protection.

Kutafin says little about the Tatars, who have been the focus of some of my own work.[34] In contemporary Russia the Tatars not only have their own republic of

[31] Moshe Lewin, *Lenin's Last Struggle* (Ann Arbor: University of Michigan Press, 2005).
[32] Kutafin, *Rossiyskaya avtonomiya*, pp. 44–5.
[33] Kutafin, *Rossiyskaya avtonomiya*, p. 45.
[34] Bowring, 'The Tatars of the Russian Federation', pp. 417–35.

Tatarstan, the most autonomous and one of the wealthiest regions in the Russian Federation, but are the largest ethnic and linguistic minority with some 5.5 million members.

Tsar Ivan IV (the Terrible) conquered Kazan in 1552, and incorporated the khanate of Kazan into the Grand Duchy of Moscow's territory. Ivan followed his victory with a policy of Christianization and Russification of his Tatar subjects and other indigenous peoples, which was not reversed until the reign of Catherine II. But the Tatar language and Muslim religion were not eliminated. Schamiloglu in 1990 provided elements of a more complete picture.[35] His article concerned Sihabäddin Märcani (1818–89), the father of modern Kazan Tatar historiography, who wrote in the nineteenth century, during the Tatar revival within the Russian Empire. Schamiloglu examined the process by which the 'modern identity of the Kazan Tatars was created'.

If, then, the creation of Tatar national identity was crystallized in the nineteenth century, that is proof positive that the tsarist Empire had not destroyed Tatar consciousness: on the contrary. Thus, Märcani was one of the leading Kazan Tatar intellectuals of the nineteenth century: following early education in a village *madrassa* in Taşkiçü, he received an Islamic education in Bukhara and Samarkand, and returned to positions in a mosque and *madrassa*, and was appointed teacher at the Russo-Tatar Teacher's School.[36]

Schamiloglu observed that the name 'Tatar' was 'originally not the self-appellation of the Muslim Turks of the Middle Volga region'. Before the Mongol conquests they were known as 'Bulğars.' The name 'Tatar' was introduced during the Mongol period, and gained broad acceptance by the Kazan Tatars only in the nineteenth century. Märcani wanted, for nationalist reasons, to emphasize that under the 'Tatar Yoke' (1223–1480) 'the Russian dukes could not act without the permission of the Tatar Khans', and emphasized the Russians' role as tax collectors.[37] It is no surprise that many Russian words—for money, treasury, horse, etc.—are of Turkic origin.

But Schamiloglu points out that there is a dearth of historical sources for the period of the khanate of Kazan from the 1430s to 1552, when Kazan was conquered by Ivan IV, not least because of Russian destruction of libraries and archives. He reminds us that

> Following the fall of the Khanate in 1552 as the first foreign conquest of the emerging Russian Empire, elements of the dynastic and tribal elite of the Khanate of Kazan either fled to other states, were incorporated into the developing Russian aristocracy, or were simply vanquished. The indigenous Muslim Turkic population in or around the

[35] Uli Schamiloglu was born in New York of Kazan Tatar ancestry, and is now professor at Wisconsin-Madison See his home page http://www.turko-tatar.com/uli/, and http://lca.wisc.edu/new_web/?q=node/50. Uli Schamiloglu, 'The Formation of a Tatar Historical Consciousness: Sihabäddin Märcani and the Image of the Golden Horde', *Central Asian Survey*, vol. 9, no. 2 (1990): pp. 39–49.

[36] Schamiloglu, 'The Formation of a Tatar Historical Consciousness', pp. 41–2.

[37] Schamiloglu, 'The Formation of a Tatar Historical Consciousness', p. 45.

city of Kazan was resettled beyond a perimeter extending many kilometres away from the city. The indigenous and newly-resettled population of the surrounding territories (again including the former core territories of the Volga Bulğarian state) would later form the core group of the modern Kazak Tatars. In the 19th century these Muslim Turks of the Middle Volga region began to acquire a shared identity under the name 'Kazan Tatar'.[38]

Märcani's work was not only an astonishing achievement in adverse circumstances, but more importantly a classic nineteenth-century 'creation of an ideology of national identity', as described by Eric Hobsbawm.[39] It was also an essential ingredient for the creation of the Tatar ASSR in 1920–1.

The situation of the so-called *inorodtsy*, the non-Slavic populations of the Empire, was defined in Russian legislation.[40] These included the *samoyedy* of Arkhangelsk *guberniya*, the '*kocheviye inorodtsy*' of Stavropol *guberniya*, the Kalmyks of Astrakhan and Stavropol, the Kyrgyz of the Inner Horde, the *inorodtsy* of the Akmola and Semipalatinsk regions of present-day Kazakhstan, and the Urals and Turgan regions, the *inorodtsy* of the Zakaspian regions, and Jews.[41] *Inorodtsy* enjoyed local government differing from the norm according to need. *Inorodtsy* in different localities used the *Kitaiskoye Ulozheniye* of 1725, the *Mongolskoye Ulozheniye* of 1798, and the *Ulozheniye* of the Mongol and Kalmyk peoples of 1690.

The Bashkirs were semi-nomadic tribes inhabiting the territory, forest and steppe, beyond the Volga. Robert Baumann has pointed out that 'despite its relative proximity to Moscow Bashkiria remain unassimilated by the late nineteenth century…an apt indication of Russia's inability to impose civil administration on the vast realms to which it had laid claim'.[42] Ivan IV penetrated the Bashkir lands following his conquest of Kazan and Astrakhan in the 1550s, and a fort was established at Ufa in 1586. There were Bashkir uprisings in 1662–4, in 1676, from 1681 to 1683, and from 1705 to 1711. Following the creation of the fortified town of Orenburg on the Ural River in 1735, Empress Anna's agent Ivan Kirillov mercilessly crushed the consequent uprising. Finally, after the influx of many Russians, bringing the population of Orenburg to 884,787, and the defeat of the Pugachev rebellion (1773–5), the Empire established a military administration for the Bashkirs similar to that of the Cossacks, named the *Bashkirskoye voisko* or Bashkir Host, with 11 cantons, each with a *nachalnik*. Bashkir light cavalry fought splendidly in the war against Napoleon.[43]

[38] Schamiloglu, 'The Formation of a Tatar Historical Consciousness', pp. 40–1.

[39] Eric Hobsbawm, 'Mass-Producing Traditions: Europe, 1870–1914', in *Inventing Traditions*, edited by Eric Hobsbawm and Terence Ranger (Cambridge: Cambridge University Press, 1983), pp. 263–307.

[40] Kutafin, *Rossiyskaya avtonomiya*, p. 77.

[41] *Svod* of laws of the Russian Empire, v. 9, art. 1.

[42] Robert F. Baumann, 'Subject Nationalities in the Military Service of Imperial Russia: The Case of the Baskirs', *Slavic Review*, vol. 46, no. 3–4 (1987): pp. 490–1.

[43] Baumann, 'Subject Nationalities in the Military Service of Imperial Russia', p. 493.

In this way, paradoxically, the Bashkirs maintained their identity into the Soviet period, and the creation of present-day Bashkortostan.[44]

Suny also observed that 'some elites like the Tatar and Ukrainian nobles, dissolved into the Russian *dvoryanstvo*, but others, like the German barons of the Baltic or the Swedish aristocrats of Finland, retained privileges and separate identities'.[45]

6.3 Religious Autonomy in Tsarist Russia

In the period immediately after World War I, Muslims enthusiastically adopted NCA as a means of asserting a separate identity in post-Imperial Russia. Crews points out that, as he was informed by a Tatar interlocutor, Islam arrived in Russia before Orthodox Christianity, so that Islam is the most 'traditional' of Russian religions.[46] By the tenth century there were substantial Muslim communities along the Volga River, in Siberia, in the Caucasus, and the oasis towns of Central Asia.[47] By the reign of Catherine II Russia had ruled the Muslim peoples settled along the Volga River for more than two centuries, while she incorporated the Muslims of Crimea and the regions north of the Caucasus and Caspian Sea. By the late nineteenth century Muslims resided in eighty-nine provinces and territories of the Empire, together with the protectorates of Khiva and Bukhara. The first Imperial census held in 1897 registered 14 million Muslims, although the true number was probably 20 million. Three and a half million lived in European Russia; twelve million spoke languages of the 'Turkic-Tatar' group.[48]

While Peter the Great had oppressed the Muslim, especially Tatar, nobility, Catherine II, inspired by Enlightenment rationality, ordered in 1787 the printing of the Qur'an for distribution free of charge to Kazakhs on the frontier, and in September 1788 ordered the establishment in Ufa of an 'Ecclesiastical Assembly of the Muhammedan Creed' (*Dukhovnoye sobraniye Magometanskovo zakona*).[49] Mukhamedzhan Khusainov was given the title mufti, with a salary, and was to be aided by 'two or three Mullahs chosen from the Kazan Tatars'. By 1800 the mufti and three judges attached to the Assembly administered oral examinations for more than 1,900 clerics.[50] The first mosque was built in Moscow in 1823, despite protests from the Orthodox Church.[51] Kazan had Tatar language schools in the time of Catherine II.[52] In this way the foundations were laid for contemporary Tatar autonomy.

[44] I am grateful to Alexander Osipov for the observation that the way in which a pre-modern 'identity' translated into a national one is a complex story.

[45] Suny, 'The Empire Strikes Out: Imperial Russia', p. 27.

[46] Robert D. Crews, *For Prophet and Tsar: Islam and Empire in Russia and Central Asia* (Cambridge, Mass: Harvard University Press, 2006).

[47] Crews, *For Prophet and Tsar*, p .11.

[48] Crews, *For Prophet and Tsar*, pp. 12–14.

[49] Crews, *For Prophet and Tsar*, pp. 52–3.

[50] Crews, *For Prophet and Tsar*, p. 56.

[51] Crews, *For Prophet and Tsar*, p. 93.

[52] Crews, *For Prophet and Tsar*, p. 200.

It was evident in the late tsarist period that the Empire must pay institutional and constitutional regard to its ethnic and linguistic complexity, outlined in part in the preceding section, or face the possibility of disintegration. The responses to these issues were surprisingly contemporary in their language and tone. Leading Russian scholars argued at length as to the nature of autonomy in the Russian Empire. In 1892 N. M. Korkunov discussed the various forms of autonomy, preserving local laws and institutions, to a greater or lesser extent.[53] V. V. Sokolovskiy also sought to prove that the existence of autonomy did not contradict the integrity of the Russian Empire.[54]

A significant number of publications followed the first Russian Revolution of 1905, which almost brought an end to the Empire. This was a time for serious re-thinking of the Empire's foundations. F. F. Kokoshkin argued in a book published in 1905 that regional autonomy did not mean the creation of a state within a state.[55] For Kokoshkin, if there were to be local laws, as existed in Russia, there must be local legislatures. The State Duma could legislate for all-Russian matters, and local legislatures on the local scale.[56] The Empire must retain its legislative supremacy.[57] According to him, regional autonomy was the highest stage of the development of decentralization. In a further publication in 1908 he distinguished between autonomous *krai* and autonomous *oblast*.[58] Kokoshkin returned to this question in 1917, and emphasized its close connection with the national (ethnic) question.[59] He argued that decentralization to a greater or lesser extent was a powerful means for satisfying the demands of ethnic groups to self-determination, especially cultural self-determination, and that this could take the form of territorial decentralization, but also other forms. He made the case that in the Russian Empire it would be impossible to build a federation on the basis of national TA. For example, Ukraine with a population of 25–30 million, more than Spain, would far outweigh other regions of Russia. To give unequal competences to the component parts of Russia would also lead to a blind alley, he thought;[60] or rather than a federation, to confederation.

In 1906 a collection *Autonomy, Federation and the National (Ethnic) Question* appeared, edited by V. M. Gessen, arguing that national autonomy should

[53] Korkunov, *Russkiye gosudarstvennoye pravo*, p. 133; Kutafin, *Rossiyskaya avtonomiya*, p. 5.

[54] V. V. Sokolovskiy, *Ktrakiy uchebnik russkovo gosudarsvennovo pravo* [Short Textbook of Russian State Law] (Odessa: Economic Typography, 1890), pp. 231–2; Kutafin, *Rossiyskaya avtonomiya*, p. 6.

[55] Fyodor Fyodorovich Kokoshkin (1871–1918), jurist, leading member of the Constitutional Democratic (Cadet) party, member of the provisional government in 1917. Fyodor Fyodorovich Kokoshkin, *Oblastnaya avtonomii i yedinstvo Rossii* [Regional Autonomy and the Unity of Russia] (Moscow: Russian Political Encyclopedia (ROSSPEN), 1905), p. 3.

[56] Kokoshkin, *Oblastnaya avtonomii i yedinstvo Rossii*, pp. 9–10.

[57] Kokoshkin, *Oblastnaya avtonomii i yedinstvo Rossii*, p. 12.

[58] Fyodor Fyodorovich Kokoshkin, *Russkoye gosudarstvennor pravo* [Russian State Law] (Moscow: Typography of M. M. Stasulevich, 1908), pp.154–5; Fyodor Fyodorovich Kokoshkin, *Lektsii po obsehmu gosudarstvennomu pravu* [Lectures on General State Law] (Moscow: Russian Political Encyclopedia (ROSSPEN), 1912, republished 2010), pp. 305–6.

[59] Fyodor Fyodorovich Kokoshkin, *Avtonomiya i federatsiya* [Autonomy and Federation] (Moscow: Russian Political Encyclopedia (ROSSPEN), 2010), pp. 3–5.

[60] Kokoshkin, *Avtonomiya i federatsiya*, pp. 9–10.

precede the establishment of a parliamentary, rule of law, state.[61] Autonomy or other forms of political independence were the best way of resolving ethnic tensions. The authors pointed out that notwithstanding the centralized political government of Russia, it preserved within itself a series of local laws.[62] Thus, in the *Privislenskiy Krai* (in Poland) the *Code Civil* of Napoleon I had been in force since 1808, while in the *Ostzeiskii Krai* (in the Baltic) a whole range of laws including Roman law were in force. In Finland the Swedish laws of 1734 were in operation. Because of its Byzantine past Bessarabiya had laws with Byzantine roots. In the Governorates of Chernigov and Poltava the Lithuanian statutes remained in force. In the Caucasus and many other places, special, particular laws were applied. Whole regions of the Russian Empire lived and had lived their own juridical life. In another chapter of the work, the question of the unity of the state was also addressed by E. Pimenova, who argued that regional autonomy could be an efficient way of resolving the national (ethnic) problem in Russia.[63]

In another key text published in 1906, G. Novotorzhskiy argued that the contemporary Russian state had come into being through conquest, and therefore consisted of a whole range of regions, formed on a national as well as administrative basis.[64] In Russia these were Finland, Poland, Ukraine, Caucasus, the Pribaltiskiy Krai, Lithuania, Siberia, and finally 'Great Russia'. He wrote:

> Finland at the present time has almost complete autonomy. The question of Polish autonomy demands resolution in the shortest possible time, as soon as the police state is abolished. The question of autonomy for the Caucasus is more complex, since many ethnicities are living there, mixed with each other. The Jewish question can be resolved by giving the Jews the full rights enjoyed by other ethnicities in Russia, and by guaranteeing the rights of the minorities which they will constitute in Poland, Ukraine, Great Russia and Byelorussia. As concerns the autonomies of Ukraine, Siberia autonomous regions in Great Russia, they can be created as required. As, so to say, autonomies of the second rank.[65]

This passage has a distinctly contemporary ring.

Other works of the same nature included A. T. Snarskiy's 1907 *Autonomy or Federation?*, and the survey published in 1907 by the Pole K. Kulchitskiy (Mazovetskiy) *Autonomy and Federation in Contemporary Constitutional States*.[66]

[61] Vladimir Matveevich Gessen, ed., *Avtonomiya, federatsiya i natsionalniy vopros* [Autonomy, Federation, and the National (Ethnic) Question] (St Petersburg: People and Freedom, 1906). Vladimir Matveevich Gessen (1868–1920) doctorate from Moscow State University, official of the Ministry of the Interior.

[62] Gessen, *Avtonomiya, federatsiya i natsionalniy vopros*, pp. 21–2; Kutafin, *Rossiyskaya avtonomiya*, p. 19.

[63] E. Pimenova, *Yedinstvo gosudarstvo i avtonomiya* [The Unity of the State and Autonomy] (St Petersburg: Azbuka, 1906).

[64] G. Novotorzhskiy, *Natsionalniy vopros, avtonomiya i federatsiya* [The National Question, Autonomy and Federation] (Moscow: Cooperative Association of USSR 'Revolutionary flag', 1906), pp. 14–15; G. Novotorzhskiy, *What is a Rule of Law State?* (Paris,1914); G. Novotorzhskiy, *The Significance of the Right to Land for the Working Class*; G. Novotorzhskiy, *The Socialisation of Land* (Sankt Petersburg: Publishing House of V. Raspopov, 1906).

[65] Novotorzhskiy, *Natsionalniy vopros, avtonomiya i federatsiya*, p. 21; Kutafin, *Rossiyskaya avtonomiya*, p. 26.

[66] Kutafin, *Rossiyskaya avtonomiya*, p. 28.

NTA was also intensively debated in this period. Kulchitskiy was one of a number of Russian authors who reflected on 'cultural-national autonomy'. In 1917, M. Y. Lazerson wrote a book entitled *Autonomy and Federation* which argued forcefully for 'personal autonomy'—that is, NTA—drawing on Karl Renner's writings.[67] In his view, one should not, in a contemporary state, consider the population as tied to particular territories. Such a state, with many ethnicities, cannot be divided into territories in each of which there is a single ethnicity.[68] However, he argued strongly against the term NCA, which in his view confused the territorial principles and the personal principle.[69]

6.4 Lenin and Bolshevik Concepts of Territorial Autonomy

Kutafin makes the point that the Bolsheviks, as convinced centralists, approached the idea of national (ethnic) autonomy very cautiously.[70] I have investigated in detail the way in which Lenin developed his position on the right of nations to self-determination in fierce argument with those such as the Jewish Bund who espoused non-territorial personal cultural autonomy on the Austro-Marxist model.[71] His understanding of self-determination followed the positions taken and language used by Marx and Engels in relation to Ireland and Britain, and Poland and Russia. For them and for Lenin there were indeed Irish and Polish nations with a right to statehood. The concept of 'nation' did not require further explanation or analysis.

In October 1913 Lenin, having stated that 'The right of nations to self-determination, i.e., the right to secede and form independent national states, will be dealt with elsewhere' declared himself in favour of local autonomy:[72]

> Obviously, one cannot conceive of a modern, truly democratic state that did not grant such autonomy to every region having any appreciably distinct economic and social features, populations of a specific national composition, etc. The principle of centralism, which is essential for the development of capitalism, is not violated by this (local and regional) autonomy, but on the contrary is applied by it *democratically*, not bureaucratically.[73]

[67] Maksim Yakovlevich Lazerson (1887–1952) sociologist and professor at St Petersburg then Petrograd State University, member of the *Saime* (Parliament) of inter-war independent Latvia, leader of the Jewish *Ceire Cion* party; from 1939 lectured at Columbia University, New York; Maksim Yakovlevich Lazerson, *Avtonomiya i federatsiya* [Autonomy and Federation] (Petrograd: Kniga po trebovaniy, 2012).

[68] Lazerson, *Avtonomiya i federatsiya*, pp. 23–4.

[69] Lazerson, *Avtonomiya i federatsiya*, pp. 25–6; Kutafin, *Rossiyskaya avtonomiya*, p. 704.

[70] Kutafin, *Rossiyskaya avtonomiya*, p. 81.

[71] Bowring, 'Austro-Marxism's Last Laugh', pp. 229–50; Bowring, 'Burial and Resurrection', pp. 191–206.

[72] V. I. Lenin, 'Centralisation and Autonomy', accessed 28 March 2011, http://www.marxists.org/archive/lenin/works/1913/crnq/6.htm#v20pp72-045.

[73] Lenin, 'Centralisation and Autonomy'.

And further:

Why national areas with populations, not only of half a million, but even of 50,000, should not be able to enjoy autonomy; why such areas should not be able to unite in the most diverse ways with neighbouring areas of different dimensions into a single autonomous 'territory' if that is convenient or necessary for economic intercourse—these things remain the secret of the Bundist Medem.[74]

This was Lenin's argument for TA and against NTA.

Lenin returned to this question in 1916, in the midst of World War I and before the October Revolution, summing up issues of self-determination, when he wrote that it was autonomy which could enable a nation, hitherto forcibly retained within an existing state (such as the Russian Empire) to 'crystallise into a nation'. He had in mind Norway's declaration of sovereignty from Denmark in 1814, and envisaged a declaration by the Polish nation that they would no longer be ruled by the Russian Tsar. He wrote:

But as everyone knows, in practice a reform is often merely a step towards revolution. It is autonomy that enables a nation forcibly retained within the boundaries of a given state to crystallise into a nation, to gather, assess and organise its forces, and to select the most opportune moment for a *declaration*... in the 'Norwegian' spirit: We, the autonomous diet of such-and-such a nation, or of such-and-such a *territory*, declare that the Emperor of all the Russias has ceased to be King of Poland, etc.[75]

Thus it is clear that before the October Revolution Lenin was in favour of the idea of creating broad regional autonomies in Russia.

In May 1917 the issue of independence for Poland and Finland was again at the top of the agenda, and Lenin drafted a *Resolution on the National Question*. His starting point was clear, namely recognition of the right of all nations forming part of Russia freely to secede and form independent states. To deny them such a right, or to fail as a Russian government to take the necessary measures to guarantee the realization of the right to secede in practice, would be in effect to support a policy of forcible seizure or annexation.[76]

From secession from the Russian Empire Lenin turned to the issue of autonomy. He meant TA: he opposed the non-territorial NCA formulated by the Austro-Marxists Otto Bauer and Karl Renner, and espoused by the Jewish Bund. He made it clear that autonomy meant support for broad regional autonomy. Moreover, he advocated the abolition of supervision from above, and the abolition of a compulsory official language, both of which were features of the assimilationist policies of the late tsarist regime. Above all, the local population itself must decide on fixing the boundaries of the autonomous territory.[77]

74 Lenin, 'Centralisation and Autonomy'.

75 V. I. Lenin, 'The Discussion on Self-Determination Summed Up', accessed 28 March 2011, http://www.marxists.org/archive/lenin/works/1916/jul/x01.htm.

76 V. I. Lenin, 'Resolution on the National Question', *Collected Works* (Moscow: Progress Publishers, 1917, 1964), pp. 302–3, Supplement to *Soldatskaya Pravda*, no. 13 (1917): p. 302. This is not to be found in the Internet Archive.

77 V. I. Lenin, 'Resolution on the National Question', p. 303.

In 1916, Lenin wrote in relation to Poland:

All those who want to stand for the freedom of nations, for the right of nations to self-determination, not hypocritically, not in the Südekum, Plekhanov, Kautsky fashion, but sincerely, must be opposed to the war because of the oppression of Poland; they must be in favour of the right of secession from Russia for those nations which Russia is now, oppressing: the Ukraine, Finland, etc.[78]

Thus, before the October Revolution Lenin was in favour not only of a right of secession from Russia by nations, but also of TA for minorities.

These policies were key components of Bolshevik policy from the moment of Bolshevik success in October 1917. In 'The Tasks of the Revolution', published in October 1917, Lenin declared that a democratic peace would be impossible without an explicit renunciation of annexation or seizure. He emphasized that every nationality without exception in Europe and in the colonies should have the right to decide for itself whether it should form a separate state.[79]

This right was enshrined in the 1918 Constitution of the Russian Soviet Federated Socialist Republic (RSFSR). Every people should decide whether they wished to participate in the RSFSR and on what basis. This was the only basis for creating a free and voluntary state. In this spirit the 1918 Constitution of the RSFSR[80] provided in Article 1, Chapter 4:

8. In its effort to create a league—free and voluntary, and for that reason all the more complete and secure—of the working classes of all the peoples of Russia, the Third Congress of Soviets merely establishes the fundamental principles of the Federation of Russian Soviet Republics, leaving to the workers and peasants of every people to decide the following question at their plenary sessions of their soviets, namely, whether or not they desire to participate, and on what basis, in the Federal government and other Federal soviet institutions.

And in Article 2, Chapter 5

11. The soviets of those regions which differentiate themselves by a special form of existence and national character may unite in autonomous regional unions, ruled by the local congress of the soviets and their executive organs.

These autonomous regional unions participate in the Russian Socialist Federated Soviet Republic upon a Federal basis.[81]

[78] V. I. Lenin, 'Peace Without Annexations and the Independence of Poland as Slogans of the Day in Russia', *Sotsial-Demokrat*, no. 51 (1916), accessed 11 November 2014, https://www.marxists.org/archive/lenin/works/1916/feb/29.htm.

[79] V. I. Lenin, 'The Tasks of the Revolution', *Rabochy Put*, nos 20 and 21 (1917), accessed 3 June 2014, http://www.marxists.org/archive/lenin/works/1917/oct/09.htm.

[80] Constitution of the Russian Soviet Federated Socialist Republic 1918, English translation, accessed 28 March 2011, http://www.marxists.org/history/ussr/government/constitution/1918/index.htm.

[81] General Provisions of the Constitution of the Russian Socialist Federated Soviet Republic, accessed 28 March 2011, http://www.marxists.org/history/ussr/government/constitution/1918/article2.htm.

On this basis, the Labouring Commune of Germans of the Volga was organized at the end of 1918, and in 1924 became an autonomous republic. The Bashkir ASSR was established within the RSFSR in 1919, followed in 1920–1 by the Kirgiz (Kazakh) ASSR, and the Tatar, Dagestan, and Gorkiy autonomous republics, the Karelian Labouring Commune, and the Chuvash, Kalmyk, Marii, Votskaya (Udmurtskaya) autonomous *oblasts* (regions). In 1921–2 the Yakutsk ASSR, and the Karachaev-Cherkess, Kabardino-Balkar, Komi, Mongol-Buryat, and a series of other autonomous *oblasts* were created.[82]

In early 1918, as the civil war raged, Lenin explained why in his view centralism was not incompatible with autonomy and federation:

> We are for democratic centralism. And it must be clearly understood how vastly different democratic centralism is from bureaucratic centralism on the one hand and from anarchism on the other. The opponents of centralism continually put forward autonomy and federation as a means of struggle against the uncertainties of centralism. As a matter of fact, democratic centralism in no way excludes autonomy, on the contrary, it presupposes the necessity of it...The example of the Russian Soviet Republic shows us particularly clearly that federation, which we are introducing and will introduce, is now the surest step towards the most lasting union of the various nationalities of Russia into a single democratic centralised Soviet state.[83]

Outside Russia, the principle of self-determination was put into practice. Independent states on the Baltic territories appeared in 1920, with the Treaty of Tartu in February of 1920 which accepted Estonian independence; the Treaty of Moscow in July of 1920 which accepted Lithuanian independence; and the Treaty of Riga in August of 1920, which accepted Latvian independence. In November 1920 Lenin declared:

> Of the small states formerly belonging to the Russian Empire, Poland has been among those that have been most of all at odds with the Great-Russian nation during the last three years, and made the greatest claims to a large slice of territory inhabited by non-Poles. We concluded peace with Finland, Estonia and Latvia also against the wishes of the imperialist Entente, but this was easier because the bourgeoisie of Finland, Estonia and Latvia entertained no imperialist aims that would call for a war against the Soviet Republic, whereas the Polish bourgeois republic had an eye, not only to Lithuania and Byelorussia but the Ukraine as well.
>
> Latvian ruling circles were also compelled to sign peace with the RSFSR, following the defeat of the foreign interventionists and the whiteguards in 1919 and the resulting consolidation of Soviet Russia's international position. On March 25, 1920, the Latvian Foreign Ministry approached the Soviet Government suggesting that peace talks be started. On April 16, the Soviet and Latvian representatives started peace talks in Moscow and on August 11 a treaty was signed with Latvia in Riga.[84]

[82] Kutafin, *Rossiyskaya avtonomiya*, pp. 133–4.

[83] V. I. Lenin, 'Original version of the article "The Immediate Tasks of the Soviet Government"', accessed 11 November 2014, https://www.marxists.org/archive/lenin/works/1918/mar/23b.htm.

[84] V. I. Lenin, 'Our Foreign and Domestic Position and Party Tasks' Speech Delivered To The Moscow Gubernia Conference Of The R.C.P.(B.)', accessed 11 November 2014, https://www.marxists.org/archive/lenin/works/1920/nov/21.htm.

I contend that the appearance, for the first time in history, of three independent states in the Baltic region was the consequence of the implementation of political principle, and not an opportunistic response to military defeat.

I also argue that Lenin, unlike Stalin, had no intention of extending the boundaries of Soviet Russia to include the former possessions of the tsarist Empire. His principled position did not change at the end of his life. In his letter of 26 September 1922, at the time of increasing conflict with Stalin as to the right of Georgia to gain independence outside the USSR—to secede—Lenin wrote:

> we consider ourselves, the Ukrainian S.S.R. and others, equal, and enter with them, on an equal basis, into a new union, a new federation, the Union of the Soviet Republics of Europe and Asia.[85]

In his Last Testament, written in 1922–3, Lenin wrote, warning against Stalin:

> It is quite natural that in such circumstances the 'freedom to secede from the union' by which we justify ourselves will be a mere scrap of paper, unable to defend the non-Russians from the onslaught of that really Russian man, the Great-Russian chauvinist, in substance a rascal and a tyrant, such as the typical Russian bureaucrat is.[86]

Lenin by then regarded Stalin as just such a Great-Russian chauvinist.

Lenin died on 21 January 1924. The 1924 Constitution of the USSR[87] of 31 January 1924, which incorporated the Treaty of December 1922 creating the USSR, contained the following, fully consistent with the principles on which Lenin insisted:

Chapter II Sovereign Rights of the Member Republics

Article 3.

The sovereignty of the member Republics is limited only in the matters indicated in the present Constitution, as coming within the competence of the Union. Outside of those limits, each member Republic exerts its public powers independently; the USSR protects the rights of the member Republics.

Article 4.

Each one of the member Republics retains the right to freely withdraw from the Union.

Article 5.

The member Republics will make changes in their Constitutions to conform with the present Constitution.

[85] V. I. Lenin, 'On the Establishment of the U.S.S.R.', accessed 28 March 2011, http://www.marxists.org/archive/lenin/works/1922/sep/26.htm.

[86] V. I. Lenin, 'The Question of Nationalities or "Autonomisation"', accessed 28 March 2011, http://www.marxists.org/archive/lenin/works/1922/dec/testamnt/autonomy.htm.

[87] Constitution of the USSR 1924, English translation, accessed 28 March 2011, http://www.answers.com/topic/1924-constitution-of-the-ussr.

Article 6.

The territory of the member Republics cannot be modified without their consent; also, any limitation or modification or suppression of Article 4 must have the approval of all the member Republics of the Union.

Article 7.

Just one federal nationality is established for the citizens of the member Republics.

The remaining history of the USSR was marked by a strong tension between regional and ethnic autonomy on the one hand and the dictatorship of the Party and its General Secretary on the other.

This leads me to my (friendly) criticism of Terry Martin. In his book *The Affirmative Action Empire: Nations and Nationalism in the Soviet Union, 1923–1939*, Martin starts with the question 'Why did the Bolsheviks adopt this radical strategy?'.[88] He asserts first of all that 'When they seized power in October 1917, they did not yet possess a coherent nationalities policy.'[89] As we have seen above, that is not quite right. He acknowledges that the Bolsheviks had a 'powerful slogan' but states that this slogan was shared with Woodrow Wilson: to me, this is a surprising proposition. It seems that Martin is not sufficiently aware of the passionate debates of the pre-war years on the question of the right of nations to self-determination, as against personal cultural NTA.[90]

According to Martin, the content of Soviet nationalities policy was 'finally delineated' at the Twelfth Party Congress in April 1923, and at a special Central Committee conference on nationalities policy in June 1923.[91] That is, in the very last months of Lenin's life, and after his conflict with Stalin over independence for Georgia.

Martin, therefore, cannot explain how, well before April 1923, most of the territorial autonomies which have continued in existence until the present day had already been created.

Nor does Martin have anything to say about the rich history of autonomy in the tsarist Empire, which I have explored above.[92] The obvious point is this: Soviet nationalities policy did not come from nothing. It had deep roots not only in Bolshevik ideology, but also in tsarist history.[93]

However, Martin does provide a series of case studies showing in detail how the Bolsheviks responded to the rising tide of nationalism 'by systematically promoting the national consciousness of its ethnic minorities and establishing for

88 Terry Martin, *The Affirmative Action Empire: Nations and Nationalism in the Soviet Union, 1923–1939* (Ithaca: Cornell University Press, 2001).

89 Martin, *The Affirmative Action Empire*, p. 2.

90 Although he cites a number of Lenin's key works at footnote 10 on p. 3.

91 Martin, *The Affirmative Action Empire*, p. 9.

92 Alexander Osipov has a different point of view. He refers to the reconceptualization of feudal heterogeneity into ethnic pluralism in the Russian Empire.

93 See Bowring, 'Minorities Protection in Russia: Is There a "Communist Legacy"?', pp. 45–58.

many of them the characteristic institutional forms of the nation-state.'[94] Thus, he notes that:

The Tatar national movement was among the strongest in the Soviet Union, and certainly the strongest in the Soviet era. The Tatar nationalist elite lobbied aggressively for and vigorously supported the Soviet policy of *korenizatsiya*: the formation of a Tatar republic, the promotion of Tatars into leadership positions, the use of the Tatar language in government and education, and support for Tatar national culture. However, this movement also faced formidable resistance. Tatars formed a narrow plurality in their own republic (48.7% Tatar and 43.1% Russian).'[95]

Martin had not seen Schamiloglu's work, apparently, since this showed that the roots of Tatar self-consciousness extended back into the tsarist period.

6.5 A Retreat from National Cultural Autonomy—or 'Autonomy' as an Empty Shell?

I have already referred, above, to Russia's accession to the CoE's FCNM, and the emphasis given in its first Report of 2000 to its experiment in NCA. On 9 April 2010 Russia published its Third Periodic Report to the Advisory Committee (AC) on the FCNM.[96] In particular, a new development in NCA was highlighted. Russia asserted that

the end of 2005 saw some changes introduced to the Federal Law 'On National and Cultural Autonomy' concerning determining of the federal executive body under which a consultative council on national and cultural autonomies was to be created. In execution of this law, the Government of the Russian Federation adopted a resolution no. 527-R of 17 April 2006 assigning the role of the above executive body to the Ministry of regional development of the Russian Federation.[97]

Further in the Report, Russia continued:[98]

Among specialized bodies ensuring interaction between national public associations and governmental authorities on the federal level, we can name the Consultative Council on National and Cultural Autonomies Affairs under the Ministry of Regional Development of the Russian Federation. Federal Law No 146-FZ of 30 November 2005 introduced changes to Article 7 of the Federal Law 'On national and cultural autonomy' that authorized the Government of the Russian Federation to determine the executive body under which a consultative council on national and cultural autonomies affairs, acting on a voluntary basis, is to be created.

[94] Martin, *The Affirmative Action Empire*, p. 1.

[95] Martin, *The Affirmative Action Empire*, p. 58.

[96] Third Report Submitted by the Russian Federation Pursuant to Article 25, paragraph 2 of the Framework Convention for the Protection of National Minorities (received 9 April 2010), ACFC/SR/III(2010)005.

[97] Third Report Submitted by the Russian Federation Pursuant to Article 25, p. 9.

[98] Third Report Submitted by the Russian Federation Pursuant to Article 25, pp. 27–9.

...The Council comprised leaders of all federal national and cultural autonomies. The first session of the Consultative Council on National and Cultural Autonomies Affairs took place on 15 June 2006.

Sessions of the Consultative Council are held twice a year.

This rather positive message was sharply contradicted on 25 July 2012 by the FCNM's AC, in its Opinion. The AC had taken the opportunity to visit Russia from 12 to 16 September 2011, and to meet a large number of official, NGO, and ethnic minority interlocutors.[99]

They turned to the topic of NCAs,[100] and reminded their readers[101] that in the first two cycles:

In the previous monitoring cycles, the Advisory Committee encouraged the authorities to restore, in collaboration with stakeholders, the central position of national cultural autonomies in federal legislation and to take measures to ensure the effective implementation of the competences of national cultural autonomies, especially in the field of language, education and culture.[102]

Russia was in this way put on the spot with regards to its NCA policy. The amending NCA Law of 2009 had enabled regional and local authorities to make payments to NCAs, but without imposing an obligation; and the new law imposed no requirement to consult.[103] Practice therefore varied widely from region to region. The AC continued that taking account of the great importance given to NCAs by state nationalities policy, in fact NCAs were restricted to 'manifestations folkloriques' and Sunday schools, thus discouraging minority communities from taking part in the much more extensive debates as to the future of Russian society, and preventing their effective participation in public life in general.[104] These concerns were reinforced[105] when the AC turned to Article 7 of the FCNM.[106] They expressed particular concern over the dissolution of the Ukrainian NCA in 2011, pursuant to an order made by the Ministry of Justice and confirmed by the Supreme Court.[107] The Ukrainian NCA was said to have exceeded its competence

[99] Advisory Committee on the Framework Convention for the Protection of National Minorities, Third Opinion on the Russian Federation (adopted on 24 November 2011), ACFC/OP/III(2011)010.

[100] Advisory Committee on the Framework Convention for the Protection of National Minorities, Third Opinion on the Russian Federation, pp. 35–6.

[101] Advisory Committee on the Framework Convention for the Protection of National Minorities, Third Opinion on the Russian Federation, para 71.

[102] My translation from the French.

[103] Law No.11 FZ, accessed 11 November 2011, http://www.rg.ru/2009/02/11/kult-avtonomia-dok.html.

[104] Advisory Committee on the Framework Convention for the Protection of National Minorities, Third Opinion on the Russian Federation, para 74.

[105] Advisory Committee on the Framework Convention for the Protection of National Minorities, Third Opinion on the Russian Federation, pp. 35–6.

[106] 'The Parties shall ensure respect for the right of every person belonging to a national minority to freedom of peaceful assembly, freedom of association, freedom of expression, and freedom of thought, conscience and religion.'

[107] See the judgment of the Supreme Court on 24 November 2010 and judgment of the Cassation Chamber of the Supreme Court of 27 January 2011.

by engaging in politics, but for the AC this was an unfortunate consequence of limiting NCAs to cultural matters. To this they added their disagreement with the federal legislation which forbids the formation of political parties on ethnic or religious grounds.

The AC criticized the Consultative Council, of which the Russian Report had made so much.[108] It regretted that by virtue of the rules governing the creation of NCAs, the Council's mandate was limited to questions of the preservation and promotion of the cultures of minorities. It could say little about the financing of NCAs.

For the AC, it was clear that the numbers of NCAs continued to grow largely as a result of the desire of the individuals creating them to attract possible finance and to gain status.

6.6 Recent Developments—The Decay of NCAs?

There have been significant changes in Russia in recent years. On 19 December 2012 President Putin signed Decree No. 1666 confirming the new 'Strategy of State National Policy for the Period to 2025' (the Strategy).[109] By 'national' is meant 'ethnic', and the two words are used interchangeably in Russian. The Strategy replaced the 'Concept of State National Policy' confirmed by President Yeltsin's Decree No. 909 of 15 June 1999. On 20 August 2013, by Order No. 718, the Russian government confirmed the Federal Strategic Programme 'Strengthening the unity of the Rossiiskiy (civic Russian) nation and the ethno-cultural development of the peoples of Russia (2014–2020)', intended to implement the Strategy.[110] The latter document makes no mention of NCA, apart from a reference to the 1996 Law.

Further insight into government strategy was given by President Putin's introductory remarks to the meeting of the Presidential Council on Inter-ethnic relations on 19 February 2013. He insisted that the main task of nationality policy must be to 'strengthen harmony and accord' among Russian citizens, so that they will see themselves as 'citizens of a single country'.[111] He outlined five key concepts of the new policy. First, he declared that the Russian language is 'the fundamental basis of the unity of the country'. Second, he called for the preparation of a single standard national history textbook. Third, he said that he supports the work of

[108] Advisory Committee on the Framework Convention for the Protection of National Minorities, Third Opinion on the Russian Federation, p. 52.

[109] 'Strategy of State National Policy for the Period to 2025', accessed 3 June 2014, http://graph.document.kremlin.ru/page.aspx?1;1644521.

[110] Presidential Decree of 19.12.2012, no. 1666 on the Strategy of State National Policy of the Russian Federation for the Period of the Year 2025, accessed 3 June 2014, http://government.ru/media/files/41d4862001ad2a4e5359.pdf.

[111] 'Putin on Rossiissky identity and Russian language', accessed 11 November 2014, http://www.odnako.org/blogs/putin-o-rossiyskoy-identichnosti-i-russkom-yazike/.

the 989 NCAs. Fourth, he opposed the return of cultural monuments confiscated by the Soviets to their original owners. Finally, he emphasized the importance of major sports events such as the Winter Olympics at Sochi in helping to fuse the many peoples of the Russian Federation into one.

The then Minister of Regional Development, Igor Slunyayev, responded to President Putin. First, he gestured to the Plan for Implementation of the Strategy drawn up by his Ministry and signed by Prime Minister Medvedev on 1 March 2013.[112] He promised reports on progress twice a year. Only a few minutes later he was to concede that practically nothing had been done.

Next he turned to statistics which showed that in 2013 there were 224,000 non-governmental organizations (NGOs) active in the Russian Federation, but only 15 NCAs at the federal level, 245 at the regional level, and 639 at the local level. He continued that 'the activities of some NCAs, unfortunately, at times remind one of elements of family business.'

In addition, he said, it was important not to miss the practical results of the activities of NCAs, and in this connection he announced that he planned to 'actualize' the work of the Consultative Council mentioned above. To be honest, he continued, the Council practically did not work. In 2011–12 it met only three times, and, unfortunately neither representatives of federal organs nor representatives of NCAs took part.

Mr Slunyayev had been in office for only 18 months, but this was a dismal account of inactivity since the Consultative Councils were created in 2006. The misgivings of the FCNM's Advisory Committee seemed to be entirely borne out.

For one commentator, Vladimir Dergachev, writing in *Izvestiya*, it was plain that Mr Putin was proposing to make the inhabitants of Russia into one nation.[113] But for the veteran historian Aleksandr Yanov, writing in *Novaya Gazeta*, Putin had not yet learned to 'distinguish patriotism from nationalism', and was seeking to replace the classic tsarist trinity of Orthodoxy, Autocracy, and Nationality (*Narodnost*) proposed by Count Uvarov in 1833 and taken up by Nikolai I in the deep reaction which followed the Napoleonic Wars, with Patriotism, Sovereignty, and Tradition. Putin is a nationalist 'of the purest water', and his new trinity will fall apart in front of our eyes.[114]

Putin's five concepts and his 'triad' are anathema to the leaders of Russia's ethnic and linguistic minorities, and their entrenched territorial autonomies. Ironically, and Putin does not understand this, the continued attraction of NCAs

[112] Prior to his appointment as Minister in October 2012 he was Governor of Kostroma Oblast. He is ethnic Russian and Russian Orthodox, and a career *chinovnik*, civil servant. He had no previous experience of work with minorities. Regulation on 15 July 2013, no. 1226, accessed 1 June 2014, http://www.minnac.ru/res_ru/0_hfile_1173_1.pdf.

[113] Vladimir Dergachov, 'Residents of Russia Offered to Make One Nation', *Izvestia.ru*, accessed 11 November 2014, http://izvestia.ru/news/545167.

[114] Aleksandr Yanov, 'The Collapse of the Putin "Triads"', *Novaya Gazeta*, no. 19, 20 February 2013, accessed 11 November 2014, http://www.novayagazeta.ru/comments/56546.html. 'The President has not learned to distinguish patriotism from nationalism.'

is based in large measure on their connection with the idea of autonomy, so deeply rooted in Russia.

On 8 September 2014 the Ministry of Regional Development, founded just ten years earlier on 13 September 2004, was dissolved by decree of President Putin, and its functions distributed between the Economic Development Ministry, the Ministry of Construction, Housing and Utilities, and the Culture Ministry.[115] The Ministry of Culture would be responsible for the protection of the rights of national minorities and indigenous peoples, and would guarantee state support for the ethno-cultural development of peoples. The Ministry of Justice would have powers in the sphere of the territorial structure of the Russian Federation, and would also look into questions of the division of powers between Federal executive authorities, and the subjects of the Federation and local authorities.[116]

The news was broken to Mr Slunyayev half an hour before he was due to start a meeting in St Petersburg of a presidium of his Ministry colleagues.[117] According to Prime Minister Dmitry Medvedev, reported on 11 September, the recent establishment of specialized ministries for the Crimea, the Far East, and the North Caucasus had made the Regional Development Ministry superfluous.[118]

6.7 Conclusion

It should be no surprise at all that the word 'autonomy' resonates so strongly in contemporary Russia. I have shown that this was no Soviet trick or show, but that territorial and indeed the concepts of NTA have deep roots in Russia and its history.

However, the Russian experiment in NTA, the NCAs, was evidently the topic of severe misgivings by no less than the (now deposed) Minister responsible for implementation of the state policy towards minorities.

And the attention of the federal government has turned elsewhere. In the May-June 2014 issue of the *Pro et Contra,* Alexander Verkhovskiy wrote a rather pessimistic article under the title 'The ethnopolitics of the federal authorities and

[115] 'Putin Liquidates Regional Development Ministry', *Russian News Agency*, September 2008, accessed 11 November 2014, http://en.itar-tass.com/russia/748551.

[116] 'Putin Signed a Decree on the Abolition of the Ministry of Regional Development and Rosoboronpostavki Rosoboronzakaz', *Newsru.com*, accessed 11 November 2014, http://www.newsru.com/russia/08sep2014/kabinet.html.

[117] 'Slunayev: Ministry of Regional Development Was a Significant Body of the Executive Power', *Baltinfo*, accessed 11 November 2014, http://www.baltinfo.ru/2014/09/08/Slyunyaev-Minregion-byl-znachitelnym-organom-ispolnitelnoi-vlasti-448246.

[118] 'Moscow Kicks Regional Development Out of Ministry', *Barentsobserver*, accessed 11 November 2014, http://barentsobserver.com/en/politics/2014/09/moscow-kicks-regional-development-out-ministry-11-09. 'Russian government management of High North developments, indigenous peoples and cross-border cooperation faces a reshuffle as President Putin abolishes the Ministry of Regional development.'

the activisation of Russian nationalism.'[119] His article is summed up: 'The federal authorities place before themselves a fully meaningful task in the sphere of ethnopolitics, but do not make any efforts which even theoretically could be sufficient for achieving a result.'

His article does not once mention NTA, or its Russian variant, NCA. The key issue is now Putin's new-found nationalism, encapsulated in his conservative 'triad'. This will come into sharp conflict with both territorial and NTA.

[119] Verkhovskiy founded that authoritative SOVA Centre: 'SOVA Center for Information and Analysis is a Moscow-based Russian nonprofit organization founded in October 2002. SOVA Center conducts research and informational work on nationalism and racism, relations between the churches and secular society, and political radicalism. We are also interested in human rights issues, especially government misuse of counter-extremism measures.' See SOVA Center for Information and Analysis, accessed 2 June 2014, http://www.sova-center.ru/en/; Council under the President of the Russian Federation the Development of Civil Society and Human Rights, accessed 2 June 2014, http://www.president-sovet.ru/composition/3057/. Verkhovskiy is also a member of the President's Council on the Development of Civil Society and Human Rights; Alexander Verkhovskiy, 'The Ethnopolitics of the Federal Authorities and the Activisation of Russian Nationalism', accessed 2 June 2014, http://carnegieendowment.org/files/ProEtContra_62_19-33.pdf.

III

TERRITORIAL AND NON-TERRITORIAL AUTONOMY IN A GLOBAL PERSPECTIVE

7

NTA as Political Strategy in Central and Eastern Europe

David J. Smith

7.1 Introduction

During the last two decades, post-communist Central and Eastern Europe (CEE) has witnessed a proliferation of new national minority legislation based on the principle of non-territorial autonomy (NTA). Such laws have been adopted by at least eight states of the region, with varying degrees of practical implementation. The best-known examples are Hungary and the Russian Federation, which are currently home to 1,200 and 900 minority cultural self-governments respectively. NTA legislation has also been revived in Estonia (based loosely on a famous law adopted during the 1920s). Thus far this has been implemented only by the country's small Finnish and Swedish minorities, though one can point to an emerging debate over the potential applicability of NTA for Estonia's much larger Russian-speaking population. NTA also formed the basis for minority legislation put before parliament in Romania at the start of 2005. In this case the proposals were not adopted. However, the question of autonomy for Romania's Hungarian minority in particular remains a key item on the national and wider regional political agenda.

NTA has thus become an increasingly salient feature of minority politics in contemporary CEE. As such, it has attracted growing attention from international organizations working in the field of minority rights, such as the Council of Europe (CoE) and the Organization for Security and Co-operation in Europe (OSCE).[1] Yet, for all this, there remain important gaps in the academic literature surrounding the revival of the model. While one can point to several excellent case studies of individual countries, there is still a surprising lack of detailed comparative research on the origins of current NTA arrangements and proposals, the

[1] Venice Commission, *The Participation of Minorities in Public Life* (Strasbourg: Council of Europe Publishing, 2008); Max van der Stoel, *Peace and Stability through Human and Minority Rights: Speeches by the OSCE High Commissioner on National Minorities* (Baden-Baden: Nomos Verlagsgesellschaft, 1999), p. 172.

political strategies behind them, and the underlying understandings of statehood, state–minority relations, and minority rights that they bring to bear.

The aim of this chapter is to examine these questions in relation to the aforementioned four country cases (Estonia, Hungary, Romania, and Russia). In so doing, it will also seek to locate these cases within wider debates around minority rights in post-communist Europe. The current minority rights agenda for the region can be seen as being driven by two imperatives: the first of these involves the political management of ethnic diversity in the interests of political stability and state consolidation, seeking to balance cultural recognition for different ethnicities with the maintenance of civic cohesion and existing state borders.[2] A second related agenda—until now more informed by western understandings of multiculturalism—is around democratization and boosting participation of minorities in public life.[3] From the standpoint of state and minority actors as well as those international organizations overseeing the European minority rights regime, NTA is seen as having the potential to support both of these agendas.[4] At the same time, the perceived viability of the model has differed according to the particular national context, and these diverse experiences have prompted an ongoing debate about the overall pros and cons of this approach.

7.2 The Origins and Main Tenets of NTA

In the western part of Europe, current debates around the political management of ethnic diversity have arisen within the framework of what were already well-established unitary nation states with relatively coherent and overarching societal cultures. In CEE by contrast, managing ethnic diversity has been a central preoccupation from the very outset of the modern state-building process.

[2] Aviel Roshwald, 'Between Balkanisation and Banalisation: Dilemmas of Ethno-Cultural Diversity', in *Cultural Autonomy in Contemporary Europe*, edited by David J. Smith and Karl Cordell (London: Routledge, 2008).

[3] Will Kymlicka, 'Nation-Building and Minority Rights: Comparing West and East', *Journal of Ethnic and Migration Studies*, vol. 26 (2000): pp. 183–212; Will Kymlicka, 'Western Political Theory and Ethnic Relations in Eastern Europe', in *Can Liberal Pluralism be Exported? Western Political Theory and Ethnic Relations in Eastern Europe*, edited by Will Kymlicka and Magda Opalski (Oxford: Oxford University Press, 2001); Will Kymlicka, 'The Rise and Fall of Multiculturalism?: New Debates on Inclusion and Accommodation in Diverse Societies', in *The Multiculturalism Backlash*, edited by Steven Vertovec and Susanne Wessendorf (London/New York: Routledge, 2010).

[4] See, e.g., High Commissioner on National Minorities, 'The Lund Recommendations on the Effective Participation of National Minorities in Public Life & Explanatory Note' (adopted September 1999), accessed 6 February 2013, http://www.osce.org/hcnm/32240?download=true, p. 29; Advisory Committee on the Framework Convention for the Protection of National Minorities, Third Opinion on Hungary (adopted on 18 March 2010), ACFC/OP/III(2010)001, accessed 27 November 2012, http://www.coe.int/t/dghl/monitoring/minorities/3_fcnmdocs/PDF_3rd_OP_Hungary_en.pdf. Note also the Council of Europe's characterization of Hungary's 1993 NTA Act as an 'ambitious law making it possible for the... [recognised]... national minorities to participate in decision-making processes'.

Within this region, movements for national self-determination originally took hold within the context of empire. Driven by disaffected new intellectual strata amongst subject peoples, they were generally grounded in identification with an ethnically defined community rather than with established political institutions.[5] In the case of larger, more compactly settled populations, nationalist demands were soon linked to particular territories, which, however imprecisely defined, were deemed to be the national homeland of the group in question. This territorial frame of reference was, however, inherently problematic given the ethnically mixed patterns of settlement within the region, which meant that however one drew the lines, ethno-national and political boundaries would never be fully congruent. In some cases, indeed, particular nationalities were so dispersed in terms of settlement that it would be hard to envisage that their demands might be satisfied to any degree at all by territorial means.

It was this contention that led Karl Renner and Otto Bauer to propound their original theory of NTA back at the turn of the twentieth century. Arguing that demands for national self-determination had to be accommodated within an ethno-federalist conception of statehood, they insisted that national rights (understood primarily as the right to maintain and practise one's distinct culture) should not be allocated to particular territorial sub-units of the state, but rather to collectivities of individual citizens who had freely affiliated themselves to a national register. This national register would form the basis for the election of national-cultural self-governments, which would assume responsibility for schooling and other cultural matters of specific concern to the particular ethnicity and would, inter alia, have the right to levy additional taxes on those who had signed up to the relevant national register.[6] This approach was diametrically opposed to the then-established nation state concept based on cultural homogenization of political space. Instead, Renner and Bauer envisaged the state as a shared territorial space inhabited by autonomously organized ethno-national groups. Their reasoning was that if each group could cater for its own cultural needs, this would leave the overall state government and territorially based local administrations to focus on more 'nationally neutral' matters of concern to all citizens.[7]

[5] Aviel Roshwald, *Ethnic Nationalism and the Fall of Empires: Central Europe, Russia and the Middle East 1914–1923* (London: Routledge, 2001), p. 5; Miroslav Hroch, *Social Preconditions of National Revival in Europe: A Comparative Analysis of the Social Composition of Patriotic Groups among the Smaller European Nations* (Cambridge: Cambridge University Press, 1985); Rogers Brubaker et al., *Nationalist Politics and Everyday Ethnicity in a Transylvanian Town* (Princeton: Princeton University Press, 2006), pp. 27–46.

[6] Otto Bauer, *The Question of Nationalities and Social Democracy* [Nationalitätenfrage und die Sozialdemokratie], with an Introduction by Ephraim Nimni and Preface by Heinz Fischer (Minneapolis: University of Minnesota Press, 2000); Karl Renner, 'State and Nation', in *National Cultural Autonomy and its Contemporary Critics*, edited by Ephraim Nimni (London/New York: Routledge, 2005).

[7] Bauer, *The Question of Nationalities*, pp. 284–8.

7.3 Institutional Legacies in Central and Eastern Europe

Renner and Bauer's ideas proved highly influential amongst democratizing movements in the Habsburg and tsarist Russian empires during the early years of the twentieth century. They were subsequently marginalized as the old empires collapsed under the combined pressures of world war and revolution, yet their thinking was in many ways vindicated by the nature of the 'new' Central and Eastern Europe that arose on the basis of the western-brokered peace settlement and the Bolshevik assumption of power in Russia. The doctrine of national self-determination may have been proclaimed as one of the cornerstones of the peace settlement, but it was largely disregarded in the case of nationalities such as the Germans, Hungarians, and Galician Ukrainians. In so far as the victorious western allies did uphold this doctrine, moreover, they applied it on a territorial basis, seeking to give selective ethno-national groups 'a state of their own'. This notion of ethnic ownership over territory was fundamentally at odds with the plural society character of the new states, all of which contained substantial ethno-national minority populations. Within the 'nationalizing' state context of interwar central Europe, belonging to a particular ethno-national minority was seen as incompatible with belonging to national political communities defined in narrowly ethnic terms. This understanding was accentuated further in the case of minorities (such as Germans and Hungarians), which could be linked by virtue of their ethnicity to a neighbouring state that harboured irredentist political elements. The 'triadic nexus' of state, minority, and external homeland nationalisms became a major source of instability and conflict within interwar Central Europe, contributing to the disaster that befell the region after 1933.[8] Interestingly, one exception to the rule (at least during the democratic 1920s) was to be found in the Baltic states of Estonia, Latvia, and Lithuania: established outside the framework of the peace settlement, these all established forms of NTA that were deemed successful in mitigating inherited tensions between the new states and their minorities.[9]

In the case of the USSR, the Soviet regime also sought to manage the multinational legacy of empire on a territorial basis. Guided by the maxim 'national in form, socialist in content', it allocated a designated 'homeland' to each of the largest ethnic groups living within the Soviet state. Once again, however, this territorially based approach could hardly accommodate the full spectrum of ethno-national diversity that existed. For instance, in the case of the Russian Republic (itself configured along federal lines) only 41 of the 127 officially

[8] Rogers Brubaker, *Nationalism Reframed. Nationhood and the National Question in the New Europe* (Cambridge: Cambridge University Press, 1996).

[9] David Smith and John Hiden, *Ethnic Diversity and the Nation State: Cultural Autonomy Revisited* (London/New York: Routledge, 2012).

acknowledged nationalities had territorial autonomy, leaving the other 86 without any form of recognition. Even where territorial autonomy had been granted, a significant proportion of the group in question typically resided outside the borders of the designated ethnic homeland. On the basis of this, Codagnone and Filippov concluded that 'only about ten million individuals in Russia, out of the 27 million non-ethnic Russians, could benefit from the protection offered by the principle of territorial autonomy'.[10] Coupled with the recording of personal ethnicity within passports, this policy thus 'institutionalized both territorial-political and personal-ethnocultural models of nationhood as well as the tension between them'.[11] The only group to benefit from any form of extra-territorial national rights under the Soviet ethno-federal system was ethnic Russians, who were encouraged to identify with the entire USSR as their homeland. The status of Russian as the language of inter-national communication within the Soviet state meant that Russians were able to live and work within the non-Russian union republics without necessarily having to learn the local language. Once again, however, this system proved to be a source of tension in the 1980s when political space was opened up for the expression of ethno-regionalism within individual union and autonomous national republics.

These institutional legacies of the past have profoundly shaped debates over the political management of ethnic diversity both within post-communist Central Europe and within the new states established following the demise of the USSR. It would clearly be inappropriate to draw too close a parallel between interwar and contemporary CEE. Nevertheless, continued trends towards ethnicization of politics within a post-communist setting, coupled with the bloodshed that occurred in former Yugoslavia and parts of the USSR during the early 1990s, elicited fears of wider conflict, instability, and continued territorial fragmentation. This in turn hastened efforts to establish a robust European minority rights framework of the kind that had previously proved so elusive during the 1920s and 1930s. While one key concern has been around issues related to ethnicity and territory in states with historically contested borders, international attention has also focused on the plight of the region's largest stateless minority, the Roma, living in dispersed fashion across several countries of the region and subject to increased socio-economic marginalization and discrimination within the context of post-communist transformation. It is against this background that contemporary manifestations of NTA must be situated. In what follows I will briefly run through four case studies and some of the debates that have surrounded them.

[10] Cristiano Codagnone and Vassily Filippov, 'Equity, Exit and National Identity in a Multinational Federation: The "Multicultural Constitutional Patriotism" Project in Russia', *Journal of Ethnic and Migration Studies*, vol. 26, no. 2 (2000): pp. 263–88. See also Vera Tolz, *Russia: Inventing the Nation* (London: Arnold, 2001), p. 251.

[11] Brubaker, *Nationalism Reframed*, p. 45.

7.4 Hungary and Hungarian Minorities in Central Europe

In looking at the revival of NTA within Central and Eastern Europe, it is appropriate to start with Hungary, which was the first state to espouse the concept following the fall of communism and which has since adopted by far the most comprehensive legal framework in this area. Hungary's pioneering work in the area of NTA can be seen to derive partly from the comparatively small share of the population that claims to belong to a national minority. While some say that the actual figure is as high as 10 per cent, the 2001 census gave a figure of 4.34 per cent.[12] With the partial exception of the Roma minority concentrated in the country's north-east, these minority populations also live in a territorially dispersed fashion, meaning that an NTA law appears well suited to this particular context. In this regard, the parliamentary debates of 1993 made reference to the similar context that lay behind Estonia's celebrated 1925 law, which catered primarily for the needs of a territorially dispersed German minority population within a state where minorities made up scarcely more than one in ten of the population.[13]

Initially adopted in July 1993 to widespread international acclaim, Hungary's minority law enshrined the right to cultural autonomy for thirteen 'indigenous' national minorities (Bulgarians, Greeks, Croatians, Poles, Germans, Armenians, Roma, Romanians, Carpatho-Rusyns, Serbs, Slovaks, Slovenes, and Ukrainians), which could trace their presence in the country back at least a hundred years. The impetus for the law came at least partly from minority representatives, apparently keen to reverse assimilationist trends that had intensified during the communist era. Minority interest in autonomy on the basis of NTA is further evidenced by the establishment of more than 1,200 cultural self-governments at various levels within Hungary during the decade or so after 1993.[14]

At the same time, the remarkable share of the parliamentary vote in favour of the 1993 legislation (96.5 per cent), testifies to overwhelming support amongst the ranks of the ethnic majority. Indeed, according to several authors, the law (at least in its initial incarnation) was very much a top-down initiative in which the specific interests of Hungary's minorities were subordinate to those of the state and its dominant ethnic group. The small numerical size of domestic minorities meant that initial post-communist state and nation-building was informed less by concerns over internal stability and political integrity than it was by the question

[12] European Commission for Democracy through Law (Venice Commission), 'Opinion on the Act on the Rights of Nationalities in Hungary' (adopted 15–16 June 2012, Venice), accessed 27 November 2012, http://www.venice.coe.int/docs/2012/CDL-AD(2012)011-e.pdf, p. 3.

[13] Krizsán Andrea, 'The Hungarian Minority Protection System: A Flexible Approach to the Adjudication of Ethnic Claims', *Journal of Ethnic and Migration Studies*, vol. 26 (2000): p. 250.

[14] Balázs Dobos, 'The Development and Functioning of Cultural Autonomy in Hungary', *Ethnopolitics*, vol. 6, no. 3 (2007): p. 456.

of negotiating the relationship between the state and the numerically significant ethnic Hungarian minorities living in neighbouring states. For András László Pap, the law was inspired at least partly by a sincere desire to compensate for the pain and suffering that the 'traditional' ethno-national communities of the region had had to endure over preceding decades.[15] Uppermost in legislators' thinking, however, was the specifically Hungarian historical experience arising from the 1920 Treaty of Trianon and its dismemberment of ethnic Hungarian areas of settlement, the legacy of which 'has never disappeared entirely'.[16] This in turn informed a 'constitutionally articulated responsibility for out-border diaspora Hungarians' within post-1989 Hungary.[17]

Most authors would share Pap's view that the July 1993 law constituted a form of 'trade currency' in Hungary's external support for claims made in relation to the Hungarian 'diaspora' living in neighbouring states.[18] According to this interpretation, Hungary sought to position itself as a pacesetter in the field of minority rights so as to acquire the moral legitimacy to ask the same of other countries, while also enhancing its credentials as a prospective member of the European Union (EU). In this respect, the championing of NTA served to strengthen Hungary's reputation as a purveyor of 'non-territorial policy innovations'.[19] Taken together with bilateral treaties signed between Hungary and neighbouring states containing Hungarian minorities, it would help to press the case for collective minority rights claims while mitigating claims that Hungarian autonomy constituted a potential threat to state sovereignty and territorial cohesion in the region.

Such an assessment of underlying strategy invites an assessment of the NTA framework from the standpoint both of Hungary's internal minorities and of Hungarian minorities abroad. As regards the former, one key question has related to the representativeness of the autonomous institutions created after 1993. At the time the law was adopted, many citizens of Hungary from a minority background were apparently reluctant to declare publicly their ethnicity, due to a collective memory of past ethnically based oppression during and after World War II. The original 1993 law thus did not use national registers as a basis for electing minority self-governments; rather, participation in elections was open to all citizens residing within the relevant electoral district. This approach, however, gave rise to the practice generally known as 'ethno-business' whereby political entrepreneurs were in some cases able to pose as

[15] András László Pap, 'Minority Rights and Diaspora-Claims: Collision, Interdependence and Loss of Orientation', in *Beyond Sovereignty: From Status Law to Transnational Citizenship*, edited by Osamu Ieda (Sapporo: Hokkaido University Slavic Research Center, 2006), pp. 243–7.

[16] George Schöpflin, 'Hungary and the EU', in *Beyond Sovereignty: From Status Law to Transnational Citizenship*, edited by Osamu Ieda (Sapporo: Hokkaido University Slavic Research Center, 2006), p. 216.

[17] Pap, 'Minority Rights and Diaspora-Claims', p. 248.

[18] Pap, 'Minority Rights and Diaspora-Claims', p. 243. In this regard see also Krizsán, 'The Hungarian Minority Protection System'.

[19] Sherill Stroschein, 'Territory and the Hungarian Status Law: Time for New Assumptions?', in *Beyond Sovereignty: From Status Law to Transnational Citizenship*, edited by Osamu Ieda (Sapporo: Hokkaido University Slavic Research Center, 2006), p. 95.

minority representatives simply in order to gain access to public office and the entitlements that flow from this.[20]

Perceived abuses of this kind were one factor behind a 2005 amendment to the NTA law, which introduced an obligatory system of enrolment on national registers for candidates and voters alike. A more recent Act on the Rights of Minorities has also sought to address the problem of ethno-business through recourse to census data: from 2014 (when new electoral provisions introduced by the Act will come into force), it will not be permissible to organize elections to a minority self-government in a district where the 2011 census indicates that the given minority group is not present above a defined numerical threshold. The 2005 amendment has also been hailed as a step forward in addressing what many commentators saw as shortcomings in the effectiveness of the minority institutions.[21] Not least, the revised law incorporated firmer guarantees relating to the functional and financial independence of minority self-governments, several of which have since been able to establish schools and take over the running of other cultural institutions.[22] Moreover, in response to external recommendations by the Council of Europe, the 2011 Act on National Minorities establishes detailed regulations governing the legal status and competences of minority self-governments and their rights of advocacy in relation to state and municipal authorities, while provisions are now in place for minority representation within the national parliament.[23] Even so, periodic monitoring reports allude to a continued lack of clarity regarding the extent of resources to be made available to minority self-governments and the modalities for accessing them. The recent economic crisis has also brought cuts in funding, which is highlighted as a particular issue in relation to Roma self-governments.[24]

Given that over half of the self-governments established between 1993 and 2002 operate in the name of the Roma minority, particular questions arise regarding the extent to which NTA has helped to further the societal integration and effective interest representation of what is Hungary's largest and most marginalized minority.[25] In this regard, early criticism of the framework pointed to the fact that NTA was not embedded within a broader overarching strategy to address issues of Roma discrimination and exclusion.[26] A more cynical view would be to see NTA as a substitute for such a strategy, enabling the state to claim symbolically that it was giving rights to the Roma, thereby drawing attention away from more substantive issues while simply entrenching pre-existing ethnic boundaries

[20] Krizsán, 'The Hungarian Minority Protection System'; Dobos, 'The Development and Functioning of Cultural Autonomy'; Balázs Visi, 'Hungary: A Model with Lasting Problems', in *Minority Rights in Central and Eastern Europe*, edited by Bernd Rechel (London/New York: Routledge, 2009), pp. 124–6.

[21] Advisory Committee, 'Third Opinion on Hungary', p. 14.

[22] Advisory Committee, 'Third Opinion on Hungary', p. 23.

[23] Act CLXXIX 2011.

[24] European Commission for Democracy through Law, 'Opinion on the Act on the Rights of Nationalities in Hungary', p. 14; Advisory Committee, 'Third Opinion on Hungary', pp. 23–4.

[25] Dobos, 'The Development and Functioning of Cultural Autonomy', p. 465.

[26] Visi, 'Hungary: A Model with Lasting Problems', pp. 128–31.

within society and encouraging the pursuit of narrow sectional interests by different groupings within the Roma ethno-political sphere.[27] Hungary has subsequently been hailed for the establishment of an Equal Treatment Authority in 2005 and the adoption of a strategic action plan to implement a 'decade of Roma integration' programme for 2007–15.[28] At the same time, there remains deep concern over a recent ongoing upsurge in discrimination and violence against Roma.

If one turns to look at the external dimension, one can clearly point to NTA as a feature of Hungarian minority political debate and practices in neighbouring countries. One case falling outside the scope of this chapter is Serbia, where Hungarian minorities have moved to implement a 2009 NTA law adopted as part of the country's ongoing discussions on accession to the EU.[29] From the standpoint of the Serbian state and the current sensitive issues relating to its territorial integrity, NTA could be seen as a useful means of undermining any potential Hungarian territorial claims focused on Vojvodina, which already benefits from devolved government. In Romania, by contrast, proposals for Hungarian NTA have also been advanced periodically, but have yet to be taken on board by the state. In this case, an ethnic Hungarian party (The Democratic Union of Hungarians in Romania (in Romanian UDMR)) has participated actively in coalition governments since the mid-1990s and has been able to secure minority rights that are far-reaching by regional standards, including provision for mother-tongue education from primary to university level, public use of the Hungarian language in areas where Hungarians make up more than 20 per cent of the local population, and a Department for Inter-Ethnic Relations which cooperates with a consultative Council of National Minorities drawn from NGO representatives.[30]

UDMR has nevertheless faced a growing challenge from smaller parties and organizations outside parliament, such as the Szekler National Council, Hungarian Civic Alliance, and the Hungarian National People's Party of Transylvania. These have accused UDMR of being unduly acquiescent to the agenda of the Romanian majority and have advanced demands for more far-reaching recognition, including territorial autonomy for the compactly settled Hungarian population in the Szeklerland area of Transylvania. Against this background, UDMR has since the

[27] Martin Kovats, 'The Good, the Bad and the Ugly: Three Faces of "Dialogue"—the Development of Roma Politics in Hungary', *Contemporary Politics*, vol. 3 (1997): pp. 55–71; Martin Kovats, 'The Political Significance of the First National Gypsy Minority Self Government in Hungary', *Contemporary Politics*, vol. 6 (2000): pp. 247–62.

[28] Advisory Committee, 'Third Opinion on Hungary'.

[29] For an initial overview of activities within this framework, see Magyar Nemzeti Tanács, 'Beszámoló a Magyar Nemzeti Tanács kétéves tevékenységéről 2010. június 30.—2012. Június 30' [Report on the Activities of the Hungarian National Council, 30 June 2010–June 30, 2012], *Magyar Nemzeti Tanács: Subotica* (2012): pp. 122–78.

[30] Melanie Ram, 'Romania: From Laggard to Leader?', in *Minority Rights in Central and Eastern Europe*, edited by Bernd Rechel (London/New York: Routledge, 2009); pp. 182–4; Second Report submitted by Romania pursuant to Article 25, Paragraph 1 of the Framework Convention for the Protection of National Minorities (received on 6 June 2005), accessed 27 November 2012, http://www.coe.int/t/dghl/monitoring/minorities/3_fcnmdocs/PDF_2nd_SR_Romania_en.pdf, pp. 5–8.

1990s pursued its own project of fuller cultural autonomy for the Hungarian minority; mindful of historically framed Romanian nationalist sensitivities over the status of Transylvania, however, it has framed autonomy in non-territorial terms.[31] In early 2005, during the run-up to Romania's EU accession, the party tabled a draft minority law based on Estonia's historic NTA model.[32] This approach was contested by UDMR's political opponents within the Hungarian community, which claimed that the proposed law would give UDMR an effective monopoly on decision-making. Additional external protection for the Hungarian minority would, they argued, only be achieved at the expense of its internal democracy.[33]

In any event, the draft tabled in 2005 failed to pass. According to the Romanian constitution, the status of national minorities is to be regulated by an organic law requiring an absolute majority in both houses of the Romanian parliament and this proved impossible to achieve.[34] In this respect, it seems that even proposals for NTA could not transcend securitized, 'nationalizing' discourses on state and nation-building within Romania, which see any prospect of further Hungarian rights as potentially threatening to the integrity of the state.[35] From an EU standpoint, moreover, the absence of such legislation did not prove to be a barrier to Romania entering the EU in 2007. At the time of writing, a general minority law has still to be adopted, with the subsequent period having seen a growth in populist nationalist rhetoric and political tensions around issues of historical commemoration, property restitution, and territorial-administrative boundaries within Transylvania. As regards the latter issue, UDMR has argued for the integration of the three Szeklerland counties into a single administrative entity, in the face of government proposals to amalgamate these into separate regions, each with an overall ethnic Romanian majority.[36]

[31] Gabriel Andreescu, 'Universal Thought, Eastern Facts: Scrutinizing National Minority Rights in Romania', in *Can Liberal Pluralism be Exported? Western Political Theory and Ethnic Relations in Eastern Europe*, edited by Will Kymlicka and Magda Opalski (Oxford: Oxford University Press, 2001).

[32] Christopher D. Decker, 'Enhancing Minority Governance in Romania: Report on the Presentation on Cultural Autonomy to the Romanian Government', *European Centre for Minority Issues Report*, no. 53 (2005), accessed 13 September 2010, http://www/ecmi.de/download/Report_53.pdf.

[33] Gabriel Andreescu, 'Cultural and Territorial Autonomy and the Issue of Hungarian Identity', *Hungarian Studies*, vol. 21, nos 1–2 (2007): pp. 61–84.

[34] European Commission for Democracy through Law (Venice Commission), 'Opinion on the Draft Law on the Statute of National Minorities Living in Romania', (adopted 21-22 October 2005), CDL-AD(2005)026, accessed 28 November 2012, http://www.venice.coe.int/webforms/documents/?pdf=CDL-AD(2005)026-e; Christopher D. Decker, 'The Use of Cultural Autonomy to Prevent Conflict and Meet the Copenhagen Criteria: The Case of Romania', in *Cultural Autonomy in Contemporary Europe*, edited by David J. Smith and Karl Cordell (London: Routledge, 2008).

[35] Decker, 'The Use of Cultural Autonomy to Prevent Conflict and Meet the Copenhagen Criteria', pp. 111–12.

[36] Ioana Lupea, 'Acceptance or Lack of Tolerance towards Minorities in Romanian Public Administration', *Accept Pluralism Policy Brief Issue*, no. 14 (2012), accessed 28 November 2012, http://cadmus.eui.eu/bitstream/handle/1814/24379/ACCEPT_PLURALISM_PB_2012_14_Romania.pdf?sequence=1.

7.5 NTA in Estonia

The fact that the draft 2005 law was ultimately rejected by Romania's parliament suggests that even proposals for a non-territorial form of autonomy can be hard-pressed to transcend nationalizing discourses on state and nation-building in today's CEE. A similar point could be made in relation to contemporary Estonia, where NTA was reintroduced against the background of a state and nation-building project predicated on the political marginalization of the large Russian-speaking settler population established during the Soviet era. Within this context—and specifically in light of international debates around Estonia's policy on citizenship—it would appear that cultural autonomy was readopted primarily with an eye to bolstering Estonia's external image and its standing in the eyes of the West. Indeed, legislators openly alluded to this function during the parliamentary debates that preceded the adoption of the law in 1993.[37] In terms of legacies, this legislation connected symbolically with a 1920s 'golden age' of democracy, which constituted a usable past in the context of Estonia's efforts to 'return to Europe' during the early 1990s. Above all, it could be held up as proof the titular nationality had historically taken a tolerant attitude towards national minorities living within Estonia, thereby ascribing all current ethnic tensions to the legacies of illegitimate Soviet rule.

The actual practical relevance of the cultural autonomy law seems more open to question. Spokespersons for Estonia's Finnish and Swedish minorities have been able to establish their own cultural councils under the terms of the law, but there are still no legal provisions governing the public-legal status or competences of these bodies. This obviously limits the possibilities for minority cultural development through NTA structures.[38] From the standpoint of the much larger Russian minority, one key issue relates to the provision that only citizens can vote for and be elected to minority self-governments. Since a significant part of the Russian population remains without full citizenship, they are not deemed to form part of a 'genuine' national minority and so remain outside the NTA framework. In spite of this, Russian representatives have submitted applications for NTA on three occasions during the past six years. All, however, have been rejected.

In recent discussions around NTA for the Russian-speaking minority, one discerns a fear on the part of ethnic majority representatives that such institutions would become a 'state within a state' and a vehicle for external influence by Russia, especially given the numerical size of the Russian-speaking minority and

[37] David J. Smith, 'Cultural Autonomy in Estonia. A Relevant Paradigm for the Post-Soviet Era?' ESRC, 'One Europe or Several?', *Working Paper 19* (2001): p. 34.

[38] Holger Berg, 'Ingerisoomlased võivad saavutada kultuurautonoomia sügiseks' [Ingrian Finns Could Achieve Cultural Autonomy in the Autumn], *Eesti Päevaleht* (2003), accessed 20 June 2012, http://www.epl.ee/news/eesti/ingerisoomlased-voivad-saavutada-kultuurautonoomia-sugiseks.d?id=50959337; T. Kabanen, 'Soome vähemusrahvuse kultuuriautonoomiast' [On Cultural Autonomy for the Finnish National Minority], 2006, accessed 7 June 2012, http://www.isamaaliit.com/category/toivo-kabanen-blogi-reformierakond/.

its territorial concentration, particularly in north-eastern Estonia.[39] Perhaps more importantly, the presence of the large Russian-speaking minority has been framed within the dominant political discourse as a threat not only to state security, but also to the societal security of the majority ethno-national group. The numerically small size of the ethnic Estonian population, coupled with the bi-national state order inherited from the USSR, means that continued recognition for the Russian language can be construed as perpetuating trends towards Russification of public life that were so evident during the Soviet era and which were held up as a threat to the longer-term survival of titular national language and culture. Such societal security considerations can be also discerned to a lesser extent in the case of Romania, but seemingly did not feature in NTA debates within Hungary. In the latter case any societal security concerns have taken the broader transnational Hungarian diaspora as their referent object rather than Hungarians living within the boundaries of the existing state.

Against this background, cultural policy in Estonia has focused squarely upon integrating the Russian-speaking minority into a common societal core, within the framework of a unitary nation state. De facto, it is still possible to speak of Russian minority autonomy, in so far as the network of Russian-language schools inherited from the Soviet era has continued to operate since 1991 under the auspices of local municipalities.[40] Under current educational legislation, however, a bilingual system of education (70 per cent Estonian to 30 per cent Russian) is being gradually phased in at upper secondary level (Grades 10–12, ages 16–19). One of the central arguments that Russian-speaking political representatives advance in favour of NTA is that it would allow Russian speakers to opt out of this system and maintain their own full system of native-language schooling, financed partly by state and municipal authorities and partly by the community itself.[41] Available evidence, however, suggests that the Russian-speaking society is divided over the way forward: many are seemingly willing to accept the transition to bilingualism, with the main point of debate relating to the speed at which the transformation should take place; other more uncompromising elements, meanwhile, have argued for preservation of the system inherited from the USSR, asking why, as taxpayers, they should not be entitled to educational provision solely under state auspices.[42] A further (very small) group would see NTA as offering insufficient recognition of Russian speakers' status within Estonia, and thus continues to argue for full territorial-political autonomy of the kind advocated by Soviet-era elites in Estonia's Russophone north-east during 1990–3.[43] In light of

[39] Aleksandr Aidarov and Wolfgang Drechsler, 'The Law and Economics of the Estonian Law on Cultural Autonomy for National Minorities and of Russian National Cultural Autonomy in Estonia', *Halduskultuur*, vol. 12, no. 1 (2011): pp. 43–61.

[40] Here Russian political representation is far more extensive than at the national level, since the local election of law of 1993 allows all permanent residents to vote in local elections and not just citizens of the state.

[41] Russkaia Kulturnaia Avtonomiia Estonii 2006 [Russian Cultural Autonomy of Estonia].

[42] E. Kekelidze, 'Eto budet estonskii variant' [It will be the Estonian Variant], *Estoniia* (1992).

[43] David J. Smith, 'Narva Region within the Estonian Republic: From Autonomism to Accommodation?', *Regional and Federal Studies*, vol. 12, no. 2 (2002): pp. 89–110; I. Oprichnin,

these divisions, numerous commentators (both ethnically Estonian and ethnically Russian) have questioned whether those advancing the NTA project are in fact genuinely representative of the minority in whose name they purport to speak, prompting claims that the Russian-speaking population is simply 'too large' to be accommodated by a framework of this kind, and that the scheme would serve only to introduce new lines of in-group division and dissension.[44]

7.6 NTA in the Russian Federation

If Estonian perceptions and experiences of NTA can be situated within what is essentially a modernist agenda of state and nation-building, the initial adoption of this model by the Russian Federation during the 1990s occurred within the context of an institutionally multinational state structure inherited from the USSR. Specifically, the 1996 National Cultural Autonomy (hereafter NCA) Act was introduced as part of a new conception of state national policy designed to strengthen 'multicultural constitutional patriotism'—an overarching civic conception of nationhood encompassing all inhabitants of the Federation.[45] In this respect, the existing model of ethno-territorial federalism inherited from the USSR was seen to have a number of limitations. First, as already noted above, this system was not seen to accommodate adequately all of the ethno-national groups within the population. A second issue, according to several authors, was a concern that territorial federalism might undermine the overall territorial integrity of the state. In August 1990 during his struggle with the Soviet leadership, Boris Yeltsin had famously invited Russia's national republics 'to take as much sovereignty as they could swallow'.[46] With a number of republican leaders taking Yeltsin at his word, the post-Soviet period saw the emergence of a separatist conflict in Chechnya and a constitutional dispute between the Federal Government and Tatarstan. Given the recent experience of the fall of the USSR, fears arose of a continued trend towards 'matrioshka nationalism' that might lead to the unravelling of the newly established Federation.[47] The overall picture that emerged in

'Chitatel' Delfi: kul'turnaia avtonomiia ne reshit problem' [Delfi Reader: Cultural Autonomy Will Not Solve the Problems], *Rus.delfi.ee*, 20 March 2011, http://journalist.delfi.ee/news/news/chitatel-delfi-kulturnaya-avtonomiya-ne-reshitproblem.d?id=42402895.

[44] See, for instance, 'Juhtkiri: Liiga suur, et olla autonoomne?' [Editorial: Too Big to Be Autonomous], *Eesti Päevaleht*, 29 December 2009. The perceived non-representative nature of the organization that originally advanced NTA in 2006 was cited as one of the key reasons for the state's rejection of the proposal. See 'MTÜ Vene Kultuuriautonoomia pöördus riigikohtusse' [Russian Cultural Autonomy NGO Turns to the Supreme Court], *Postimees*, 2 July 2010, http://www.postimees.ee/283338/print/mtu-vene-kultuuriautonoomia-poordus-riigikohtusse.

[45] Codagnone and Filippov, 'Equity, Exit and National Identity', p. 266.

[46] Christopher Marsh, *Unparalleled Reforms: China's Rise, Russia's Fall, and the Interdependence of Transition* (Lanham: Lexington Books, 2005), p. 55.

[47] Ray Taras, 'Conclusion: Making Sense of Matrioshka Nationalism', in *Nations and Politics in the Soviet Successor States*, edited by Ian Bremmer and Ray Taras (Cambridge: Cambridge University Press, 1993); Ray Taras, 'Conclusion: From Matrioshka Nationalism to National Interests', in

the 1990s was one of asymmetrical federalism, whereby local leaders indeed sought to grab as much power and resources as possible, to the detriment of overall state cohesion. There were also concerns over trends towards 'nationalizing' practices at the level of the national republics that might provoke local level horizontal conflicts between different ethnicities inhabiting these territories.

It was against this background that the new state conception and the NCA law were launched in June 1996. These were associated first and foremost with Valery Tishkov, academic expert on ethnicity and nationalism and Russian Federation Nationalities Minister during 1992. Tishkov never proposed the abolition of territorial autonomy: the 1996 conception made it plain that NCA was to be a complement to the system of national republics, the constitutional position of which remained unchanged. All the same, it was clearly hoped that NCA would serve as a counterbalance to the republics and thus help to limit from below the power of 'ethnocratic' elites within these territories. Overall, the conception was notable for its emphasis on consolidating 'a civic and spiritual-ethical community of all Russia' and its lack of any reference to the role of ethno-territorial autonomy in this regard.[48] Especially revealing in this regard is perhaps Yeltsin's address to the opening session of Russia's parliament in 1994, which asserted that 'no single ethnic group can possess an exclusive right to control over territory, political institutions, and resources'.[49]

Writing in 2000, Codagogne and Filipov claimed that the new state conception of nationality policy had been negatively received by leaders in many of the established territorial republics, who had portrayed this as a strategy of 'divide and rule' designed to promote a long-term policy of assimilation. In this regard, they asserted, republican leaders tried to draw a line of continuity back to the old Soviet-era rhetoric about 'fusion' of the USSR's manifold nationalities into a new 'Soviet people', portraying this as an overtly assimilationist rather than simply integrationist policy.[50] Yet the practical experience of NTA, both in the 1990s and subsequently, suggests that this view is in need of qualification. In the overwhelming majority of cases, existing territorially based authorities have not sought to block the establishment of national cultural autonomies (NCAs) within their territories; on the contrary, it seems that they have viewed this as a key means of bolstering their own legitimacy and power base at the regional level.[51] More broadly, it would seem that fears of continued territorial fragmentation and centre-periphery conflict within Russia were greatly exaggerated during the 1990s, and that Russia's 'stateness' has proved to be far more robust than many predicted at the outset.[52]

New States, New Politics: Building the Post-Soviet Nations, edited by Ian Bremmer and Ray Taras (Cambridge: Cambridge University Press, 1997).

[48] Codagnone and Filippov, 'Equity, Exit and National Identity', pp. 276–8.

[49] Codagnone and Filippov, 'Equity, Exit and National Identity', p. 274.

[50] Codagnone and Filippov, 'Equity, Exit and National Identity', p. 283.

[51] Alexander Osipov, 'National Cultural Autonomy in Russia: A Case of Symbolic Law', *Review of Central and East European Law*, no. 35 (2010): p. 45.

[52] Elise Giuliano and Dmitry Gorenburg, 'The Unexpectedly Underwhelming Role of Ethnicity in Russian Politics, 1991–2011', *Demokratizatsiya. The Journal of Post-Soviet Democratization*, vol. 20

A more salient issue with regard to NCA—and to Russia's 'multicultural constitutional patriotism' project more generally—concerns the growing centralization of state power over the course of the past decade and the prospect of increased pressure both from advocates of a unitary and ethnically neutral approach to state and nation-building and from more 'nationalizing' forces adhering to an overtly ethnic Russian conception of nationhood.[53] In light of these centralizing trends, Bill Bowring claimed in 2006 that, ten years on from the adoption of the NCA law, Russia was 'witnessing the end of a fascinating but doomed experiment'.[54]

This view would seem to require some qualification, in so far as the number of NCAs at various levels in Russia has continued to grow, from 504 in 2005 to 717 by January 2009.[55] There remains, however, the question of what practical, social, and political role NCAs actually perform within contemporary Russia. As Bowring has observed, the new bodies of NCA have possessed little in the way of actual powers and resources, to the extent that there was little if anything to differentiate them from pre-existing NGOs.[56] Alexander Osipov echoes this assessment in a more recent article, pointing to the 'puzzling' fact that there is so much demand to establish NCAs when they apparently do so little. Perhaps equally curious is the fact that few commentators, be they state officials, ethnic activists, or academics, have routinely drawn attention to the practical limitations of the NTA model, but have rather continued to discuss the issue in highly abstract terms. This state of affairs leads Osipov to the conclusion that NCA has a largely symbolic function within a Russian context that is still heavily shaped by ethnicized, 'groupist' understandings of political participation.[57] In the latter regard, Osipov suggests, NCA has served to divert attention away from issues of equality and non-discrimination, allowing the authorities to explain 'exclusion and conflicts in terms of cultural differences rather than institutional deficiencies and social deprivation'.[58]

(2012): pp. 175–88; Oleh Protsyk and Benedikt Harzl, eds, *Managing Ethnic Diversity in Russia* (Abingdon/New York: Routledge, 2012).

[53] Codagnone and Filippov, 'Equity, Exit and National Identity', p. 284; Hans Oversloot, 'The Homogeneity of Russia, or the Remains of an Empire (Federalism and Regionalism)', in *Managing Ethnic Diversity in Russia*, edited by Oleh Protsyk and Benedikt Harzl (Abingdon/New York: Routledge, 2012).

[54] Bill Bowring, 'The Tatars of the Russian Federation and National-Cultural Autonomy: A Contradiction in Terms?', in *Cultural Autonomy in Contemporary Europe*, edited by David J. Smith and Karl Cordell (London/New York: Routledge, 2008), p. 95.

[55] Osipov, 'National Cultural Autonomy in Russia', p. 42.

[56] Bill Bowring, 'Burial and Resurrection: Karl Renner's Controversial Influence on the "National Question" in Russia', in *National Cultural Autonomy and its Contemporary Critics*, edited by Ephraim Nimni (London: Routledge, 2005), p. 203.

[57] Osipov, 'National Cultural Autonomy in Russia', p. 54; Alexander Osipov, 'National-Cultural Autonomy in Russia: A Matter of Legal Regulation or the Symbolic Construction of an Ethnic Mosaic?', in *Managing Ethnic Diversity in Russia*, edited by Oleh Protsyk and Benedikt Harzl (Abingdon/New York: Routledge, 2012). See also Chapter 9 in this volume.

[58] Osipov, 'National Cultural Autonomy in Russia', p. 54.

7.7 Conclusions

The last two decades have seen the establishment across Central and Eastern Europe of various arrangements bearing the label of NTA. In the same period, international organizations engaged with the region have also referenced the NTA model as a potential mechanism both for regulating state–minority conflicts and for boosting minority participation in public life. Much of the existing literature on the topic, however, has adopted a normative standpoint, focusing on what could and should be done rather than on 'what actually exists', why it came into being and how NTA arrangements are understood and evaluated within the societies concerned.[59] This chapter has briefly examined the political strategies and practices that have driven the creation and informed the operation of relevant institutional frameworks in Hungary, Estonia, and Russia. It has further analysed the case of Romania, where vigorous debates around the NTA model have yet to give rise to actual legislation.

Of the various countries studied, it is Hungary that has the most comprehensive framework in place. The original law adopted in 1993 has twice been amended in line with external recommendations intended to boost the representativeness and effectiveness of minority self-governments. The self-government model has been widely embraced by minority activists, and yet questions remain regarding the actual capacity of these bodies to address issues of central concern to particular groups, especially in the case of the large and socially marginalized Roma minority. Ultimately, most authors concur that the NTA law was originally adopted with an eye not so much to the needs of domestic minorities, but rather to set an example which it was hoped might be replicated (on the basis partly of anticipated EU backing for the model) in neighbouring states containing sizeable ethnic Hungarian minorities. This strategy, however, raised the obvious question of whether those minorities themselves—not to mention the states in question—would embrace the NTA approach.

In the case of Serbia (largely beyond the scope of this chapter), NTA legislation has been developed as part of post-2000 processes of democratization, and this has been implemented by Hungarian activists operating within the framework of an autonomous and multicultural province of Vojvodina. In Romania, NTA has been advocated by the largest ethnic Hungarian political party (UDMR), which has sought to advance minority interests through participation in coalition government. It has, however, been difficult to build a broader consensus over this model amongst Hungarian minority activists. In this regard, political forces within the Hungarian elite have criticized the UDMR approach as overly accommodationist and have advanced their own further-reaching proposals for territorial autonomy based on the compactly Hungarian region of Szeklerland. In any event, political forces representing the Romanian majority have remained

59 Osipov, 'National Cultural Autonomy in Russia', p. 30.

opposed to any form of autonomy, which is still viewed in securitized terms, as a potential threat to the unitary character and integrity of the state as a whole.

Securitization of minority issues has also been a defining factor in the Estonian case, where the 1993 law on minority cultural autonomy has never developed beyond a loose and ill-defined framework. While this law has been utilized by activists belonging to the numerically small Finnish and Swedish minorities, the state has so far rejected attempts to initiate autonomy in the name of the much larger ethnic Russian population. In analysing the situation in Estonia, most authors see the 1993 law as having a mainly symbolic function, within an overall project of building a unitary nation state. Within this context, the relevance of autonomy has been questioned amongst Russian minority activists, who have focused their attentions on issues of citizenship and equality. Beyond this, there seems to be no underlying consensus regarding a framework of 'positive' rights for the Russian minority.

In the final case considered here—that of the Russian Federation—NTA appears to have been adopted as part of top-down initiatives designed to consolidate the post-Soviet political community and address imbalances and sub-state nationalizing trends arising from the inherited system of ethno-territorial federalism. In line with practices during the Soviet era, the framework of NCA has allowed for largely symbolic cultural recognition of minority cultures rather than structures geared to boosting minority representation and participation in public life. Seen in terms of its original objectives, however, the approach could be deemed as successful, in so far as NCA has been widely embraced by minority activists as well as local authorities within the various constituent republics of the Federation.

By way of overall conclusion, the various cases discussed in this chapter call to mind Aviel Roshwald's observation that pointing to the practicalities of NTA is one thing, winning the support of majorities and minorities quite another.[60] In assessing the potential applicability and viability of NTA as a model, attention clearly has to be paid to issues such as overall ethno-demographic composition of society, settlement patterns, and the degree of minority socio-political cohesion and actorness, as well as to the specific collective memory frames and institutional legacies governing each case.

These cases also bring into focus issues of representativeness, legitimacy and effectiveness of NTA bodies, and a key question raised by Osipov in relation to Russia, namely: why, if cultural autonomy has little practical impact or significance, have so many cultural self-governments been established? This 'puzzle' might also be seen as relevant in the case of Hungary. One explanation would be to point to the continued role of inherited communist (and pre-communist) institutional legacies in shaping the understandings of minority rights held by public officials and minority activists alike. By this reading, such rights are interpreted largely through the prism of culture and guaranteeing equal possibilities for the

[60] Roshwald, 'Between Balkanisation and Banalisation', p. 37.

development of all national *groups* (and the prevention of group-based conflicts), rather than through a western liberal paradigm stressing individual rights of representation and participation in the public sphere. In a post-communist context still shaped by informal practices, moreover, minority political entrepreneurs have seen establishment of autonomy bodies as a means of ensuring access to key officials and obtaining influence and funding, regardless of whether the body in question genuinely represents the wider community in whose name it purports to speak.

All of this suggests that in those states where it has been implemented on a significant scale, NTA has had a role in 'normalizing' the relationship between states and minorities and consolidating political community according to inherited principles implemented in a top-down manner. Such a state of affairs can hardly be seen as corresponding with the liberal understanding of minority rights currently promoted by European and Euro-Atlantic international organizations, although further comparative work is needed to ascertain more fully the roles performed by extant NTA bodies in different settings.[61] In the more 'nationalizing' state contexts of Romania and Estonia, meanwhile, multinational legacies arising from the communist past have been rejected and proposals for autonomy (at least in the case of larger, more mobilized minorities) viewed as inimical to the vision of constructing a unitary nation state. Against this background, it remains to be seen whether workable NTA arrangements could still be established as part of a longer-term convergence around the minority rights paradigm.

[61] In this regard, note the claim by Dobos, 'The Development and Functioning of Cultural Autonomy'—echoed by a later 2010 Council of Europe report—that Hungary's cultural autonomy law of 1993 has in fact significantly boosted minority representation and participation in public life.

8

Autonomy as Symbolic Production

The Case of Contemporary Russia

Alexander Osipov

8.1 Introduction

It is already common wisdom among academics and policymakers that autonomy can and must serve as a mechanism for the accommodation of ethnic or cultural diversity. This general view usually encapsulates three concepts: the notion of autonomy implies the existence of autonomous *entities*—structural units within systems of governance; for the purpose of resolving ethnic problems autonomous units must be *ethnicity-based*; and autonomous arrangements must be positioned with regard to *territory*—the entire debate on autonomy asserts the dichotomy of territorial and non-territorial autonomy (hereinafter TA and NTA accordingly).[1] These three components respectively beg at least three general questions. (1) What kinds of institutional settings can be regarded as autonomous entities given that all kinds of organizations have some degree of decision-making powers? (2) In what way do autonomous arrangements relate to ethnicity? (3) What kinds of linkages between territory and ethnicity allow us to qualify an autonomy arrangement as TA or NTA? Answers follow regularly from politicians and academia, and the common underpinning of most explanations either implies or explicitly states that autonomy means shaping a target ethnic 'community' or a combination of minority 'communities' as political or administrative units. Respectively, the debate rests on the assumption that ethnic groups can be regarded as cohesive social entities able to behave as a single actor. In other words, the debate is propelled by and structured around the tacit tendency to regard ethnicity as agency.

[1] Maria Ackrén, *Conditions for Different Autonomy Regimes in the World. A Fuzzy-Set Application* (Åbo: Åbo Akademis Förlag—Åbo Akademi University Press, 2009); Thomas Benedikter, *The World's Modern Autonomy Systems. Concepts and Experiences of Regional Territorial Autonomy* (Bozen/Bolzano: European Academy of Bozen/Bolzano, 2009); Hans-Joachim Heintze, 'On the Legal Understanding of Autonomy', in *Autonomy: Applications and Implications*, edited by Markku Suksi (The Hague/Boston: Kluwer Law International, 1998), pp. 7–32; Ruth Lapidoth, *Autonomy: Flexible Solutions to Ethnic Conflicts* (Washington, D.C.: United States Institute of Peace Press, 1997).

One may ask what happens if this core and rather arbitrary assumption is discarded. My suggestion here is to explore an alternative perspective for interpreting 'ethnic' and 'territorial' profiles of autonomous arrangements. The guiding principle here will be an interpretation of ethnicity as structure, or as merely socially acceptable systems of categorizations, which allow for framing administrative and political arrangements as related to or dissociated from ethnicity and territory. This approach will be tested here with empirical evidence from the Russian Federation. Russia is a country which has extensively employed notions of NTA and TA in its domestic politics and legislation over decades. Russia's predecessor, the Soviet Union (USSR) was founded on the idea of ethnicity-based federalism, and although official Soviet ideologists rejected the concept of NTA, similar ideas were in fact present in Soviet ideological developments and administrative arrangements.[2] Most importantly, the system has proved to be viable, stable, and legitimate in the eyes of the Russian public. In other words, this chapter is about the ways in which ethnic categorizations can be framed as autonomous arrangements and how ethnicity is discursively and institutionally linked to territory or decoupled from territory in legislation and public administration. The core question here is whether the analysis requires such assumptions regarding autonomous arrangements as organizations embodying collective ethnic agencies.

8.2 TA and NTA—Organizational Models or Discursive Frames?

NTA is interpreted in a multiplicity of ways in scholarly publications and political statements. They can be lumped in three major categories: (1) activities pursued on behalf of an ethnic group for the sake of preserving and expressing ethnic identity in a variety of organizational forms;[3] (2) the special shaping of an organization on ethnic grounds;[4] or (3) the endowment of the said organizations with public

[2] Dina Amanzholova, *Formatirovaniye sovetskosti: Natsionalnye menshinstva v ethncopoliticheskom landshafte SSSR. 1920–1930-t gg* [The Formatting of the Sovietness: National Minorities in the Ethnopolitical Landscape of the USSR. 1920–1930s] (Moscow: Sobraniye, 2010); Vadim Musaev, 'Kul'turnaya avtonomiya kak sredstvo razresheniya natsional'nyh problem: istoriya i perspektivy' [Cultural Autonomy as a Means of Resolving National Problems: History and Prospects], in *Perekrestok kul'tur: mezhdisciplinarnye issledovaniya v oblasti gumanitarnyh nauk* (Moscow: Logos, 2004), pp. 95–7; Alexander Osipov, *Natsional'no-kul'turnaia avtonomiia: idei, resheniia, instituty* [National-Cultural Autonomy: Ideas, Decisions, Institutions] (St. Petersburg: Tsentr nezavisimykh sotsiologicheskikh issledovanii, 2004), pp. 45–54.

[3] Brendan O'Leary, 'The Logics of Power-Sharing, Consociation and Pluralist Federations', in *Settling Self-Determination Disputes: Complex Power-Sharing in Theory and Practice*, edited by Barbara Metzger, Marc Weller, and Niall Johnson (Leiden: Martinus Nijhoff Publishers, 2008), pp. 47, 54–5; Heintze, 'On the Legal Understanding of Autonomy', pp. 15–16.

[4] Christopher Decker, 'Contemporary Forms of Cultural Autonomy in Eastern Europe: Recurrent Problems and Prospects for Improving the Functioning of Elected Bodies of Cultural Autonomy', in *The Participation of Minorities in Public Life* (Strasbourg: Council of Europe Publishing, 2008), pp. 89–90; Yash Ghai, 'Ethnicity and Autonomy: A Framework for Analysis', in *Autonomy and Ethnicity: Negotiating Competing Claims in Multi-ethnic States*, edited by Yash Ghai (Cambridge/

functions or competences.[5] The three categories or framework approaches (which partly overlap) share the same common assumption that ethnic groups are building blocks of governance, but prioritize different aspects of their incorporation. In the first instance, the emphasis is placed on the *fundamental* recognition of ethnic groups as collective agencies and thus quasi-polities as such regardless of the organizational framework. In the second case, the focal issue is on the *organizing* of an ethnicity in a corporate-type body able to reflect the group's interest and will within an electoral system. In the third case, the focal issue is on the *functioning* of ethnicity-based organizational settings as public bodies. But if the framework approach to NTA as an embodiment of group agency is rejected, then the entire concept becomes superfluous. Although the ethnic profile of autonomy arrangements can be explained and justified (because of the goals, functions, or membership principles of the respective settings), the term 'autonomy' begs questions since a clear and uniform explanation of what kinds of entities deserve 'autonomous' status and for what reasons is fully lacking in this context. The adjective 'non-territorial' as well as other related terms such as 'cultural', personal', or 'functional' also lack clarity and uniformity in utilization. The usage of the word 'non-territorial' means the opposition of NTA to TA, and this implies that the understanding of TA is fully clear; while (as described in section 8.5) this may be equally nebulous.

In practical terms, NTA quite often means unnecessary multiplication of entities, that is, tagging (done by involved policymakers as well as external observers) segregated organizational settings or various forms of ethnic activism as 'autonomy' although these phenomena can be adequately described without resorting to this terminology. Over the last hundred years there have been very few workable models in terms of corporate-type bodies formed on ethnic basis. One should rather talk about implementation of individual elements of the framework concept, such as publicly elected coordinative councils of individual ethnic groups or delegation of public functions in education and of respective resources to private organizations. Another development is failure of practical implementation, that is, situations when the autonomy arrangement on paper does not work out in reality as expected. For example, the statehood of Cyprus based on parallel coexistence of self-governing Greek and Turkish communities collapsed in two and a half years after its inception in 1960.[6] Obstacles on NTA's way to practical implementation are numerous and unrelated to this chapter's main content. I will

New York: Cambridge University Press, 2000), p. 8; Benedikter, 'On the Legal Understanding of Autonomy', pp. 39–40.

5 Tove H. Malloy, 'The Lund Recommendations and Non-Territorial Arrangements: Progressive De-territorialization of Minority Politics', *International Journal on Minority and Group Rights*, vol. 16, no. 4 (2009): pp. 665–79; Markku Suksi, 'Personal Autonomy as Institutional Form—Focus on Europe Against the Background of Article 27 of the ICCPR', *International Journal on Minority and Group Rights*, vol. 15, nos 2–3 (2008): pp. 157–78.

6 Reed Coughlan, 'Cyprus: From Corporate Autonomy to the Search for Territorial Federalism', in *Autonomy and Ethnicity: Negotiating Competing Claims in Multi-ethnic States*, edited by Yash Ghai (Cambridge/New York: Cambridge University Press, 2000), pp. 219–41; Albert F. Reiterer, *Cyprus: Case Study about a Failure of Ethno-National Understanding* (Frankfurt am Main/New York, NY: Lang, 2003).

point out just one: there is an inherent contradiction between the basic idea of segregated ethnicity-based institutions, on the one hand, and lacking guarantees of their financial self-sufficiency and thus the need (inevitably controversial and contestable) for the distribution of public resources, on the other.[7]

TA is usually described as a quasi-statehood or political community based on ethnic majority within the respective territory and thus a form of a specific ethnicity's organization.[8] This view reflects rather a normative than a descriptive or analytical approach and too often contradicts empirical realities. TA is not something self-evident and uniform; territorial arrangements take place in territories with a different demographic composition and not necessarily with a core ethnic majority. In practice entities referred to as TA or in a similar way differ because of rationales behind their establishment (self-determination of the core group, prevention of conflicts, respect for historical legacies, optimization of governance, etc.), forms of justification (formal or informal, explicit or implicit) or of beneficiaries (TA may be established on behalf of a concrete ethnic group or for creating a certain mode of governance in a multi-ethnic region), and so forth.

In general, both TA and NTA as concepts for arrangements involving ethnicity also beg the question about what the linkage between ethnicity and territory or decoupling of ethnicity and territory may mean. The multiplicity of ways TA and NTA are formed, named, interpreted, and justified makes this question not easy to answer. If NTA is understood as an organization of an ethnic group and as such opposed to TA, then the term NTA makes sense if TA is also interpreted as organization of a single designated ethnicity. However, the latter model would be in conflict with empirical realities. If TA refers to accommodation of ethnic diversity in multiple ways and not necessarily through privileging one core ethnicity, then the term NTA becomes meaningless because in all three major interpretations of NTA the linkage with territory or administrative divisions is irrelevant for the very essence of the concept.

8.3 Symbolic Policies as Production of Meanings

Everything falls in place, when NTA and TA are regarded as practical categories with multiple and shifting meanings. In this perspective, TA and NTA will not necessarily have one 'true' interpretation each independent of the context, which in concrete situations may serve as framing the reality in certain ways and for the delivery of various messages to target audiences. Also needless to say, both NTA and TA can be implemented in practice (or non-implemented because of failure or imitation) in a variety of ways, and the outcomes can be explained by different actors through an array of arguments.

[7] For more on contradictions of NTA see Rainer Bauböck, 'Territorial or Cultural Autonomy for National Minorities?', in *The Politics of Belonging: Nationalism, Liberalism and Pluralism*, edited by Alain Dieckhoff (Lanham, MD: Lexington Books, 2004), pp. 221–58.

[8] Benedikter, 'On the Legal Understanding of Autonomy'; Lapidoth, *Autonomy*.

Respectively, both concepts may be approached as denominators for two areas of discourse, political as well as legal and administrative solutions. The relevant research task would be a study of how different interpretations of autonomy emerge and evolve in concrete circumstances and what kinds of practical impacts they generate. This chapter suggests testing through a case study the hypothesis that autonomy arrangements as practice are independent of their alleged 'objective' ethnic fundamentals or group agency.

Furthermore, the symbolic and discursive dimension of autonomous arrangements (termed 'talks' by Nils Brunsson[9]) may be regarded as an area independent from 'actions', that is, activities entailing direct practical consequences. This analytical perspective allows for examining the interrelation of the so-called 'symbolic' and 'instrumental' policies. Symbolic policies can be conceptualized as a sphere where publicly relevant narratives and meanings are produced while instrumental policies are actions resulting in enforcement of concrete strategies and decisions. Instrumental policies are viewed as activities having 'resource effects' while 'symbolic' policies have 'interpretative' ones.[10] There is no clear division between the two spheres: rhetoric can be open to different interpretations while actions may have a symbolic meaning or do not necessarily embody the related rhetoric.[11] By no means can symbolic policy be interpreted as a fiction or camouflage unrelated to 'real' policy; although it does not have a direct substantive effect, by creating and imposing meanings and interpretations as well as forming and channelling public claims and expectations, it indirectly shapes the political action.[12] In fact, by generating a legitimate world view, symbolic policy turns out to be a tool of hegemony.[13] One can assume that the disjuncture between symbolic and instrumental policies may manifest itself in two forms. The first one is the phenomenon of 'systemic hypocrisy',[14] that is, discrepancy between public representation of an organization (a government in particular) and its actual functions. The difference between systemic hypocrisy, on the one hand, and merely intended or unintended incoherence in performances, on the other, is that a certain kind of rhetoric is employed to camouflage and substitute activities completely different in purpose and direction. The second phenomenon can be called hidden transcript,[15] or avoidance of explicit narrations on certain issues

[9] Neil Brunsson, *The Organization of Hypocrisy. Talk, Decisions and Actions in Organizations* (Chichester, NY: John Wiley & Sons, 1989).

[10] Anne L. Schneider and Helen Ingram, *Policy Design for Democracy* (Lawrence: University Press of Kansas, 1997), pp. 206–7.

[11] Thomas A. Birkland, *An Introduction to the Policy Process: Theories, Concepts, and Models of Public Policy Making* (Armonk, NY: M. E. Sharpe, 2005); Schneider and Ingram, *Policy Design for Democracy.*

[12] Murray Edelman, *Politics as Symbolic Action. Mass Arousal and Quiescence* (Chicago: Markham Publishing Company, 1971), pp. 7–45.

[13] Antonio Gramsci, *Selections from the Prison Notebooks* (New York: International Publishers, 1971).

[14] Brunsson, *The Organization of Hypocrisy.*

[15] James C. Scott, *Domination and the Arts of Resistance: Hidden Transcripts* (New Haven, CT: Yale University Press, 1990).

in the set-up of public representation. In other words, representational components or 'talks' are shaped and designed in a way to increase their discursive appropriateness and the degree of their compliance with public expectations. 'Hidden transcript' often appears as a part of 'officialization' (as termed by Bourdieu), that is, a process that includes beyond recognition and acceptance of a rule also 'a public declaration of reverence for the group and for the self-representation it presents to others and to itself'.[16] Officialization requires a certain level of simplification and distortion of the social knowledge; a certain degree of ignorance turns out to be a precondition for non-conflictual existence in a complex social environment. The guidelines through which people can navigate in the social world must be consistent and based on a coherent world view, and this requires bracketing out certain information that does not fit in the dominant interpretation, or in other words, substituting the objective relations with acceptable subjective images.[17] The 'talks' and 'actions' of autonomy offer a good opportunity for studying the interplay between symbolic and instrumental policies since both notions, NTA and TA, are open to numerous interpretations and allow for multiple strategies of implementation and justifications.

8.4 National Cultural Autonomy in Russia: De-Territorialization of Ethnicity?

The very idea of NTA goes back to the European liberal and socialist thought of the late nineteenth century.[18] NTA labelled as 'personal' or 'cultural' autonomy was a topical issue in the early twentieth-century discussions on the left of Russia's political spectrum; the idea was vigorously rejected by the communist rulers, but reconsidered and extensively debated in the 1980s and 1990s. The notion of NCA was introduced into Russia's legislation in the aftermath of the USSR's breakdown; the basic act determining the respective policies—the Federal Law 'On National-Cultural Autonomy' (hereinafter, 'the NCA Law') was adopted in 1996.[19] NTA and related terms have acquired popularity and are widely used in Russian legislation as well as in official, academic, and popular discourses.

16 Pierre Bourdieu, 'A Paradoxical Foundation of Ethics', in *Practical Reason. On the Theory of Action* (Stanford, CA: Stanford University Press, 1998), p. 141.

17 Pierre Bourdieu, *The Logic of Practice* (Stanford, CA: Stanford University Press, 1990), pp. 108–9.

18 [Karl Renner] Synopticus (pen name), *Staat und Nation* (Wien: Dietl, 1899). Reprinted as Karl Renner, 'State and Nation', in *National-Cultural Autonomy and its Contemporary Critics*, edited by Ephraim Nimni (London/New York: Routledge, 2005), pp. 15–47; Otto Bauer, *The Question of Nationalities and Social Democracy* [Nationalitätenfrage und die Sozialdemokratie] with an introduction by Ephraim Nimni and preface by Heinz Fischer (Minneapolis: University of Minnesota Press, 2000); Asbjørn Eide, Vibeke Greni, and Maria Lundberg, 'Cultural Autonomy: Concept, Content, History and Role in the World Order', in *Autonomy: Applications and Implications*, edited by Markku Suksi (The Hague/Boston: Kluwer Law International, 1998), pp. 251–76.

19 Federal'nyi zakon 'O natsional'no-kul'turnoi avtonomii' [Federal Law 'On National-Cultural Autonomy'] (with subsequent amendments), No. 74-FZ from 17 June 1996.

The term 'autonomy' in connection with NCA has acquired two basic and interchangeable meanings in Russian domestic law.[20] Firstly, one refers to a general principle by which individuals use various institutional formats to collectively pursue their rights and interests related to their ethnic origin, language, and culture; secondly, it indicates a specific form of ethnicity-based non-governmental organization (hereinafter NGO). In sum, NCA is interpreted as an entity on a par with being a general principle. Clearly it is regarded as an ethnic organization; and it is often referred to with such adjectives as 'non-territorial' or even 'exterritorial'.[21]

From this angle, the answers to the three basic questions put forward at the beginning of this chapter—why autonomy? why ethnic? why non-territorial?—look simple if not self-evident. 'Autonomy' relates to autonomous agency of ethnic groups or implies a corporate bearer of specific functions or competences. In a formal sense, the non-territoriality of NCA is explicitly underlined in the legislation and multiple official policy statements. The NCA Law stipulates that 'the right to national-cultural autonomy does not amount to the right to national-territorial self-determination' (art 4). The Concept of the Nationalities Policy in the Russian Federation,[22] which was approved by a presidential decree in 1996 and which until 2012 served as a conceptual guideline for public authorities, refers to NCA as a form of cultural self-determination for dispersed ethnicities and also as an 'exterritorial public formation'. The Strategy approved by the presidential decree as a replacement for the 1996 Concept refers to NCA as one of two modes (on a par with federalism) of diversity policies and also mentions that NCA as a civil society institution provides for the enjoyment of ethnocultural rights regardless of citizens' place of residence.[23]

A deeper analysis reveals, however, a limited instrumental value of NCAs, and this puts under question the relevance of the term 'autonomy'.[24] An 'ordinary' non-profit NGO (which may also be ethnicity-based), while enjoying all the rights that NCAs are endowed with (including rights in the spheres of culture,

[20] Alexander Osipov, 'National Cultural Autonomy in Russia: A Case of Symbolic Law', *Review of Central and East European Law*, vol. 35, no.1 (2010): pp. 27–57; Valerii Stepanov, 'Natsional'no-kul'turnaia avtonomiia v Rossii kak ideia i pravovaia norma' [National-Cultural Autonomy in Russia as an Idea and a Legal Norm], in *Pravovye aspekty etnicheskih otnoshenii v Rossii* [Legal Aspects of Ethnic Relations in Russia] (Moscow: Delovaia Stolitsa, 2004), pp. 91–117; Nicky Torode, 'National Cultural Autonomy in the Russian Federation: Implementation and Impact', *International Journal on Minority and Group Rights*, vol. 15, nos 2–3 (2008): pp. 179–93.

[21] Vladimir Yu. Zorin, 'Razmyshleniya o natsionalino-kulturnoi avtonomii' [Considerations on National-Cultural Autonomy], *Zhisn' Natsional'nostei*, no. 3 (2010): p. 59.

[22] Kontseptsiia Natsional'noi Politiki Rossiiskoi Federatsii [Conceptual Outline of the Nationalities Policy of the Russian Federation], Ukaz Presidenta No. 909 ot 15 iyunia 1996 goda [President's Decree No. 909 of 15 June 1996].

[23] Strategiya gosugarstvennoi natsionalnoi politiki na period do 2025 goda [Strategy of State Nationalities Policy for the Period to 2025], Ukaz Presidenta No. 1666 ot 19 Dekabria 2012 goda [President's Decree No. 1666 of 19 December 2012].

[24] Alexander Osipov, 'National-Cultural Autonomy in Russia: A Matter of Legal Regulation or the Symbolic Construction of an Ethnic Mosaic?', in *Managing Ethnic Diversity in Russia*, edited by Benedikt Harzl and Oleh Protsyk (New York: Routledge, 2012), pp. 62–84.

mass media, and education), has advantages vis-à-vis NCAs because 'autonomies' (a) enjoy fewer rights than ordinary public associations; (b) cannot choose their organizational forms; and (c) face numerous procedural restrictions with respect to their establishment and operation. The NCA Law contains an exhaustive list of permissible activities (art 1) exclusively in the spheres of language, culture, and education. The rights granted to NCAs (art 4) are explicitly limited to a few spheres, such as preservation of identities, promotion of the language, education, and national (ethnic) culture, strengthening the unity of the Russian nation, harmonization of interethnic relations, facilitation of inter-religious dialogue, and adaptation of migrants,[25] while such a specification of permissible activities is absent in the general laws on non-profit organizations. The 2003 amendments to the NCA Law prescribe only one institutional shape based on registered individual membership, while less burdensome and more flexible forms have been excluded. The creation and maintenance of an NCA is more complex in comparison with other kinds of NGOs,[26] and this makes NCAs vulnerable (more than other NGOs) to control and interference of registering and supervisory authorities.

There is no specific obligation for the government to provide funding for NCAs, and the NCA Law fails to identify specific mechanisms and criteria for funding allocation or authorize specific government bodies to make funding decisions. In fact, the legislation on public associations and non-profit organizations in theory offers ordinary non-profit organizations more forms and grounds on which to request state support. NCAs are financed from public resources on an ad hoc and irregular basis, and there have not been any motions to delegate to NCAs functions or competences with respect to cultural activities or education. In fact there have been only a few limited attempts to treat NCAs differently (in practical, but not symbolic terms) from other NGOs.

The establishment and functioning of NCAs are strictly linked to administrative-territorial divisions of the country, and in this sense can hardly be considered 'exterritorial.' NCAs can be local, regional (created within a federation unit), pan-Russian, or federal. A local NCA can be set up only within a municipal unit (according to art 6 of the NCA Law). The founders of a local NCA can be either physical persons permanently resident (i.e. administratively registered) within the given territory or ethnicity-based NGOs also having registration in the same territorial unit. Local NCAs can establish a regional organization, and subsequently regional NCAs can form the federal one. Last, but not least is that activities of an NCA as well as of any other NGO are allowed only within the administrative territory where the respective organization is registered.

A more important question arises then as to why the concept looks so attractive to ethnic activists, although NCA is neither an 'autonomy arrangement' different in a positive sense from ordinary NGOs nor a non-territorial entity. Despite

[25] The last four items were added in November 2014.
[26] Osipov, 'National Cultural Autonomy in Russia', pp. 39–42.

legislative restrictions and bureaucratic burdens, the number of NCAs has grown over the years. By early 1999, 227 NCAs had been registered, of which 160 were local, 60 regional, and 7 federal.[27] On 1 April 2010, there were 759 organizations, of which 532 were local, 210 regional, and 17 federal; by June 2014 the total number of registered NCAs reached 1,025 throughout the country, of them 753 local, 256 regional, and 16 federal.[28] NCAs represent around sixty ethnicities including ethnic Russians, even in the regions where Russians constitute the majority, as well as groups traditionally deemed to be sub-ethnic or ethnographic categories.

NCAs coexist with other, more numerous, ethnicity-based NGOs, and the models of coexistence vary. In practice, NCAs like all other ethnocultural NGOs are preoccupied primarily with folk arts. Few engage in long-term projects related to education, research, mass media, public advocacy, or inter-regional ties.[29] Nevertheless, the contradictions in and around the law drew no public attention and brought about no public protests or criticisms. Official spokespersons, ethnic activists, and academics basically pay attention to abstract issues (like which groups should be entitled to create NCAs) and neglect practically relevant problems such as NCAs rights and procedures of establishment. Ethnic activists en masse do not demonstrate any kind of objection to the fundamentals of the ideology of NCA as the government formulates it; their criticism does not go beyond mere requests for some public funding.

8.5 Ethnic Federalism: Territorialization of Ethnicity?

If a national cultural autonomy has not been set up by law as a public body and its 'non-territorial' status remained obscure, it would be logical to look at TA or territorial settings to which NCA is juxtaposed in the Russian public discourse. In terms of law, territorialization of ethnicity in the Russian Federation has little to do with autonomy. Only a part of Russia's constituent regions are referred to as 'autonomous' entities, namely four autonomous districts (*okrugs*) and one (Jewish) autonomous province (*oblast*). These units are constituent parts of the federation equal with other types of regions, and the adjective 'autonomy' should be understood rather as a legacy in historical terms.[30] A common assumption taken by

[27] Vladimir Zorin, 'Etnopoliticheskii faktor v razvitii rossiiskogo federalizma: opyt zakonotvorchestva' [Ethnopolitical Factor in the Development of Russian Federalism: the Experience of Law-Making], *Etnopanorama*, 1, no. 2 (1999): p. 16.

[28] According to the data placed on the Ministry of Justice official website—http://unro.minjust.ru/NKAs.aspx.

[29] For an overview, see Vladimir Mukomel, *Natsional'nye men'shinstva. Pravovye osnovy i praktika obespecheniia prav lits, prinadlezhashchikh k natsional'nym men'shinstvam, v sub'ektakh Iuga Rossiiskoi Federatsii* [National Minorities. Legal Fundamentals and Practices of Securing the Rights of Persons Belonging to National Minorities in the Subjects of the Russian Federation] (Moscow: CEPRI, 2003); Osipov, *Natsional'no-kul'turnaia avtonomiia*, pp. 161–224.

[30] Alexei Shatilov, 'Avtonomiya—poniatiye, soderzhaniye, vidy' [Autonomy—The Notion, Meaning, Types], *Pravo i Zhizn'*, no. 38 (2001): pp. 75–84.

default is that the Russian Federation is built on two principles, namely the territorial and 'national-territorial' (i.e. ethnicity-based) ones. Twenty-one republics, the Jewish autonomous *oblast* and four autonomous *okrugs* are believed to be 'national', that is, ethnicity-based entities while forty-six provinces (*oblasts*), nine territories (*krais*) and two federal cities are regarded as purely territorial units.[31] If we examine the scholarly literature on Soviet and Russian federalism, we can see that most territorial units are regarded as the 'property' of, or a form of organization for one or more ethnic groups. The latter are informally referred to as 'titular nations', that is, eponymic nationalities that gave their names to the respective territorial entities. It should be noted that, according to the 2010 Census, in twelve out of the twenty-one constituent republics as well as in the autonomous *oblast* and all autonomous *okrugs* of the Russian Federation, the 'titular' ethnic group does not constitute the majority of the local population.

Federalism is traditionally considered the basis of and an area of prime concern to Soviet and later Russian nationalities policy. Moreover, it is widely believed that Russian federalism grants a special status to, and bestows special advantages on, the 'titular nationalities,' thus creating a formal hierarchy of ethnic communities. However, it would be appropriate to scrutinize how these perceptions are enshrined in the existing legislation and institutional settings. In a strictly formal sense, the idea of ethnicity-based federalism and TA started to be institutionalized with the Bolshevik takeover in 1917. The Declaration of the Rights of Working and Exploited People, adopted on 12 January 1918 at the III Congress of Soviets (at that time the Congress formally constituted the supreme body of power), stipulated in its Article 1(2) that the Russian Soviet Republic constituted a 'free union of free nations as the federation of Soviet national republics' (*natsionalnykh respublik*). In July 1918, the Declaration was incorporated into the first Constitution of the Russian Soviet Federative Socialist Republic (RSFSR) as its Chapter I. All subsequent Soviet constitutional acts were less straightforward. The USSR Constitutions of 1924 and 1936 did not imply that the union republics amounted to 'national states' and autonomous territorial units as ethnic entities, nor did the constitutions of the union republics. The USSR Constitution of 1977 did not describe the union republics and autonomies as 'national states'. The same vagueness and ambiguity mark the sectoral legislation. The RSFSR Law 'On the Autonomous *Okrugs* of the RSFSR' enacted in 1980, made no reference to the 'ethnic' character of these territories. Neither did the five laws on the status of autonomous *oblasts* of Russia (1981) mention the 'ethnic' status of these regions.

From the perspective of constitutional law and ordinary legislation, the 'ethnic' statehood of Soviet republics and autonomies was rather a figure of speech. In institutional terms, 'national territorial structure' served as a vehicle of economic modernization and Sovietization which included levelling of social and economic positions of different ethnicities and regions as well as creation of

[31] The Republic of Crimea and the city of Sevastopol, illegally occupied and annexed by the Russian Federation in February–March 2014, are not counted here.

some institutions of nation statehood.[32] The concept of 'nationality statehood', although virtually absent in the legislation, was unanimously acknowledged in multiple publications and statements of the communist party ideologists and scholars, particularly lawyers; for all of them there was no doubt that Soviet federalism was ethnicity-based, and that it was its main substantive feature.[33] In legal terms a landmark was the USSR Law 'On the Free National Development of the USSR Citizens Residing outside their Own National-State Unit or not Possessing Such Units on the Territory of the USSR' of 26 April 1990. For the first time the law clearly (albeit indirectly) linked ethnicity and statehood by referring to 'citizens residing outside their own national-state units, or not possessing such units.'

In the aftermath of the USSR's breakdown this situation remained basically unchanged. The Russian Constitution of 1993 contains the terms 'multi-national people' and 'peoples' in multiple meanings. The Constitution does not define the units of federation as 'ethnic' entities, while the current legislation addresses this issue vaguely and indirectly. A few laws, including the Fundamentals of the Legislation on Culture, the Law on Languages, the Law on Education, and the Federal Law on National-Cultural Autonomy, mention 'citizens living outside their nation-state and nation-territorial entities'[34] and 'ethnic communities with a corresponding republic, autonomous *okrug*, autonomous *oblast*'.[35] Such provisions imply a connection between specific ethnic communities and specific federation units, but fail to define the nature and the legal content of this connection. Beyond these formulations, the Russian federal legislation does not establish territorial units as a form of organization for certain ethnic groups. No references to ethnicity can be found in the basic laws concerning the structure of the federation and the division of powers adopted in 1999–2001. The same is true of the Federal Constitutional Law 'On the Creation within the Russian Federation of the New Subject as a Result of Merger of Perm *Oblast* and the Komi-Permyak Autonomous *Okrug*' of 25 March 2004.[36]

At the regional level, constitutions and charters of republics and autonomous *okrugs* often contain ambiguous provisions. They fail either to mention the 'titular' groups altogether, or to speak about 'self-determination of the titular nation.' Instead, they state that the entire population is the source of political

[32] Ronald Suny, *The Revenge of the Past: Nationalism, Revolution, and the Collapse of the Soviet Union* (Stanford: Stanford University Press, 1993); Walker Connor, *The National Question in Marxist-Leninist Theory and Strategy* (Princeton, NJ: Princeton University Press, 1984); Terry Martin. *The Affirmative Action Empire: Nations and Nationalism in the Soviet Union, 1923–1939* (Ithaca, NY: Cornell University Press, 2001).

[33] Alexei Lepeshkin et al., *Kurs sovetskogo gosugarstvennogo prava* [Course of the Soviet State Law], vol. 2 (Moscow: Gosyurizdat, 1962), p. 166.

[34] See for example Zakon RF 'O yazykakh narodov Rossiiskoi Federatsii' [Law of the Russian Federation 'On Languages of the Peoples of the Russian Federation'] (with subsequent amendments) No. 1807-1 from 25 October 1991, *Vestnik SND i VS RSFSR*, No. 50 (1991), item 1740.

[35] Federal'nyi zakon 'O natsional'no-kul'turnoi avtonomii'.

[36] *SZFR*, No. 13 (2004), item 1110.

power, or otherwise emphasize a special role reserved to the 'titular' group without reference to government. For example, the 1994 Constitution of Buryatia declares that 'the multi-national people is the holder of statehood and the source of [political] power in Buryatia' (art 3, part 1), and at the same time that 'the Republic of Buryatia, established to realize the right of the Buryat nation to self-determination, protects the interests of the entire multi-national people of Buryatia' (art 60, part 1).[37] The Constitution of Yakutia (Sakha) (eastern Siberia) uses the term 'national-state status' [of the Republic] (Chapter 3), but declares that the Republic's people consisting of citizens of all nationalities is the source of state power and that no one segment of the population can usurp the right to exercise it (art 1, part 4). Regional laws do not contain more specific definitions. Moreover, regions are not allowed to establish any special legal treatment of any group because only the federation, and not its subjects, is authorized to regulate issues of human rights and civil liberties.

According to some regional constitutions and charters, the government is obliged to support the language and culture of certain groups; this obligation can hardly be regarded as a sign of 'ethnic' statehood. Firstly, such provisions appear in the constitutions and charters of some constituent republics and autonomous *okrugs*, but not in others; secondly, charters and laws of some regions other than republics and 'autonomies' also refer to the specific role of certain ethnicities or contain pledges to support their cultures and customs. For example, Article 2, part 1 of the Charter of Krasnodar territory (*krai*) defines the region as the historical territory of Cossacks and a place where Russians constitute a majority. All charters of the autonomous *okrugs* contain provisions concerning indigenous peoples; similar formulations appear in the Charters of Kemerovo and some other *oblasts*. However, unlike the *oblasts*, autonomous *okrugs* are widely perceived as 'ethnic' statehoods.

In all but one constituent republic (Karelia), the languages of 'titular' ethnic groups are declared state languages, alongside the Russian language, as provided by Article 68, part 2 of the Russian Constitution. The republics are entitled to establish their own state languages while the other constituent units are not. However, the latter have the right to provide legal support to local languages with a similar effect, and some autonomous *okrugs* do this. Besides, in some cases official status is granted to languages of groups other than the 'titular' ethnicity. For example, in Karachayevo-Cherkessia five, and in Dagestan all local languages are formally acknowledged as state languages. In fact, governments in constituent republics repeatedly grant preferences to 'titular' nationalities. This may include symbolic recognition of a special role played by 'titular' groups, or an official status for local languages and support of their public use, as well as funding of cultural and educational institutions. In addition, a number of republics (primarily Tatarstan, Bashkortostan, Chuvashia, and Mordovia) provide some support to cultural projects and institutions serving their 'titular' nationalities living outside

[37] Quoted from the official legal database *Garant*, available at www.constitution.garant.ru.

'their' republics. The issue at stake here is how 'ethnic statehood' of the republics, the autonomous *oblast* and autonomous *okrugs* is set up in the legislation, and what it means in institutional terms. The general answer would be the lack of a clear correlation between the legal fundamentals of the republics, the autonomous *oblasts* and *okrugs*, and their respective domestic policies. As such, the legal status of an 'ethnic' entity does not determine the extent and nature of protection it offers its 'titular' ethnic group or groups.

One may also ask how the links between territory and ethnicity in the framework of TA in Russia correspond with de-territorialization of ethnicity in the framework of NTA. The question may sound odd from a legal perspective since the Russian republics and other supposedly 'ethnic' territorial entities are statehoods while NCAs are merely NGOs with limited entitlements and capacities. In the framework of political and scholarly debates, the very idea of NCA has been explained and justified as an alternative to territorialized ethnicity, a remedy for ethnic rivalries over territories. This is done in very general terms and as a rule without further specification. No federal governmental official or policymaker has ever suggested a strategy of lifting territorial institutionalization of ethnicity and dissembling ethnic federalism; on the contrary, all have clearly denied such a possibility. Vladimir Zorin, chair of the State Duma Nationalities Committee (1996–9) and the state minister in charge of nationalities affairs (2001–4), often said that NCA would never replace ethnic territorial federalism but that it could prevent further claims to create new ethnic territorial autonomies.[38] More often, experts and policymakers comment on NCA as a supplement to ethnic federalism, and this means separation between those ethnicities, which symbolically possess 'their own' administrative units, and the rest. The former are not allowed to establish NCAs while the latter can channel their activities into NCA but not territorial claims. This dichotomy of TA and NTA makes little if any practical sense: most ethnicities are numerical minorities all over the country; all territorial units are subject to the same over-centralized and homogenizing policies; NGOs, including NCAs, are under a strict control and have limited capacities by definition.[39] Thus, they are incomparable with federation units.

[38] 'Derzhava. Dostoinstvo. Dostatok. Interv'iu s predsedatelem Komiteta Gosudarstvennoi Dumy Rossiiskoi Federatsii po delam natsional'nostei V. Yu. Zorinym' [Country. Dignity. Wealth. Interview with the Chair of the Nationalities Committee of the State Duma of the Russian Federation V. Yu. Zorin], *Zhizn' Natsional'nostei*, no. 6 (1996), p. 12; Vladimir Zorin, *Dnevnik ne dlia sebia—Kn.2: Strasti Okhotnogo riada* [A Diary for Myself; Book 2—Passions of Okhotny Ryad] (Moscow: Violanta, 1999), p. 265; Vladimir Zorin, 'Federalizm—nashe istoricheskoe budushchee' [Federalism is Our Historic Future], *Budushchee federalizma v Rossii: Rossiia i Respublika Bashkortostan. Materialy mezhregional'noi nauchno-prakticheskoi konferentsii* [The Future of Federalism in Russia: Russia and the Republic of Bashkortostan. Proceedings of the Inter-regional Scientific—Practical Conference] (Ufa: Institut povysheniia kvalifikatsii pri Administratsii Prezidenta Respubliki Bashkortostan, 2002), pp. 62–6.

[39] Federica Prina, 'Homogenisation and the "New Russian Citizen": A Road to Stability or Ethnic Tension?', *Journal on Ethnopolitics and Minority Issues in Europe*, vol. 10, no.1 (2011): pp. 59–93.

8.6 Autonomy, Ethnicity, and Territoriality as Symbolic Entities

In the Russian Federation, NTA, termed as national cultural autonomy (NCA), is explicitly referred to as an exterritorial ethnicity-based formation as well as a general principle. However, no organizations established under the logo of NTA can be deemed public bodies, because they do not acquire public functions and competences and public funding remains optional. 'Non-territoriality' remains under question, because incorporation, functioning, and public funding (whenever available) turn out to be closely bound to the administrative-territorial division of the country. Moreover, the legislation on NCA puts autonomies in a position worse than other non-governmental associations. These circumstances make the entire topic of ethnic groups' agency manifested in self-organization and participation in public life irrelevant in this context. Generally, the respective legal provisions may be deciphered in a way that the lawmakers welcome organizations on ethnic grounds outside the institutional settings of territorial polities.

NTA makes sense only as something set against TA, but what does TA mean in the Russian context? How is 'ethnic statehood' of the republics, autonomous *okrugs*, and the autonomous *oblast* set up in the legislation? The answer is that it manifests itself in name only while the implementation presents a multiplicity of different and inconsistent practices. In other words, 'ethnic federalism' does not guarantee any protective treatment of the 'titular' ethnic groups and does not automatically imply discrimination against the 'non-titular' population. While 'ethnic statehood' lacks a clear definition in both the legal system and practical policies, it persists outside this framework, in semi-official, media, and scholarly discourses.

What deserves attention here is the general and durable consent of all stakeholders in Russia—that is, governmental bodies, policymakers, ethnic activists, academic experts, media, and so forth—about the relevance and importance of both NTA and TA. From the opposite perspective, over the last almost three decades following political liberalization, there have been very few critical voices questioning the very validity of the core ethno-political ideas or pointing out major contradictions in their formulation and implementation. These contradictions can be explained if one assumes that Russian ethnicity-related policies must be to a large extend regarded as a tool for symbolic production of multi-ethnicity; that is, to use Pierre Bourdieu's definition, 'the production of the value of the work or, which amounts to the same thing, of belief in the value of the work or production of cultural and symbolic values and meanings'.[40] In a broader perspective, political institutionalization of ethnicity, or 'the process by which organizations

[40] Pierre Bourdieu, 'The Field of Cultural Production, or the Economic World Reversed', *The Field of Cultural Production: Essays on Art and Literature*, edited and introduced by Randal Johnson (New York: Columbia University Press, 1993), p. 37.

and procedures acquire value and stability'[41] should be analysed as a symbiosis of symbolic and instrumental politics. Political institutionalization includes 'officialization', that is, 'the process whereby the group (or those who dominate it) teaches itself or masks from itself its own truth, binds itself by a public profession which sanctions and imposes what it utters, tacitly defining the limits of the thinkable and the unthinkable and so contributing to the maintenance of the social order from which it derives its power'.[42] Symbolic production and its part, officialization, generate legitimizing macro-narratives, a kind of social mythology for different social and political actors,[43] a 'circle of belief',[44] which provides for the general ideological cohesion. All stakeholders share the same assumptions and expectations and are bonded and constrained by the same discursive matrix; this prevents demand for practically relevant action, which the official authorities would not welcome. Joint rituals symbolize political participation and thus substitute the harmonization of interests.[45] 'The problem is when states do not want a plural ethos upon which to build its polity. Such states are forced to find a social cohesion myth that conceals the real aim while purporting to promote pluralism. This type of inclusive fiction, or that I would term "fictive pluralism" thus renders the basis for social cohesion dubious.'[46] Symbolic production in ethnic policies allows for delimiting the socially acceptable agenda and silencing the issues that can generate discord and conflicts. One tool is the substitution of agendas: debates about the legitimacy of distinction between 'titular' and 'non-titular' ethnicities in fact leave no room for addressing the problems of exclusion and discrimination; the general notions of 'self-determination' and 'group development' keep aside the efficacy of language policies or transparency and fairness of cultural programmes.

The picture becomes even more complex if we take into account the opportunities of different context-dependent interpretations and thus a multiplicity of narratives targeting different audiences. NCA makes sense if it countered to TA; praising of NTA is a way to express a negative attitude to ethnic inequalities implied by TA. When the state endorses the idea of NTA it signals that it is in favour of ethnic pluralism and against granting privileges to 'titular' ethnicities. Indeed, since the early 1990s, NCA has been portrayed as a way to depart from the erroneous Soviet tradition of creating hierarchies of peoples; on the contrary, as some

[41] Samuel Huntington, *Political Order in Changing Societies* (New Haven, CT/London: Yale University Press, 1968), p. 12.

[42] Bourdieu, *The Logic of Practice*, p. 108.

[43] Jean-François Lyotard, *The Postmodern Condition: A Report on Knowledge*, translated by Geoffrey Bennington and Brian Massumi (Minneapolis: University of Minnesota Press, 1984).

[44] Pierre Bourdieu, 'The Production of Belief: Contribution to an Economy of Symbolic Goods', in *The Field of Cultural Production: Essays on Art and Literature*, edited and introduced by Randal Johnson (New York: Columbia University Press, 1993), p. 80.

[45] Murray Edelman, *Constructing the Political Spectacle* (Chicago/London: University of Chicago Press, 1988), pp. 122–30.

[46] Tove Malloy, 'Social Cohesion Estonian Style: Minority Integration Through Constitutionalized Hegemony and Fictive Pluralism', in *Minority Integration in Central Eastern Europe. Between Ethnic Diversity and Equality*, edited by Timofey Agarin and Malte Brosig (Amsterdam/New York: Rodopi, 2009), p. 245.

scholars and ideologists argued, cultural autonomy would mean the acknowledgement of all groups as equal participants in the country's 'nationalities policy'.[47] Issues of non-discrimination are not salient in Russian public discussions, either in terms of the treatment of individuals or structural conditions for social dynamics and mobility. Public attention is focused on extreme manifestations of ethnic enmity or on cultural policies and thus diverted from equality issues, which are overshadowed by such rhetorical exercises as 'non-territorial self-determination', 'equal opportunities in cultural development', or just 'development'.[48]

In a different context and to a different audience, not critical but rather supportive of 'ethnic federalism,' NTA means not only recognition of ethnic diversity but also a reaffirmation of a taxonomy of ethnic groups, and thus reproducing the agenda of group statuses and entitlements. Russians constitute the country's demographic core, 'titular nations' possess 'their own' statehoods, while all the rest can organize themselves into NCAs and 'develop' themselves through the NCAs or other NGOs. Such perceptions lead to claims for symbolic recognition and, conversely, fight against misrecognition and thus they require legitimization by official narratives. The demand for the latter comes from two sides: from the government's need for a tool of self-representation, and from the ethnic elites' appetite for a better position in the symbolic hierarchy. In parallel, an overt discussion of certain issues does not fit into this protocol of communication and is thus avoided; the Russian authorities and the general public resort to 'hidden transcript'. On the other hand, people who can be ethnic spokespersons, or 'ethnic entrepreneurs' (to use Joseph Rothshild's term[49]) need to be in contact with the government and to resolve certain issues concerning funding, representation, maintenance of cultural institutions; they are placed in a position when they can be allowed to communicate and to achieve their goals only if they stick to the imposed agendas and scenarios of communication. According to Russian law, NCAs are the major officially authorized type of ethnicity-based organizations. When ethnic activists establish NCAs, they signal their loyalty to the authorities; this rather burdensome ritual of accepting the rules of the games turns out to be beneficial rather than public criticism of the NCA impracticalities.

[47] Emil Pain, *Etnopoliticheskii mayatnik. Dinamika i mekhanizmy etnopoliticheskikh protsessov v postsovetskoi Rossii* [Ethnopolitical Pendulum. Dynamics and Mechanisms of Ethnopolitical Processes in Post-Soviet Russia] (Moscow: Institut sotsiologii RAN, 2004), p. 169; Leokadia Drobizheva, 'Zavoyevaniya demokratii i ethnonatsionalnye problemy' [Achievements of Democracy and Russia's Ethnonational Problems], *Obshestvennye nauki i sobremennost'*, no. 2 (2005): pp. 16–28; Victor Saveliev, *Nationalno-kulturnaya avtonomiya kak forma ethnokulturnogo samoopredeleniya narodov Rossii* [National-Cultural Autonomy of a Form Self-Determination for Peoples of Russia] (Moscow: RAGS, 2008), pp. 37–8.

[48] Olga Samoilenko, 'Formy samoopredeleniia ravnopravnykh narodov Rossiiskoi Federatsii' [Forms of Self-Determination of Russia's Equal Peoples], *Pravo i politika*, vol. 9, no. 11 (2008): pp. 2633–8; Michael Fomichenko, 'Natsional'no-kul'turnaia avtonomiia kak forma samoopredeleniia narodov v Rossii' [National-Cultural Autonomy as a Form of Self-Determination of Peoples in Russia], *Natsional'nye interesy*, vol. 8, no. 3 (2005): pp. 35–41.

[49] Joseph Rothschild, *Ethnopolitics: A Conceptual Framework* (New York: Columbia University Press, 1981).

The idea of TA implies that 'titular' ethnic groups shall enjoy a special beneficiary regime within their 'homelands'. In both TA and NTA, hidden and blurry implications do not translate into clear requirements of the law. 'Systemic hypocrisy' and 'hidden transcript' keep official policies flexible and able to satisfy many contradictory demands. The state and social actors operate within the same discourse; the demand for symbolic recognition often takes precedence over the demand for concrete resources. The state avoids making concrete promises while its citizenry lacks legal or political remedies to force the government to fulfil its declarations. Along with the direct interconnection of symbolic and instrumental policies one can single out the situations of their disjuncture. Direct and consistent implementation of the principles pertaining to TA would mean discrimination against certain classes of citizenry on ethnic or linguistic grounds. Respectively, in many national contexts and in international organizations the mainstream public figures refrain from debating the essence of 'ethnic statehood' since the opposite would mean a clear emphasis on the existence of first- and second-class citizens on certain territories. Also a clear rejection or criticism of TA would be an encroachment on the deeply entrenched moral and ideological justifications of the existing statehoods. Therefore, all stakeholders resort to 'hidden transcript', avoid implementation of the respective principles and use them selectively and inconsistently. Likewise, a real cultivation of NTA would mean creation of segregated organizational settings, growing budgetary expenditures for the support of minority institutions, fights over the distribution of public resources along ethnic lines, and probably discrimination against NGOs or even individuals on the grounds of their legal status or ethnic affiliation. On the other hand, stressing the impracticality of NTA in public would compromise one of the main pillars of the official policies and a brand welcomed by the general public.

8.7 Conclusion

In the Russian context, both TA and NTA demonstrate three kinds of discrepancies: one is between institutional settings and 'objective' ethnic underpinnings (or ethnic agency embodied in activism or electoral constituencies); the second one is between the framework notions and their specifications (i.e. within the domain of 'talks'), and the third one is between 'talks' and 'actions'. Both NGO activities and administrative-territorial units can be adequately described as such without resorting to ethnic groups as self-organizing social entities and collective actors. NTA and TA, even being embedded in the legislation, are not specified in the official discourses or are specified inconsistently, while implementation lacks uniformity or is pursued in a way contradicting the initial basic idea. In all cases 'hidden transcript' is present, and that results in bracketing out certain issues and 'systemic hypocrisy', meaning a gulf between representation and practice.

The discrepancies and the fact that they are accepted and tolerated by the general public can be explained if one assumes that NTA and TA appear at first as core components of the dominant narrative on ethnicity rather than a tool of resource distribution or exercise of political power. By forming the public agendas and setting up limits and scenarios for public deliberations, both notions indirectly generate 'resource effects',[50] shaping the relation of domination and hegemony. In other words, reproduction and dissemination of socially acceptable narratives in combination with sidelining inacceptable ones, turn out to be a mechanism of power. Symbolic policies directly unrelated to practical issues create a basic interpretative scheme which establishes a non-controversial basis for communication. On top of this is that narrowly understood institutional settings stemming from the ideas of group agency and clear-cut group divisions (such as corporate organizations with strictly defined ethnic membership in the framework of NTA or privileges for 'core' ethnicities within TA) remain optional.

The Russian case cannot be deemed unique. All over the world, minds are 'colonised' with ethnicity or, more precisely, with a 'groupist'[51] world view. The ideas of self-determination, equality of groups, and value of group cultural authenticity have gained global acknowledgement. Meanwhile, straightforward and consistent implementation is hardly compatible with a market-based and individualistic open society. Symbolic production of multi-ethnicity entailing 'systemic hypocrisy' and 'hidden transcript', seem to become a tool for reconciling the irreconcilables. The repertoires of systemic hypocrisy and usage of 'hidden transcript' should be looked for first and foremost when ethnic policies and the respective legislations are analysed. In a broader perspective, when one sets up the research agenda of political institutionalization of ethnicity, one should pay attention to its symbolic dimension. As one can see, symbolic production is an alienable part of the processes leading to the emergence of durable rules and repertoires of social interactions (i.e. institutions) determining the role of ethnic divisions and related terminologies.

50 Schneider and Ingram, *Policy Design for Democracy.*

51 Rogers Brubaker, 'Ethnicity without Groups', *Archives Européennes de Sociologie*, vol. XLIII, no. 2 (2002): p. 164.

9

Indigenous Autonomy in the Americas

Alexandra Xanthaki

9.1 Introduction

The American continent has a long tradition of autonomous regimes, both territorial and non-territorial. Autonomous regimes of American indigenous communities in particular have not been the subject of intense discussion and comparison, partly because the task of discussing such autonomous regimes in the whole of the Americas represents a huge challenge. Although all American indigenous peoples have as common denominator the European colonization and their subsequent extinction to a large degree, their stories certainly differ. 'Caught within colonial systems, whether through imperialism as settlers arrived in their territories or through the nation-state system and its hierarchy of categories designed to protect and promote the powerful',[1] their situation has been shaped considerably by their specific history of colonization. In Latin America, the Spaniards tried to rule the already existing indigenous societies through the *encomieda* system which allowed prominent Spaniards to be in charge of indigenous communities. In exchange for their labour and resources, the Spanish lord would guarantee protection and education. It was 'thinly masked slavery'. In North America, the English chose to create new societies separate from the existing indigenous communities. After wars, enslavement, and forced relocations, they often concluded treaties of co-existence, albeit at times with dire consequences for indigenous groups.[2] The different strategies of colonizers were determined also by the circumstances, for example the large numbers of indigenous inhabitants in Latin America and the rather smaller numbers of indigenous inhabitants in North America. As time went by, the lines between Spaniards and indigenous Americans became blurred in Latin America, whereas such lines remained rather obvious in North America. At the same time,

[1] Mario Blaser, Ravi de Costa, Deborah McGregor, and William D. Coleman, 'Reconfiguring the Web of Life: Indigenous Peoples, Relationality, and Globalisation', in *Indigenous Peoples and Autonomy, Insights for a Global Age*, edited by Mario Blaser, Ravi de Costa, Deborah McGregor, and William D. Coleman (Vancouver: UCB Press, 2010), p. 17.

[2] Christopher Minster, 'Spain's American Colonies and the Encomienda System', accessed 3 March 2015, http://latinamericanhistory.about.com/od/theconquestofperu/p/Spain-S-American-Colonies-And-The-Encomienda-System.htm.

the Spaniards were more focused on taking the natural resources of the territories they occupied, whereas the English spent more time developing trade and agriculture. Nothwithstanding the different ways, both strategies led to the extinction, structural discrimination, and historical injustices of the American indigenous communities.

Indigenous peoples of the whole of the Americas suffered intensely from centuries of assimilation polices imposed on them by the newcomers. Panama and Brazil are notable examples of assimilation for centuries, but so are Guatemala and its adopted policies 'of containment, if not overt extermination',[3] Bolivia in the pre-Morales era, Canada, and the US.[4]

Indigenous peoples in North America have in the last decades seen an improvement in their rights, although their relationship to the states is defined 'by the historical exercise of hierarchical power by the state over Aboriginal peoples, the marginalization and suppression of Aboriginal cultures, and lack of imagination in relation to Aboriginal forms of governance—features central to the colonial project in Canada'.[5] The US has so called government-to-government relations with approximately 566 American Indian and Alaska Native tribes and villages. Native Hawaiians do not have the same status, although they have some form of federal recognition, whereas other indigenous groups are not federally recognized, even though some have acquired status at the state level.[6] The federally recognized tribes have reservations or other lands set aside for them, over which they exercise powers of self-government.

In Canada, in 1996 the state recognized that indigenous peoples have 'an inherent right to self-government' under Section 35 of the (1982) Constitution Act[7] and promised the negotiation of new institutions of indigenous self-government in education, health, social services, language, culture, religion, policing, property rights, and the administration and enforcement of indigenous laws. This went further than the conditional powers available to indigenous communities under the Indian Act.[8] Still, 'power imbalance, cultural dominance, and the challenge of reimagining governmental relationships between Aboriginal peoples and the state continue to dominate Canada's political landscape and influence contemporary negotiations aimed at altering their relationship'.[9]

[3] Jonathan T. Hiskey and Gary L. Goodman, 'The Participation Paradox of Indigenous Autonomy in Mexico', *Latin American Politics and Society*, vol. 53, no 2 (2011): p. 62.

[4] E.g. see James Anaya, 'The Situation of Indigenous Peoples in the United States of America', UN Doc A/HRC/21/47/Add.1 (2012); Marc Chevrier, *Canadian Federalism and the Autonomy of Quebec: A Historical Viewpoint* (Québec: Gouvernement du Québec, 1996); Michael Asch, *On Being There to Stay, Treaties and Aboriginal Rights in Canada* (Toronto: Toronto University Press, 2014).

[5] Michael Coyle, 'Negotiating Indigenous Peoples' Exit from Colonialism: The Case for an Integrative Approach', *Canadian Journal of Law and Jurisprudence*, vol. 27 (2014): p. 286.

[6] See Anaya, 'The Situation of Indigenous Peoples in the United States of America', p. 5.

[7] See 'The Government of Canada Recognizes the Inherent Right of Self-Government as an Existing Aboriginal Right under Section 35 of the Constitution Act, 1982', *Aboriginal Affairs and Northern Development Canada*, accessed 3 March 2015, http://www.aadnc-aandc.gc.ca.

[8] See Indian Act, RSC 1985, ch 1–5, ss 81–85.1, as mentioned in Coyle, 'Negotiating Indigenous Peoples' Exit from Colonialism'.

[9] Coyle, 'Negotiating Indigenous Peoples' Exit from Colonialism', p. 286.

In Latin America, currently large numbers of indigenous peoples are found mainly where pre-colonial civilizations prospered: very large numbers in Bolivia and Guatemala, a significant percentage in Peru and Ecuador, and some smaller groups in Belize, Honduras, and Mexico.[10] The past two decades have witnessed a process of change in many Latin American states. In some countries indigenous peoples are still far from reaching effective political rights and autonomy, but in other countries they have achieved a lot. Hiskey and Goodman note: 'From the election of Evo Morales as president of Bolivia in 2006 to the ongoing Zapatista conflict in southern Mexico, the collective voice of indigenous peoples across the region has grown increasingly louder, albeit in different forms, as their respective political systems have continued to open up to them.'[11] Several Latin American states have recently acknowledged their multicultural and pluri-ethnic character. Within this framework, several states, including Colombia, Bolivia, and Panama, have established or renewed legal arrangements for indigenous territorial autonomy that allow indigenous peoples to govern themselves according to their own principles and beliefs and through their own social institutions and systems. These arrangements 'purport to institutionalize forms of what could be called official (constitutional) political and legal pluralism'.[12] These are important steps away from the statist legal and political model that marginalized and oppressed indigenous peoples. However, such developments have stayed to a large degree on paper and have not been fully implemented, as this would require a complete overhaul of the relations between indigenous peoples and non-indigenous peoples in Latin America.[13] Van Cott has argued that while indigenous peoples in North America seem to be struggling to get more extensive autonomy over their affairs, the struggle of indigenous peoples in Latin America seems to be the reconciling of the duality between having the right to be indigenous and having rights as full and equal citizens of the states.[14]

9.2 Definitional Issues

Indigenous autonomy as a term is used rather loosely in the literature to denote a number of concepts ranging from political representation to development of

[10] Ana Lucia Salinas de Dosch, 'Understanding Latin America Indigenous Movements: From Marginalisation to Self-Determination and Autonomy?', Paper delivered at 3rd International Seminar and Workshop on Latin American and Asian Studies (LASA III), Institute of Occidental Studies, Universiti Kebangsaan Malaysia, 17–18 October 2012.

[11] Hiskey and Goodman, 'The Participation Paradox of Indigenous Autonomy in Mexico', p. 62.

[12] Joris van de Sandt, 'Communal Resource Tenure and the Quest for Indigenous Autonomy on State Law and Ethnic Reorganisation in Two Colombian *Resguardos*', *Journal of Legal Pluralism* vol 48 (2003): p. 125.

[13] Sandt, 'Communal Resource Tenure'.

[14] Donna Lee Van Cott, 'Indigenous Struggles', *Latin American Research Review*, vol. 38, no. 2 (2003): p. 221; Donna Lee Van Cott, 'Building Inclusive Democracies: Indigenous Peoples and Ethnic Minorities in Latin America', *Democratization*, vol. 12, no. 5 (2005): pp. 825–42.

indigenous languages and identities to organized political resistance.[15] For example, de Costa notes that 'the richness and complexity of indigenous peoples autonomy projects are visible in interpersonal relations, struggles at the community level, regional arrangements regarding resource development, and the symbolic meanings that others attach to Indigenous peoples struggles'.[16]

In North America claims for autonomy are seen through the lens of the term 'sovereignty', as this concept is often used in relation to autonomous regimes. Although the concept of sovereignty has been used by US tribes to assert their previous independence, Anghie has criticized it as a mainly Eurocentric concept, arisen in the process of delegitimizing the claims of 'nomadic colonial peoples' and legitimizing the grabbing of their territories.[17] Young has favoured a hybridized 'principle of local self-determination enacted in the context of global governance structures' manifested as a decentralized democratic federalism patterned on Iroquois concepts of federalism.[18]

For the purposes of this chapter, it seems that the best guide to understand the various aspects of American autonomous regimes is the draft American Declaration on the Rights of Indigenous peoples (draft American Declaration). Its elaboration started in 2006. Negotiations were stalled in 2012 and started again in 2015, though without evidence of serious progress. Nevertheless, the text of the draft American Declaration, quite similar to the United Nations Declaration on the Rights of Indigenous Peoples (UNDRIP), but modified to reflect the particularities of the region and the region's indigenous claims, offers a real insight into the understandings and categories of autonomous regimes in the region.

Provisions related to autonomy are scattered in the current text of the draft Declaration. The main relevant provision is Article XX, an article not yet adopted by the American states. Currently it reads:

1. Indigenous peoples, [as one of the ways to exercise their] [in the exercise of] the right to self-determination [within the states], have the right to autonomy or [and] self-government with respect to inter alia, culture, language, spirituality, education, [information, means of communication,] health, housing, employment, social well-being, maintenance [of community security], [of jurisdictional functions in matters of territory,] family relations,

[15] For example, Erich Fox Tree, 'Global Linguistics, Mayan Languages, and the Cultivation of Autonomy', in *Indigenous Peoples and Autonomy, Insights for a Global Age*, edited by Mario Blaser, Ravi de Costa, Deborah McGregor, and William D. Coleman (Vancouver: UCB Press, 2010), p. 91: 'Autonomy means that every mayan language is discrete, complete, and productive'.

[16] Ravi de Costa, 'Afterword', in *Indigenous Peoples and Autonomy, Insights for a Global Age*, edited by Mario Blaser, Ravi de Costa, Deborah McGregor, and William D. Coleman (Vancouver: UCB Press, 2010), p. 241.

[17] Antony Anghie, *Imperialism, Sovereignty and the Making of International Law* (Cambridge: Cambridge University Press, 2007), p. 310–11; also Radhika Mongia, 'Historicizing State Sovereignty: Inequality and the Form of Equivalence', *Comparative Studies in Society and History*, vol. 49, no. 2 (2007): pp. 384–411.

[18] Iris Marion Young, 'Hybrid Democracy: Iroquois Federalism and the Postcolonial Project', in *Political Theory and the Rights of Indigenous Peoples*, edited by Duncan Ivison, Paul Patton, and Will Sanders (Cambridge: Cambridge University Press, 2000), p. 254.

economic activities, administration of land and resources, environment and [entry of non-members]; [and to determine with states the ways and means of financing {the exercise of these rights} these autonomous functions].

2. Indigenous peoples have the right to maintain and develop their own decision-making institutions.

The current draft provision is a detailed version of the corresponding Article 4 of UNDRIP, which recognizes that 'indigenous peoples, in exercising their right to self-determination, have the right to autonomy or self-government in matters relating to their internal and local affairs, as well as ways and means for financing their autonomous functions'.

9.3 Territorial Autonomy

In addition to Article XX, the draft American Declaration currently acknowledges in Article VI that indigenous peoples have the right 'to their social, political, and economic organisation; [to their legal systems]; [and to administer their lands, territories and natural resources].' Although states have not yet agreed on the recognition of indigenous peoples' legal systems and administration of their lands, it seems that the indigenous right to social, political, and economic organization is agreed.

9.3.1 Territorial autonomy in North America

The past policies of separation between indigenous and non-indigenous peoples have particularly favoured territorial autonomy in North America. Indigenous band governments in Canada have had authority over their reserves for a long time, set out by the Indian Act. However, the system had a lot of problems. In 1983, the Special Committee of the House of Commons on Indian Self-Government recommended that the federal government recognize indigenous bands as a distinct order of government within the Canadian federation and begin to negotiate self-government agreements with Indian bands. In 1996, the Royal Commission on Aboriginal Peoples also recommended that Aboriginal governments become recognized as the third level of government in Canada, in addition to the federal government and the provinces; however, the shift had moved on from constitutional recognition to negotiation between the state and the various indigenous communities. Despite a large number of such negotiations since the 1990s, only about twenty such agreements have been reached, most of them closely linked to land claims. More than eighty negotiations are still pending and the federal government recently concluded that the self-government negotiation process is 'not sustainable',[19] while the Supreme Court of Canada has thus far declined invitations

[19] Coyle, 'Negotiating Indigenous Peoples' Exit from Colonialism', pp. 286–7.

to declare that self-governance is a constitutionally protected Aboriginal right. Tired of waiting for the negotiations to bear fruit, some indigenous communities have now started to act unilaterally. In January 2014, the Nipissing First Nation adopted what is believed to be the first constitution for a First Nation in Ontario that replaces the Indian Act as the supreme law on the governance of the First Nation. The initiative has not yet been tested in court.[20]

Such autonomous arrangements are in most cases related to land claims. Indeed, in order to make autonomous regimes effective, a number of other rights must also be recognized, such as the indigenous rights to manage the environment and their lands (art XVIII.2 of the draft American Declaration), indigenous rights to free, prior, and informed consent related to the environment of their lands (art XVIII.3), and rights to create their own protected areas of conservation on their lands. The Inter-American Court for Human Rights has also recognized the important link between indigenous autonomy and land rights. In *Awas Tingi v. Nicaragua*, *Saramaka v. Suriname*, and *Sarayaku v. Ecuador*, the Court used the right to property, as recognized in Article 21 of the American Convention on Human Rights (ACHR), as the basis to discuss violations to indigenous autonomy.[21] Unfortunately, the above-mentioned provisions have not yet been agreed in the American Declaration, even though of course both the US and Canada have consented—after their initial reluctance—to similar provisions of UNDRIP. Indigenous autonomy cannot be disentangled from indigenous struggle for control over their territories. In Canada, when the Québec government started hydroelectric projects after a period of intense forestry and mining development without Cree involvement, the Crees began to oppose such projects that harmed their lands.[22] After resorting to the courts and rejecting a quick settlement, negotiations began with the federal government and Québec that led to the James Bay and Northern Québec Agreement (JBNQA), signed in 1975.[23] The agreement allowed the project to continue but recognized the rights of the Crees to live their own way of life and established measures to ensure the Crees' land use and participation in decision-making. It established co-management in many areas of policymaking, but the state decisions would still be subject to the final authority of the state. Despite the agreement, Crees continued to be excluded from decision-making regarding the development of the land, their governance in the territory, and their participation in resource development and benefits.[24]

[20] 'Nipissing First Nation Passes First Ontario Aboriginal Constitution', CBCNEWS, 21 January 2014, accessed 5 March 2015, http://www.cbc.ca/news/canada/sudbury/nipissing-first-nation-passes-first-ontario-aboriginal-constitution-1.2505488.

[21] Tom M. Antkowiak, 'Resources, and Rhetoric: Indigenous Peoples and the Inter-American Court', *University of Pennsylvania Journal of International Law*, vol. 35, no.1 (2014): pp. 113–87.

[22] Harvey A. Feit, 'Neoliberal Governance and James Bay Cree Governance', in *Indigenous Peoples and Autonomy, Insights for a Global Age*, edited by Mario Blaser, Ravi de Costa, Deborah McGregor, and William D. Coleman (Vancouver: UCB Press, 2010), p. 60.

[23] Feit, 'Neoliberal Governance and James Bay Cree Governance', p. 61.

[24] Feit, 'Neoliberal Governance and James Bay Cree Governance', p. 62.

Currently, the Cree autonomous regime in Québec is also not subject to the Indian Act. The Cree-Naskapi (of Québec) Act of 1984 recognized that nine Cree communities are not subject to the Indian Act or the band system, but are represented by the Grand Council of the Crees (Eeyou Istchee) or GCCEI and governed by the Cree Regional Authority. The Grand Council of the Crees signed an agreement in 2012 with the province of Québec that would abolish the municipalities in the region and merge them with the Cree Regional Authority in a new regional government called the Eeyou Istchee James Bay Territory. They are still in talks with the federal government on a Cree Nation Governance Agreement to refine the new structure's relationship to the federal authorities. Coyle has discussed the negative effects of asymmetries in negotiation power on negotiations relating to self-government between indigenous peoples and the state.[25]

In addition to the land element, two self-government agreements in Canada recognize indigenous autonomy over educational matters: In Nova Scotia and British Columbia, law-making authority has been conferred on the indigenous communities, with the government of Canada providing education programme and governance funding through a transfer agreement to the signatory groups. In Nova Scotia, an education self-government agreement has been in place since 1997. As part of this agreement, the First Nations that operate on-reserve schools do so through the Mi'kmaw Kina'matnewey (MK) education organization. MK has a Master Education Agreement with the Nova Scotia Ministry of Education, which formalizes collaboration between the two organizations. In British Columbia, eleven First Nation bands have been given self-government on education matters after agreements with the government and the province. The Agreement allows participating communities to 'provide primary, elementary, and secondary education programs and services comparable to those provided by other education systems in Canada, so as to permit the transfer of students between education systems without academic penalty.'[26]

A notably wide autonomous regime was agreed following the Nunavut Agreement in Canada. A new federal territory, Nunavut, was created in 1999, separate from the North Territories, where other indigenous communities lived. Nunavut is not reserved exclusively for the Inuit, and any Canadian can move there and vote in its elections.[27] However the strong Inuit majority is reflected in the governance of the territory.

In addition to the political strategies and lobbying for more self-government, Canadian indigenous peoples have also resorted to litigation, with mixed results.

[25] Michael Coyle, 'Transcending Colonialism? Power and the Resolution of Indigenous Treaty Claims in Canada and New Zealand', *NZULR*, vol. 24 (2011): p. 596.

[26] 'Education Partnership in Nova Scotia', *Aboriginal Affairs and Northern Development Canada*, 9 September 2011, accessed 5 March 2015, https://www.aadnc-aandc.gc.ca/eng/1312900494134/1312900618854.

[27] Elections Nunavut, 'Voter Information', http://www.elections.nu.ca/apps/authoring/dspPage.aspx?page=qualify, accessed 8 June 2015.

As Peach notes, 'whereas Canadian courts have, on occasion, provided Indigenous peoples with significant victories, in cases such as *Haida Nation* v *British Columbia (Minister of Forests)* and *Taku River Tlingit First Nation* v *British Columbia (Project Assessment Director),* the courts have also provided them with a number of painful defeats and have only rarely questioned the legitimacy of the fundamental legal underpinnings of colonialism.'[28]

Although indigenous territorial autonomy units in Canada and the US have many similar characteristics, unlike Canada, the US Supreme Court has recognized that Indian tribes are inherently sovereign nations with powers of self-government. However, first, only recognized nations have self-government powers. This leaves indigenous peoples in Alaska and Hawaii in a very vulnerable position. Secondly, even recognized tribes who enjoy self-government, had surrendered both their sovereignty and their original land rights parts and are now under the power of the US.[29] Anaya notes: 'tribes are sovereign nations with certain inherent powers of self-government and original rights, but they are rendered, in words penned by the famous Supreme Court Justice John Marshall, "domestic dependent nations," subject to the overriding power of the federal Government'.[30] Many self-government structures are connected to treaties that were signed between the US and the tribes. Although the treaty-making stopped in 1871, 'many of the historical treaties with tribes continue in force as part of federal law and to define United States-tribal relations'.[31] The (1924) Indian Reorganization Act included provisions that protected Indian lands and provided for establishing reservation-based governments similar to local municipalities. However, it served as a way of gradual assimilation. Many Indian tribes today continue under the IRA regime of the Indian Self-Determination and Education Assistance Act of 1975, by which tribes are able to assume the planning and administration of federal programmes that are devised for their benefit. The UN Special Rapporteur on the Rights of Indigenous Peoples has highlighted some of the problems of territorial autonomous regimes for reservation autonomies. US courts have consistently restricted the self-government of such units, to limit the powers of tribal decision-making bodies and judiciary.[32]

9.3.2 Territorial autonomy in Latin America

Territorial autonomy is not restricted by any means to North America. Although some Latin American states have not established autonomy for their indigenous populations, for example Argentina, other states include such arrangements in their constitution. Article 2 of the Constitution of Mexico

[28] Ian Peach, 'The Power of a Single Feather: Meech Lake, Indigenous Resistance and the Evolution of Indigenous Politics in Canada', *Review of Constitutional Studies*, vol. 16, no. 1 (2011): p. 1.

[29] Anaya, 'The Situation of Indigenous Peoples in the United States of America', para 14.

[30] Anaya, 'The Situation of Indigenous Peoples in the United States of America', para 15.

[31] Anaya, 'The Situation of Indigenous Peoples in the United States of America'.

[32] Anaya, 'The Situation of Indigenous Peoples in the United States of America', paras 50–5.

'guarantees and protects the rights of indigenous peoples and communities to self-determination and consequently to autonomy'. The examples of Oaxaca and the Chiapas autonomous regimes (and their failures to move effectively from promises to reality) offer important lessons.[33] In addition, Article 260 of the Constitution of Venezuela states that 'the legitimate authorities of the native peoples shall have the power to apply, *within their territorial competence* levels of administration of justice', whereas the Constitution of Bolivia (2009) recognizes in Article 190 the indigenous 'jurisdictional functions and competency through their authorities'. Even in cases where constitutionally territorial autonomy is not that strong, in practice, many indigenous groups in Latin America enjoy forms of territorial autonomy.

In some cases, autonomy is used as a way to weaken the rights of indigenous communities. Peru has no autonomy regimes in general for its indigenous populations, but only for the indigenous peoples in isolation and initial contact in its territory to which it refers as 'autonomous peoples'. 'Reserves' have been created for these communities since the 1980s, but the 2006 Law 28736 was adopted to further strengthen the framework of 'indigenous reserves'. This law created a weaker system of protection for these communities because it permits extractive activities within these units when such activities are found to be of national interest and an environmental impact assessment (EIA)—rather than a human rights impact assessment—has been approved by the state. This is catastrophic for these communities.[34]

On the other hand, Nicaragua's indigenous autonomy has been considered a model to be followed.[35] Although Central and Pacific Coast indigenous communities lack recognition,[36] indigenous communities on the Atlantic coast of Nicaragua enjoy both territorial and non-territorial autonomy (NTA). Both the North Atlantic Autonomous Region and the South Atlantic Autonomous Region are governed by regional councils, while their indigenous inhabitants also enjoy non-territorial 'cultural autonomy'.[37] After the Miskitu rebellion against the Sandinistas, autonomy was used in the 1980s as the prize of an ethnically exclusive, pan-indigenous movement. Law 28 on an Autonomy Statute for the

[33] Rodolfo Stavenhagen, 'Politics, Identity, and Mexico's Indigenous Rights Movement (review)', *Human Rights Quarterly*, vol. 33, no. 4 (2011): pp. 1169–76.

[34] Jorge Agurto, 'Peru', in *The Indigenous World 2014*, edited by Cæcilie Mikkelsen (Copenhagen: IWGIA, 2014), pp. 164–5.

[35] Jose Maria Arraiza, 'Squaring Indigenous Circles: The Making of Nicaragua's Indigenous Communal Property Regime', *International Journal on Minority and Group Rights*, vol. 69, no. 19 (2012): p. 72, also quoting Mary Finley-Brook and Karl Offen, 'Bounding the Commons: Land Demarcation in Northeastern Nicaragua', *Bulletin of Latin American Research*, vol. 28, no. 3 (2009): p. 345.

[36] M. M. Idiaquez, 'Ethnic Communities of the Pacific and North-Central Nicaragua', *Envio*, no. 136 (1992), accessed 5 March 2015, www.envio.org.ni/articulo/2557. Also, Juliet Hooker, '"Beloved Enemies": Race and Official Mestizo Nationalism in Nicaragua', *Latin American Research Review*, vol. 40, no. 3 (2005): pp. 38–9.

[37] Michael Tkacik, 'Characteristics of Forms of Autonomy', *International Journal on Minority and Group Rights*, vol. 15 (2008): p. 371.

Regions of the Atlantic Coast of Nicaragua ('Autonomy Law') recognized the Spanish-speaking mestizos, who were of mixed indigenous and Spanish origin and usually came from the Pacific coast of Nicaragua, the indigenous Miskito, Sumo, and Rama as well as the Garifunas and the Creoles, who were native-born descendants of African slaves[38] and established concrete rights for them, including to communal forms of property. The governments of the 1990s largely ignored the Autonomy law, while backing private natural resources exploitation projects in the Atlantic. After years of struggles, the constitution now guarantees rights of indigenous peoples to non-discrimination, free association, free expression, education in their mother tongue, and the right to administer their own affairs in conformity with traditions[39] as well as the approval of regional councils for any concessions and exploitation projects of natural resources in the Atlantic coast.[40] Although the implementation of the Autonomy law remains under question, at least it put an end to the rhetoric of a monocultural Nicaragua and opened a dialogue on the relationship between national politics and indigenous identity.[41] In 2001, indigenous autonomy resurfaced after a ruling by the Inter-American Court for Human Rights found that the Nicaraguan government had violated the rights to communal property of the Mayangna community of Awas Tingni.[42] The Court held that Nicaragua had to adopt the necessary measures to create an effective mechanism for demarcation and titling of the indigenous communities' territory, in accordance with their customary law, values, customs, and mores. Today, Nicaragua is again under Sandinista rule and the international debate on autonomy and indigenous–state relations is still lively.[43] Since 2001, the Inter-American Court for Human Rights has also held judgements where indigenous autonomy is linked to the right to property.

9.4 Autonomy and Representation

In certain contexts, particularly in South America, indigenous peoples who form majorities of the states seek to increase their collective autonomy through electoral

[38] Law 28 on an Autonomy Statute for the Regions of the Atlantic Coast of Nicaragua, art 2; Baron L. Pineda, *Shipwrecked Identities, Navigating Race in Nicaragua's Mosquito Coast* (New Jersey: Rutgers University Press, 2006), pp. 53–65; William Grigsby, 'Caribbean Coast: Multilingual, Multicultural and… Finally Autonomous?', *Envio*, no. 266 (2003).

[39] Constitution of the Republic of Nicaragua 1987, art 89, s 2, as amended by the Law on a Partial Reform of the Political Constitution, Law No. 192, 1 February 1995, Law No. 330, 18 January 2002, and Law No. 527, 8 April 2005.

[40] Arraiza, 'Squaring Indigenous Circles', p. 73.

[41] Eric Rodrigo Meringer, 'Accommodating Mestizaje on Nicaragua's Rio Coco, Miskitu Activism before the Sandinista's Revolution', *AlterNative: An International Journal of Indigenous Peoples*, vol. 10, no. 3 (2014): p. 204.

[42] *Awas Tingi v. Nicaragua, The Mayagna (Sumo) Awas Tingni Community v. Nicaragua*, Inter-American Commission of Human Rights Series C No. 79 (31 August 2001).

[43] Meringer, 'Accommodating Mestizaje on Nicaragua's Rio Coco, Miskitu Activism before the Sandinista's Revolution', p. 204.

politics. In the recent post-liberal governments in several Latin American states, including Bolivia, Venezuela, and Ecuador, new opportunities for indigenous political rights have arisen. In Bolivia, Evo Morales, an Ayamara leader, came to power with the support of the indigenous peoples. In Guatemala, indigenous leaders worked towards a unified pan-Mayan identity that runs through different linguistic and cultural communities.

An important issue that arises relates to the administrational units of autonomy for indigenous communities. Hernández-Díaz maintains that in Mexico, the construction of municipalities 'have been reserved by indigenous peoples as a space from which they can defend their right to be different and counter central government policies. In local spaces, free of political positions and ideological debates, indigenous peoples have maintained, recreated, or developed forms of government different from those localities considered to be of mixed race or non-indigenous. Communities, at different moments in history, have used this institution as a means to defend themselves from, resist, and challenge the politics of the state.'[44] The question whether the autonomous area coincides with the boundaries of an indigenous territorial unit, or is bigger to incude an autonomous municipal territorial unit that includes indigenous peoples is important for the rights of indigenous communities. In the second scenario, indigenous voices may get lost among other voices. In several places in Latin America, the indigenous party-controlled 'alternative municipalities' incorporate indigenous political and cultural elements, but does not go as far as being an indigenous autonomous area.[45] However, in some cases, the institution of the municipality works quite well for indigenous communities.

Certainly, autonomy in Latin America is not only a top-down approach. A notable example of a more organic formulation is the *ayllu* system, the traditional form of a community in the Andes, defined as 'a territory of a community of kin and...a socio-economic organisation unit of the Andean culture that is based on solidarity and reciprocity'.[46] *Ayllus* are self-sustained groups that own a piece of land and have specific hierarchies and obligations to one another. Schilling-Vacaflor discusses how the *ayllu* structures have been maintained in some areas of the highlands and valleys of Bolivia until today, despite the top-down syndical *campesino* organizations that have existed since 1952. Today, in some areas the *ayllu* continue to be the main autonomous organization of indigenous nations, whereas in others they have been substituted by the syndical organizations. Representatives of the *ayllus* are sent to the National Council

[44] Jorge Hernández-Díaz, 'The Construction of Post-Liberal Citizenships: Claims of Municipal Autonomy and Indigenous Demands in Mexico', *Latin American Research Review*, vol. 45 (2010): p. 138.

[45] Jonas Wolff, 'The New Constitutions and the Transformation of Democracy in Bolivia and Ecuador', in *New Constitutionalism in Latin America: Promises and Practices*, edited by Detlef Nolte and Almut Schilling-Vacaflor (Farnham: Ashgate, 2012), pp. 183–202.

[46] Marcelo Francesco Osco, 'Ayllu: Decolonial Critical Thinking and (AN)other Autonomy', *Indigenous Peoples and Autonomy, Insights for a Global Age*, edited by Mario Blaser, Ravi de Costa, Deborah McGregor, and William D. Coleman (Vancouver: UCB Press, 2010), p. 30.

of Ayllus and Markas of Qullasuyu (CONAMAQ), founded in 1997 to restore autonomy of indigenous peoples, including their 'collective rights to land and natural resources, re-definition of administrative units and self-determination exercised through indigenous autonomies and direct representation in state institutions'.[47] CONAMAQ has a clear political vision for the indigenous peoples, that is, the return to pre-colonial relations between communities and the state, the rejection of existing political parties and syndicates as a dilution of indigenous power and claims, and the direct representation in state institutions, similar to Zapatistas' claims in Mexico. The rejection of political parties and of syndicates has put them in conflict with their former political allies—MAS, the political movement led by Evo Morales. CONAMAQ opposed the tendency to extend indigenous rights also to the *campesino* populations (peasants) and disagreed with the incorporation of indigenous *originario campesino* autonomies established in the new constitution. This case highlights the difficulties that arise in the construction of specific autonomous areas where indigenous peoples live; and the tensions between indigenous peoples and other vulnerable parts of the population in their quest for effective political participation. Similar tensions exist between some of the indigenous *ayllus* in the highlands and the Confederación Sindical Única de Trabajadores Campesinos de Bolivia (CSUTSB), the most important indigenous-*campesino* organization in Bolivia with the most members, founded in 1979. CSUTSB uses a 'pan-indigenous face', but being rather close to the government, it seems to promote autonomy of municipalities with rights equal to indigenous autonomies. The dual identity of indigenous peoples as indigenous and as members of the *campesino* syndicates has created challenges, deriving from the state's insistence on treating indigenous peoples in a similar manner to other vulnerable groups. The ratification of UNDRIP as state law in October 2007 is powerful ammunition for indigenous peoples in Bolivia, because it explicitly recognizes special rights to indigenous peoples because of historical injustices, level of distinctiveness, and historical continuity of these nations.

In addition to the tensions that arise at times in constructing indigenous autonomies in the Americas (and beyond), and states' attempts to treat indigenous claims for autonomy in similar ways to other such claims or other administrative divisions, this case also shows how indigenous identity in some Latin American indigenous individuals coexists with other powerful identities, for example the identity of the peasant, and how indigenous peoples have to manage these identities. In similar ways, their vision for indigenous autonomy is also shared with other visions in the political sphere, such as the socialist vision or the post-liberal agenda; again such visions have to be managed and are on occasions in conflict. Zapatistas in Mexico have been criticized for pursuing autonomy, when

[47] Almut Schilling-Vacaflor, 'Indigenous Identities and Politico-Juridical Demands of CSUTCB and CONAMAQ in the Constitutional Change Process of Bolivia', *T'inkazos, La Paz* vol. 11 (2008): pp. 23–4.

their struggle should join the voices for globalization, deregulation, and open markets.[48] This parallel struggle for more indigenous rights and other visions is not that obvious in North America, where indigenous struggles have not so actively joined other struggles. To a large degree, this may be explained as a consequence of the policy of separation that was pursued by colonizers in North America, which may have prevented indigenous peoples from actively sharing political agendas with non-indigenous peoples.

State interference in the way indigenous local governments are run is often justified on the basis of improving the system or ensuring democratic structures. However, in reality many of these structures weaken the indigenous political units and their representation. Oaxaca was the first state in Mexico to recognize in 1995 the practice of *usos y costumbres*, or customary law, as a legal means of selecting local leaders and managing day-to-day municipal operations. Since colonial times, 412 out of 570 municipios in Oaxaca have run their affairs locally by a form of *usos y costumbres*. Most of these municipios were indigenous communities and the *usos y costumbres* included traditional customs and customary law to elect their local leaders. Since being included in state law, *usos y costumbres* has competed with the open-list electoral political party regime that prevails in the rest of the *municipios* and in the rest of the state. The *usos y costumbres* system was not based on democratic structures, ballot was not secret and some communities have systematically excluded some sections of the population, such as women, from participation in local political affairs. So, in 1995, the state gave citizens living in *usos* municipalities the option of voting for whomever they wanted in state and national elections while being formally allowed to continue their use of non-partisan, customary selection methods for local government offices. This was envisaged as a positive reform. However, as Stavahagen argues, '[w]hatever its original purpose, making it legal gave the governing PRI party an edge over its political rivals in assuming ownership over these communities in the face of increasing hard-ball party politics in a democratizing Oaxaca, where left-wing political movements were on the rise.'[49] Hiskey and Goodman also criticize the initiative:

> Without explicit efforts to strengthen indigenous citizens' ties to the national political community, however, the *usos* legislation effectively insulated these municipalities from the state's rapidly increasing multiparty electoral competition, increasing the chances that they would simply continue their clientelist relations with the PRI. This study argues that Oaxaca offers a textbook case of flawed and incomplete reforms producing consequences far beyond the immediate realm of the institutions in question.[50]

[48] Todd A. Eisenstadt, *Politics, Identity, and México's Indigenous Rights Movements* (Cambridge: Cambridge University Press, 2011); and the reply to the criticism in Stavenhagen, 'Politics, Identity, and Mexico's Indigenous Rights Movement (review)'.

[49] Stavenhagen, 'Politics, Identity, and Mexico's Indigenous Rights Movement (review)', p. 1173.

[50] Hiskey and Goodman, 'The Participation Paradox of Indigenous Autonomy in Mexico', pp. 64–6.

9.5 Non-Territorial Autonomy: Autonomy in Juridical Matters

Non-territorial autonomous regimes in the Americas include a variety of arrangements. The provision of the draft American Declaration that recognizes the right of indigenous peoples 'to promote, develop and maintain their institutional structures and their distinctive customs, spirituality, traditions, procedures, practices and, in the cases where they exist, juridical systems or customs, in accordance with international human rights standards' has not yet been agreed. Article XXII—on the participation of indigenous peoples in decision-making in matters that affect them—is also controversial, 'including those that the state agrees to with other states and multilateral institutions, as well as in the process of development of legislative, administrative and juridical measures'.

9.5.1 Free, prior, and informed consent as an expression of non-territorial autonomy

There can be no discussion on indigenous autonomy in the Americas without touching on the requirement of free, prior, and informed consent of indigenous peoples (FPIC) on decisions that affect them. Today, this is a major concern of indigenous peoples all around the Americas. Having the autonomy to put a stop on big development projects is essential to their survival and prosperity. Rights to participation and consultation, seen as political rights, are included in several legislative texts of the Americas, but do not go far enough to protect indigenous peoples in situations of natural resources exploitation. In Bolivia, for example, the participation of indigenous peoples is promoted, and permits for energy production are judged on the basis of referendums at the municipal and departmental levels. However, there the voices of the indigenous communities, who are much more affected by such projects than other local populations, are continuously obscured by the majority views.[51]

FPIC is included in seven articles of UNDRIP, an instrument supported eventually by all American states. Article 19 of UNDRIP recognizes a collective right to giving or withholding consent by the indigenous peoples, according to the rules and procedures determined by the group itself, whereas Article 32(2) requires States to 'consult and cooperate in good faith with the indigenous peoples concerned through their own representative institutions in order to obtain their free and informed consent prior to the approval of any project affecting their lands or territories and other resources, *particularly in connection with the development, utilization or exploitation of mineral, water or other resources.*'[52] In 2009, the Human

[51] Secretariat of the Convention on Biological Diversity, 'Recognising and Supporting Territories and Areas Conserved by Indigenous Peoples and Local Communities, Global Overview and National Case Studies', *CBD Technical Series*, no. 64 (2012): p. 30, accessed on 2 March 2014, http://www.cbd.int/doc/publications/cbd-ts-64-en.pdf.

[52] United Nations Declaration on the Rights of Indigenous Peoples (adopted 13 September 2007), art 32, s 2 (emphasis added).

Rights Committee noted in *Angela Poma Poma v. Peru*,[53] which involved the impact on water beneath indigenous peoples' lands, that 'participation in decision-making process must be effective, which requires not mere consultation but the free, prior and informed consent of the members of the community'.[54] In the context of its Early Warning Urgent Action procedure the Committee on the Elimination of Racial Discrimination (CERD) has examined cases in Brazil, Canada, and Peru on their failure to obtain the FPIC of the affected indigenous peoples.[55] The UN Committee on Economic, Social and Cultural Rights also affirmed in 2009 the duty of States 'to respect the principle of free, prior and informed consent of indigenous peoples in all matters that affect them'.[56] In its concluding observations to Colombia, the Committee repeated in 2010 that the right of indigenous peoples to FPIC should be respected before any project that affects indigenous peoples is implemented and that legislation must be enacted to ensure the respect of this indigenous right.[57]

How strong is the requirement for consent in development projects? The Mexican former Special Rapporteur on the Human Rights and Fundamental Freedoms of Indigenous Peoples, Rodolfo Stavenhagen, has referred to the 'right to free prior informed consent by indigenous peoples' which includes their 'right to say no' describing it as being of 'crucial concern' in relation to large-scale or major development projects and 'essential' for the protection of their human rights.[58] His successor, James Anaya, has also adopted this line, explaining it further. Anaya has adopted a nuanced approach emphasizing that the strength of the requirement for FPIC would vary according to 'the circumstances and the indigenous interests involved'.[59] He noted that a 'direct impact on indigenous peoples' lives or territories establishes a strong presumption that the proposed measure should not go forward without indigenous peoples' consent', and that 'in certain contexts, that presumption may harden into a prohibition of the measure or project in the absence of indigenous consent'.[60] The Special Rapporteur has

[53] Human Rights Committee, 'Ángela Poma Poma v. Peru' (adopted 24 April 2006) UN Doc. CCPR/C/95/D/1457/2006.

[54] Human Rights Committee, 'Ángela Poma Poma v. Peru', para 7.6.

[55] CERD, 'Summary Record of the First Part (Public) of the 1901st Meeting', 26 September 2008, UN Doc. CERD/C/SR.1901 (2008).

[56] Committee on Economic, Social and Cultural Rights (CESCR), 'General Comment No. 21 on the Right of Everyone to Take Part in Cultural Life' (adopted 21 December 2012) UN Doc. E/C.12/GC/21 (2009), paras 36–7.

[57] 'Concluding Observations on Colombia' (adopted 21 May 2010) UN Doc. E/C.12/COL/CO/5 (2010); 'Concluding Observations on New Zealand' (adopted 30 May 2012) UN Doc. E/C.12/NZL/CO/3 (2012).

[58] CHR, 'Report of the Special Rapporteur on the Situation of Human Rights and Fundamental Freedoms of Indigenous People' (adopted 21 January 2003) UN Doc. E/CN.4/2003/90 (2003), paras 13 and 66. He points out that FPIC is necessary as too many major developments do not respect the consultation and participation criteria that are laid out in ILO Convention No. 169.

[59] Human Rights Council, 'Promotion and Protection of all Human Rights, Civil, Political, Economic, Social and Cultural Rights, Including the Right to Development, Report of the Special Rapporteur' (adopted 15 July 2009) UN Doc. A/HRC/12/34 (2009), para 47.

[60] Human Rights Council, ' Promotion and Protection of all Human Rights, Civil, Political, Economic, Social and Cultural Rights, Including the Right to Development, Report of the Special Rapporteur'.

recognized the development of an international norm requiring the consent of indigenous peoples when their property rights are impacted by natural resource extraction.[61] He has confirmed that the

> general rule [is] that extractive activities should not take place within the territories of indigenous peoples without their free, prior and informed consent. Indigenous peoples' territories include lands that are in some form titled or reserved to them by the State, lands that they traditionally own or possess under customary tenure (whether officially titled or not), or other areas that are of cultural or religious significance to them or in which they traditionally have access to resources that are important to their physical well-being or cultural practices. Indigenous consent may also be required when extractive activities otherwise affect indigenous peoples, depending upon the nature of and potential impacts of the activities on the exercise of their rights. In all instances of proposed extractive projects that might affect indigenous peoples, consultations with them should take place and consent should at least be sought, even if consent is not strictly required.[62]

The Inter-American System of Human Rights has been vocal on FPIC. The Inter-American Commission on Human Rights has confirmed the need for consultation in cases of natural resource extraction since 2001.[63] In 2007, the Court held in *Saramaka People v. Suriname*[64] that in the case of large-scale development or an investment project that would have an impact on indigenous communities, the State 'has the duty, not only to consult with the [indigenous group], but to obtain their free, prior and informed consent, according to their customs and traditions'.[65] The Court was asked to decide on whether logging and mining concessions awarded by the State to third parties on indigenous lands violated indigenous rights and affirmed that in some cases the scope of Article 21 of the ACHR[66] may comprise the exploitation of indigenous sub-soil resources.[67] Unfortunately, the 2012 case of *Kichwa v. Ecuador*[68] does not refer to the right to FPIC as such, but discusses instead the 'right to consultation with the aim of

[61] The Special Rapporteur qualified this requirement by adding that FPIC may not be essential for projects that do not have these potential impacts as long as this was in line with the requirements of arts 46 and 32(3) of UNDRIP. James S. Anaya, 'Indigenous Peoples' Participatory Rights in Relation to Decisions about Natural Resource Extraction', *Arizona Journal of International and Comparative Law*, vol. 22, no. 1 (2005): pp. 7–8; Human Rights Council, 'Promotion and Protection of all Human Rights, Civil, Political, Economic, Social and Cultural Rights, Including the Right to Development' (adopted 11 August 2008) UN Doc. A/HRC/9/9/Add. 1.

[62] Human Rights Council, 'Report of the Special Rapporteur on the Rights of Indigenous Peoples, Extractive Industries and Indigenous Peoples' (adopted 1 July 2013) UN Doc. A/HRC/24/41 (2013), para 27.

[63] *Marie and Carrie Dann v. United States Case 11.140* (Report 75/02 (2002), para 130) Inter-American Commission of Human Rights; *Mayagna (Sumo) Awas Tingni Community v. Nicaragua* (Merits, Reparations and Costs) Inter-American Court of Human Rights Series C No. 79, para 25 (31 August 2001).

[64] *Saramaka People v. Suriname* (Preliminary Objections, Merits, Reparations, and Costs) Inter-American Court of Human Rights Series C No. 172.

[65] *Awas Tingi v. Nicaragua, The Mayagna (Sumo) Awas Tingni Community v. Nicaragua*, para 134.

[66] ACHR, 'OAS Treaty Series No. 36' (ACHR) (adopted 22 November 1969).

[67] *Saramaka People v. Suriname*, para 126.

[68] *Pueblo Indigena Kichwa de Sarayaku v. Ecuador* (Merits and Reparations) Inter-American Court of Human Rights Series C No. 245 (27 June 2012).

reaching an agreement or obtaining consent'.[69] The Court held that 'the State did not conduct an appropriate and effective process that would guarantee the right to consultation of the *Sarayaku* people before undertaking or authorizing the program of exploration or exploitation of resources on their territory'.[70]

9.5.2 Autonomy in judicial matters

Contrary to FPIC, that falls below the existing international law standards in the Americas, indigenous autonomy in judicial matters is more accepted than in other parts of the world. The recognition of indigenous juridical systems (art 34 of UNDRIP) has been quite a controversial issue during the elaboration of UNDRIP. In contrast, Article XI of the draft American Declaration which recognizes 'the juridical personality of the indigenous peoples, respecting indigenous forms of organisation' has already been agreed by member states whereas American States approved in 2011 that 'the indigenous law and legal systems shall be recognised and respected by the national, regional and international legal systems'.

Several American Constitutions are vocal on indigenous jurisdiction, both territorial and non-territorial. The Constitution of Bolivia 2009 states in Article 190 that 'the nations and native indigenous rural peoples shall exercise their jurisdictional functions and competency through their authorities and shall apply their own principles, cultural values, norms and procedures'. However, limitations are set in the next paragraph: 'The rural native indigenous jurisdiction respects the right to life, the right to defence and other rights and guarantees established in the Constitution.' Article 149 of the Constitution of Peru also states that 'The authorities of the Native and Peasant Communities, with the support of the Peasant Rounds [Rondas Campesinas], may exercise jurisdictional functions within their territory in accordance with common law, provided that they do not violate the fundamental rights of the individual.'

More cautiously, Article 260 of the Constitution of Venezuela proclaims: 'The legitimate authorities of the native peoples shall have the power to apply, within their territorial competence levels of administration of justice based on their ancestral traditions and affecting their members only, in accordance with their own rules and proceedings, provided the same are not contrary to this Constitution, law and public order. The manner in which this special competence shall be co-ordinated with the national judicial system shall be determined by law.'

Article 246 of the Constitution of Colombia also sets domestic law as a limitation to indigenous jurisdiction: 'The authorities of the indigenous peoples may exercise their jurisdictional functions within their territorial jurisdiction in accordance to their own laws and procedures, provided that these are not contrary to the Constitution and to the laws of the Republic. The law will establish the

[69] *Human Rights Committee, Communication No. 1457/2006, Ángela Poma Poma v. Peru*, para 185.

[70] *Pueblo Indigena Kichwa de Sarayaku v. Ecuador*, para 211.

forms of coordination of this special jurisdiction with the national judicial system.' The Constitution of Ecuador also explicitly recognizes in Article 1910 that indigenous authorities have judiciary functions in which they can apply customary norms and procedures 'so long as they do not contest the constitution and the laws. Finally, the Constitution of Mexico in Article 2.II:

> guarantees and protects the rights of indigenous peoples and communities to II. Apply their own normative systems in the regulation and solution of their internal conflicts, subject to the general principles of this Constitution, respecting individual guarantees, human rights and, in relevant manner, the dignity and integrity of women. The law will establish the cases and procedures of validation by the corresponding judges or courts.[71]

The Court held in *Chavez* that Article 2 does not create 'an independent and exclusive legal sphere only for indigenous communities. On the contrary, it is a statement that entails special care.'[72]

It is interesting that some of these constitutions, for example Peru, do not require that indigenous jurisdiction be in conformity with all legislation, but only with Constitutional guarantees. Making indigenous jurisdiction stand only when in conformity with domestic law defeats the point and sweeps away the essence of autonomy. Even the prevalence of the Constitution over indigenous jurisdiction seems questionable; the condition of having indigenous jurisdiction dependent on international human rights law seems adequate to ensure human rights protection and also to be in the spirit of indigenous real autonomy and self-determination.[73] Any such assessment about the indigenous cultural norm must allow for a certain deference to the group's 'own interpretive and decision-making processes in the application of universal human rights norms, just as states are accorded such deference'.[74] The Supreme Court of Colombia seems to lean towards such interpretation: the Court has held that limiting the community's autonomy, when it comes to situations regarding internal control, should be 'the minimum acceptable', and therefore 'can only relate to what is truly intolerable in

[71] Constitución Política de los Estados Unidos Mexicanos 1917 [Political Constitution of the United Mexican States], art 2.

[72] Helga Maria Lell, 'The Concept of Citizenship: Multicultural Challenges and Latin American Constitutional Democracy', *Birkbeck Law Review*, vol. 87, no. 2 (2004): p. 110. For the case, see Juicio para la Protección de los Derechos Politico Electorales del Ciudadano, Expediente SUP-JDC-1 1/2007, Tribunal Electoral del Poder Judicial de la Federacion (Distrito Federal) *Joel Cruz Chavez y Otros. [The State v. Chavez and others* (Trial to Protect the Political and Electoral Rights of Citizens) SUP-JDC-1 1/2007 Mexican Electoral Tribunal of the Federal Judiciary].

[73] Alexandra Xanthaki, 'Normative Directions', in *Indigenous Peoples' Access to Justice*, edited by Wilthon Littlechild and Elsa Stamatopoulou (New York: Institute for the Study of Human Rights, Columbia University, 2014), pp. 21–40; also Alexandra Xanthaki, 'Multiculturalism and International Law: Discussing Universal Standards', *Human Rights Quarterly*, no. 1 (2010): pp. 21–48.

[74] James Anaya, 'International Human Rights and Indigenous Peoples: The Move Towards the Multicultural State', *Arizona Journal of International and Comparative Law*, vol. 21, no. 1 (2004): p. 26.

that they endanger *man's most precious assets*.'[75] Gomez Isa elucidates that 'the Constitutional Court included in 'this core of untouchable rights only the *right to life*, the *prohibition of slavery* and the *prohibition of torture*'[76] as well as 'the *legality of proceedings* and, in criminal matters, the *legality of offences and sentences*'.[77] Very interestingly, the Constitutional Court held that 'only in relation to these can the existence of true *intercultural consensus* be predicated'.[78] This of course limits a lot the leeway that the state has to restrict the rules deriving from indigenous autonomous regimes that relate to wholly internal indigenous situations, in cases when 'all the elements defining a particular situation involve an indigenous community: both the perpetrator of the conduct and the injured party belong to the community, and the events have taken place within the territory of that community'.[79] Gomez Isa discusses some cases where the community itself revisited and revised its own cultural rules. For example, she mentions how the U'wa community revisited their cultural practice of rejecting babies with serious defects or as a result of multiple births.[80]

Notable on this point is the recognition of the indigenous family norms and rules in the American draft Declaration, an important addition to provisions of UNDRIP. Agreed Article XVI recognizes 'the various indigenous forms of family, in particular the extended family, as well as the forms of matrimonial union, filiations, descent, and family name'. However, the current text also proclaims that states should 'take into account, primarily, the applicable indigenous law' in family matters and that 'the indigenous institutions, and indigenous courts where they exist' shall have jurisdiction (art XVI), an addition which has not yet been accepted by States.

Another interesting discussion that arises relates to the binding power of tribal laws in reservations on non-indigenous people. In the US, laws such as the Major Crimes Act of 1885 and Public Law 280 of 1953 have extended state criminal and civil jurisdiction in Indian country whether it relates to an indigenous or non-indigenous. The application of indigenous reservation laws to non-indigenous is a very important one as reports of a rape or sexual assault 'epidemic' among US indigenous women have recently surfaced. According to the US Department of Justice, 'in at least 86 per cent of the reported cases of rape or sexual assault against American Indian and Alaska Native women, survivors report

[75] Corte Constitucional de Colombia (C.C.) (Colombian Constitutional Court), Sentencia T–349/96, 8 August 1996, 2.3 (Colom.) As translated and quoted in Gomez F. Isa, 'Cultural Diversity, Legal Pluralism, and Human Rights from an Indigenous Perspective: The Approach by the Colombian Constitutional Court and the Inter-American Court of Human Rights', *Human Rights Quarterly*, vol. 36, no. 4 (2014): p. 738.

[76] Gomez, 'Cultural Diversity, Legal Pluralism, and Human Rights from an Indigenous Perspective'.

[77] Gomez, 'Cultural Diversity, Legal Pluralism, and Human Rights from an Indigenous Perspective'.

[78] Gomez, 'Cultural Diversity, Legal Pluralism, and Human Rights from an Indigenous Perspective'.

[79] Gomez, 'Cultural Diversity, Legal Pluralism, and Human Rights from an Indigenous Perspective', p. 738.

[80] Gomez, 'Cultural Diversity, Legal Pluralism, and Human Rights from an Indigenous Perspective', p. 742.

that the perpetrators are non-Native men'; and many such assaults happen within reservations.[81] Amnesty International notes that 'the complex interrelation between federal, state and tribal jurisdictions... undermines tribal authority and often allows perpetrators to evade justice';[82] and ultimately fails victims. The concern about strict indigenous norms and laws is balanced by the need that such norms follow international human rights standards.

9.6 Conclusions

Autonomous regimes in the Americas differ substantially, a legacy of different circumstances, different colonial strategies, and different evolution of the states in which they live. In Latin America, indigenous claims for autonomy have run parallel to other political visions. Accordingly, Latin American indigenous groups seem to be in constant interaction (support but also competition) with other vulnerable groups. North American indigenous peoples are more separate in their struggle, which at times limits their impact on non-indigenous support. Still, the main challenges for the autonomy of all indigenous peoples in the Americas are similar: their primary concern is the impact of transnational corporations in their lands and territories. Autonomy in matters that affect them in the form of FPIC of indigenous peoples in such decisions is essential to protect their survival. Autonomy to apply their norms and rules is also important to them, for their cultural, political, and social development but also as a token of states' respect of their identity and self-determination. Territorial autonomy has been a way in some states to promote indigenous control over their lives. However, transcribing such autonomous regimes from paper to reality has been a real challenge. New international instruments, regional and international human rights bodies, and the transnational indigenous movement work hard in highlighting such weaknesses and promoting further indigenous quests for real and effective autonomy.

[81] 'Maze of Injustice, A Summary of Amnesty International's Findings', *Amnesty International*, accessed 5 March 2015, http://www.amnestyusa.org/our-work/issues/women-s-rights/violence-against-women/maze-of-injustice.

[82] 'Maze of Injustice, A Summary of Amnesty International's Findings'.

10

Autonomy in South Asia

Evidence for the Emergence of a Regional Custom

Joshua Castellino

10.1 Introduction

One of the difficulties in studying regional autonomy regimes at a global level is that the literature often tends to focus heavily on some, while leaving swathes of others untouched by scrutiny. Studies on autonomy often lay heavy emphasis on 'usual suspects' such as Québec,[1] Catalonia,[2] South Tyrol,[3] and Tibet,[4] while there are fewer attempts to understand how others configure such regimes.[5] While South Asia attracts more attention than most other parts of the world in general research literature, there is surprisingly little concerted work on questions of its regional autonomy regimes, be it territorial or non-territorial.[6]

In undertaking this chapter a few caveats therefore need clear articulation. First, 'South Asia' is defined as including India, Pakistan, Bangladesh, Sri Lanka, Nepal, the Maldives, and Bhutan.[7] For reasons of space, Bangladesh, Afghanistan,

[1] See Marc Chevrier, *Canadian Federalism and the Autonomy of Quebec: A Historical Viewpoint* (Québec: Gouvernement du Québec, 1996).

[2] Sue Wright, ed., *Language, Democracy and Devolution in Catalonia* (Clevedon: Multilingual Matters, 1999).

[3] Jens Woelk, Francesco Palermo, and Joseph Marko, eds, *Tolerance through Law: Self-Governance and Group Rights in South Tyrol* (Leiden/Boston: Martinus Nijhoff Publishers, 2008).

[4] Barry Sautman and June Teufel Dreyer, eds, *Contemporary Tibet: Politics, Development and Society in a Disputed Region* (New York: ME Sharpe Inc., 2006).

[5] More recent innovative works have cast this net considerably further. Yash Ghai and Sophia Woodman, eds, *Practising Self-Government: A Comparative Study of Autonomous Regions* (Cambridge: Cambridge University Press, 2013). For an authoritative work including theory as well as case studies, see Sujit Choudhary, *Constitutional Design for Divided Societies: Integration or Accommodation?* (Oxford: Oxford University Press, 2008). An older book that broke new ground in this respect is Hurst Hannum, ed., *Autonomy, Sovereignty and Self-Determination: The Accommodation of Conflicting Rights* (Revised Edition, Pittsburgh: University of Pennsylvania Press, 1996).

[6] A notable exception that has been cited several times in this chapter is Marendra Prasad Singh and Veena Kukreja, eds, *Federalism in South Asia* (New Delhi: Routledge, 2014).

[7] This classification is discussed in Joshua Castellino and E. Dominguez Redondo, *Minority Rights in Asia: A Comparative Legal Analysis* (Oxford: Oxford University Press, 2006), p. 28.

Bhutan, and the Maldives will not merit significant analysis: it could be said that Afghanistan is a *sui generis* entity not readily classifiable as South Asia in any case.[8] Second, this analysis is based on constitutional design, paying attention to attempts to engage autonomy and those aimed at forging such models or federations. The general lack of existing information requires significant descriptions restricting the space for analysis as a consequence. Third, as issues of 'live' political discussion, the material offered here is subject to change, and as a result the commentary stays with broad frameworks rather than narrow detail. Fourth, it is important to assert that territorial autonomy (TA) is only one form of autonomy in the region, with considerable developments in the realm of non-territorial autonomy (NTA) or personal autonomy, which remain beyond the scope of this work.[9] While South Asia may be one of the most fascinating regions in which to study the question of non-territorial autonomies, the scope of this chapter is defined by the title of the work within which it sits, namely the question of minorities and territory. While society-wide discussions about South Asia's multitude of minorities being engaged with questions concerning NTA are visible and prominent in practice,[10] the emphasis of this chapter is on TA. The main reason for this lies in the unfulfilled promises and frustrations with such types of autonomy, and the extent to which they remain at the forefront of public debate.

Despite their conspicuous absence from the literature, questions of autonomy in South Asia have become, and are likely to become, more central in the next few decades. Three reasons could be attributed to this: (a) the general wave of populist protest commencing with the Arab Spring which has provided a fillip for public protest, much being channelled through identity-based politics;[11] (b) the States in the region are relatively young, with decisions taken at their birth driven by political expediencies which are coming under pressure; (c) the scope for public expression of identity is creating preconditions likely to be exploited (for beneficial or malicious reasons) by a range of new assertive actors. Thus the prediction here is that questions of autonomy (territorial and non-territorial) are likely to become accentuated in South Asia, where they have merited relatively low levels of public engagement, caused by the distance of vulnerable groups from sites of power.

[8] See Martin McCauley, *Afghanistan and Central Asia: A Modern History* (London: Pearson, 2002).

[9] Personal autonomy regimes, also known as NTA regimes are discussed in Castellino and Dominguez, *Minority Rights in Asia*, pp. 78–86. For a more general work that outlines the underpinning theory and practice, see Ephraim Nimni, Alexander Osipov, and David J. Smith, eds, *The Challenge of Non-Territorial Autonomy: Theory and Practice* (Oxford: Peter Lang, 2013).

[10] For a discussion on non-territorial autonomy in India, especially the design and conflict around Muslim personal law, see Castellino and Dominguez Redondo, *Minority Rights in Asia*, pp. 78–86. For a historical perspective, see R. M. Baxamus, *A Historic Perspective on Muslim Personal Law in India* (Bombay: SNDT Women's University, 1984). Perhaps the widest-ranging commentary on the issue is available in Partha S. Ghosh, *The Politics of Personal Law in South Asia: Identity, Nationalism and the Uniform Civil Code* (New Delhi: Routledge, 2007). For a well-articulated gendered lens on this question, see Faustina Pereira, *The Fractured Scales: The Search for a Uniform Personal Code* (Calcutta: Stree Publishers, 2002).

[11] See Joshua Castellino, *International Law and Self-Determination: The Politics of Possession with Formulations of Post-Colonial 'National' Identity* (The Hague: Martinus Nijhoff, 2000), pp. 167–74.

With the objective of providing readers with a general introduction to the South Asian treatment of the question of TA, and in order to identify starting points enabling researchers to draw on South Asian examples, this chapter is divided into two sections. Section 10.2 provides the historical background to the emergence of the States, specifically within the contested external boundaries.[12] This is followed by a brief exploration of the basic legal tenets of the States concerned. Any analysis of autonomy arrangements needs to be situated within the overall constitutional make-ups of the States, which is what the second part of this section hopes to achieve. Section 10.3 seeks to present the regional autonomy regimes as articulated in constitutions and statutes in India, Pakistan, Sri Lanka, and Nepal. The States are chosen to show how autonomy questions remain either at the forefront of, or as the ostensible solution at the national level to, ingrained questions of the sustainable sub-national identities. The conclusion will emphasize the prevalence of live conflict-laden autonomy questions that reverberate within the States, presenting these within an overall commentary of the experience of regional autonomy. The main conclusion advanced is that there is significant evidence for the existence of regional custom concerning TA. This is visible in legislative design and national and regional politics. This, in conjunction with the predicted rise in the resonance of such questions, will likely lead to South Asia being the most dynamic (if not necessarily the most successful) of the world's regions in seeking the accommodation of competing identities over the next few decades.

10.2 Manufacturing Boundaries, Accommodating Identities

In seeking to understand how autonomy regimes are configured within States, the starting point in every post-colonial State has to be the physical demarcation of the territory itself.[13] While the following quote from Lord Salisbury from 1890 pertains to Africa, the sentiment underlying it is equally applicable to colonial line-drawing in the region:

> We [the colonial powers] have engaged...in drawing lines upon maps where no white man's feet have ever trod; we have been giving away mountains and rivers and lakes to

[12] For more on boundary issues in South Asia, see V. Fazila-Yacoobali Zamindar, *The Long Partition and the Making of Modern South Asia: Refugees, Boundaries and Histories* (New York: Columbia University Press, 2007).

[13] For a general outline of the issue of boundaries in international law, see M. N. Shaw, 'The Heritage of States: The Principle of Uti Possidetis Juris Today', *British Yearbook of International Law*, vol. 67 (1996): pp. 97–101; Kaiyan Homi Kaikobad, 'Some Observations on the Doctrine of Continuity and Finality of Boundaries', *British Yearbook of International Law*, vol. 49 (1983): pp. 119–27; and Steven R. Ratner, 'Drawing a Better Line: Uti Possidetis and the Borders of New States', *American Journal of International Law*, vol. 90 (1996): pp. 590–624. For a specific assessment of the impact of this discourse on post-colonial States, see Castellino, *International Law and Self-Determination*; Joshua Castellino and Steve Allen, *Title to Territory in International Law: A Temporal Analysis* (Dartmouth: Ashgate, 2005) and Joshua Castellino, 'Territorial Integrity and the "Right" to Self-Determination: An Examination of the Conceptual Tools', *Brooklyn Journal of International Law*, vol. 33, no. 2 (2008): pp. 503–68.

each other, but we have only been hindered by the small impediment that we never knew exactly where those mountains and rivers and lakes were.[14]

As a consequence of such line-drawing, all subsequent constitutional arrangement occurred within a fixed, artificially imposed territorial frame.[15] Sri Lanka, as an island, is easiest to address since geographic factors were a key determinant to its emergence as a separate state. This new State did, however, inherit a significant Tamil population concentrated in the north of the island, closest to India and the Indian state of Tamil Nadu.[16] The boundary between India and Pakistan was determined by a combination of internal negotiation in the pre-independence movement, and subsequent reiteration, occupation, unaddressed claim, or clarification between the States.[17] When the idea of an undivided India became untenable, negotiations began between the two leading claimants to power: the Indian National Congress, and the Muslim League, itself emerging from the Indian National Congress. The fear of Muslim submersion into a Hindu India led to the articulation of a claim for a separate State consisting of West Pakistan (Baluchistan, North-West Frontier Province (NWFP), Sindh, Muslim-dominated Punjab), and East Pakistan (consisting of Muslim-dominated Bengal). Claims for other Muslim-dominated areas such as Kashmir, Hyderabad, and Allahabad were not realized, and these remained within India. The well-documented emergence of Bangladesh was achieved through covert and overt Indian involvement in support of the Mukhti Bahini and Mukhti Fauj who mobilized around the linguistic movement initiated by the Awami League, who technically won the national elections of 1971 on a separatist agenda.[18] The Kingdom of Nepal had been maintained with clear administrative boundaries under British colonial rule and gained its independence as a separate entity,[19] similar to Bhutan.[20] A third formerly independent Himalayan kingdom, Sikkim, was, however, incorporated into India, meriting little global attention or scrutiny.[21]

At independence each State under consideration here had to overcome ethnic, linguistic, and religious fault lines to forge a common national identity linking its communities. This challenge should not be underestimated: India itself is extremely diverse, with its billion-strong population consisting of six main ethnic

[14] As cited by Judge Ajibola in *Libya v Chad* [1994] ICJ Reports, p. 53.

[15] India's external boundary with China is equally problematic. See A. G. Noorani, *India–China Boundary Problem 1846–1947: History and Diplomacy* (New Delhi: Oxford University Press, 2011).

[16] For more, see Jeyaratnam A. Wilson, *Sri Lankan Tamil Nationalism: Its Origin and Development in the 19th and 20th centuries* (New Delhi: Penguin, 2000).

[17] See Anna Orton, *India's Borderland Disputes: China, Pakistan, Bangladesh, Nepal* (New Delhi: Epitome Books, 2010).

[18] Richard Sisson and Leo E. Rose, *War and Secession: Pakistan, India and the Creation of Bangladesh* (Berkeley: University of California Press, 1991).

[19] See John Whelpton, *A History of Nepal* (Cambridge: Cambridge University Press, 2005).

[20] Karma Phuntso, *The History of Bhutan* (New Delhi: Random House Press, 2013).

[21] See Saul Mullard, *Opening the Hidden Land: State Formation and the Construction of Sikkimese History* (Leiden: Brill, 2011).

groups, 52 major tribes, six major religions, and 6,400 castes and sub-castes besides 18 major languages and 1,600 minor languages and dialects.[22] The challenge of welding these communities into a modern State while accommodating competing 'national' and sub-national aspirations was possibly among the most complex faced by any emerging State. External frontiers were demarcated on grounds of religion between India and Pakistan, posing additional problems for the large Muslim population within India, and, to a marginally lesser extent, for the Hindus and Christians within Pakistan.

Each State took different approaches in seeking to address the varied emerging, submerged and dormant sub-State aspirations, usually framing the debate within articulations of constitutional and administrative law, as demonstrated in Section 10.2. In legal terms India is defined as a 'secular socialist republic' with a strong federal structure and power devolved between the central government based in New Delhi, and the regional governments. The demarcations of the regions was determined on linguistic grounds and commenced commensurate with significant debate in constituent assemblies. The idea of re-drawing the Indian map on the basis of language was envisaged as enabling greater coherence and linguistic protection, rather than relying on the boundaries of princely states from which India was originally derived. In the Indian context power between the centre and state governments is clearly defined within the constitution (see section 10.3.1.1) which also envisaged special consideration for specific regional autonomies such as that of Kashmir.[23]

In the decades since independence Pakistan has followed an uncertain journey towards constitutional democracy, culminating in modern challenges that have left it floundering on the shores of being a failed State. Its early years were dominated by power exercised via the army, and the State went through a traumatic severance when Bangladesh emerged in 1971. That war of secession (or independence from a Bangla perspective) and the ongoing hot–cold war between Pakistan and India over Kashmir has meant that identity and territorial issues have never been far from mainstream politics. On the surface Pakistan is a federal State in ways similar to its neighbour: its administrative state boundaries are derived primarily on ethno-linguistic grounds with the Pakhtoons dominant in NWFP, Sindhis dominant in Sindh, Baluchis, who are now agitating for ever-greater autonomy and even secession, the dominant group in Baluchistan, with the dominant nationwide group, the Punjabis, playing a prominent role in national politics and within the armed forces.[24]

[22] *TMA Pai Foundation and Ors v State of Karnataka and Ors*, WP (Civil) No. 317/1993 (31 October 2002), para 158.

[23] For a succinct summary of these issues, see Thomas Benedikter, *The World's Working Regional Autonomies: An Introduction and Comparative Analysis* (New Delhi: Anthem Press, 2007), pp. 305–16.

[24] See Hamid Khan, *Constitutional and Political History of Pakistan* (Oxford: Oxford University Press, 2009).

After emerging from the shadow of Pakistan, Bangladesh is now in a period where old wounds around its establishment as a sovereign State in the aftermath of the 1971 Indo-Pakistan War are being re-opened. The State itself has remained democratic since the emergence of the Awami League in 1971 as the principal political power, though original claims about homogeneity have been challenged by Bangladesh's own indigenous people, the Chakma in the Chittagong Hills.[25] In this context the Peace Accord signed between the Bangladesh government and the Parbattyo Chattagram Jana Sanghati Samiti is relatively well known as a model of autonomy. However as Matin et al. show in their assessment of the impact of ethnic inequality on forestry management, this accord changed very little. While its premise was the need to bring an end to the low-intensity dispute, the underlying causes of the dispute was the dispossession and displacement of the hill tribes, which has continued unabated in the post-Accord period through the in-migration of Bengalis and compulsory acquisition of land by the government.[26]

At Sri Lankan independence the challenge that immediately became apparent was how the two large communities on the island (Sinhala and Tamil) could co-exist in harmony. The geographic division of the communities was apparent: Tamils were predominantly located in the north of the island around the Jaffna peninsula, while the Sinhala were prominent over the rest of the island.[27] Sri Lanka also has a significant Muslim population (estimated at 7 per cent) but not being based in a geographically contiguous area, it has had minimal impact on discussions concerning autonomy. While Sri Lanka has been through significant periods of rapprochement, these failed to stave off what became a long-running civil war, ended in 2009 through brutal force, accompanied by serious allegations of gross violations of human rights. The State that has emerged from that war has become increasingly totalitarian and thus any attempt to understand autonomy regimes within it becomes even more subject to the diktats of contemporary politics.[28]

The displacement of the monarchy in Nepal and the emergence of a modern constitutional democracy sent shock waves through the international community. Commencing from a Maoist movement, the surge towards popular democracy was sealed when the Maoists won the right to form the government. The success of the transition remains dependent on the extent to which adequate structures are designed to safeguard Nepal's ethnic and caste-based communities. While the

[25] For a discussion on the Chittagong Hill Tracts, see Faustina Pereira, 'The Chittagong Hill Tracts Peace Accord and the Long Road to Peace: A Case Study', in *International Law and Indigenous Peoples*, edited by Joshua Castellino and Niamh Walsh (Leiden: Martinus Nijhoff Publishers, 2005), pp. 293–302.

[26] Nilufar Matin, Mohammad S. Islam, Musingo T. E. Mbuvi, Bernard O. Odit, Paul O. Ongugo, and Mohammad A. Syed, 'Group Inequality and Environmental Sustainability: Insights from Bangladesh and Kenyan Forest Commons', *Sustainability*, vol. 6, no. 3 (2014): pp. 1462–88.

[27] See Gnanapala Welhengama and Nirmala Pillay, *The Rise of Tamil Separatism in Sri Lanka: From Communalism to Secession* (London: Routledge, 2014).

[28] See Human Rights Watch, 'Sri Lanka', in *World Report on Human Rights 2014* (New York: Human Rights Watch, 2014), accessed 24 October 2014, http://www.hrw.org/world-report/2014/country-chapters/sri-lanka.

decision to orient the State towards a pluralist democracy is to be commended, much remains to be achieved if this aspiration can be meaningfully fulfilled.[29]

10.3 The States, Federalism, and Regional Autonomy

Having established a brief background for each State, this section seeks to identify the applicable law for each within this purview.

10.3.1 India

As Mahajan contends, federalism in India has 'helped...curb, or at least minimize, the dominance of the majority and provided space for different groups and communities to share power...It has resulted in the emergence of diverse and plural elites in the political arena',[30] and has had numerous benefits in: (i) expanding the public sphere; (ii) curtailing interference from the centre; (iii) generating regional autonomies; (iv) decentralizing power away from national elites; and in (v) dampening and, in some cases, resolving ethnic conflict.[31]

Of the States reviewed here, India is the most federalist, with the clearest demarcation for regional autonomy. However the State shows strong centralist tendencies in comparison with federal States outside South Asia. It leads Wheare to concede that while India is 'strictly and fully federal': (a) the issues under exclusive mandates of the states tend to be of subordinate concern;[32] (b) the Union retains power of intervention over state affairs in normal and emergency times;[33] and (c) the Indian Parliament has the mandate to reorganize states in consultation with them, but without consent.[34]

10.3.1.1 The Indian constitution and regional autonomy

While it is not possible to dwell on the rich historical discussions that framed the Indian constitution in these pages,[35] it will suffice to highlight that its architecture at the outset bore strong principles of power devolution, evidenced in: (a) the

[29] See Bhuwan Chandra Upreti, *Nepal: Transition to Democratic Republican State* (New Delhi: Kalpaz Publications, 2010).

[30] Gurpreet Mahajan, 'Federal Accommodation of Ethnocultural Identities in India', in *Federalism in Asia*, edited by Baogang He, Brian Gallidan, and Takashi Inoguchi (Cheltenham: Edward Elgar, 2007), p. 92.

[31] Kenneth C. Wheare, *Federal Government* (New York: Oxford University Press, 1964), pp. 26–7.

[32] 'state' with a lower case 's' is used to denote the sub-national entities within India, whereas 'State' with a capital 'S' is reserved for references to the country.

[33] Constitution of India 1950, amended by various constitutional amendments as notified, art 365.

[34] Wheare, *Federal Government*, pp. 26–7.

[35] For a summary of some of these, see Castellino and Dominguez Redondo, *Minority Rights in Asia*, pp. 61–5.

reorganization of states on the basis of linguistic communities with separate legislatures; (b) the articulation (via a Union, state, and concurrent lists) of the mandates between centre and state; (c) specially designated autonomy for Kashmir and the states in the north-east of India, with these states further subdivided into thirteen autonomous districts.[36]

The fundamental aim of federalist provisions in the Indian constitution could be expressed as the safeguarding of the rights of linguistic communities, with the reorganizing of boundaries envisaged as enabling such communities self-governance rights.[37] Yet despite the demarcation of explicit spheres in the constitution, the 'national' is privileged over the 'state', with the latter subject to revision by Parliament's right to demarcate new states,[38] albeit with a role for presidential approval.[39] Thus while Parliament has the power of redrawing the federal map, Baxi points out that in reality it is 'peoples movements' (most recently in the creation of the state of Telengana in 2014)[40] that exercise this power; as a result:

> New states are almost constantly born within the Indian federation, along linguistic/cultural/identity axes. No doubt, both insurgent and state violence mark the birthing of new state 'communities'.[41]

These often violent contestations of power are not restricted to agitations for federal status, but may extend to calls for secession.[42] The struggles[43] have, by

[36] For more, see David Stuligross, 'Autonomous Councils in Northeast India: Theory and Practice', *Alternatives*, vol. 24 (1999): pp. 497–526; also see Sajjad M. Hassan, 'Understanding the Breakdown in Northeast India: Explorations in State–Society Relations', *Working Paper*, no. 07–83 (2007).

[37] One of the reasons for the length of the Indian constitution is the amount of detail with regards to the features of federalism contained within the document itself. Thus the constitution is, at once, a constitution for the State as well as for its federal components. The demarcation of power between the centre and the states is contained in the Schedules that identify various 'lists' of competence—national, state, and 'mixed'.

[38] Constitution of India, art 3, as demonstrated by the carving out of three new states in the mid-2000s.

[39] After modification by the Constitution (Fifth Amendment) Act 1955, s 2 and the Constitution (Seventh Amendment) Act 1956.

[40] Andhra Pradesh Reorganisation Act 2014. For a historical overview of the challenges to the creation of Telengana, see Kingshuk Nag, *Battleground Telengana: Chronicle of an Agitation* (New Delhi: Harper Collins, 2012); Putchalapalli Sundarayya, *Telengana People's Struggles and its Lessons* (New Delhi: Foundation Books, 1972, reprinted 2006); Louise Tillin, *Remapping India: New States and their Political Origins* (London: Hurst, 2013). For the report arguing for the merger of Telengana with Andhra Pradesh, see S. Ali, K. M. Panikker, and H. N. Kunzru, *Report of the States Reorganization Committee* (New Delhi: Government of India, 1955).

[41] See Upendra Baxi, 'The Rule of Law in India: Theory and Practice', in *Asian Discourses on the Rule of* Law, edited by Randall Peerenboom (London: Routledge, 2004), p. 334.

[42] The better known of these are Kashmir and Punjab, but calls for secession have also come from Nagaland and Tamil Nadu. See Pradip Phanjoubam, 'Surrogate Wars, Surrogate Governments', *Outlook Magazine*, 27 May 2003 and Pradip Phanjoubam, 'The Fourteen Spokes of a Revolution', *Outlook Magazine*, 20 October 2003.

[43] These armed struggles are primarily 'identity-based' agitations rather than socio-economic ones, namely in Andhra Pradesh which pits the so-called Peoples War Group (PWG) against the state government. For a report on this issue and the peace treaty, see Suhas Chakma, 'Guns and Talks in India's Wretched of the Earth', *Kashmir Times*, Index: Review/42/2004, accessed 13 October 2004.

and large been contained within the Union through a range of means from police action[44] to the negotiating of peace treaties.[45]

Three features of the Indian federal system are particularly distinctive:

(a) National Parliament retains power;
(b) Cooperative federalism is the norm rather than the exception;
(c) The democratic deficit stands structured by the federal power to suspend the federal principle in situations of an armed rebellion and external aggression.[46]

The specific provisions for autonomy are contained in Article 244 of the constitution[47] with Articles 339 and 340 dealing with the relationship of the central administration in these issues, including a description of the control of the Union over the administration of Scheduled Areas[48] and the appointment of a commission to investigate the conditions of groups unfortunately named 'backward classes'.[49] The original constitutional design has been significantly altered by amendments, the net effect of which has been to augment the scope of Union powers, concurrently reducing the issues under the exclusive domain of states.[50] Within India's federal system the regional autonomy guaranteed to Jammu and Kashmir, Nagaland, and Mizoram also merit further comment. The problematic history of the accession of Kashmir into India was key to the framing of Article 370, which restricts the powers of the national Parliament. However, governments of India have staunchly resisted demands for self-rule as articulated by the People's Democratic Party, while keeping the dialogue open on 'shared rule'.[51]

While meriting less attention, the special autonomy regimes of Nagaland and Mizoram are equally important to understanding regional autonomy regimes in India.[52] These provisions contained in Articles 371 (A to G) restrict the impact of laws passed by the national Parliament in the realm of customary and other laws, making them conditional on concurrent consensus from state legislatures. Provisions on regional autonomy in the north-east of India also pertain to sub-state autonomies, pertaining to special representative bodies within the tribal areas in Assam, Meghalaya, Tripura, and Mizoram. These districts are jointly administered under the sixth schedule of the constitution by the Union

44 As in Punjab, Kartar Singh Duggal, *Understanding the Sikh Psyche: Reflections on the Current Punjab Crisis* (New Delhi: Siddhartha, 1992).

45 As in Nagaland, H. K. Barpujari, *North-East India: Problems, Policies and Prospects since Independence* (New Delhi: Spectrum, 1998).

46 Baxi, 'The Rule of Law in India', p. 335.

47 For a commentary see Asian Centre for Human Rights, *The Maladministration of Indigenous and Tribal Peoples of India* ACHRF 33/2004, (4 August 2004).

48 Constitution of India, art 339.

49 Constitution of India, art 340.

50 Mahendra Prasad Singh and Veena Kukreja, *Federalism in South Asia* (New Delhi: Routledge, 2014), pp. 19–23.

51 Singh and Kukreja, *Federalism in South Asia*, p. 93.

52 For an informative though dated commentary on tribal movements and their constitutional accommodation in the north-east of India, see K. S. Singh, ed., *Tribal Movements in India* (Delhi: Manohar Publishers, 1982, reprinted in 2006).

and state governments alongside elected district or regional councils. The law provides districts/councils with the mandate to pass legislation pertaining to a host of issues including land, agriculture, irrigation, forest, education, public health, administration (including justice), appointment or succession of tribal chiefs or headmen, marriage and divorce, and social custom. As currently framed these laws are subject to the proviso that where conflict between laws may arise, that of the state legislatures prevails.[53] While these provisions appear to be robust, the constitution provides the Union government with emergency powers to govern, particularly relevant in the manner in which this has enabled the central government to deploy the army through the draconian Armed Forces (Special Powers) Act.[54] A study into the insurgencies in the north-eastern region was heavily critical of this approach which included, in addition, reliance on ethnic strongmen to deliver peace and security in return for a freer hand in governance, and the establishment of personal fiefdoms. As Lacina argues:

> This departure from democratic norms and constitutionalism for short-term practical gains is fraught with negative consequences for federal governance in the long run.... [a] tendency [that] surface[es] in Mizoram, Tripura, Nagaland, Manipur, the Bodo areas of Assam, as well as in case of the Gorkhaland movement in the Darjeeling hill district in West Bengal, where the Union and state governments have yielded to the temptation for pragmatic and provisional gains but long-term losses.[55]

The result of these measures is that the Indian performance on regional (state) autonomy is mixed and can be summed up in the following six points. First, regional autonomy is reflected in a system that distinguishes the central government from states, usually drawn or redrawn on the basis of language. Second, where religious minorities have been territorially based there has been some attempt to create autonomous regimes, though this pertains as much to language as ethnicity, namely Muslims and Sikhs are majorities in Jammu and Kashmir and Punjab respectively. Instead the system of NTA, in the form of the prevalence of religious laws, is the main point of accommodation of religious minorities (and the Hindu majority). Third, the constitutional guarantee for the special regime for Kashmir remains in place, persisting despite criticism from the incumbent regime of this prior to its election,[56] but further discussion concerning self-rule has stalled. Fourth, special regimes are in place in the north-eastern states, including, in some, for sub-regional autonomy as discussed above. Fifth, the federal system is based on a clear articulation of the mandates of the Union government vis-à-vis state governments, however Union lists have grown while those of the states have shrunk. Finally, while the system is federal in outlook, the centre retains power to

[53] Singh and Kukreja, *Federalism in South Asia*, p. 94.

[54] See Armed Forces (Special Powers) Act 1958.

[55] Bethany Lacina, 'The Problem of Political Stability in Northeast India: Local Ethnic Autocracy and the Rule of Law', *Asian Survey* XLIX (2009): pp. 998–1020.

[56] For a recent discussion on Kashmir, see Arup K. Sen, 'Kashmir: A State of Exception', *Economic and Political Weekly*, vol. L, no. 8 (2015) and Paul D'Souza, 'Conflict of Kashmir and the Problem of Disappearance', *Economic and Political Weekly*, vol. L, no. 5 (2015).

intervene within the state affairs and frequently does, citing emergency powers, and in some cases including especially in the north-east and Kashmir, through draconian deployment of armed forces, whose track record of rights abuses undermines India's democratic credentials.[57]

There have been recent attempts to redraw the Indian map, which now consists of twenty-nine states in addition to seven Union territories governed directly from New Delhi. Some of the newer states have been created as knee-jerk responses to popular demand, with inadequate attention paid to their viability, and many are likely to struggle to thrive in an increasingly competitive neo-liberal economy.[58] There continue to be sub-state demands for more states, the latest being the emergence of Telengana on linguistic grounds through secession from Andhra Pradesh.[59] Each territorial unit retains considerable diversity and minorities within minorities, including kin communities divided by state boundaries. In addition there continues to be identity-based tension as a consequence of caste discrimination and discrimination against indigenous peoples (*adivasis*).[60] The simmering discontent of economic disparity plays a growing role in support for a Maoist Naxalite movement, which is often brutally suppressed through police action that creates fear.[61]

10.3.2 Pakistan

While from the outset Pakistan was envisaged as a federal State as promised in the Lahore Resolution by the Muslim League in 1940, in actual fact it has been highly centralized.[62] Further, as the federal idea withered in Pakistan's first twenty-five years, the exclusiveness of the power elite and the short-sighted and discriminatory policies pursued heightened social exclusion, and generated governance structures that proved inappropriate in accommodating the 'multiple social identities in a context shaped by regional diversities and inequalities'.[63] The result of the various crises of federalism, in addition to other general governance failures, has led to Pakistan being labelled 'a defunct', 'lopsided', 'confused' or 'failed' federation.[64] Thus even though Pakistan could notionally be considered a federation,

[57] See Human Rights Watch, 'India: Getting Away with Murder: 50 Years of the Armed Forces Special Powers Act', *Human Rights Watch* (2008). Also see Amnesty International India, 'Briefing: The Armed Forces Special Powers Act: A Renewed Debate in India on Human Rights and National Security', *Amnesty International India* (2013). For additional commentary, see [Editorial] 'An Empty Verdict', *Economic and Political Weekly*, vol. XLIX, no. 47, 22 November 2014; A. Pervez, 'Fallout of Continued Use of AFSPA', *Economic and Political Weekly*, vol. XLVI, no. 9 (2011).

[58] Singh and Kukreja, *Federalism in South Asia*, p. 115.

[59] For a history of these efforts, see Sundarayya, *Telengana People's Struggle*.

[60] See Sanjukta Das Gupta and Raj Sekhar Basu, eds, *Narratives from the Margins: Aspects of Adivasi History in India* (London: Primus, 2012).

[61] See generally V. R. Raghavan, *The Naxal Threat: Causes, State Responses and Consequences* (New Delhi: Vij Books, 2011).

[62] Singh and Kukreja, *Federalism in South Asia*, p. 213.

[63] Singh and Kukreja, *Federalism in South Asia*, p. 51.

[64] Singh and Kukreja, *Federalism in South Asia*, p. 51.

it operates as a unitarian State, while reiterating the promise of federalism to appease sub-national communities and nations. As Ahmad puts it: 'Since its creation in 1947 it has failed to establish an organic and effective covenant between the federation and the federating units, despite some incremental forward movements toward provincial autonomy and devolution'.[65]

In tracing the development of federalist concepts through Pakistan's three constitutions, a few landmarks can be highlighted. These have been selected to show how notions of federalism have continued to be viewed as a potential solution. However these discussions have not yet succeeded in changing the basic underlying national governance fabric. Pakistan's constitutional history has been classified by Waseem as encompassing two eras: a pre-federalisation era (1947–71) and a federalization era (1973 to date). The gap relates to the war, secession, and resulting constitutional and territorial adjustments after the establishment of Bangladesh. In characterizing (or perhaps caricaturing) the two eras Waseem finds:

> the first phase was characterized by centralization of authority and elimination of the federal structure within West Pakistan. In the second phase, federalism bounced back and gradually moved forward in the formidable challenge from the centralist framework of state authority.[66]

Any attempt to understand Pakistan's attempt to create a federalist State with regional autonomies has to commence with the 1940 Lahore Resolution. The text of the Lahore Resolution was proposed on 23 March 1940 at Minto Park, Lahore, by A. K. Fazul Haq, then Chief Minister of Bengal.[67] The Resolution made five key points, the three reproduced below of salience to our discussion:

- that no constitutional plan would be…acceptable to Muslims unless… designed on the following basic principle, namely, that geographically contiguous units are demarcated into regions which should be so constituted, with such territorial readjustments as may be necessary, that the areas in which the Muslims are numerically in a majority, as in the North-Western and Eastern Zones of India, should be grouped to constitute 'Independent States' in which the constituent units shall be autonomous and sovereign.
- That adequate, effective and mandatory safeguards should be specifically provided in the constitution for minorities…for the protection of their religious, cultural, economic, political, administrative and other rights and interests in consultation with them; and in other parts of India where Mussalmans are in a minority, adequate, effective and mandatory safeguard[s] shall be specially provided in the constitution for them and other minorities for the protection

[65] Raza Ahmad, 'The Endemic Crisis of Federalism in Pakistan', *The Lahore Journal of Economics* (2010): p. 15.

[66] Mohammad Waseem, 'Federalism in Pakistan', 2010, p. 5, accessed 16 October 2014, http://www.forumfed.org/pubs/Waseem-Fed-Overview.pdf.

[67] For more on the events leading up to this, see Jaswant Singh, *Jinnah: India–Pakistan Independence* (New Delhi: Rupa, 2009).

of their religious, cultural, economic, political, administrative and other rights and interests in consultation with them.

– This session further authorizes the Working Committee to frame a scheme of constitution in accordance with these basic principles, providing for the assumption finally by the respective regions of all powers such as defence, external affairs, communications, customs and such other matters as may be necessary.[68]

The following points can be emphasized as central to the text and spirit of Lahore. First, it emphasized the demarcation and designation, (including through territorial adjustment) of Muslim-populated areas of undivided India as independent and autonomous states with a degree of sovereignty. Second, that specific minority protection provisions be constructed within new territorial units, as well as ensuring such protection for Muslims left in India, to be realized with their full participation. Third, a call for the design of a new constitution adhering to basic principles of federalism, with the suggestion that these extend to models akin to sovereign States. Thus the Lahore Resolution visualized Pakistan as a federal State where communities or nations with distinct historical, linguistic, social, and cultural backgrounds would function as federal provinces. This articulation was viewed by Bengali, Sindhi, Baluchi, Pakhtun, and Pakistan nationalists as akin to a social contract urging them to become part of the emerging State.[69] It is worth reiterating that NWFP (home to the Pathans) originally voted against joining the union of Pakistan in 1946, and were swayed by the promise of federated governance, to which it had become accustomed during British rule.[70]

While the design of Pakistan may have well been flawed at the outset, the failure to live up to the Lahore Resolution promises of a federated structure were mitigating factors in the ultimate demise of East Pakistan. In (West) Pakistan, the resultant loss of the East increased pressure for a move towards regional autonomy, with many arguing for a fairer distribution of power and resources between the centre and provinces.[71] While this pressure did result in a minor attempt to address issues of federalism in the 1973 constitution, these fell short of the Lahore promise, and faded away in the midst of the dominance of Pakistan's ruling classes. The result of the power matrix in Pakistan is often presented as Punjabi dominance in forming central government and controlling the armed forces, but also in dictating the nature of the relationship between the centre and provinces such as NWFP, Baluchistan, and Sindh.

Through the Independence Act of 1947[72] Pakistan adopted an amended version of the Government of India Act 1935[73] as its new constitution, incorporating

[68] See Ikram Ali Malik, *Muslim League Session 1940 and the Lahore Resolution 1940: Documents* (Islamabad: National Institute of Historical and Cultural Research, 1990).

[69] Singh and Kukreja, *Federalism in South Asia*, p. 209.

[70] Ian Talbot, 'The Punjabization of Pakistan: Myth or Reality', in *Pakistan: Nationalism without a Nation*, edited by Christophe Jaffrolot (New Delhi: Manohar, 2002), pp. 54–65.

[71] Singh and Kukreja, *Federalism in South Asia*, p. 51.

[72] Malik, *Muslim League Session 1940*, p. 88.

[73] Malik, *Muslim League Session 1940*, p. 88.

the promise of the Lahore Resolution that the country would function as a federal State.[74] However while the three constitutions that have been passed since (1956, 1962, 1973) have enshrined a two-level structure, they have left Pakistan as a unitary centralized State. Along the way there have been significant discussions clarifying the notion of federalism and its application, but they have rarely been incorporated into the constitution, and where they have, the implementation of these has been left vague enough to avoid structural change. The 'Basic Principles Committee Report', also known as the 'Bengali–Punjabi Crisis Report 1951', was one of the earliest articulations of how such a structure could be realized.[75] The issue of seeking a balance of power between Bengal and Punjab was presented as the Mohammad Ali Bogra Formula (1953).[76] This formula was subsequently accepted in a modified form by the Constituent Assembly (CA) in 1954, but this did not enter force. When the Assembly did eventually reconvene it did so with far greater representation of non-Muslim League Bengalis. Some progress was made on the agenda of achieving structural change, though the trend moved away from federalization, as the four provinces of West Pakistan were subsumed into a single federal unit (West Pakistan), which came into existence in October 1955.[77] Thus the attempt at greater representation for one region reduced the overall thrust of regional autonomy for the (current) provinces of (West) Pakistan. The goal of this move was twofold: to concede greater representation to the Bengalis, but to suppress emerging sub-national movements in NWFP and Baluchistan. This could be considered the point in the State-building process of Pakistan where the dominance of Punjab over the smaller nationalities became fully established.[78] As Ali put it, the move constituted, 'short-sighted bureaucracy, desperate to balance "East with West, [which] infected the national question into the heart of West Pakistani politics"'.[79] In any case while there was greater representation for Bengalis, Ali argued that this constitution and arrangement institutionalized political discrimination against Bengalis, giving them an ostensibly greater voice while augmenting the rights of the president and central government and reducing provincial autonomy to a 'farcical status'.[80]

Even the facade of federalism disappeared in the 1962 constitution which took the concept out of Article 1, absorbing it into the preamble. The federal question was engaged negatively, with the publication of a single list of subjects for central legislature leaving residual authority to provincial legislatures, with

[74] Singh and Kukreja, *Federalism in South Asia*, p. 210.

[75] Safdar Mahmood, *Pakistan: Political Roots and Development 1947–1999* (Oxford: Oxford University Press, 2002), pp. 40–1.

[76] See generally Yunas Samad, *A Nation in Turmoil: Nationalism and Ethnicity in Pakistan 1937–1958* (New Delhi: Sage, 1995).

[77] This is described by Ali as a short-sighted bureaucratic scheme in a book that offers very harsh criticism in general; see Tariq Ali, *Can Pakistan Survive? Death of a State* (New Delhi: Penguin, 1983). Also see Hamza Alavi, 'Nationhood and Nationalities in Pakistan', *Economic and Political Weekly*, vol. 24, no. 27 (1989): pp. 1527–34.

[78] Satish Kumar, 'Problems of Federal Politics in Pakistan' in *Society and Politics in Pakistan*, edited by Pandav Nayak (New Delhi: South Asian Publisher, 1984), p. 23.

[79] Ali, *Can Pakistan Survive?*, p. 49.

[80] Ali, *Can Pakistan Survive?*, p. 49.

any interpretation of autonomy from these further restricted by the provision of Article 131(2) which further minimized any exercise of this limited mandate.[81] The federal agenda received a brief fillip during the martial law regime of General Yahya Khan (1969–70), with his Legal Framework Order, intended to be the basis of the future constitution, proposing what Raza deemed a 'relatively decentralized federation'.[82] In any case any discussion on this question stalled as Pakistan went through a traumatic war which eventually led to the secession of the East and its subsequent recognition as Bangladesh.

The severance of the East left Punjab, within the Single Unit, subsequently the State of Pakistan, as its most dominant ethno-national community, accounting for the majority (56 per cent) of the population. This reiterated the question of federal delineation of power, and the 1973 constitution proposed a federal system with representative provincial quotas within the central bureaucracy.[83] Once again however the constitution was seen as a facade: while federal in nature it was unitary in character. The provincial autonomy provisions were countered by strong emergency powers, enabling central governmental interference into provinces, a power utilized often.[84] Further, regional autonomy provisions were curbed by Article 142(b) which reserved the legislative agenda for the central government enabling greater involvement in issues within provincial jurisdictions. To make this more assertive, Article 143 explicitly identified central governmental supremacy over provincial government over the concurrent list, effectively making that list a federal list.[85] While this constitution has survived further periods of martial law (Zia ul-Haq 1978–88) and Musharraf (2001–8) and remains in force, the federal question has rarely left mainstream Pakistani politics. However, the presidential powers to dissolve provincial governments were strengthened (Eighth Constitutional Amendment, rescinded by the Thirteenth Amendment, reasserted by the Seventeenth Amendment). In a step that took Pakistan further away from the Lahore vision, Musharraf's creation of the National Security Council in 2003 formalized the political role of the armed forces, extending the power base of a Punjabi-dominated institution.[86]

One route to assessing the devolutionary credentials within a system is to look at how the fiscal system is managed between centre and regions. Pakistan's has clear federal bias, with federal taxes accounting for 90 per cent of total revenue collected, and the federal government retaining 93 per cent of the revenue collection mandate. The provinces have the ability to raise the residual 7 per cent of the revenue but spend 28 per cent of it.[87] This means that provinces rely heavily on central grants, which impinge on their ability to operate autonomously.

[81] Rafi Raza, ed., *Pakistan in Perspective 1977–1997* (Karachi: Oxford University Press, 1997), p. 8.
[82] Raza, *Pakistan in Perspective 1977–1997.*
[83] Singh and Kukreja, *Federalism in South Asia*, p. 216.
[84] Singh and Kukreja, *Federalism in South Asia*, p. 223.
[85] Singh and Kukreja, *Federalism in South Asia*, p. 223.
[86] Singh and Kukreja, *Federalism in South Asia*, p. 227.
[87] Singh and Kukreja, *Federalism in South Asia*, p. 227.

The monies were distributed to provinces on the basis of population until 2009, which guaranteed a significantly larger share for Punjab (57.88 per cent) than the rest of the provinces put together (Sindh 23.28 per cent, NWFP 13.54 per cent, Baluchistan 5.3 per cent).[88] While NWFP and Baluchistan do receive special 'development grants', these are nowhere commiserate with their contribution to the economy in terms of energy, where NWFP (hydroelectric power) and Baluchistan (gas) contribute heavily to development in Punjab. The manner in which the money has been negotiated and distributed through a 'National Fiscal Committee Award' has, as is to be expected, been subject to significant political manoeuvring. Singh and Kukreja highlight that while the provinces have won leeway on the award, their demands have been half met by the Eighteenth Constitutional Amendment.[89]

In recent years the pressure for self-determination has increased in Pakistan. There are many factors to this: the ongoing governance struggles in crises in such as in the Swat Valley where ex-Taliban fighters form the de facto government; the inevitable consequences of being engaged as a 'frontline State' in the attempt to combat terrorism; and from tensions arising from the disagreement about the extent to which religion should penetrate the public sphere. The disparities in wealth distribution, unbalanced fiscal policies, suppression of regionalism, and the now systematized failure to implement the spirit and the modalities of the Lahore Resolution have strengthened calls for secession. Protests, demonstrations, and violent incidents against the central government have become commonplace in Baluchistan, NWFP, and Sindh. Instead of engaging with the underlying substance of these arguments for divorce, the government has sought to combat them through reiterations of Islamic ideology or militarized solutions,[90] neither of which appear effective in the medium or long run. The last time in recent years that federalism was genuinely addressed was through discussions that led to the Eighteenth Amendment to the Constitution (April 2010). This amendment, restoring parliamentary democracy to Pakistan after General Musharraf's military rule, also contained provisions for greater cession of power from the centre towards the provinces. This change had not really been tested, coming as it did in the face of various other pressures, including natural disasters. As a consequence, whether due to errors of commission or omission, little has been done to change Pakistan's bureaucratized structure, and the discussions are viewed as more failed devolutionary promises.[91]

Like others in South Asia, Pakistan is ethnically and linguistically complex, consisting of five major ethnic groups which do not always correspond to

[88] Singh and Kukreja, *Federalism in South Asia*, p. 227.

[89] Singh and Kukreja, *Federalism in South Asia*, p. 229.

[90] The issue of governance through military rule in general, with some focus on how this affects the provinces is discussed generally in R. A. Singh, *Military Governance in Pakistan* (New Delhi: Raj Publications, 2007).

[91] For a view through a Baluchi lens, see Aasim Sajjad Akhtar, 'Balochistan versus Pakistan', *Economic and Political Weekly*, vol. XLII, nos 45–6 (2007).

linguistic communities.[92] The federal model with regional autonomy would seem the logical starting point for a nation-building process, as acknowledged in the Lahore Resolution. This section has shown how this promise has come unstuck, and endorses Singh and Kukreja's view that many of 'Pakistan's ethno-national conflicts are rooted in the mismatch between diversity and political institutional arrangements'.[93] For change to occur the ruling elite would need to agree to abdicate hegemony,[94] and accept the plural composition of modern Pakistan.

10.3.3 Sri Lanka

Unlike India and Pakistan, which entertained federalist options from the outset, Sri Lanka has identified as a unitary State. Early articulations that federal power-sharing arrangements could be called upon to build a viable society, notably in 1926 by S. W. R. D. Bandaranaike,[95] did not achieve traction, though the ideologue behind their articulation rose to become Sri Lankan prime minister. Instead the unitary State created discriminatory regimes against its territorially based Tamil population, leading to disaffection and a bloody civil war that dominated the State's post-colonial history. Issues remain about how effective any post-conflict solutions could be, since peace has been 'won' through brutal militarization accompanied by a slide towards personal autocracy.

Commentators highlight that the Sinhalese–Tamil conflict was triggered by government-sponsored policies that actively discriminated against Tamils in land rights, language policy, education, employment, and power-sharing.[96] To maintain Sri Lanka as a clearly separate entity with its distinct culture from that of its much larger neighbour India, with its own Tamils, Sri Lanka's post-colonial governance was driven by the need to maintain Sinhala political hegemony by exerting control, excluding, discriminating, and resisting power-sharing ventures with its Tamil population.[97] Thus the right to vote was withdrawn from Indian Tamils (1949–50), Sinhalese was instituted as the sole official language replacing English (1956), Tamils were actively excluded from government jobs, and barred from serving in the police and military.[98] The State took over the administration

[92] For more, see Stephen Cohen, *The Idea of Pakistan* (New Delhi: Oxford University Press, 2005).

[93] Singh and Kukreja, *Federalism in South Asia*, p. 242.

[94] For more on the 'vice-regal culture' of Pakistan's ruling elite, see Kumar, 'Problems of Federal Politics in Pakistan', p. 30.

[95] For a detailed discussion of this proposal and the subsequent pact, see Welhengama and Pillay, *The Rise of Tamil Separatism in Sri Lanka*, pp. 203–6.

[96] See Ved Pratap Vaidik, *Ethnic Crisis in Sri Lanka: India's Options* (New Delhi: National Publishing House, 1980) and Robert C. Oberst, 'Policies of Ethnic Preferences in Sri Lanka', in *Ethnic Preference and Public Policy in Developing States*, edited by Neil Nevitte and Charles H. Kennedy (Boulder: Lynne Rienner, 1996), pp. 135–54. Also see Robert C. Oberst, 'Federalism and Ethnic Conflict', *Publius*, vol. 18 (1988): p. 182.

[97] See Kē. En. Ō. Dharmadāsa, *Language, Religion and Ethnic Assertiveness: The Growth of Sinhalese Nationalism in Sri Lanka* (Ann Harbor: University of Michigan Press, 1992).

[98] See Satchi Ponnambalam, *Sri Lanka: The National Question and the Tamil Liberation Struggle* (London: Zed Books and Tamil Information Centre, 1983).

of Christian schools and established quota systems to promote Sinhalese access to universities.[99] Oberst highlights widespread electoral fraud, State-instigated anti-Tamil riots and 'systematic and recurrent policies of exclusion and denial of power sharing'.[100] These policies eroded Sri Lanka's secular institutions impacting the bureaucracy, legislature, and judiciary.[101] Fledgling externally sponsored attempts at consociational power-sharing models floundered due to a lack of political will and the inability of the political elite across the ethnic divide to agree suitable models.[102]

The result was the marginalization of minorities and subsequent distrust of them, creating an ambience which facilitated the Liberation Tigers of Tamil Eelam (LTTE) to tap into resentment to launch an armed struggle for a separate Tamil state from 1983 onwards.[103] The Tamil quest for self-determination received covert and overt support from India and the global Tamil diaspora, which served to equalize the war effort. Significant efforts were made to arrive at a negotiated settlement, each falling short of engineering a genuine peace process. One effort brokered by India brought together Tamil stakeholders with Sri Lankan representatives in 1985 in Bhutan. With negotiations stalling, the Tamils put together the Thimpu Declaration which articulated a four-point demand:

- the recognition of the Tamils on the island as a nation;
- the recognition of the existence of an identified homeland for Tamils on the island of Sri Lanka;
- the recognition of the right to self-determination of the Tamil nation; and
- the recognition of the right to citizenship and the fundamental rights of all Tamils in Sri Lanka.[104]

The nature of these demands, especially concerning self-determination, the identification of a homeland, and recognition of Tamils as a nation were held to violate the basic sovereignty of Sri Lanka, and as a consequence the declaration was rejected outright.

The notion of federalism, alongside consociationalism, regional autonomy, and power-sharing were mooted and gained attention at various times. Federalism was

[99] Oberst, 'Federalism and Ethnic Conflict', p. 141.

[100] Oberst, 'Federalism and Ethnic Conflict', p. 141.

[101] See Lakshmanan Sabaratnam, 'The Boundaries of the State and the State of Ethnic Boundaries: Sinhala–Tamil Relations in Sri Lankan History', *Ethnic and Racial Studies*, vol. 10 (1987): pp. 291–315.

[102] See A. G. Noorani, 'The Challenge of Power-Sharing in Sri Lanka', *Economic and Political Weekly*, vol. XXX, no. 12 (1995).

[103] For a report that assesses the situation prior to the descent into a civil war, see Paul Sieghart, 'Sri Lanka: A Mounting Tragedy of Errors' [Report of a Mission to Sri Lanka in January 1984 on behalf of the International Commission of Jurists and its British Section] (Dorchester: Justice, 1984).

[104] K. M. De Silva, *Regional Powers and Small State Security: India and Sri Lanka 1977–1990* (Washington DC: Woodrow Wilson Centre Press, 1995), p. 164. Also see Visvanather Dharmalingam, 'Tamil Demands at Thimpu', *Tamil Times* (1985); Nadesan Satyendra, 'Thimpu Declaration: The Path of Reason', *Tamil Times*, vol. 6, no. 4 (1987): pp. 11–14.

given serious consideration in 2002, with the model envisaged seeking to create regional autonomy for the north, where the Tamil community was dominant, with general protections facilitated by the adoption of a federalist constitution guaranteeing the territorial integrity and sovereignty of Sri Lanka. These sentiments were defeated by the ascendancy to power of Rajapakse in 2005 on a campaign of anti-federalism. While federalism and devolution are seen as panaceas and have stimulated debate, Rajapakse has dismissed them, exploiting genuine Sinhala angst of being overrun. While the Sinhalese outnumber Tamils three to one in Sri Lanka, they are outnumbered six to one by the Tamil-speaking population of South Asia.[105] As a result there has long existed a fear of submergence, much like Muslims in India in the days leading up to Indian partition. On the Tamil side, a significant proportion feared that power-sharing was unlikely to work, a claim that gained currency after the brutal 2009 war and its aftermath.

The early articulation of federalism as a constitutional response to Sri Lanka's diversity, mooted in 1926 by S. W. R. D. Bandaranaike, has never been close to becoming a reality. Even during his own reign as Ceylon's fourth post-independence prime minister in 1956, the idea was sidelined due to political expediencies. When Bandaranaike put forward his forthright arguments in a series of six articles, they did not gain the acceptance of the Tamil leadership.[106] Thirty years later when these articles were re-invoked and presented by the Tamil leadership, they were opposed by Bandaranaike, who was unwilling to concede.[107] The work of the Donoughmore Commission (1927) constitutes another milestone on the road of failed federalism, when federalist proposals submitted for its consideration were rejected.[108] An admittedly simplistic proposal, by Tamil leader Ponnabalam, which envisaged a legislature with half the seats for the Sinhala and the remainder shared between Tamils, Muslims, Burghers, and others, was also rejected.[109] The early scepticism towards federalism from the Tamil leadership changed from the mid-1950s to the mid-1970s when the Freedom Party robustly advocated for this solution.[110] The passage of the Official Language Act,[111] including a subsequent legal challenge,[112] accentuated demands for regional autonomy, with S. J. V. Chelvanayakam, leader of the (Tamil) Federal Party engaging in a vigorous federalist campaign, dismissed and branded as racist and separatist in the mainstream press.[113]

[105] See Nira Wickramasinghe, 'Producing the Present: History as Heritage in Post-War Patriotic Sri Lanka', *Economic and Political Weekly*, vol. XLVIII, no. 43 (2013).

[106] William Clarance, 'Woolf and Bandaranaike: The Ironies of Federalism in Sri Lanka', *Political Quarterly*, vol. 72, no. 4 (2002): p. 482.

[107] Clarance, 'Woolf and Bandaranaike', p. 485.

[108] See Jane Russell, *Communal Politics under the Donoughmore Constitution 1931–1947* (Colombo: Thisara Prakasakayo, 1982).

[109] Welhengama and Pillay, *The Rise of Tamil Separatism in Sri Lanka*, pp. 114–37.

[110] Wilson, *Sri Lankan Tamil Nationalism*, pp. 82–112.

[111] Official Language Act No. 33 of 1956.

[112] *Kodeswaran v AG of Ceylon* [1970] AC 1111, PC. The language issue had already come up in cases before the Privy Council; see *Liyanage et al v Regina* [1966] 2 WLR 682.

[113] Singh and Kukreja, *Federalism in South Asia*, p. 499.

Sri Lanka did come close to implementing decentralization, in the offer to devolve power to a provincial council in the Tamil-majority areas in 1987. Following the Indo-Lanka Accord,[114] this effort included the Thirteenth Amendment to the constitution calling for the establishment of provincial councils in each of nine provinces.[115] The resistance to such a move included a challenge heard by the Sri Lanka Supreme Court, claiming that the move violated Sri Lanka's constitutionally guaranteed unitary status (Article 2), and required a referendum and a two-thirds majority in Parliament before implementation.[116] The Court rejected the claim in a 5–4 decision, but even though incorporated, the devolved powers merely provided a 'veneer of devolution', with plenty of leeway for the centre to retake powers through an overwhelmingly powerful presidency.[117] The amendment thus failed to respond to Tamil aspirations while also undermining the potential impact of any real devolution.

A more serious attempt at peace, accompanied by devolution, came under the premiership of Chandrika Kumaratunga, whose campaign for power included seeking to create the conditions for peace that would enable redress of Tamil grievances.[118] Her initial devolution package, articulated in August 1995, sought to roll back the constitutional impediments to devolution which guaranteed Sri Lanka's existence as a unitary State (such as arts 2 and 76 in the 1978 constitution). While the measures were not posited as 'federal' in proposing Sri Lanka to be an 'indissoluble union of regions' and subsequently as consisting of a 'centre and regions', they re-opened the possibility of regional autonomy as being the way forward to create an environment where all Sri Lankans could live in peace and harmony.[119] The package went through several rounds of negotiations and was ultimately presented to Parliament as a constitutional amendment bill in October 1997, where it failed to gather the necessary support.[120] In the meantime Tamil aspirations moved from internal renegotiation of rights to demands for the

[114] For a discussion of this accord, its treatment within the Sri Lankan legal system, and subsequent developments, see Welhengama and Pillay, *The Rise of Tamil Separatism in Sri Lanka*, pp. 231 f.

[115] For more, see M. L. Marasinghe, 'Ethnic Politics and Constitutional Reform: The Indo-Sri Lanka Accord', *International and Comparative Law Quarterly*, vol. 37 (1988): pp. 551–87.

[116] The claim was analogous to the 'Basic Structure' claim over the Indian constitution as arose in *Golaknath v State of Punjab* AIR [1967] SC 1643 and *Keshavananda Bharati v State of Kerala* AIR [1973] SC 1461. For a commentary on this doctrine and how it limits the federal government's ability to change the 'basic structure' of the constitution, see S. P. Sathe, *Judicial Activism in India: Transgressing Borders and Enforcing Limits* (New Delhi: Oxford University Press, 2002), pp. 63–99.

[117] Rohan Edrisinha, 'The Federal Debate in Sri Lanka', in *Varieties of Federal Governments: Major Contemporary Models*, edited by Rekha Saxena (New Delhi: Foundation Books/Cambridge University Press, 2011), pp. 452–3.

[118] Gamini Keerawella and Rohan Samarajiva, 'Sri Lanka in 1994: A Mandate for Peace', *Asian Survey*, vol. 35, no. 2 (1995): p. 156.

[119] For a critique as this 'package' developed from election onwards prior to its attempted passage, see S. L. Gunasekera, *Tigers, Moderates and Pandora's Package* (Colombo: Multi Packs (Ceylon) Ltd, 1996).

[120] See Select Committee Report, Parliamentary Select Committee, 'Report on Constitutional Reforms' (1997).

establishment of a new State through a process of external self-determination, captured in the Thimpu Principles (referred to in n 104).

Norwegian efforts to broker peace were premised on a common framework with two components: (i) the creation of a united Sri Lanka; and (ii) the substantial meeting of Tamil aspirations.[121] The negotiations led to the Oslo Agreement (December 2002)[122] which among other things, dampened the Tamil claim for external self-determination to one for internal self-determination within Sri Lanka. This re-opened the door for a negotiated federal framework, with strong Tamil autonomy within the sovereignty of Sri Lanka, but with attention paid to the aspirations of the island's significant Muslim minority.[123] The call resulted in a backlash among the Sinhala who viewed discussions for regional autonomy or federalism as a clarion call for Sri Lanka's eventual disintegration. Sinhala hardliners felt empowered to make a distinct claim for power, catapulting Rajapakse into the presidency in 2005. Campaigning and winning on the basis that federalism would eventually lead to disintegration, Rajapakse swept to power with a mandate to find a different solution to 'the Tamil problem'. His mandate stemmed from victories in the parliamentary elections (April 2004) and his successful claim for the presidency in November 2005. Described as a vote for dominant 'majoritarian nationalism'[124] it was accompanied by the belief in a military solution to what was presented as a terrorist problem, tapping into the post-September 11 zeitgeist. Thus the discussion around federalism and power-sharing was replaced by brutal military action, with the international community stunned into silence and apathy as anti-terrorist rhetoric enabled States to deal with 'minority problems'. While Rajapakse's election manifesto highlighted the need for an 'undivided country, national consensus and an honorable peace',[125] the accompanying rhetoric favoured militarized routes to their achievement. His effective silencing of Sri Lanka's democratic institutions since the 2009 war and his attempt to avoid international scrutiny suggest that the Tamil issue was probably an excuse for what appears to be a power grab. Rather than seeking appeasement or confidence-building measures within Tamil communities, Rajapakse has categorically ruled out federalism, insisting that the State will remain unitary.[126]

Many commentators and activist believe that regional autonomy for Tamils within a federal State remains the only viable route to inclusive peace on the

[121] For a commentary on the peace process leading up to Oslo, see Paikiasothy Sarvanamuttu, *Democratization of the Peace Process: Sri Lanka* (Colombo: Centre for Policy Alternatives, 2005).

[122] 'Declaration in Support of the Peace Process in Sri Lanka' (adopted 25 November 2002, Oslo).

[123] E. Premratane, 'Sri Lanka: From a Unitary to a Federal State', Paper presented at Euro Region Summer University, Institute of Federalism, University of Fribourg, Switzerland, September 2003, p. 9. For a more general historical view, see Vijaya Samaraweera, 'The Muslim Revivalist Movement, 1880–1915', in *Collective Identities, Nationalism and Protest in Sri Lanka*, edited by Michael Roberts (Colombo: Marga Institute, 1979), pp. 261–3.

[124] Singh and Kukreja, *Federalism in South Asia*, p. 536.

[125] Mahinda Rajapakse, 'Mahinda Chinthana: Victory for Sri Lanka Presidential Election', 2005, accessed 16 October 2014, http://www.president.gov.lk/pdfs/MahindaChinthanaEnglish.pdf.

[126] See interview with *The Times*, London, 13 July 2009 and *The Hindu*, New Delhi, 6 July 2008.

island. For these commentators, such a mechanism would be a crucial political device which could maintain the island's unity and diversity, instilling and safeguarding the democracy recently shredded by the incumbent government. It would be necessary, if and when Sri Lanka is ready to engage anew with this question, to focus on the manner in which meaningful relations can be built to enable discussion of crucial issues such as fair distribution of resources and opportunities, to prevent the background matrix that led to years of war that have robbed generations of Sri Lankans of their futures. Blueprint solutions articulated consist of: (a) a negotiated resolution to the ethnic conflict and its aftermath; (b) a federal-type constitutional settlement that accommodates the ethno-territorial Tamil minority in the north and east; and (c) a united Sri Lanka through regional autonomy and power-sharing at the centre.[127] The road towards achieving this is fraught with difficulty, but could consist of:

> a three-stage process of peace and democratization. Stage one may begin with a civil society initiative at a reconciliation commission barring the political class and a dialogue across religions. After about six months, stage two may take over and an all-party negotiation process should take over and seek to produce in the next six months a template for a broad political consensus for a common multinational, consociational, and federal power-sharing. Finally, stage three should aim at a constitution-making by a constituent assembly elected by an electoral college consisting of the members of the parliament and the provincial councils.[128]

10.3.4 Nepal

This attempt to understand how regional autonomy and federalism function in South Asia comes, in Nepal's context, at an intriguing time. A traditional monarchy, Nepal has undergone major change in the last decade, and while this is posited as a move from monarchy towards federalism, this could easily be viewed through the lens of communities in Nepal seeking to make governance more relevant to their needs. The ascendancy of the Maoists has created historical landmarks such as the Jana Andolan II (Peoples' Movement II) in April 2006 and the Madhesi Revolt in early 2007. The consequence of this change is a firm decision to move towards a federalist State structure, though its negotiation, through a new constitution, is proving complicated.[129]

Among the myriads of challenges faced in the design of such a federation lie fundamental questions concerning: (a) the coherence of the emerging regional units, and whether they ought to be based on ethnic or linguistic lines; (b) how many autonomous territorial units are ideal and sustainable in a relatively small country governed by its mountainous terrain; (c) what fiscal policies ought to

[127] Singh and Kukreja, *Federalism in South Asia*, p. 544.
[128] Singh and Kukreja, *Federalism in South Asia*, p. 544.
[129] Srinivasan Ramani, 'Moment for Peace and Constitution Building in Nepal', *Economic and Political Weekly*, vol. XLVI, no. 41 (2011).

govern relations between Kathmandu and the regional governments; and (d) how emerging federalism can guarantee against territorial dismemberment.[130] With the decision to move towards a federation having been taken, Nepal is currently in the throes of ensuring that its design and implementation can provide a stabilizing influence, stimulating the national economy and addressing its significant development challenges, exacerbated by the devastation of the earthquakes in May 2015. These sentiments have led commentators to label Nepal as 'an aspiring federation'.[131]

The foundation for Nepal's push towards federalism is provided in the Peace Agreement between Nepal's interim government and the Madhesi leaders, signed on 28 February 2007 which makes clear that 'Nepal will become a federal democratic republic state', in which 'states will be fully autonomous and empowered'.[132] The Comprehensive Peace Agreement between the Government of Nepal and the Communist Party of Nepal (Maoists), signed on 21 November 2006, had already paved the way for major structural change to society. The preamble, which includes a reiteration of the mandate of the agreement as being significantly nationwide, includes the following clauses:

> Pledging for forward-looking restructuring of the state by resolving the prevailing problems related to class, ethnicity, regional and gender differences;
>
> Reiterating commitments to competitive multiparty democratic system, civil liberties, fundamental rights, human rights, complete press freedom and all other democratic norms and values including the concept of rule of law.[133]

This was made explicit when the Interim Constitution was amended on 13 April 2007, and Article 138 was inserted, labelled 'Progressive restructuring of the State', to the following effect:

> (1) There shall be made progressive restructuring of the State with inclusive, democratic federal system of governance, by doing away with the centralized and unitary structure of the State so as to end discriminations based on class, caste, language, gender, culture, religion and region.
>
> (1a) Recognizing the desire of the indigenous peoples and of the people of backward and other area including *Madhesi* people towards autonomous provinces Nepal shall be a federal democratic republican state. Provinces shall be autonomous and vested with full authority. The boundaries, number, names and structures, as well as full details of

130 For more on each of these issues, see Mara Malagodi, *Constitutional Nationalism and Legal Exclusion: Equality, Identity Politics and Democracy in Nepal* (Delhi: Oxford University Press, 2013).

131 Singh and Kukreja, *Federalism in South Asia*, p. 47.

132 Townsend Middleton and Sara Shneiderman, 'Reservations, Federalism and the Politics of Recognition in Nepal', *Economic and Political Weekly*, vol. XLIII, no. 19 (2008).

133 'Unofficial Translation of the Comprehensive Peace Agreement concluded between the Government of Nepal and the Communist Party of Nepal (Maoist)' (adopted 21 November 2006), available on the website of the Ministry of Foreign Affairs, Government of Nepal and also on the website of the United States Institute of Peace, Washington, at http://www.usip.org/sites/default/files/file/resources/collections/peace_agreements/nepal_cpa_20061121_en.pdf.

the lists, of autonomous provinces and the center and allocation of means, resources and powers shall be determined by the Constituent Assembly, while maintaining the sovereignty, unity and integrity of Nepal.

...

(3) The final settlement on the matters relating to the restructuring of the State and the form of federal system of governance shall be as determined by the Constituent Assembly.

Another amendment, also in April 2007, specifies that the CA would make the final decision on the 'federal system of state', putting federalism firmly on the agenda.[134]

While the quest for federalism is posited as a modernist post-monarchical quest, evidence for such calls exist from as early as the 1950s, when Tarai groups, based in the plains, sought a form of autonomy.[135] That call lay dormant until its re-articulation by the Maoists who posited federalism as a central plank for the future governance of Nepal in their decade-long struggle against the government. Until that time Nepal presented itself to the international community as a country with a common, shared national identity.[136] Assertions of caste or ethnic affiliations were suppressed as disruptive to nation-building, and advocates of these identities were viewed as unpatriotic. One commentator perhaps uncharitably commented that the period from 1960 to 1990 was concerned with nation-building, while the subsequent period has been about 'ethnicity-building'.[137] The watershed of 1990 is important because it signalled the restoration of democracy.[138] In that discussion some political parties and activists had demanded new structures designed to create greater room for ethnic rights and autonomy, with some fledgling arguments towards federalism.[139] It was around this time that the Maoists began articulating claims for the development of a policy for ethnic autonomy, unveiled in 1995 at their first National Conference.[140] The policy entitled 'Ethnic Policy of Nepal' became a framework for their grievances against the State, and this remained at the forefront of their demands for greater coherence in governance. It included a

[134] Menaka Guruswamy, 'Integration of the Army and New Constitutionalism in Nepal', *Economic and Political Weekly*, vol. XLV, no. 9 (2010).

[135] David N. Gellner, 'Caste, Ethnicity and Inequality in Nepal', *Economic and Political Weekly*, vol. XLII, no. 20 (2007).

[136] See 'Report submitted by Nepal to United Nations Human Rights Committee under Article 40 of the Covenant' (adopted 18 May 1994) UN. Doc. CCPR/C/74/Add.2, para 1.

[137] Khrisna Khanal, 'Federalizing the Nepali State: Challenges and Opportunities', in *South Asia: Envisioning a Regional Future*, edited by Smruti P. Pattanaik (New Delhi: Pentagon Security International, 2011), p. 141.

[138] Surendra S. Bhandari, *Self-Determination and Constitution Making in Nepal: Constituent Assembly, Inclusion and Ethnic Federalism* (Singapore: Springer, 2014), pp. 4–8.

[139] Bhandari, *Self-Determination and Constitution Making in Nepal*, pp. 131–66. Also see Krishna Bhattachan identified as a strong advocate of ethnic autonomy and federalism, in Lovise Aalen and Magnus Hatlebakk, 'Ethnic and Fiscal Federation in Nepal', 2008, accessed 17 October 2014, http://www.cmi.no/publications/publication/?3082=ethnic-and-fiscal-federalism-in-nepal.

[140] Singh and Kukreja, *Federalism in South Asia*, p. 405.

proposal (2001) for the establishment of nine autonomous regions based on ethnic affiliation, a claim that remained a campaigning platform in their subsequent victory in the 2008 elections.[141]

Prior to these developments, claims for cultural affiliations were viewed as narrow, backward, and constituting serious impediments to the tasks of modernization and the project of building a new form of nationalism towards harmonious and unified development.[142] This experience of constructing the new national identity, like in other post-colonial countries with multi-ethnic, multi-religious and multi-linguistic populations, centred around the extension of a single dominant narrative to others. In Nepal, the consensus settled on a specific choice: the effort commenced in seriousness to construct a homogenous Parbatiya (hill dweller) culture as encompassing the national identity. The result was the articulation, subsequent imposition, and active suppression of differing narratives of personal identity. This exacerbated inequalities between Nepal's diverse ethnic and caste-based communities.[143] In other words:

> the kind of national identity that was propagated in schools and through government organizations was experienced as highly exclusionary by lower castes, by ethnic groups (Janajatis), by religious minorities (Buddhists, Muslims, and increasingly now by Christians), and by people of Indian ethnicity (Madhesis) living in the economically crucial Tarai region in the south of the country.[144]

The approach inevitably strengthened the hands of specific dominant groups, namely Bahuns (Brahmins) and Chhetris (Kshatriyas) who benefited from their identity emerging as the 'national identity' enabling them to spread throughout the country as landowners, priests, administrators, soldiers, and policemen.

The challenge of the transition in Nepal towards federalism should not be underestimated. Since independence Nepal has been presided over by the ruling monarchy as a 'highly centralized, feudal, monarchic, exclusive and unitary Hindu state',[145] perched atop a mountainous territory where diverse ethno-linguistic groups developed relatively autonomously from each other due to physical barriers. The resultant diversity is further compounded by the inherited divisions from its Hindu tradition, specifically, the caste system. The national census of 2001 reveals an interesting picture about Nepal: Paharis (hill dwellers) constitute 66.2 per cent of the total population, Madhesis (who live mainly in the plains) account for 28.4 per cent, with 'others' listed at 5.4 per cent. Yet when assessed through the lens of caste and ethnicity the picture that emerges is more complex. Caste-based groups compromise 58.6 per cent of the population while ethnically

[141] These nine autonomous regions had an ethnic base, i.e. Seti-Mahakali, Bheri-Karnali, Thruwan, Magarant, Tamuwan, Tamang Saling, Newar, Kirant, and Madhesh, were the names that indicated their ethnic base. Cited by Singh and Kukreja, *Federalism in South Asia*, p 406.

[142] Gellner, 'Caste, Ethnicity and Inequality in Nepal', p. 1826.

[143] For more, see Rajendra Pradhan and Ava Shreshta, 'Ethnic and Caste Diversity: Implications for Development', *NMR Working Paper Series*, no. 4 (2005).

[144] Gellner, 'Caste, Ethnicity and Inequality in Nepal', p. 1823.

[145] See Singh and Kukreja, *Federalism in South Asia*, p. 411.

identifiable groups comprise 36.4 per cent, with 'others' listed as 6.2 per cent. It is important to bear in mind that whichever the dominant analysis, there is no caste-based or ethnic group that forms the majority, with the largest such group, the Chhetri, constituting 15.8 per cent of the population.[146]

Commenting on the drivers for federalism, Sharma identifies two key motivating factors: first, the wrenching free from the shackles imposed by an over-centralized governance system that benefitted the upper castes (Bahuns and Chhetris); second, the belief that federalism is the only governance mechanism that would enable the reflection of the plural and diverse composition of society.[147] Thus Nepal's seeking out federalism as a solution is in the best traditions of the discourse as articulated by Ghai and Cotterell, as an attempt to re-engineer the State and society based on democratic principles and community rights.[148] It also seeks to draw on federalism's strengths in using institutional and legal architecture to dampen identity-based conflict and create a more inclusive form of governance.

The challenges that remain have been clearly summarized by Singh and Kukreja as consisting of:

> six major but interrelated contentious issues, namely, carving out of territorial units, system of government, multi-level division of power and distribution of jurisdictional authority, creation of sub-state federal structure, issue of inclusion and rights, and fiscal federalism.[149]

10.4 Conclusion

In concluding this chapter on federalism and regional autonomy in four South Asian States, a few key points need to be emphasized. First, the States analysed here are young republics, drawn over older nations, with governance structures influenced by their shared colonial experience. Colonial rule encompassed genuine attempts to understand how best regions of this size and complexity could be governed. Against this, territories that came under Crown's realm were relatively autonomous, with many being independent sovereign kingdoms. Many of these became vassal states under British India, with the return and retention of sovereignty, a key post-colonial demand, met differently in each of the different post-colonial national contexts. Thus discussions around federalism and regional

[146] Latest census data will be published on http://cbs.gov.np, accessed 17 October 2014.

[147] Pitamber Sharma, *Unraveling the Mosaic: Spatial Aspects of Ethnicity in Nepal* (Kathmandu: Himal Books, 2008), p. 83.

[148] Yash Ghai and Jill Cotterell, 'Federalism and Political Inclusion: Choices for Nepal', in *Varieties of Federal Governance: Major Contemporary Models*, edited by Rekha Saxena (New Dehli: Foundation Books/Cambridge University Press, 2011), pp. 291–4. Also see Yash Ghai and Jill Cotterell, *Federalism and State Restructuring in Nepal: The Challenges for the Constituent Assembly* (Kathmandu: UNDP, 2007).

[149] See Singh and Kukreja, *Federalism in South Asia*, p. 436.

autonomy are not new discussions in the region. Second, state practice within South Asia provides strong evidence for the emergence of regional autonomy as the accepted and idealized governance route. This conclusion is drawn from a study of the underlying state formation discussions concurrent to the founding of the States themselves, and in the regularly reiterated discussions within each State. Significant gaps remain between agreed parameters and their implementation. While the Indian federal example is viewed of as a model, its flaws are clearly visible and may not be suitable for the various types of design questions posed within South Asia. Third, there is evidence from civil society discussions and their imprint on national and regional politics that demands for regional autonomy and self-governance are growing. Each State under scrutiny has used a series of different measures to engage or dismiss this discussion. The claims keep arising and these questions are going to become a heightened priority on the governance agenda of each State reviewed here. This does not mean that State practice on regional autonomy will grow in the short or medium term: the Sri Lankan example shows how the backlash from such discussions are equally prevalent in the political space. However it is possible to view the longer-term future of the States as encompassing compromises or principles that would enable greater self-governance: indeed this appears the only sustainable solution at this point in time. Finally, despite the growth in the rhetoric and the complex discussions that have spanned the last six decades of politico-legal developments in the region on the issue of autonomy, there are some fundamental peace and security questions that dominate the landscape. This includes the failed aspirations for self-determination in Kashmir, Nagaland, and to a significant lesser extent in other Indian states; the demands over new internal boundary-drawing; the Baluchi and Sindhi question gaining in vehemence in Pakistan with question marks over how Pathan claims can be addressed in a Punjabi-dominated State. The Tamil question has been frozen in the current climate but it is hard to see how a peaceful and unified Sri Lanka can emerge without the significant distrust towards the regime being overcome. Nepal continues to wrestle with idealized forms of regional autonomy and its constituents. Bangladesh's model of regional autonomy in the Chittagong hill tracts has not yet been fully developed or explored, nor is there an understanding of whether regional autonomy per se can provide the ideal governance platform for the country. In short, South Asia provides fertile ground for the continued study of questions of regional autonomy. The diversity of each State and the discussions to date suggest that serious attempts to work with communities, nations, civil society, and other stakeholders (including governmental bodies where they invite it), to design and articulate regional autonomy models would be welcome.

Conclusions: Beyond the Illusion of Ethno-culturally Homogeneous Territory

Karl Kössler

1. Introduction

More than a decade ago, autonomy was described as 'a loose and disparate concept that contains many threads but no single strand'.[1] This regrettable state of affairs has not changed in the meantime. Yet, what certainly has changed over the last two decades is an incremental dissociation of autonomy from *territorial* autonomy. While these two notions had, for a long time, been equated,[2] autonomy has been increasingly perceived as an umbrella term that comprises both territorial and non-territorial autonomy (hereinafter TA and NTA). This development is a result of an increased interest in NTA among both academic experts and political decision-makers. The political rediscovery in non-territorial arrangements is clearly reflected by the change of emphasis from TA to NTA in international documents, which occurred between the Copenhagen Document of 1990 and the Lund Recommendations of 1999.[3] Moreover, it is, of course, epitomized by a number of laws in the 1990s, which (re)introduced NTA to countries of Central and Eastern Europe (CEE).[4] Put simply, TA, as a result, is characteristic today of Western Europe and other parts of the world, while NTA, for various reasons,[5] is particularly popular in CEE.

[1] Tim Potier, *Conflict in Nagorno-Karabakh, Abkhazia and South Ossetia: A Legal Appraisal* (The Hague: Kluwer Law International, 2001), p. 54. Around the same time Matti Wiberg stated similarly that it 'is fair to claim that no clear account of the concept of autonomy is available.' (Matti Wiberg, 'Political Autonomy: Ambiguities and Clarifications', in *Autonomy: Applications and Implications*, edited by Markku Suksi (The Hague: Kluwer Law International, 1998), p. 43.)

[2] See the classical definitions mentioned by Nootens in this volume, section 2.2, many of which pretend to define autonomy, but in fact refer only to TA.

[3] 'The aim of the NTA provisions of the Lund Recommendations was to lead governments away from fearing territorial autonomy claims towards contemplating NTA as alternatives' (Tove Malloy, 'The Lund Recommendations and Non-Territorial Arrangements: Progressive De-Territorialization of Minority Politics', *International Journal on Minority and Group Rights*, vol. 16, no. 4 (2009): p. 677).

[4] See Smith in this volume, sections 7.4–7.6.

[5] See sections 4.2 and 4.3.

Similar to this geographic divide, the scientific communities focusing on TA and NTA, respectively, have so far been largely separated. In recognition of this fact, it has been the aim of this volume to integrate these two communities and engage them in a mutually fruitful cooperation. Integration is not only the leitmotif for the involvement of experts on both TA and NTA, but also for the inclusion of scholars from different disciplines such as political theory, comparative politics, and comparative constitutional law. A greater focus on autonomy seems to be imperative in particular for the latter discipline, which has been rightly criticized for not dedicating sufficient research efforts to the vast and highly topical area of 'constitutionalism in plurinational contexts'.[6] As regards content, the book has been aimed at reconceptualizing autonomy and territory and the nexus between the two (Chapters 1–4), at uncovering the historical origins and evolution of autonomy (Chapters 5–6), and at illustrating how TA and NTA are actually put into practice in different parts of the world (Chapters 7–10). The following conclusions loosely follow this structure.

2. Reconciling Diversity, Autonomy, and (Non-)Territoriality

'Macedonia's sovereignty and territorial integrity, and the unitary character of the State are inviolable and must be preserved. There are no territorial solutions to ethnic issues.'[7] This famous statement, which was intended to illustrate the specific rationale of the 2001 Ohrid Framework Agreement, is remarkable for two reasons. First, it reflects the widespread belief that 'territorial solutions' would inevitably threaten a state's 'sovereignty and territorial integrity'.[8] Secondly, it declares such solutions for this very reason to be generally unfeasible.[9] Yet, territoriality is to some degree essential in any attempt to introduce autonomy in the context of culturally diverse societies.

At a first level, even the basic distinction between the majority and minorities is a matter of the territorial scope of law because the relations between these two categories of groups, in terms of both numbers and power,[10] take shape only

[6] Stephen Tierney, 'Beyond the Ontological Question: Liberal Nationalism and the Task of Constitution-Building', *European Law Journal*, vol. 14, no. 1 (2008): p. 136. Instead, comparative constitutional law has largely focused since its revival in the mid-1980s on three topics: fundamental rights, democracy, and judicial review (see Sujit Choudhry, 'Rethinking Comparative Constitutional Law: Multinational Democracies, Constitutional Amendment, and Secession', Paper presented at the annual meeting of the Law and Society Association, Berlin, 25 July 2007, p. 1).

[7] Article 1(2) of the Ohrid Framework Agreement of 2001 (adopted 13 August 2001).

[8] See, on this belief, section 4.1.

[9] Contrary to this declaration, a core element of the agreement was actually territorial, i.e. the redrawing of municipal boundaries to the benefit of the Albanian minority (see Joseph Marko, 'The Referendum on Decentralization in Macedonia in 2004: A Litmus Test for Macedonia's Interethnic Relations', *European Yearbook of Minority*, vol. 4, no. 2 (2004): pp. 695–721).

[10] Both numerical and power relations are essential in Capotorti's famous definition (see Francesco Capotorti, 'Study on the Rights of Persons Belonging to Ethnic, Religious and Linguistic Minorities', UN Doc. E/CN.4/Sub.2/384/Rev.1.

within certain boundaries. Once established in this manner, minorities may also be classified according to their relation to state borders: they may be entirely contained within their state of residence, be a minority in this state but a dominant majority in another one, or be in a minority position in more than one state.[11] Yet, the way that state borders affect the legal definition of a minority and, as a consequence, the access to minority rights has recently changed. Generally, there is a marked tendency for citizenship of the state of residence no longer to be the sole requirement for this definition.[12] This decreasing significance of citizenship is not only characteristic of minority rights, but constitutes a broader trend, which also encompasses access to social rights and certain political rights. The mismatch between the binary logic of formal state membership and a reality of growing diversification of legal statuses is illustrated by the fact that today for non-citizens 'the real prize is legal residency, not citizenship'.[13] Even though legal residency has therefore gained importance at the expense of formal state membership, it is of course likewise based on a territorial link to a specific state.

At a second level, territoriality is inextricably associated with any form of autonomy. In the case of NTA this link is evidently much weaker, as non-territoriality is by definition its very essence. Actually, it is the least common denominator of NTA, which is itself not a clear-cut concept but rather an umbrella term encompassing quite diverse forms of autonomy.[14] But even in these cases territoriality still matters, as any NTA regime requires a precisely delimited territorial scope of application. In this regard, the personality principle itself does not provide any guidance. For instance, Karl Renner intended his pioneering model of national cultural autonomy (NCA) to be implemented in the entire Austro-Hungarian Empire. However, he could have equally taken only one of the halves of the empire, that is, *Cisleithanien* or *Transleithanien*, or entities at still lower government levels as his territorial frame of reference. Anyway, determining the territorial scope of NTA is therefore an arbitrary and not a principled decision. This decision may then follow the pre-existing territorial structure or depart from it. In the Russian Federation, the current arrangement of NCA reflects the country's federal structure and foresees a multilevel design by providing the opportunity to establish NCA institutions at the federal, regional, and local levels.[15] As only the respective lower-level institutions are authorized to form their counterparts at

[11] See John McGarry, Michael Keating, and Margaret Moore, 'Introduction: European Integration and the Nationalities Question', in *European Integration and the Nationalities Question*, edited by John McGarry and Michael Keating (London/New York: Routledge, 2006), p. 1.

[12] See Palermo in this volume, section 1.3.2 with reference to ECJ case law, opinions of the ACFC, to several opinions of the Venice Commission, as well as its *Report on Non-Citizens and Minority Rights*, adopted at the Commission's sixty-ninth plenary session (Venice, 15–16 December 2006), Study no. 294/2004, CDL-AD(2007)001.

[13] Peter J. Spiro, *Beyond Citizenship: American Identity after Globalization* (Oxford: Oxford University Press, 2007), p. 159.

[14] Suksi differentiates in this volume, sections 4.2.2–4.2.4 three forms of NTA: institutional forms of civil law turning into functional autonomy, functional autonomy within line administration, and national cultural autonomy.

[15] See Osipov in this volume, section 8.4.

the next higher level, this design follows a bottom-up logic and creates a 'pyramid of NCAs'. While the territorial scope of application follows in the Russian case the country's administrative structure, it is, in the case of the self-government[16] of the Sami within Finland, defined specifically.[17] The area relevant for their cultural autonomy is marked on a map on the basis of what is considered the Sami homeland.[18] In contrast to Russia, this area cross-cuts administrative boundaries because it encompasses three municipalities and parts of a fourth one.[19] Interestingly, merely the territorial scope of application of self-government is limited to this area, whereas individual affiliation to cultural autonomy is open to all Sami with either Finnish citizenship or merely domicile in the country.

While territoriality thus matters to NCA because it requires a basic definition of its territorial scope, it does not matter, in contrast to TA, regarding the identification of the concrete subjects of autonomy. Individual affiliation to an NCA regime is according to the personality principle determined by self-identification. Whereas in Renner's conception everyone was 'forced to choose', self-identification is, in today's common practice of NCA, a voluntary process.[20] On the one hand, a legal obligation may, from a purely pragmatic perspective, take away real or perceived pressure from people who are otherwise afraid of publicly declaring themselves.[21] On the other hand, this seems problematic with regard to the principle of voluntary self-identification as a recognized European and international standard.[22] Since NCA is supposed to be targeted exclusively at minorities, the act of declaring one's affiliation is commonly not open to everyone,[23] but reserved to a predetermined circle of potential members. Thus, access to NCA usually requires, beyond citizenship, residence, or both, the belonging to a recognized minority, as demonstrated by the fulfillment of certain subjective and objective criteria.[24]

[16] In line with a quite common usage of terms, 'self-government' is understood here as synonymous with 'autonomy' (see also, for instance, Zelim A. Skubarty, 'Introduction', in *Beyond a One-Dimensional State: An Emerging Right to Autonomy?*, edited by Zelim A. Skubarty (Leiden/Boston: Martinus Nijhoff Publishers, 2005), pp. xxxi–lviii). There are of course other authors who differentiate in one way or another between these two notions (e.g. Yoram Dinstein, 'Autonomy', in *Models of Autonomy*, edited by Yoram Dinstein (Tel Aviv: Tel Aviv University Press, 1981), p. 219; Ruth Lapidoth, *Autonomy: Flexible Solutions to Ethnic Conflicts* (Washington, D.C.: United States Institute of Peace Press, 1996), p. 54).

[17] For details see Suksi in this volume, section 4.3.

[18] The map is attached to the Decree on the Sami Assembly (1727/1995).

[19] s 4 of the Act on the Sami Assembly.

[20] See, however, the arrangement in the Brussels-Capital Region which requires all citizens to make a declaration as soon as they are old enough to vote (see Philippe van Parijs, 'Must Europe be Belgian? On Democratic Citizenship in Multilingual Polities', in *The Demands of Citizenship*, edited by Catriona McKinnon and Iain Hampsher-Monk (London/New York: Continuum, 2000), p. 242).

[21] See, with regard to Hungary in the 1990s, Smith in this volume, section 7.4.

[22] See art 3(1) of the FCNM and art 3(2) of the UN General Assembly's Declaration on the Rights of Persons Belonging to National or Ethnic, Religious and Linguistic Minorities, 3 February 1992, A/RES/47/135.

[23] Note, however, that Hungary's original 1993 law had opened participation in elections of the minority self-governments to all citizens residing within the relevant electoral district (on this see Smith in this volume, section 7.4).

[24] See, on different models of determining individual affiliation, Suksi in this volume, section 4.5.

On balance, the personality principle offers some advantages in comparison to TA's territoriality principle, which are, however, also subject to certain limits. First, the subjects of autonomy are through voluntary individual affiliation self-defined so that self-government is only exercised by those people who have deliberately chosen to be part of it. By contrast, the subjects of TA are defined without their explicit consent through the boundaries of the autonomous territory. As a consequence, 'voting with one's feet',[25] that is, physically moving away from this territory, is the only option to not being forced into autonomy. Even though the personality principle therefore guarantees more voluntariness, this advantage is limited by the fact that both Renner's model and most of today's practices do not foresee the option to choose affiliations others than those predetermined, no affiliation at all, or multiple affiliations. The latter implies the inability to match the reality of multiple identities. An early example of this was the break-up of the religiously defined *millets* along linguistic lines during the last decades of the Ottoman Empire.[26] A second main advantage associated by Renner himself with the personality principle pertains to its ability to 'secularize' language, that is, to separate governance from language as it was already separated from religion and thus end territorial domination based on the majority language.[27] Fully overcoming what Renner called, by analogy with the famous principle of the 1555 Peace of Augsburg, 'cuius regio, illius lingua'[28] has of course proved difficult. Whereas a legal framework can take a neutral position towards religion, it cannot do the same towards language. In practice, it simply requires for its daily functioning the choice of one or more languages for official purposes.

It is self-evident, not least by its very name, that TA has stronger and much more immediate links with territoriality. After all, the latter determines the subjects of self-government. The fact that these are according to the territoriality principle *all* people within the boundaries of the autonomous entity contrasts sharply with a widespread perception of TA as a means of empowering exclusively or at least predominantly one culturally distinct group, that is, a nationwide minority with a compact area of settlement. In academia, this view is in the first place reflected in numerous minority-limited definitions of autonomy in general and thus by implication also of TA as one of its specific forms.[29] Secondly, this

[25] See Charles M. Tiebout, 'A Pure Theory of Local Expenditures', *Journal of Political Economy*, vol. 64, no. 5 (1956): pp. 416–24.

[26] See Erk in this volume, section 5.6.

[27] See Synopticus (pen name of Renner), 'State and Nation', translated by Joseph O'Donnell, in *National-Cultural Autonomy and its Contemporary Critics*, edited by Ephraim Nimni (London/New York: Routledge, 2005), pp. 27–8.

[28] Rudolf Springer (pen name of Renner), *Der Kampf der österreichischen Nationen um den Staat* (Leipzig/Vienna: Deuticke, 1902), p. 61.

[29] For instance, according to Yash Ghai's classic definition, 'autonomy is a device to allow minorities claiming a distinct identity to exercise control over affairs of special concern to them'. (Yash Ghai, 'Autonomy as a Participatory Right in the Modern Democratic State: Public Participation, Autonomy and Minorities', in *Beyond a One-Dimensional State: An Emerging Right to Autonomy?*, edited by Zelim A. Skubarty (Leiden/Boston: Martinus Nijhoff Publishers, 2005), p. 38. Similarly, John McGarry and Margaret Moore define autonomy as 'a form of self-rule that gives ethnic and national minorities substantial powers to govern their own affairs' (John McGarry and Margaret

perception is characteristic of much scholarly work endorsing what has been variously termed multinational, plurinational, ethnic, or post-conflict federalism. This concept promotes the idea of drawing or even redrawing the boundaries between autonomous territories within a state in such a way that nationwide minorities are turned into regional majorities.[30] Since the 1990s this transformation of minorities by playing with the territorial scope of legal norms has gained considerable support not only from academics but also in constitutional practice.[31] The fact that autonomy is meant to benefit only or primarily one specific culturally distinct group is illustrated by several constitutions of this period in terms of both statements of identity and provisions about territorial (re)organization. As to the first dimension, ex-Article 1 of the 1992 constitution of the Republika Srpska provides a prime example, as it explicitly defined this entity of Bosnia and Herzegovina as 'a State of the Serb people and of all its citizens'.[32] As to the second dimension, Article 47(1) of the 1995 constitution of Ethiopia first names most constituent states after one specific titular group and draws the boundaries between them along ethnic lines.[33] Then it also facilitates in Article 47(2) the later redrawing of these boundaries for the same reason by granting 'nations, nationalities and peoples within the states... the right to establish, at any time, a state of their own'. The notion of a regionally dominant group owning the autonomous territory and, as a consequence, territorially based power is the *raison d'être* not only of the two above-mentioned cases, but also of many others. However, it is imperative to recognize that concrete TA arrangements differ considerably regarding the strength of this ownership relation, which finds its institutional expression in the balance between ethnic and territorial elements. There are, as a consequence, many different positions on a sliding scale between a strong and weak ethnic-territorial link.[34]

The limitation of TA to empowering one culturally distinct group entails that existing relations between dominant and dominated groups are not done away with, but are merely reversed. After all, this target group of autonomy is a nationwide minority in Capotorti's sense regarding both numbers and power, which is

Moore, 'Karl Renner, Power Sharing and Non-Territorial Autonomy', in *National-Cultural Autonomy and its Contemporary Critics*, edited by Ephraim Nimni (London/New York: Routledge, 2005), p. 79).

[30] See Will Kymlicka, *Multicultural Citizenship: A Liberal Theory of Minority Rights* (Oxford: Oxford University Press, 1995), pp. 27–8.

[31] For useful overviews, see Sujit Choudhry and Nathan Hume, 'Federalism, Secession and Devolution: From Classical to Post-Conflict Federalism', in *Research Handbook on Comparative Constitutional Law*, edited by Tom Ginsburg and Rosalind Dixon (Cheltenham: Edward Elgar, 2011), pp. 363–72; John McGarry and Brendan O'Leary, 'Federation and Managing Nations', in *Multinational Federations*, edited by Michael Burgess and John Pinder (London/New York: Routledge, 2007), pp. 189–91.

[32] The wording 'a State of the Serb people and' was later declared unconstitutional by the Constitutional Court of Bosnia and Herzegovina in its seminal Partial Decision U 5/98 III of 1 July 2000.

[33] See Yonatan Tesfaye Fessha, *Ethnic Diversity and Federalism: Constitution Making in South Africa and Ethiopia* (Farnham: Ashgate, 2010), pp. 201–7.

[34] For a categorization of the three main abstract approaches to this link, see Palermo in this volume, section 1.2.

transformed within the autonomous territory into a regional majority in numerical terms and hence—in the context of majoritarian democracy inevitably—also in terms of power. As long as an arrangement of self-government is embedded in such a context and may thus be called 'majoritarian ethnic TA',[35] it reproduces the nation state model, only on a smaller scale. Ironically, such 'nation regions' typically emphasize the cultural diversity *of the state* as the main argument in the political struggle for self-government, but at the same time negate or at least downplay cultural diversity *of the region*, that is, the presence of internal minorities.

This biased and somewhat schizophrenic approach towards diversity entails that other groups within the autonomous territory, which have been variously termed 'internal minorities',[36] 'intra-unit minorities',[37] and the like, are not recognized and at risk of being marginalized. It is certainly true that this does not lead necessarily to the worst case, that is, 'sons of the soil politics',[38] which blatantly discriminates against these groups. But even in a best-case scenario, 'majoritarian ethnic TA' still fails to extend to them most benefits of self-government because it is based on the strict dualism between those groups recognized through the assignment of their 'own' territory and those in this sense unrecognized. Under the paradigms of the nation state/nation region and majoritarian democracy, internal minorities are differently affected by the risk of marginalization. This risk will be in most cases greater for 'minorities within minorities',[39] which are, like indigenous people in Quebec, numerically inferior on both the national and sub-national scale. By contrast, 'majorities within minorities', which belong, like Anglophones in Quebec, to the nationwide majority,[40] will generally be in a better position. First, they may benefit from the protective role of the central government and its package deals with the regional government. Secondly, they are only a minority in decision-making on subject matters assigned to the regional government, but not regarding those still remaining with the central government. Their minority status is therefore in this sense not only affected by the drawing of the boundaries of the autonomous territory, but also by the concrete vertical

[35] See Karl Kössler, 'Beyond Majoritarian Autonomy? Legislative and Executive Power-Sharing in European Regions', in *Law, Territory and Conflict Resolution*, edited by Francesco Palermo, Enrico Milano, and Matteo Nicolini (Leiden/Boston: Martinus Nijhoff Publishers, forthcoming).

[36] Sujit Choudhry, 'Does the World Need More Canada? The Politics of the Canadian Model in Constitutional Politics and Political Theory', in *Constitutional Design for Divided Societies: Integration or Accommodation?*, edited by Sujit Choudhry (Oxford: Oxford University Press, 2008), p. 158.

[37] Ronald L. Watts, 'Multinational Federations in Comparative Perspective', in *Multinational Federations*, edited by Michael Burgess and John Pinder (London/New York: Routledge, 2007), p. 232.

[38] Choudhry, 'Does the World Need More Canada', p. 153.

[39] Internal minorities are usually divided according to their numerical position in the overall state context into two subcategories: 'minorities within minorities' and 'majorities within minorities' (see Avigail Eisenberg and Jeff Spinner-Halev, eds, *Minorities within Minorities: Equality, Rights and Diversity* (Cambridge: Cambridge University Press, 2005).

[40] It was precisely due to this belonging to the nationwide majority that the UN Human Rights' Committee refused to qualify English speakers as minority in the sense of art 27 of the ICCPR (see *Ballantyne, Davidson, McIntyre v Canada*, Communications Nos 359/1989 and 385/1989, UN Doc. CCPR/C/47/D/359/1989 and 385/1989/Rev.1 (1993), para 11.2).

distribution of powers. In other words, it has both a territorial and a functional dimension. In conclusion, the zero-sum game of reversing majority–minority relations within the limits of an autonomous territory to the benefit of one group and to the detriment of others has prevented TA from living up, at least as much as possible, to its above-mentioned rationale, that is, the self-government of *all* people within the boundaries of the autonomous entity. We will see in the following two sections that the view of 'majoritarian ethnic TA' has been prevailing throughout much of history and in most parts of the world. However, as illustrated in the final outlook it has recently come to be challenged, not least through the rediscovery of NTA.[41]

3. Autonomy and Sovereignty in Historical Perspective

From a historical perspective, autonomy in a broad sense undoubtedly preceded the advent of the modern state and of sovereignty as, according to the famous definition of Jean Bodin,[42] distinctive characteristics of this state.[43] Since medieval times, a complex network of multiple and overlapping political entities enjoying local or corporate autonomy within a multilevel order, was, for instance, over centuries a main feature of the Holy Roman Empire. After all, it was the existence of, in this sense, self-governing intermediary powers like cities, bishoprics, and professional corporations, which led Samuel von Pufendorf to famously describe this empire as an 'irregulare aliquod corpus et monstro simile', that is, as some kind of irregular body resembling a monster.[44] Autonomy of nested political entities within a larger imperial framework was equally characteristic of the Ottoman Empire, as soon as it rapidly expanded its territory in the late Middle Ages. Another early example of self-government is Navarra, which had already been granted its first written *fueros*, that is, special rights, in the thirteenth century.[45] The constellation of all these quite different pre-sovereignty forms of autonomy within medieval multilevel orders bears a remarkable resemblance to the present (European) condition of what has been termed 'late sovereignty'.[46] Similar to the

41 See section 5 of this chapter.

42 See Jean Bodin, *Les six Livres de la République* [The Six Books of the Republic] (Paris: Jacques du Puis, 1576), p. I:8.

43 See, for a concise analysis of this link between the modern state and sovereignty, Dieter Grimm, *Souveränität. Herkunft und Zukunft eines Schlüsselbegriffs* [The Origins and the Future of a Key Concept] (Berlin: Berlin University Press, 2009), pp. 16–34.

44 The original Latin wording is 'irregulare aliquod corpus et monstro simile' (Severinus de Monzambano Veronensis (pen name of Samuel von Pufendorf), *De Statu Imperii Germanici ad Laelium fratrem, Dominum Trezolani, liber unus* [About the State of the Empire, to Laelius, the Brother of Germanicus, the Lord, Trezolani, One Book] (Genevae: P. Columesium, 1667), VI:9).

45 Note that the *fueros* of the provinces Navarra, Guipúzcoa, Vizcaya, and Álava are still today recognized in Additional Provision I of the Spanish Constitution. The province of Navarra is at the same time an Autonomous Community, while the latter three provinces form the Autonomous Community of the Basque Country.

46 Neil Walker, 'Late Sovereignty in the European Union', in *Sovereignty in Transition*, edited by Neil Walker (Oxford: Hart, 2003), p. 3.

latter, it was characterized by 'functionally limited polities within a multidimensional order', which do not claim 'comprehensive jurisdiction over a particular territory' and thus allow for 'territorial overlap without subsumption'.[47] In between these two constellations of pre-sovereignty autonomy and 'late sovereignty', there was, of course, the Westphalian *intermezzo*. In this period sovereignty was precisely distinguished by the claims of states to *comprehensive* jurisdiction over *mutually exclusive* territorial entities. This period, however, has gradually come to an end in the wake of the post-World War II proliferation of international and supranational institutions and legal regimes.[48]

Yet, the widespread overestimation of 1648 as *the* turning point, which brought into being like a big bang so-called Westphalian sovereignty, that is, independence of any external power (external dimension) and ultimate authority to make decisions regarding a specific territory (internal dimension), should be put into perspective. This is not to deny the importance of 1648 as *one* milestone on an evolutionary path towards the modern state and sovereignty. But one should avoid the quite common excessive focus on this event,[49] which has produced a 'both decontextualized and ahistoricized'[50] understanding of sovereignty. 1648 should be put into perspective at both the theoretical and the legal-political levels.

In terms of theory, there is evidence that the essential principle of ultimate authority over a specific territory, that is, the internal dimension of sovereignty, was only articulated in a clear and explicit way in the mid-eighteenth-century writings of Christian Wolff and Emer de Vattel and thus roughly a century after the peace of Westphalia.[51] As to the level of legal and political practice, it is demonstrated in this book that the sovereign state with its alleged attributes of being territorially compact and legally unified did not actually come into being with the peace of Westphalia.[52] Instead, many states were in fact unable to transform their claim to ultimate authority over their territory into effective direct control and were thus forced to allow for diverse forms of autonomy and legal pluralism.[53] This necessity stemmed above all from the problem of overstretching territory beyond administrative capacities, which was, until the nineteenth century or in many areas even later, additionally aggravated by poorly developed communication and

[47] Walker, 'Late Sovereignty in the European Union', p. 23.

[48] See Richard Falk, 'Revisiting Westphalia, Discovering Post-Westphalia', *The Journal of Ethics*, vol. 6, no. 4 (2002), pp. 311–52.

[49] See, for instance, Daniel Philpott, 'The Religious Roots of Modern International Relations', *World Politics*, vol. 52 (2000): pp. 211–12.

[50] Peer Zumbansen, 'Carving Out Typologies and Accounting for Differences Across Systems: Towards a Methodology of Transnational Constitutionalism', in *The Oxford Handbook of Comparative Constitutional Law*, edited by Michael Rosenfeld and András Sajó (Oxford: Oxford University Press, 2012), p. 84.

[51] See Stephen D. Krasner, *Sovereignty: Organized Hypocrisy* (Princeton: Princeton University Press, 1999), pp. 14–20.

[52] See Erk and Bowring in this volume, sections 5.2 and 6.2–6.3 respectively.

[53] This legal pluralism was actually quite similar to how this idea is understood today (for an introduction, see Margaret Davies, 'Legal Pluralism', in *The Oxford Handbook of Empirical Legal Research*, edited by Peter Cane and Herbert M. Kritzer (Oxford: Oxford University Press, 2010), pp. 805–27).

transportation. Due to the limited reach of direct control, states had to rely on the existing local personnel of conquered territories and, in connection therewith, leave in place traditional legal systems.

This has been pointed out, for instance, with regard to the Russian Empire, where the expansion of the Muscovite state in the mid-sixteenth century into areas predominantly inhabited by non-Russians practically necessitated the maintenance of existing local rules and institutions. Autonomy within the ensuing multinational empire became in certain peripheral areas in the late nineteenth century even so far-reaching that it included a bilingually Swedish–Finnish administration with no official role whatsoever for the Russian language.[54] Similarly, the Ottoman Empire encountered in the process of its expansion the practical limits of exercising direct control and succumbed to the pressure to concede varying degrees of autonomy. Due to the ensuing individual bargains the *millets* were then characterized by a wide array of local variations rather than a uniform system prescribed in a top-down manner.[55] These limitations inherent to expansionism sooner or later affected a number of states with vast territory[56] and made them, in this sense, necessarily 'negotiated empires'.[57] Under these circumstances, self-government within an imperial context was granted due to the obvious needs of practicality and had little to do with the recognition of diversity-related demands for autonomy.

As such demands for self-government and even independent statehood became commonplace with the nineteenth-century rise of nationalism, autonomy entered a new stage regarding both its conceptualization and practical implementation. As to the conceptual dimension, research has so far dedicated much effort to scrutinizing the writings of Renner and Bauer in Austria–Hungary as well as the intense TA–NCA debate in the Russian Empire, which saw Lenin and other Bolsheviks on the one hand and followers of Austro-Marxist ideas on the other. Beyond that, this volume also draws attention to certain lesser-known authors such as those of the late Tsarist period whose theories even preceded the aforementioned debate by twenty years.[58] As to the practical dimension, nationalism sparked attempts, albeit too hesitant, in the Habsburg and Ottoman Empires to introduce or reform NTA arrangements.[59] TA found in both cases even less

[54] See Bowring in this volume, section 6.2. [55] See Erk in this volume, section 5.6.

[56] Among many other examples, one might think in this context of the self-government enjoyed by the princely states of India under British suzerainty and of the complex and historically changing relations between China and Tibet. Interestingly, the British in the nineteenth century also applied their (European) category of suzerainty to Sino–Tibetan relations, which had typically been characterized with the non-legal notion of a 'priest-patron relationship'. Thus, they saw China as exercising some sort of control falling short of sovereignty and Tibet as enjoying within these limits a high level of autonomy (see Michael Van Walt van Praag, *The Status of Tibet: History, Rights, and Prospects in International Law* (Boulder: Westview Press, 1987), pp. 105–6).

[57] With regard to the Ottoman Empire: Karen Barkey, 'Islam and Toleration: Studying the Ottoman Imperial Model', *International Journal of Politics, Culture, and Society*, vol. 19 (2005): p. 10.

[58] See Bowring in this volume, section 6.3.

[59] The Ottomans reformed in this period the *millet* system, albeit in an overall context of increasing centralization of power. Austro-Hungarian efforts were confined to the 1905 Moravian compromise. This solution of creating separate language-based electoral lists for Germans and

support. The majority of Young Turks staunchly opposed any claims to reverse the nineteenth-century trend of centralization.[60] Emperor Charles I of Austria only promised federalization in his *Völkermanifest* of 16 October 1918 and thus far too late to have any practical impact. Quite evidently, the declining multinational empires provided a fertile ground for the conceptualization of autonomy. By contrast, the actual implementation of arrangements of self-government only gained impetus after their demise. The cumbersome process of reorganizing Europe after World War I gave rise to a number of new autonomy regimes, with Estonia from 1925 to 1940 being the most notable example of NTA. As far as TA is concerned, arrangements mandated by the peace treaties were, like the Memel Territory, equally short-lived or, as in the case of Transcarpathia and Ruthenia, not even implemented in the first place. However, the interwar period also entailed in 1920 the establishment of the autonomy[61] of the Åland Islands, which was not based on a peace treaty and is still, with some modification,[62] in force today.

4. Global Practice of Autonomy

It has been the decided aim of this book to also offer, beyond a reconceptualization of autonomy and an exploration of its historical evolution, some insights into how TA and NTA are put into practice. Most contributions to this volume, which cover the implementation of autonomy across different parts of the world, examine this subject within the timeframe since the just-discussed interwar period to the present day. From the evidence gathered in these chapters, three issues seem to merit particular attention: first, the emergence of autonomy as a political bargain between the main parties involved (section 4.1); secondly, the main factors influencing whether and how autonomy is put into practice through this bargain (section 4.2); thirdly, what constellations of TA/NTA such bargains give rise to (section 4.3).

4.1. Autonomy as a political bargain

'The good law-giver and the true statesman must have their eyes open not only to what is absolute best, but also to what is best in relation to actual conditions.'[63]

Czechs fell clearly short of the far-reaching ideas of the Austro-Marxists and met with their criticism (Otto Bauer, *The Question of Nationalities and Social Democracy* [Nationalitätenfrage und die Sozialdemokratie] with an Introduction by Ephraim Nimni and Preface by Heinz Fischer (Minneapolis: University of Minnesota Press, 2000), pp. 308–10).

[60] See Stanford J. Shaw, 'Ottoman Empire', in *The Oxford Encyclopedia of the Islamic World. Vol. 4*, edited by John L. Esposito (Oxford: Oxford University Press, 2009), pp. 280–95.

[61] The legal sources are the Autonomy Act of 1920 and the Decision of the Council of the League of Nations on the Åland Islands, September 1921, League of Nations Official Journal, 697.

[62] The Autonomy Act was revised in 1951 as well as in 1991.

[63] Aristotle, *Politics*, translated by Ernest Barker (2nd edition, Oxford: Oxford University Press, 1948), p. 181.

With regard to an autonomy arrangement, the assessment of what is best in concrete circumstances is incumbent on the main actors involved, that is, the principle conflict parties and sometimes kin-states.[64] Put differently, the viability of an arrangement depends on whether its institutional design succeeds in solving commitment problems by providing incentives to *all* main actors to adhere to these institutions.[65] Precisely because viable autonomy is a political bargain sustained by these actors, it is typically a very pragmatic ad hoc solution. The fact that arrangements thus take, from case to case, so many different forms and escape easy generalizations is not only a main reason for the above-mentioned lack of conceptual clarity.[66] More importantly, the absence of common practice has also prevented the emergence of a right to autonomy under international customary law.[67] Evidently, support from the main actors does not have to amount to unbridled enthusiasm. After all, the old formula applies that 'autonomy is most often only reluctantly granted, and usually ungratefully received'.[68] Sometimes, support from the parties involved may contrast strikingly with the assessment of an arrangement's viability by academic experts or external political actors. A case in point is the much-cited conundrum of NCA in Russia.[69] Whereas scholars[70] and the ACFC[71] see autonomy in this case as diluted by legislative gaps, restrictions of activities, and undue bureaucratic hurdles, recent years have been marked by a steep increase in the number of NCA organizations. A similar contrast has been observed with regard to cultural self-governments in Hungary.[72] Thus, the two, at least in quantitative terms, best developed examples of NTA are at the same time among those with quite little instrumental value. Basically, the nonetheless considerable support for these arrangements may be attributed to the fact that the groups in question either do not seek more or are not in a position to realistically expect more.[73]

64 See Miek Boltjes, 'The Implementation Challenge in Intrastate Peace Processes: An Analysis', in *Implementing Negotiated Agreements: The Real Challenge to Intrastate Peace*, edited by Miek Boltjes (The Hague: TMC Asser Press, 2007), pp. 6–8.

65 See James D. Fearon, 'Commitment Problems and the Spread of Ethnic Conflict', in *The International Spread of Ethnic Conflict: Fear, Diffusion, and Escalation*, edited by David A. Lake and Donald S. Rothchild (Princeton: Princeton University Press, 1998), pp. 107–26.

66 See section 1 of this chapter.

67 See Stefan Oeter, 'Minderheiten im institutionellen Staatsaufbau' [Minorities in the Institutional Structure of the State], in *Das Minderheitenrecht europäischer Staaten* [Minority Law of European States], Teil 2, edited by Jochen Abr. Frowein, Rainer Hofmann, and Stefan Oeter (Berlin: Springer, 1994), p. 494; Commission for Democracy through Law (Venice Commission) CDL–INF (1996), 4, Opinion on the interpretation of art 11 of the Draft Protocol to the European Convention on Human Rights appended to Recommendation 1201 of the Parliamentary Assembly, para 3c.

68 Dinstein, 'Autonomy', p. 302.

69 See Bowring, Smith, and Osipov in this volume, sections 6.1, 7.6, and 8.4 respectively.

70 See Alexander Osipov, 'National Cultural Autonomy in Russia: A Case of Symbolic Law', *Review of Central and East European Law*, vol. 35, no. 1 (2010): pp. 27–57.

71 See ACFC, Third Opinion on the Russian Federation. Adopted on 24 November 2011 (adopted 25 July 2012) ACFC/OP/III(2011)010.

72 See Smith in this volume, section 7.4.

73 See also on this section 4.3.

While support from the main actors is crucial, one should be wary of perceiving these parties as monolithic blocks. Sometimes the claims of different factions within them, each purporting to represent the same group, may diverge fundamentally and thus further complicate the process of striking a bargain. A case in point is the demand for TA for the Hungarian minority in Romania, which was endorsed in the early 2000s by several parties in explicit opposition to the NTA proposal from the Democratic Union of Hungarians in Romania (UDMR).[74] Another important thing to bear in mind, especially for national governments fearing secessionism, is that a minority's support of an arrangement does not necessarily require in each case very extensive self-government, but always appropriateness. As long as an arrangement is in the above-mentioned sense tailored to actual conditions, a 'thin autonomy' might prove equally successful.[75] Good timing, by contrast, seems to be indispensable for the chances of initial arrangement of its reform to win sufficient support. The course of history opens and closes windows of opportunity because of changing demographics, economic relations, geopolitical contexts, political attitudes and claims, etc. For instance, the increasing Catholic share of Northern Ireland's population has profound repercussions on what options of institutional design are acceptable to the parties of the conflict.[76] Similarly, autonomy negotiations are today facilitated in the case of the Åland Islands by the fact that, unlike in the nineteenth century, they are no longer a geopolitical hotspot for Sweden and Finland.

4.2. Five main influencing factors

Among the numerous factors, which may have an impact on whether and how autonomy is put into practice,[77] five seem to be highlighted in particular by the chapters of this book: a context of a stable democracy and rule of law; international actors; historical structural legacies (especially from colonialism, communism, and traditional liberalism); competing nation-building projects; and the association of TA with secession.

First, the context of a stable democracy and rule of law is beyond doubt of utmost importance for autonomy's success. This has been underlined by previous research[78] and is equally evident from the cases covered in this book.[79] In many

[74] See Smith in this volume, section 7.4.

[75] John Packer, 'Reflections on Implementation Mechanisms of Selected Autonomy, Self-Rule and Similar Arrangements', in *Implementing Negotiated Agreements: The Real Challenge to Intrastate Peace*, edited by Miek Boltjes (The Hague: TMC Asser Press, 2007), p. 71.

[76] See John McGarry and Brendan O'Leary, 'Consociation and its Critics: Northern Ireland after the Belfast Agreement', in *Constitutional Design for Divided Societies: Integration or Accommodation?*, edited by Sujit Choudhry (Oxford: Oxford University Press, 2008), p. 399.

[77] For a table listing such factors, see Sophia Woodman and Yash Ghai, 'Comparative Perspectives on Institutional Frameworks for Autonomy', in *Practising Self-Government: A Comparative Study of Autonomous Regions*, edited by Yash Ghai and Sophia Woodman (Cambridge: Cambridge University Press), p. 452.

[78] See, e.g., Kjell-Åke Nordquist, 'Autonomy as a Conflict-Solving Mechanism: An Overview', in *Autonomy: Applications and Implications*, edited by Markku Suksi (The Hague: Kluwer Law International, 1998), pp. 69–71.

[79] See Chapters 7–10 of this volume.

young democracies, throwing off the yoke of authoritarian rule has gone hand in hand with some form of decentralization. This has been just as characteristic of early post-colonial democracies as of those emerging during democracy's 'third wave'[80] or as in the case of Nepal even more recently. However, in many of these young and still unstable democracies enthusiasm and solemn declarations have soon given way either to very weak autonomy regimes such as in Nigeria[81] or even to an outright failure of implementation as in Nepal.[82]

Secondly, international actors often have a significant impact. Quite obviously, this includes the role(s) played by a kin-state, which may take unilateral steps to support a national minority abroad or facilitate through 'benign intervention' both the conclusion of an autonomy arrangement and its subsequent maintenance. Beyond a kin-state, the involvement of other international actors may at times also have great influence on whether and how autonomy is put into practice. Whereas the role of the United States in brokering the 1998 Belfast Agreement is in this regard one of the more positive examples,[83] the essential equilibrium between interventionism and furthering local ownership was clearly absent in other instances. Even if it seems true that sustaining an autonomy arrangement from the outside may have the short-term benefit of overcoming stalemate caused by continued disagreement of local actors, it is unlikely to have a positive effects in the long run, as it exempts these very actors from the need to negotiate and compromise. This is amply demonstrated by such glaring examples as Bosnia and Herzegovina,[84] as well as Lebanon under the French mandate and even after independence.[85] In other instances, international actors have had an impact on the establishment of self-government even without direct intervention. It has been contended, for example, that the introduction of cultural autonomy in Hungary in 1993 was to some extent a message to other states in order to justify a proactive policy of demanding from neighbouring countries more protection of Hungarians minorities.[86] In a similar vein, the Estonian law of the same year appears

[80] Samuel P. Huntington, *The Third Wave: Democratization in the Late Twentieth Century* (Oklahoma: University of Oklahoma Press, 1993).

[81] This is reflected in characterizations of Nigeria as a 'hollow federation' or a 'unitary state in federal disguise' (Rotimi Suberu and Larry Diamond, 'Institutional Design, Ethnic Conflict Management, and Democracy in Nigeria', in *The Architecture of Democracy. Constitutional Design, Conflict Management and Democracy*, edited by Andrew Reynolds (Oxford/New York: Oxford University Press: 2002), p. 406).

[82] For a short overview of the most salient issues in the (since 2007) stalled process of constitutional reform, see Yash Ghai, 'Ethnic Identity, Participation and Social Justice: A Constitution for New Nepal?', *International Journal on Minority and Group Rights*, vol. 18, no. 3 (2011): pp. 309–34.

[83] See McGarry and O'Leary, 'Consociation and its Critics', pp. 379–82.

[84] This is of course epitomized most clearly by the High Representative whose role has with the 'Bonn Powers' arguably changed 'from that of a supervisor of the peace implementation process to its main actor' (Jens Woelk, 'Bosnia-Herzegovina: Trying to Build a Federal State on Paradoxes', in *Constitutional Dynamics in Federal Systems: Sub-National Perspectives*, edited by Michael Burgess and G. Alan Tarr (Montreal/Kingston: McGill-Queen's University Press, 2012), p. 119).

[85] See Marie-Joëlle Zahar, 'Power Sharing in Lebanon: Foreign Protectors, Domestic Peace, and Democratic Failure', in *Sustainable Peace: Power and Democracy after Civil Wars*, edited by Philip G. Roeder and Donald Rothchild (Ithaka: Cornell University Press, 2005), pp. 219–40.

[86] See András László Pap, 'Minority Rights and Diaspora-Claims: Collision, Interdependence and Loss of Orientation', in *Beyond Sovereignty: From Status Law to Transnational Citizenship*,

to have been addressed at least partly to critics of the country's controversial citizenship legislation.[87] What both these cases have in common is the functional character of autonomy with a view to the external image of these countries and to enhancing their chances of integration in international and supranational organizations, above all, of course into the European Union.

Thirdly, autonomy arrangements tend to be influenced considerably by historical structural legacies, which reinforce themselves by limiting creative imagination of the bargaining parties and, as a consequence, the variety of acceptable institutional designs. This path dependence[88] seems to be particularly strong regarding the legacies of colonialism, communism, and traditional liberalism. While the above-mentioned practical necessities of administering large empires forced colonial powers to establish locally at least some form of self-government, this process often went hand in hand with the political manipulation of both cultural diversity and of autonomy itself. In Africa, for instance, the powerful local arm of colonial rule was typically organized along (sometimes invented) ethnic and/or religious lines, which perverted pretended self-government into 'decentralized despotism' of one group at the expense of others.[89] Even though autonomy arrangements were at the time of independence quite common and additional ones were introduced during decolonization, many of them have fallen victim, to the colonial legacy of a negative perception of autonomy as an instrument of one group to dominate others.

The similar penchant of formerly communist countries for ethnic TA has of course much stronger theoretical underpinnings, which date back to the position developed by Lenin and other Bolsheviks against Austro-Marxist ideas of NCA. In practice, however, the Soviet Union only implemented the concept of ethnic TA to a very limited extent because the reality of mixed settlement areas necessarily produced minorities within minorities instead of an 'own' territory for each group.[90] It has been pointed out, for example, that in the Russian Soviet Federative Socialist Republic (RSFSR) only 41 of the 127 officially recognized nationalities enjoyed autonomy in Lenin's sense.[91] Today, the situation is similar. Conventional wisdom has it that the list of constituent entities in Article 65(1) of the 1993 constitution of Russia establishes territorially defined units on the one hand and ethnic-based units with numerically dominant titular groups on the other. In fact, however, the titular group is according to the 2010 census only in a

edited by Osamu Ieda and Balázs Majtényi (Sapporo: Hokkaido University Slavic Research Center, 2006), p. 243.

87 See David J. Smith and John Hiden, *Ethnic Diversity and the Nation State: National Cultural Autonomy Revisited* (London/New York: Routledge, 2012), p. 111.

88 On the concept, see Paul Pierson, 'Increasing Returns, Path Dependence, and the Study of Politics', *American Political Science Review*, vol. 94, no. 2 (2000): pp. 251–67.

89 See Mahmood Mamdani, *Citizen and Subject: Contemporary Africa and the Legacy of Late Colonialism* (Princeton: Princeton University Press, 1996), pp. 23–4.

90 See section 2 of this chapter.

91 See Cristiano Codagnone and Vassily Filippov, 'Equity, Exit and National Identity in a Multinational Federation: The "Multicultural Constitutional Patriotism" Project in Russia', *Journal of Ethnic and Migration Studies*, vol. 26, no. 2 (2000): p. 266.

majority position in 12 of the 21 republics.[92] Even though more a myth than a reality, Lenin's ethnic TA legacy has had an enormous impact. It was not only translated into the constitutional law of the Soviet Union, but as an idea likewise adopted in a number of other communist countries, such as the People's Republic of China and Ethiopia under military rule (1974–91). Whereas 'nationality regional autonomy' in China is a formal concept with only limited autonomy in practice,[93] Lenin's legacy is today in Ethiopia more relevant than ever before. The idea of ethnic TA has since the end of the 1960s become so widespread and deeply rooted among most political forces that the new government formed by the Ethiopian People's Revolutionary Democratic Front (EPRDF) decided in 1991, in contrast to the lip services of the preceding military regimes, to really put the concept into practice.[94] And this coalition of mostly ethnic-based parties did so in a particularly radical way. The Ethiopian constitution of 1995 not only creates ethnic-based states, but also vests 'the Nations, Nationalities and Peoples of Ethiopia'[95] with 'all sovereign power' (art 8) and confers upon them 'the unrestricted right to self-determination up to secession' (art 39(1)). While the spirit of these provisions can be traced back almost a century to Lenin's ideas, his concept of ethnic TA is in more complex ways also linked to today's NTA arrangements in CEE. Here it did not serve as a model but quite the contrary, as a communist legacy to get rid of. This is particularly true for what has been called the 'Baltic arena',[96] where NTA had been introduced in the 1920s in opposition to the Soviet logic of ethnic TA. For Estonia, the reestablishment of NTA in 1995 was thus also a means to emphasize state continuity with the interwar period and to foster the country's post-communist identity.[97] On the whole, CEE is therefore today, with some exceptions such as the Sami in Nordic countries or the Maori in New Zealand, once again the core area of NTA.

While communism was from a global perspective a major force in spreading the false idea of ethnic TA being a practically viable concept, another influential ideology argued against any form of autonomy. Ever since John Stuart Mill's famous words that 'free institutions are next to impossible in a country made up of different nationalities',[98] traditional liberalism has been guided by the strong

[92] See Osipov in this volume, section 8.5.

[93] This limited self-government of the recognized nationalities contrasts strikingly with the genuine autonomy granted to the Special Administrative Regions Hong Kong and Macao (see Qianfan Zhang, *The Constitution of China: A Contextual Analysis* (Oxford/Portland: Hart, 2012), pp. 109–12).

[94] See Fessha, *Ethnic Diversity*, pp. 169–86.

[95] These categories are not differentiated but covered by a common definition in art 39(5): 'A "Nation, Nationality or People" for the purpose of this Constitution, is a group of people who have or share large measure of a common culture or similar customs, mutual intelligibility of language, belief in a common or related identities, a common psychological make-up, and who inhabit an identifiable, predominantly contiguous territory.'

[96] Smith and Hiden, *Ethnic Diversity*, p. 111.

[97] See Aleksandr Aidarov and Wolfgang Drechsler, 'The Law and Economics of the Estonian Law on Cultural Autonomy for National Minorities and of Russian National Cultural Autonomy in Estonia', *Halduskultuur—Administrative Culture*, vol. 12, no. 1 (2011): pp. 46–8.

[98] John Stuart Mill, *Considerations on Representative Government* (London: Parker, Son and Bourn, 1861), p. 289.

belief that the homogeneous nation state would be a prerequisite for democracy. Due to its monolithic idea of both the nation and the state and the purported neutrality of its constitution,[99] the liberal-democratic nation state typically denies the need for any form of autonomy that would contravene the dual order of the unitary state on the one hand and individual citizens on the other. Even though these views have been contested by some nineteenth-century liberals,[100] later by the Austro-Marxists[101] and, since the 1990s, by liberal nationalists,[102] traditional liberalism has greatly influenced numerous countries both under colonial rule and during decolonization. Especially in Africa, the homogeneity of the nation and its state came to be seen, also due to this legacy, as an indispensable prerequisite for democracy, political stability, and modernization.[103] Diversity became, in turn, stigmatized as an archaic remnant of the past. This general tendency also captured a predominantly left-wing movement like the Mozambique Liberation Front (FRELIMO), whose slogan 'to kill the tribe to build the nation'[104] strikingly echoed even in the 1970s what Mill had written more than a century before: 'Nobody can suppose that it is not more beneficial for a Breton or a Basque of French Navarre to be a member of the French nationality than to sulk on his own rock, the half-savage relic of past times. The same remark applies to the Welshman and the Scottish Highlander.'[105]

This leads us directly to a fourth factor, which impacts on whether and how autonomy is put into practice, namely competing nation-building projects. Essentially, this competition follows from the fact that the nation state pursues such a project in order to *produce ex post* the common national identity,[106] which traditional liberalism actually *presupposes*. Minority groups often counter these efforts, with a focus on 'their' part of the state territory, with an own

[99] For a critique of this, see Ferran Requejo, 'European Citizenship in Plurinational States: Some Limits of Traditional Democratic Theories: Rawls and Habermas', in *European Citizenship, Multiculturalism and the State*, edited by Ulrich Preuss and Ferran Requejo (Baden-Baden: Nomos, 1998), pp. 29–49.

[100] See John Emerich Edward Dalberg Acton, 'Nationality', *Home and Foreign Review*, vol. 1 (1862): pp. 1–25.

[101] See Bauer, *The Question of Nationalities*, pp. 224–7. For a discussion of Bauer's critique of the liberal nation state as having a 'centralist-atomist structure' and its implication for NTA, see Nimni in this volume, section 3.4.

[102] For a concise overview of this school of thought, including among many others Charles Taylor and Will Kymlicka, and its argument that liberalism and nationalism are compatible, see Wayne Norman, *Negotiating Nationalism: Nation-Building, Federalism, and Secession in the Multinational State* (Oxford: Oxford University Press, 2006), pp. 1–3.

[103] See Francis M. Deng, 'Ethnicity: An African Predicament', *The Brookings Review*, vol. 15, no. 3 (1997): p. 28.

[104] Quoted in Solomon A. Dersso, *Taking Ethno-cultural Diversity Seriously in Constitutional Design: A Theory of Minority Rights for Addressing Africa's Multiethnic Challenge* (Leiden/Boston: Martinus Nijhoff Publishers, 2012), p. 67.

[105] Mill, *Considerations on Representative Government*, p. 293. In a similar vein, Seymour Martin Lipset also characterized claims of minorities as a 'revolt against modernity' (Seymour Martin Lipset, 'The Revolt against Modernity', in *Mobilization, Center-Periphery Structures and National Building*, edited by Per Torsvik (Bergen: Universitets Forlaget, 1981), p. 451).

[106] See Eugen Weber, *Peasants Into Frenchmen: The Modernization of Rural France, 1880–1914* (Palo Alto: Stanford University Press, 1976).

nation-building project. The result is then an obvious clash between majority nationalism justifying the established order and minority nationalism contending against it.[107] In other instances, minorities are assimilated into a uniform national identity, which is typically constructed by 'extending' the identity of the dominant group. This occurred, for instance, in a number of African and South Asian countries,[108] particularly in the process of decolonization and again during democracy's 'third wave'. That democratization is indeed closely intertwined with nation-building projects is particularly clearly demonstrated by the example of Nepal. In the times of monarchy until 1990 the explicit aim was to forge a uniform national identity, which was to be based on one language (Nepali), one religion (Hindu) and the culture of one caste (hill Bahun-Chhetri).[109] Then this project was countered in the wake of transition to democracy by formerly suppressed minority nationalisms and also, linked to these, demands for ethnic TA, which have been promoted decisively by the powerful Maoists.

On a more general note, competing nation-building seems to have two important implications for autonomy. First, the construction of a uniform national identity by 'extending' the identity of the dominant group makes it for members of the latter often inconceivable that identities other than this fused nationalized one may exist: 'English Canadians outside Québec largely think of themselves as Canadians-who-happen-to-speak-English, rather than as a distinct national group within Canada.'[110] This inability to conceive of multiple identities entails that minority claims for self-government sometimes meet with little understanding. Minority nationalism, in turn, often attempts to portray the majority as a coherent group.[111] In this sense, some Québécois, for instance, use the term 'rest of the country (ROC)',[112] which implies, in disregard of other groups like the First Nations, a strictly dualist view of Canada.

A second implication of rival nation-building for autonomy pertains to the contestation of territory. Both majority and minority nationalisms are commonly characterized by a strong attachment to a specific territory. This most often results from a group's traditional settlement there and from this area being the location of historical events, which are still seen as identity-relevant according to the present

[107] See André Lecours and Geneviève Nootens, 'Understanding Majority Nationalism', in *Contemporary Majority Nationalism*, edited by Alain-G. Gagnon, André Lecours, and Geneviève Nootens (Montreal/Kingston: McGill-Queen's University Press, 2011), pp. 3–18.

[108] See Castellino in this volume, sections 10.2–10.3.

[109] See David N. Gellner, 'Caste, Ethnicity and Inequality in Nepal', *Economic and Political Weekly*, vol. 42, no. 20 (2007): pp. 1823–8.

[110] David Miller, 'Nationality in Divided Societies', in *Multinational Democracies*, edited by Alain-G. Gagnon and James Tully (Cambridge/New York: Cambridge University Press, 2001), p. 314.

[111] Michael Keating, 'Rival Nationalisms in a Plurinational State. Spain, Catalonia, and the Basque Country', in *Constitutional Design for Divided Societies. Integration or Accommodation?*, edited by Sujit Choudhry (Oxford: Oxford University Press, 2008), p. 317.

[112] See, for instance, Alain-G. Gagnon and Raffaele Iacovino, *Federalism, Citizenship, and Quebec. Debating Multinationalism* (Toronto: University of Toronto Press, 2007).

nationalist narrative.[113] A first problem is then that usually more than one group claims a territory on the basis of these arguments, albeit usually referring to different time periods, as inextricably linked to their respective identity. Kosovo and Palestine are only two obvious of numerous examples. The second problem is that these putative homelands are perceived by each side as exclusive, which is then supposed to justify the demand not only for some sort of self-government but for governing 'their' territory according to the idea of ethnic TA. Autonomy thus becomes a zero-sum game.

A fifth factor, which impacts on whether and how self-government is put into practice, is what may be called a climate of 'autonomy-phobia',[114] that is, the widespread fear of states that autonomy will be a stepping stone to secession. Thus, it would threaten not only the state's territorial integrity, but also, due to the often violent character of separatism, national security. Even though typically only (ethnic) TA sparks this fear and, as a consequence, a securitized autonomy discourse, they are in a few cases even provoked by claims for NTA. A glaring example is the Romanian government's rejection of such demands raised by the UDMR in 2005.[115] That states typically view secession with utmost suspicion hardly comes as a surprise. After all, they are guided by the inherent interest of self-preservation. Their constitutions are therefore, paraphrasing Thornberry's remarks regarding international law,[116] 'no suicide pacts'. With very few exceptions like the above-mentioned Ethiopian case, they thus refrain in the spirit of Madisonian constitutionalism from adopting 'provisions that prevent the defeat of the basic enterprise',[117] that is, self-preservation. As a consequence, they explicitly prohibit secession, simply remain silent on this issue or, as ruled in the *Quebec Secession Reference*,[118] grant a right to merely *negotiate* separation rather than to separation itself.[119] This fear of secession has profound repercussions on the

[113] This link between past and present is best expressed by Ernest Renan: 'A nation is a soul, a spiritual principle. Two things, which, in truth, are really one, constitute this soul, this spiritual principle. One is in the past, the other in the present. One is the possession in common of a rich legacy of memories; the other is the present-day consent, the desire to live together, the will to continue to value the undivided heritage one has received.' (Ernest Renan, 'What is a Nation?', in *Nation and Narration*, edited by Homi Bhabha (London/New York: Routledge, 1990), p. 19.

[114] Francesco Palermo, 'Central, Eastern and South-Eastern Europe and Territorial Autonomy: Are They Really Incompatible?' in *Political Autonomy and Divided Societies. Comparative Territorial Politics*, edited by Alain-G. Gagnon and Michael Keating (Basingstoke: Palgrave Macmillan, 2012), p. 82.

[115] See Smith in this volume, section 7.4.

[116] 'International Law is not a suicide club for states' (Patrick Thornberry, 'The Democratic or Internal Aspect of Self-Determination with Some Remarks on Federalism', in *Modern Law of Self-Determination*, edited by Christian Tomuschat (Dordrecht/Boston: Martinus Nijhoff Publishers, 1993), p. 118).

[117] Cass R. Sunstein, 'Constitutionalism and Secession', *University of Chicago Law Review*, vol. 58, no. 2 (1991): p. 633.

[118] *Reference re Secession of Quebec* [1998] 2 S.C.R. 217.

[119] See, for a comparison of constitutional positions towards secession, Karl Kössler, 'Constitutions and Secession: From "Perpetual Union" to a Right to Separate?', in *Qualified Autonomy versus Secession*, edited by Annegret Eppler, Charlie Jeffery, and Stefan August Lütgenau (Innsbruck: StudienVerlag, forthcoming).

perception of TA. As states often directly associate notions like TA and the even more infamous 'F-word', federalism, with disintegration, these evoke responses almost as negative as secession itself. A case in point is the cautious political pragmatism applied when international documents, which evidently deal with issues of self-government, deliberately use less explicit wording so as to cater to the concerns of certain states.[120]

The crucial question is whether the assumption that states granting TA are more likely to break apart is correct and thus justifies its refusal. From a state's perspective, there is much insecurity involved in responding to this question because a group's preference for autonomy or secession often changes over time and it may do so for a variety of reasons. Little more than a decade ago, it had been claimed with reference to globalization and European integration that in 'the stateless nations of the United Kingdom, Spain, Belgium and Canada, nationalist leaders have increasingly eschewed separatism in favour of seeking a place within the new complex systems of multi-level government'.[121] Since then, however, the secession option has gained support, albeit not necessarily majority support, in all of the above-mentioned European stateless nations: a development, which has been controversially stigmatized as a 'form of irredentist Euro-tribalism'.[122] The question is then in these and other cases whether TA is to blame because it would inevitably fuel secessionism. Unfortunately, the evidence from the seemingly endless debate on this issue is far from being conclusive and rather suggests that there simply is no easy and generally applicable answer.[123] For this to be possible, institutional designs of TA are just too diverse and extra-institutional determinants like social and economic factors or political culture too numerous and influential. Irrespective of whether the undeniable risk of secession eventually materializes in a single case or in a majority of cases, TA has arguably offered in many instances better prospects to dampen secessionism than its refusal.[124] As opposed to the inherent unilateralism of the latter option, it takes demands for self-government seriously and thus at least provides a *chance* to find a mutually accepted solution, which occupies some position on the broad spectrum between the two extremes of secession and complete denial of self-government. This intrinsic character as a

[120] Examples are the Lund Recommendations (see John Packer, 'Reflections on Implementation Mechanisms', p. 71) and the Council of Europe Reference Framework for Regional Democracy (see Mario Heinrich, 'Regionale Selbstverwaltung, Chancen und Probleme: Bemühungen des Europarats um eine Europäische Charta der regionalen Demokratie' [Local Self-Government, Opportunities and Problems: Europe's Efforts to Establish a European Charter of Regional Democracy], in *Volksgruppen und regionale Selbstverwaltung in Europa*, edited by Anna Gamper and Christoph Pan (Vienna/Baden-Baden: facultas.wuv and Nomos, 2008), p. 69.

[121] Michael Keating, 'Plurinational Democracy in a Post-Sovereign Order', *Queen's Papers on Europeanisation*, no. 1 (2002): p. 1.

[122] Joseph Weiler, 'Editorial', *European Journal of International Law*, vol. 23, no. 4 (2012): p. 911.

[123] For an introduction into this debate see Choudhry and Hume, 'Federalism, Secession and Devolution', pp. 363–72; Jan Erk and Lawrence Anderson, 'The Paradox of Federalism: Does Self-Rule Accommodate or Exacerbate Ethnic Divisions?', *Regional and Federal Studies*, vol. 19, no. 2 (2009): pp. 191–202.

[124] See Nancy Bermeo, 'The Import of Institutions', *Journal of Democracy*, vol. 13, no. 2 (2002): pp. 96–110.

compromise is reflected in a number of constitutions, which introduce TA and emphasize in the very same provision the limit of territorial integrity.[125] It remains doubtful whether the refusal of such a compromise or, even worse, processes of further centralization and, particularly in a post-September 11 context, securitization,[126] will on the whole produce better outcomes. Such strategies might even give rise to demands for secession, where they previously did not exist. Autonomy-phobia's prediction of separation would then become a self-fulfilling prophecy.

4.3. TA and/or NTA?

If we understand autonomy as a political bargain influenced by various impact factors, the question of how the final arrangement may look like remains. In few exceptional cases, autonomy is put into practice for various reasons as a transitional solution. As far as TA is concerned, such arrangements are an intermediate stage either towards the abolition of self-government (e.g. Hong Kong and Macau) or towards full independence (e.g. New Caledonia).[127] As for transitional NTA, some observers have suggested such a solution as a stage towards eventual TA for situations in which the latter seems, due to a lack of democratic consolidation and unstable internal or international boundaries, momentarily unfeasible.[128] Leaving these exceptional cases aside, autonomy arrangements, which are intended to function for an indefinite period of time, most often introduce either TA or NTA and rather rarely combine them.

It has been pointed out in this volume with reference to a rich literature on this point that TA is commonly the only realistic option in the case of large and territorially concentrated groups.[129] Such groups typically aim to underpin a nation-building project, which is closely entwined with a specific geographical area,[130] with far-reaching competences regarding issues like economic development, infrastructure, policing, or immigration. These are by their very nature territory-related powers impossible to be exercised by NTA institutions.[131] As

[125] Among many examples see, for instance, art 2 of the Spanish constitution, art 5 of the Italian constitution, and art 4 of the Chinese constitution.

[126] For examples of such processes in India, Pakistan, and Sri Lanka see Castellino in this volume, sections 10.3.1–10.3.3.

[127] See Yash Ghai, 'Introduction: Nature and Origins of Autonomy', in *Practising Self-Government: A Comparative Study of Autonomous Regions*, edited by Yash Ghai and Sophia Woodman (Cambridge: Cambridge University Press, 2013), pp. 9–10.

[128] See Rainer Bauböck, 'Territorial or Cultural Autonomy for National Minorities?', *IWE Working Paper*, no. 22 (2001): pp. 30–31; Will Kymlicka, 'Western Political Theory and Ethnic Relations in Eastern Europe', in *Can Liberal Pluralism be Exported? Western Political Theory and Ethnic Relations in Eastern Europe*, edited by Will Kymlicka and Magda Opalski (Oxford: Oxford University Press, 2001), p. 67.

[129] See Nootens in this volume, section 2.3.

[130] See section 4.2.

[131] See John Coakley, 'National Territories and Cultural Frontiers: Conflicts of Principle in the Formation of States in Europe', *West European Politics*, vol. 5, no. 4 (1982): p. 36; McGarry and Moore, 'Karl Renner', pp. 82–3.

the modern state expanded massively during the twentieth century, by exercising more and more such powers among other things, this inherent practical limitation of non-territorial solutions seems nowadays far greater than in Renner's time. Against this backdrop, NTA is for large and territorially concentrated groups hardly an attractive option, unless they are politically too weak to have realistic hopes for TA or they do not seek TA at all. As a consequence, NTA has become linked with small and/or dispersed communities, which are from an empirical perspective clearly the primary target group and actual beneficiaries of such arrangements. This is true today, for instance, in the case of Hungary with a (for NTA) downright 'ideal' constellation of mostly small and dispersed minorities. A historical example is Estonia's law of 1925, which was primarily designed to meet the demands of the German minority.[132]

Beyond the focus on small and/or dispersed groups, there are also similarities between NTA today and in the interwar period concerning the extent of self-government. It has been underlined that the draft of the 1925 Estonian law was only passed when substantial fiscal and political powers were removed and NTA institutions thus made 'sufficiently harmless from the standpoint of the majority'.[133] This statement seems to be equally applicable to a number of contemporary arrangements. It is obvious that non-territorial solutions are perceived by states in terms of secessionism much less threatening and therefore preferable surrogates for TA.[134] But most NTA arrangements do not only lag behind the possibilities offered by TA, which is, due to the above-mentioned exclusion of territory-related powers, inevitable. They also fail to realize the thus necessarily more limited potential of NTA and do not even come close in practice to the extent of autonomy envisaged by Renner.[135]

The function of NTA as a harmless substitute for TA is characteristic of several cases in CEE, where territorial solutions are viewed by states for a number of reasons with utmost suspicion. Among these reasons is the image that minorities are disloyal and a potential fifth column, an obstacle to a strong state and an issue of national security.[136] Others are efforts of post-communist majority nation-building in the face of weak civic cohesion, Lenin's conceptual legacy of ethnic TA and, not least, the direct association of any territorial solution with the violent disintegration of the Soviet Union and Yugoslavia.[137] This perception of NTA as a surrogate is epitomized by two decisions of the Supreme Court of Estonia in 1993, which found two referendums in the predominantly Russian-speaking

[132] See Smith in this volume, section 7.5.

[133] Kari Alenius, 'The Birth of Cultural Autonomy in Estonia: How, Why and for Whom?', *Journal of Baltic Studies*, vol. 38, no. 4 (2007): p. 458.

[134] See on autonomy-phobia in section 4.2.

[135] McGarry and Moore, 'Karl Renner', p. 84. After his comparative analysis in this volume, Suksi also arrives at the conclusion that 'generally speaking, it seems that non-territorial cultural autonomies have not been vested with broad powers' (section 4.4).

[136] See Kymlicka, 'Western Political Theory', p. 67.

[137] See Jennifer Jackson-Preece, 'Minority Rights Enforcement in Europe: A Difficult Balancing Act', *International Journal of Peace Studies*, vol. 3, no. 2 (1998): pp. 35–55.

towns of Narva and Sillamäe about 'a status of national-territorial autonomy' to be unconstitutional.[138] While ruling out TA, this judgment referred explicitly to the opportunities of cultural autonomy, which Section 50 of the Estonian constitution would provide instead of territorial self-government. In particular the aforementioned traumatic disintegration processes of the 1990s also impacted strongly on the position of international organizations. They gave rise to a feeling at the end of this decade that 'insufficient attention has been given to the possibilities of cultural autonomy'.[139] This change of attitude is also reflected in the Lund Recommendations' deliberate turn towards emphasizing non-territorial solutions.[140] TA has lost support since the 1990s not only in comparison to NTA, but also to other instruments of minority participation such as the design of electoral systems and reserved seats.[141] Essentially, TA has only found endorsement when the outcome political and/or military confrontation had already made it an accomplished fact. Obviously, such an approach of selective *ex post facto* support of what has been termed 'seized autonomies'[142] makes international organizations vulnerable to criticism for incoherence and double standards.

Compared to the establishment of either TA or NTA, a combination of both forms of autonomy is much less common. If combined, however, their relationship is typically quite asymmetrical, with NTA serving as a supplement to an overall predominantly TA-focused arrangement. This is the case, for instance, in South Tyrol or in the Brussels-Capital Region. Of course, such a minor role contrasts starkly with Renner's comprehensive model of the *Nationalitätenbundesstaat*, which treated territorial and non-territorial elements as equally important. In fact, he foresaw a 'double network on the map' so that the populations at all government levels, from municipalities to the state level, would be organized twice, 'once nationally and once according to administrative requirements'.[143] In view of the considerable complexity of Renner's institutional design, it seems true that his legacy today is less the details of the specific model than the idea of combining NTA and TA as equally significant elements. Closest to this idea was probably the original 1992 proposal for NCA in Russia. This early draft aimed at curbing ethnocratic tendencies associated with the territorial structure of the Russian Federation by putting NCA institutions in legal terms on an equal footing with the republics.[144] In the end, however, this proposal failed to be implemented

[138] Decision No. III-4/A-2 of the Constitutional Review Chamber of the Supreme Court of Estonia of 11 August 1993 and Decision No. III-4/A-3 of 6 September 1993 of the Constitutional Review Chamber of the Supreme Court of Estonia. For details, see Suksi in this volume, section 4.3.

[139] Max Van der Stoel, *Peace and Stability through Human and Minority Rights: Speeches by the OSCE High Commissioner on National Minorities* (Baden-Baden: Nomos Verlagsgesellschaft, 1999), p. 172.

[140] See section 1 of this chapter.

[141] With reference to both the OSCE-HCNM and the Venice Commission, see Palermo, 'Central, Eastern and South-Eastern Europe', pp. 90–1.

[142] Nordquist, 'Autonomy', p. 64.

[143] Robert A. Kann, *The Multinational Empire: Nationalism and National Reform in the Habsburg Monarchy. 1848–1918. Vol. 2* (New York: Octagon Books, 1983), p. 159.

[144] See Smith and Hiden, *Ethnic Diversity*, p. 111.

in a way similar to Renner's model due to political opposition. Non-territorial self-government under the 1996 law then turned out to be quite limited rather than 'Austro-Marxism's last laugh'.[145] Nonetheless, the example seems to suggest that in conducive political circumstances there would be potential to combine TA and NTA in a meaningful way.

5. Outlook

There are several reasons to believe that autonomy will, in the foreseeable future, continue to be a crucial instrument of institutional design. On a global scale, this relevance seems to result, for instance, from the current downfall of the post-cold war geopolitical order, from claims for self-government in the wake of the 'Arab Spring' and increasing pressure on many of the still comparatively young post-colonial states to reform structures, which often still reflect political bargains at the time of independence.[146] As for Europe in particular, it is true that the heyday of autonomy in the 1990s has given way in the new millennium, at least regarding TA, to a dramatic decrease of efforts both to introduce self-government and to reform existing arrangements.[147] This trend, however, has not made autonomy irrelevant but in light of growing secessionist tendencies, for instance in Scotland and Catalonia, even more topical.

Precisely such examples of large and territorially concentrated groups also suggest that more comprehensive TA will, as far as possible and appropriate, combined with NTA, continue to be important. This does not only result from the above-mentioned tendency that such groups are simply unlikely to settle for anything less. From a more general perspective, territory has not ceased contrary to Renner's belief to be crucial for both group identities and for political and legal organization. Whereas he was convinced that the transformation of peasants into workers through the Industrial Revolution would entail the replacement of territory-bound groups by class-based communities,[148] attachment to territory is still strong today.[149] Similarly, the territoriality principle is, in contrast to Renner's prediction about its decreasing importance,[150] still the fundamental organizational principle. As far as Europe is concerned, this is true even in the face of globalization and European integration, which some had regarded in the 1990s

[145] Bill Bowring, 'Austro-Marxism's Last Laugh?: The Struggle for Recognition of National-Cultural Autonomy for Rossians and Russians', *Europe-Asia Studies*, vol. 54, no. 2 (2002): pp. 229–50.

[146] See Castellino in this volume, section 10.1.

[147] See Francesco Palermo, 'Concluding Remarks: New Regionalism in Central, Eastern and South-Eastern Europe: Traditional Models and Beyond', in *Regional Dynamics in Central and Eastern Europe*, edited by Francesco Palermo and Sara Parolari (Leiden/Boston: Martinus Nijhoff Publishers, 2013), pp. 241–3.

[148] See Karl Renner, *Das Selbstbestimmungsrecht der Nationen* (Leipzig/Vienna: Deuticke, 1918), p. 79.

[149] See section 4.2.

[150] See Renner, *Das Selbstbestimmungsrecht*, p. 79.

as giving rise to the 'end of territory'.[151] Against this hypothesis, it is contended that instead of de-territorialization there is a recurrent process of rescaling, which means the diversification and relocation of functions to different levels (sub-state, state, transnational, and supranational) and thus the reconstruction of territory at multiple scales.[152]

As TA therefore remains crucial in many cases, the major challenge is to design arrangements, which provide for comprehensive self-government but at the same time avoid the pitfalls most commonly associated with this form of autonomy, more precisely with the prevailing notion of majoritarian ethnic TA.[153] In other words, the challenge consists in finding appropriate solutions on the broad spectrum between 'balkanization and banalization' of diversity.[154] Already Renner was fully aware that majoritarian ethnic TA, which he equated like so many others with TA per se, is fundamentally at odds with a reality of culturally non-homogenous territory and inevitably entails the issue of internal minorities.[155] In such cases it would mean 'if you live in my territory, you are subject to my domination, my law, and my language! It is the expression of domination, not of equal rights; the domination by the established inhabitants of the newcomers, by the propertied, who is held fast by his property, of the propertyless, who must follow demand where it leads, at least by the majority of the minority.'[156]

Renner's solution to alleviate these adverse effects of TA on internal minorities was obviously its combination with strong elements of NTA. Instead of being a weak surrogate, the latter is then a strong supplement.[157] Two other instruments applied to reduce potential marginalization of internal minorities include the assignment to the national government of the power to intervene on behalf of these groups in certain sensitive policy fields[158] and a comprehensive

[151] See Bertrand Badie, *La fin des territoires: Essai sur le désordre international et sur l'utilité sociale du respect* [The End of Territories: Essay on the International Disorder and the Social Utility of Respect] (Paris: Fayard, 1995). The 'end of territory' hypothesis paralleled in the 1990s the debate about the 'end of history' (Francis Fukuyama, 'The End of History?', *The National Interest*, no. 16 (1989): pp. 3–18).

[152] See Michael Keating, *Rescaling the European State: The Making of Territory and the Rise of the Meso* (Oxford: Oxford University Press, 2013), pp. 48–73. Similarly, Kevin Cox, Murray Low, and Jenny Robinson, 'Political Geography: Traditions and Turns', in *Handbook of Political Geography*, edited by Kevin Cox, Murray Low, and Jenny Robinson (London: Sage, 2008), pp. 1–14.

[153] See section 2 of this chapter.

[154] Aviel Roshwald, 'Between Balkanization and Banalization: Dilemmas of Ethno-Cultural Diversity', *Ethnopolitics*, vol. 6, no. 3 (2007): pp. 365–78.

[155] See section 2 of this chapter.

[156] Karl Renner, 'State and Nation', pp. 27–8. Note that the notion of internal minorities usually does not include immigrants. It seems, however, interesting for future research to also explore if and to what extent NTA may be equally applied to these 'new minorities'. This would be much in line with the spirit of the early ideas of the Austro-Marxists Renner and Bauer on NCA. These were, as reflected also in this quote, in part developed to benefit itinerant workers, who were forced into mobility within the Habsburg Empire.

[157] See section 4.3.

[158] E.g., arts 349–51 of the constitution of India (see Joshua Castellino and Elvira Domínguez Redondo, *Minority Rights in Asia. A Comparative Legal Analysis* (Oxford: Oxford University Press, 2006), pp. 88–9).

catalogue of fundamental rights in the national constitution.[159] Both these instruments set like NTA some *external substantive limits* to the scope of majoritarian decision-making within an autonomous territory. However, they do not change this form decision-making as such and thus fail to address the fundamental problem of internal minorities being outnumbered in this process. A fourth instrument, namely regional power-sharing, tackles precisely that problem.[160] It does so by introducing in an autonomous region *internal procedural limits* to majoritarian decision-making. In concrete terms, diverse mechanisms of sharing territorially based power, essentially in its legislative and executive dimensions,[161] protect internal minorities against being outnumbered, at least *partially*. This means that regional power-sharing does not fully supplant but merely supplements majoritarian democracy, as its application is confined to a certain range of issues. If this instrument is supposed to work in such a way, this evidently presupposes some degree of TA. Otherwise, there is just no power to share. Recent years have witnessed in many respect a noticeable trend towards regional power-sharing. First, there is a veritable proliferation of peace agreements including this instrument since the 1990s, especially in Asia and Europe.[162] Secondly, academic work on TA as a means of conflict resolution has closely tracked these developments and increasingly directed its attention to power-sharing at the subnational level. This is epitomized in particular by substantial research efforts on what has been termed 'regional consociations'[163] and 'complex power-sharing'.[164] Thirdly, some cautious allusions to the link between TA and regional power-sharing appear to emerge even at the level of international soft law. In this regard, the 2012 Ljubljana Guidelines on Integration of Diverse Societies of the OSCE-HCNM stated that 'institutions of self-governance' must ensure 'that they can legitimately claim to reflect the views of all the communities settled in the concerned territory' and that 'in this context, power-sharing arrangements, where in place, should not be constructed in a manner that excludes any communities from representation'.[165]

159 For instance, the Canadian Charter of Rights and Freedoms 1982 (see Peter Hogg, *Constitutional Law of Canada* (5th edition, Scarborough: Carswell, 2000), 36.1–36.4.

160 For an analysis of the potential and limits of regional power-sharing, see Kössler, 'Beyond Majoritarian Autonomy?'.

161 Examples of legislative power-sharing are special voting procedures, which grant pre-defined identity-related groups within the legislature a right to suspend or prevent a draft law, or less powerful mechanisms like reserved seats. Executive power-sharing includes, for instance, rules regarding the inclusiveness of governments and proportional representation in public administration.

162 For an overview of many of these cases see Stefan Wolff, 'Complex Power-Sharing and the Centrality of Territorial Self-Governance in Contemporary Conflict Settlements', *Ethnopolitics*, vol. 8, no. 1 (2009): pp. 27–45.

163 John McGarry and Brendan O'Leary, 'Introduction: The Macro-Political Regulation of Ethnic Conflict', in *The Politics of Ethnic Conflict Regulation: Case Studies of Protracted Ethnic Conflicts*, edited by John McGarry and Brendan O'Leary (London/New York: Routledge, 1993), pp. 1–47. Opposed to the (until then) exclusive focus on classical 'sovereign consociations' at the national level, McGarry and O'Leary started to pay increasing attention to these 'regional consociations'.

164 Carmen Kettley, James Sullivan, and Jessie Fyfe, 'Self-Determination Disputes and Complex Power Sharing Arrangements: A Background Paper for Debate', *Cambridge Centre of International Studies Working Paper* (2001): pp. 4–5.

165 Ljubljana Guidelines, Explanatory Note to Guideline no. 39.

In terms of supplementing TA with one or more of the four above-mentioned instruments, there emerges the key question of how to justify such substantive and/or procedural limits to majoritarianism. Put simply, anti-majoritarian mechanisms may be defended in the case of autonomous territories with similar arguments as in relation to states. After all, a 'tyranny of the majority', a main concern of liberal political thinkers about democracy,[166] is equally conceivable. According to some it is even more likely in territories of a smaller scale.[167] This implies that justifications for anti-majoritarian constraints regarding states in national constitutions may be applied by analogy to autonomy arrangements. After all, the latter are, irrespective of whether they have in a specific case formal constitutional status, from a functional perspective the constitution-like basic law of autonomous territories. In national constitutions, the 'tyranny of the majority' problem is addressed by what has been described as their *regulative function*, that is, the function to enable *and* disable political decision-making.[168] While they enable in liberal democracies (majoritarian) decision-making by regulating institutions, powers, and processes, they also disable it. They do so by setting, similar to the four above-mentioned instruments to supplement TA, both procedural limits, for example through supermajority requirements, and substantive limits, most notably through a catalogue guaranteeing the rights of individuals and minorities.[169]

In a state, which is characterized by cultural diversity, the *constitutive function* of its basic law is arguably equally important as this regulatory role. In such cases, the basic law's task of constituting the demos and forging a common political identity is due to weaker pre-constitutional bonds particularly difficult and at the same time particularly important.[170] Fulfilling this task is, in turn, indispensable for the constitutional framework to be legitimate and stable. While one should nonetheless be wary of naively overestimating a constitution's influence in this regard, it surely can to a certain degree 'foster the development of a common political identity by creating the institutional spaces for shared decision making... without recourse to force or fraud'.[171] In this light, substantive and procedural

[166] While this notion was of course first popularized by Tocqueville (Alexis de Tocqueville, *Democracy in America*, translated by Harvey C. Mansfield and Delba Winthrop (Chicago: University of Chicago Press, 2000), vol. 1, chap. 15), its prominence was later multiplied through its use by Mill, Acton, and numerous other liberal theorists.

[167] This was, for instance, in Federalist no. 10 one of the main reasons for James Madison to prefer a 'large republic' (see Clinton Rossiter, ed., *The Federalist Papers* (New York: The New American Library, 1961). See also Franz L. Neumann, 'Federalism and Freedom: A Critique', in *Federalism: Mature and Emergent*, edited by Arthur W. Macmahon (Garden City: Doubleday, 1955), pp. 44–57.

[168] See Stephen Holmes, *Passions and Constraint* (Chicago: University of Chicago Press, 1995).

[169] See Ronald Dworkin, *Taking Rights Seriously* (Cambridge: Harvard University Press, 1977), p. 133.

[170] See Jan-Werner Müller and Kim Lane Scheppele, 'Constitutional Patriotism: An Introduction', *International Journal of Constitutional Law*, vol. 6, no. 1 (2007): pp. 67–71.

[171] Sujit Choudhry, 'Bridging Comparative Politics and Comparative Constitutional Law: Constitutional Design for Divided Societies', in *Constitutional Design for Divided Societies: Integration or Accommodation?*, edited by Sujit Choudhry (Oxford: Oxford University Press, 2008), pp. 5–6.

constraints to majoritarianism do not only matter from the pragmatic perspective of preventing a 'tyranny of the majority', but also for efforts to construct a demos and common political identity on the basis of sharing rather than domination. The success of these efforts seems to be essential in order for a basic law to gain and maintain empirical legitimacy,[172] and, as a consequence, lasting stability. This reasoning equally applies to the basic laws of states and autonomous territories, which are culturally diverse rather than homogeneous. On this account, there appears to be no reason why justifications for anti-majoritarian instruments in nation states should not be likewise applicable to nation regions, which is characterized by a similar logic, only on a smaller territorial scale.

[172] Empirical legitimacy 'involves the capacity of a political system to engender and maintain the belief that existing political institutions are the most appropriate and proper ones for the society' (Seymour Martin Lipset, *Political Man: The Social Bases of Politics* (2nd edition, London: Heinemann, 1983), p. 64. Habermas points out that legitimacy in this empirical sense is inextricably linked with legitimacy in a normative sense, i.e. the potential for legitimacy (see Jürgen Habermas, 'Legitimationsprobleme im modernen Staat', in *Legitimationsprobleme politischer Systeme*, edited by Peter Graf Kielmansegg (Opladen: Verlag für Sozialwissenschaften, 1976), pp. 39–42.

Bibliography

BOOKS

Ackrén, Maria. *Conditions for Different Autonomy Regimes in the World. A Fuzzy-Set Application* (Åbo: Åbo Akademis Förlag—Åbo Akademi University Press, 2009).

Agranoff, Robert. ed. *Accommodating Diversity: Asymmetry in Federal States* (Baden-Baden: Nomos, 1999).

Ali, S., K. M. Panikker, and H. N. Kunzru. *Report of the States Reorganization Committee* (New Delhi: Government of India, 1955).

Ali, Tariq. *Can Pakistan Survive? Death of a State* (New Delhi: Penguin, 1983).

Amanzholova, Dina. *Formatirovaniye sovetskosti: Natsionalnye menshinstva v ethncopoliticheskom landshafte SSSR. 1920–1930-t gg* [The Formatting of the Sovietness: National Minorities in the Ethnopolitical Landscape of the USSR. 1920–1930s] (Moscow: Sobraniye, 2010).

Amatulli, Giuseppe. *The Legal Position of the Sami in the Exploitation of Mineral Resources in Finland, Norway and Sweden* (Åbo: Institute for Human Rights of Åbo Akademi University, 2015).

Anderson, Benedict. *Imagined Communities: Reflections on the Origin and Spread of Nationalism* (London: Verso, 1991).

Anghie, Antony. *Imperialism, Sovereignty and the Making of International Law* (Cambridge: Cambridge University Press, 2007), pp. 310–11.

Aristotle, *Politics*, translated by Ernest Barker (2nd edition, Oxford: Oxford University Press, 1948).

Asch, Michael. *On Being There to Stay, Treaties and Aboriginal Rights in Canada* (Toronto: Toronto University Press, 2014).

Ashbrook, John. *Buying and Selling the Istrian Goat: Istrian Regionalism, Croatian Nationalism, and EU Enlargement* (Bruxelles: Peter Lang, 2008).

Axtmann, Roland. *Liberal Democracy into the Twenty-First Century: Globalization, Integration and the Nation-State* (Manchester: Manchester University Press, 1996).

Badie, Bertrand. *La fin des territoires: Essai sur le désordre international et sur l'utilité sociale du respect* [The End of Territories: Essay on the International Disorder and the Social Utility of Respect] (Paris: Fayard, 1995).

Barkey, Karen. *Empire of Difference: The Ottomans in Comparative Perspective* (Cambridge: Cambridge University Press, 2008).

Barpujari, H. K. *North-East India: Problems, Policies and Prospects since Independence* (New Delhi: Spectrum, 1998).

Bauer, Otto. *Die Nationalitätenfrage und die Sozialdemokratie* [The Question of Nationalities and Social Democracy] (Vienna: Verlag der Wiener Volksbuchhandlung Ignaz Brand, 1907 (1924)).

Bauer, Otto. *The Question of Nationalities and Social Democracy* [Nationalitätenfrage und die Sozialdemokratie]. With an Introduction by Ephraim Nimni, Preface by Heinz Fischer (Minneapolis/London: University of Minnesota Press, 2000).

Baxamus, R. M. *A Historic Perspective on Muslim Personal Law in India* (Bombay: SNDT Women's University, 1984).

Benedikter, Thomas. *The World's Modern Autonomy Systems. Concepts and Experiences of Regional Territorial Autonomy* (Bozen/Bolzano: European Academy of Bozen/Bolzano, 2009).

Benton, Lauren. *A Search for Sovereignty: Law and Geography in European Empires 1400–1900* (New York: Cambridge University Press, 2010).

Bhandari, Surendra. *Self-Determination and Constitution Making in Nepal: Constituent Assembly, Inclusion and Ethnic Federalism* (Singapore: Springer, 2014).

Birkland, Thomas A. *An Introduction to the Policy Process: Theories, Concepts, and Models of Public Policy Making* (Armonk, NY: M. E. Sharpe, 2005).

Bodin, Jean. *Les six Livres de la République* [The Six Books of the Republic] (Paris: Jacques du Puis, 1576).

Bohman, James. *Democracy Across Borders: From Demos to Demoi* (Cambridge, MA: The MIT Press, 2007).

Bourdieu, Pierre. *The Logic of Practice* (Stanford, CA: Stanford University Press, 1990).

Bowring, Bill. *Law, Rights and Ideology in Russia: Landmarks in the Destiny of a Great Power* (Abingdon: Routledge, 2013).

Braude, Benjamin and Bernard Lewis. *Christians and Jews in the Ottoman Empire: The Functioning of a Plural Society* (New York: Holmes and Meier, 1982).

Brubaker, Rogers. *Ethnicity without Groups* (Cambridge, MA: Harvard University Press, 2004).

Brubaker, Rogers. *Nationalism Reframed. Nationhood and the National Question in the New Europe* (Cambridge: Cambridge University Press, 1996).

Brubaker, Rogers, et al. *Nationalist Politics and Everyday Ethnicity in a Transylvanian Town* (Princeton: Princeton University Press, 2006).

Brunsson, Neil. *The Organization of Hypocrisy. Talk, Decisions and Actions in Organizations* (Chichester, NY: John Wiley & Sons, 1989).

Castellino, Joshua. *International Law and Self-Determination: The Politics of Possession with Formulations of Post-Colonial 'National' Identity* (The Hague: Martinus Nijhoff Publishers, 2000).

Castellino, Joshua and Elvira Domínguez Redondo. *Minority Rights in Asia: A Comparative Legal Analysis* (Oxford: Oxford University Press, 2006).

Castellino, Joshua and Steve Allen. *Title to Territory in International Law: A Temporal Analysis* (Dartmouth: Ashgate, 2005).

Carr, Leslie G. *'Colour-Blind' Racism* (Thousand Oaks, CA: Sage, 1997).

Chevrier, Marc. *Canadian Federalism and the Autonomy of Quebec: A Historical Viewpoint* (Québec: Gouvernement du Québec, 1996).

Choudhary, Sujit. *Constitutional Design for Divided Societies: Integration or Accommodation?* (Oxford: Oxford University Press, 2008).

Claude, Inis L. *National Minorities: An International Problem* (Cambridge: Harvard University Press, 1955).

Cohen, Stephen. *The Idea of Pakistan* (New Delhi: Oxford University Press, 2005).

Connolly, William E. *The Ethos of Pluralism* (Minneapolis: University of Minnesota Press, 1995).

Connor, Walker. *The National Question in Marxist-Leninist Theory and Strategy* (Princeton, NJ: Princeton University Press, 1984).

Crews, Robert D. *For Prophet and Tsar: Islam and Empire in Russia and Central Asia* (Cambridge, Mass: Harvard University Press, 2006).

Cross, William Paul. ed. *Democratic Reform in New Brunswick* (Toronto: Canadian Scholars' Press, 2007).

Deci, Edward L. and Richard M. Ryan. *Intrinsic Motivation of Self-Determination in Human Behaviour* (New York: Plenum, 1985).
Dersso, Solomon A. *Taking Ethno-Cultural Diversity Seriously in Constitutional Design: A Theory of Minority Rights for Addressing Africa's Multiethnic Challenge* (Leiden/ Boston: Martinus Nijhoff Publishers, 2012).
De Silva, K. M. *Regional Powers and Small State Security: India and Sri Lanka 1977–1990* (Washington DC: Woodrow Wilson Centre Press, 1995).
Dharmadāsa, Kē. En. Ō. *Language, Religion and Ethnic Assertiveness: The Growth of Sinhalese Nationalism in Sri Lanka* (Ann Harbor: University of Michigan Press, 1992).
Duggal, Kartar Singh. *Understanding the Sikh Psyche: Reflections on the Current Punjab Crisis* (New Delhi: Siddhartha, 1992).
Dworkin, Gerald. *The Theory and Practice of Autonomy* (Cambridge: Cambridge University Press, 1988).
Edelman, Murray. *Constructing the Political Spectacle* (Chicago/London: University of Chicago Press, 1988).
Edelman, Murray. *Politics as Symbolic Action. Mass Arousal and Quiescence* (Chicago: Markham Publishing Company, 1971).
Eisenberg, Avigail and Jeff Spinner-Halev. eds. *Minorities within Minorities: Equality, Rights and Diversity* (Cambridge: Cambridge University Press, 2005).
Eisenstadt, Todd A. *Politics, Identity, and México's Indigenous Rights Movements* (Cambridge University Press, 2011).
Farrelly, Michael. *Discourse and Democracy: Critical Analysis of the Language of Government* (Abingdon: Routledge, 2014).
Fessha, Yonatan Tesfaye. *Ethnic Diversity and Federalism: Constitution Making in South Africa and Ethiopia* (Farnham: Ashgate, 2010).
Gagnon, Alain-G. *L'âge des incertitudes. Essais sur le fédéralisme et la diversité nationale* [The Age of Uncertainity: Essays on Federalism and National Diversity] (Québec: Presses de l'Université Laval, 2012).
Gagnon, Alain-G. and Raffaele Iacovino. *Federalism, Citizenship, and Quebec. Debating Multinationalism* (Toronto: University of Toronto Press, 2007).
Gagnon, Alain-G. and Michael Keating. *Political Autonomy and Divided Societies: Imagining Democratic Alternatives in Complex Settings* (London: Palgrave Macmillan, 2012).
Gál, Kinga. ed. *Minority Governance in Europe* (Budapest: Local Government and Public Service Reform Initiative of the Open Society Institute, 2002).
Gauthier, David. *Morals by Agreement* (Oxford: Clarendon Press, 1986).
Gessen, Vladimir Matveevich. ed. *Avtonomiya, federatsiya i natsionalniy vopros* [Autonomy, Federation and the National (Ethnic) Question] (St Petersburg: People and Freedom, 1906).
Ghai, Yash. ed. *Autonomy and Ethnicity* (Cambridge: Cambridge University Press, 2000).
Ghai, Yash and Jill Cotterell. *Federalism and State Restructuring in Nepal: The Challenges for the Constituent Assembly* (Kathmandu: UNDP, 2007).
Ghai, Yash and Sophia Woodman. *Practising Self-Government: A Comparative Study of Autonomous Regions* (Cambridge: Cambridge University Press, 2013).
Ghosh, Partha S. *The Politics of Personal Law in South Asia: Identity, Nationalism and the Uniform Civil Code* (New Delhi: Routledge, 2007).
Gramsci, Antonio. *Selections from the Prison Notebooks* (New York: International Publishers, 1971).
Grimm, Dieter. *Souveränität. Herkunft und Zukunft eines Schlüsselbegriffs* [The Origins and the Future of a Key Concept] (Berlin: Berlin University Press, 2009.

Gunasekera, S. L. *Tigers, Moderates and Pandora's Package* (Colombo: Multi Packs (Ceylon) Ltd, 1996).

Gupta, Sanjukta Das and Raj Sekhar Basu. *Narratives from the Margins: Aspects of Adivasi History in India* (London: Primus, 2012).

Gurr, Ted Robert. *Minorities at Risk* (Washington, D.C.: United States Institute of Peace Press, 1993).

Hannum, Hurst. *Autonomy, Sovereignty, and Self-Determination: The Accommodation of Conflicting Rights* (revised edition, Philadelphia: University of Pennsylvania Press, 1996).

Hayday, Matthew. *Bilingual Today, United Tomorrow* (Montreal/Kingston: McGill-Queen's University Press, 2005).

Hechter, Michael. *Containing Nationalism* (Oxford: Oxford University Press, 2000).

Held, David. *Models of Democracy* (Cambridge: Polity Press, 2006).

Hogg, Peter. *Constitutional Law of Canada* (5th edition, Scarborough: Carswell, 2000), 36.1–36.4.

Holmes, Stephen. *Passions and Constraint* (Chicago: University of Chicago Press, 1995).

Hroch, Miroslav. *Social Preconditions of National Revival in Europe: A Comparative Analysis of the Social Composition of Patriotic Groups among the Smaller European Nations* (Cambridge: Cambridge University Press, 1985).

Hueglin, Thomas O. and Alan Fenna. *Comparative Federalism: A Systematic Inquiry* (Toronto: Broadview Press, 2006).

Huntington, Samuel. *Political Order in Changing Societies* (New Haven, CT/London: Yale University Press, 1968).

Huntington, Samuel P. *The Third Wave: Democratization in the Late Twentieth Century* (Oklahoma: University of Oklahoma Press, 1993).

Ignatieff, Michael. *Blood and Belonging: Journeys into the New Nationalism* (Toronto: Penguin, 1994).

İnalcık, Halil and Donald Quataert. *An Economic and Social History of the Ottoman Empire* (Cambridge: Cambridge University Press, 1994).

Jackson Preece, Jennifer. *National Minorities and the European Nation-States System* (Oxford/New York: Clarendon Press, 1998).

Jelavich, Barbara. *History of the Balkans* (Cambridge: Cambridge University Press, 1983).

Kann, Robert A. *The Multinational Empire: Nationalism and National Reform in the Habsburg Monarchy. 1848–1918. Vol. 2* (New York: Octagon Books, 1983).

Kant, Emanuel. *Groundwork of the Metaphysics of Morals*, translated by Mary Gregor (Cambridge: Cambridge University Press, 1997).

Keating, Michael. *Rescaling the European State: The Making of Territory and the Rise of the Meso* (Oxford: Oxford University Press, 2013).

Keating, Michael. *Nations against the State. The New Politics of Nationalism in Quebec, Catalonia and Scotland* (2nd edition, Hampshire/New York: Palgrave, 2001).

Keating, Michael. *Plurinational Democracy. Stateless Nations in a Post-Sovereignty Era* (Oxford: Oxford University Press, 2001).

Kedourie, Elie. *Nationalism* (London: Hutchinson, 1960).

Kerr, Donal A. ed. *Religion, State, and Ethnic Groups* (Aldershot: Dartmouth, 1992).

Khan, Hamid. *Constitutional and Political History of Pakistan* (Oxford: Oxford University Press, 2009).

Kokoshkin, Fyodor Fyodorovich. *Avtonomiya i federatsiya* [Autonomy and Federation] (Moscow: Publishing House 'Russian Political Encyclopedia' (ROSSPEN), 2010 (republished)).

Kokoshkin, Fyodor Fyodorovich. *Lektsii po obsehmu gosudarstvennomu pravu* [Lectures on General State Law] (Moscow: Publishing House 'Russian Political Encyclopedia' (ROSSPEN), 2010 (republished), 1912).

Kokoshkin, Fyodor Fyodorovich. *Oblastnaya avtonomii I yedinstvo Rossii* [Regional Autonomy and the Unity of Russia] (Moscow: Publishing House 'Russian Political Encyclopedia' (ROSSPEN), 1905).

Kokoshkin, Fyodor Fyodorovich. *Russkiye gosudarstvennoye pravo* [Russian State Law] (St Petersburg: Typography of Russian Association, 1892).

Krasner, Stephen D. *Sovereignty: Organized Hypocrisy* (Princeton: Princeton University Press, 1999).

Kutafin, Oleg Emelyanovich. *Rossiyskaya avtonomiya* [Russian Autonomy] (Moscow: Prospekt, 2006).

Kymlicka, Will. *Multicultural Citizenship* (Oxford: Oxford University Press, 1995).

Lapidoth, Ruth. *Autonomy. Flexible Solutions to Ethnic Conflicts* (Washington, D.C.: US Institute of Peace Press, 1997).

Laponce, J. A. *The Protection of Minorities* (Berkeley: University of California Press, 1960).

Lazerson, Maksim Yakovlevich. *Avtonomiya i federatsiya* [Autonomy and Federation] (Petrograd: Kniga po trebovaniy, 2012).

Lenin, V. Ilyin. *Collected Works*, vol. 20 (Moscow: Progress Publishers, 1972).

Lepeshkin, Alexei et al. *Kurs sovetskogo gosugarstvennogo prava* [Course of the Soviet State Law], vol. 2 (Moscow: Gosyurizdat, 1962).

Lewin, Moshe. *Lenin's Last Struggle* (Ann Arbor: University of Michigan Press, 2005).

Lijphart, Arend. *Democracy in Plural Societies: A Comparative Exploration* (New Haven, CT: Yale University Press, 1977).

Lijphart, Arend. *The Politics of Accommodation: Pluralism and Democracy in the Netherlands* (Berkeley: University of California Press, 1968).

Lipset, Seymour Martin. *Political Man: The Social Bases of Politics* (2nd edition, London: Heinemann, 1983).

Lyotard, Jean-François. *The Postmodern Condition: A Report on Knowledge*, translated by Brian Massumi and Geoff Bennington (Minneapolis: University of Minnesota Press, 1984).

Macartney, Carlile Aylmer. *National States and National Minorities* (London: Oxford University Press, 1934).

Macpherson, C. B. *Democratic Theory: Essays in Retrieval* (Oxford: Clarendon Press, 1973).

Magord, André. *The Quest for Autonomy in Acadia* (Brussels: Peter Lang, Editiones Scientifiques Internationales, 2008).

Mahmood, Safdar. *Pakistan: Political Roots and Development 1947–1999* (Oxford: Oxford University Press, 2002).

Maitland, Frederic W. *Township and Borough: The Ford Lectures 1897* (Cambridge: Cambridge University Press, 1964).

Malagodi, Mara. *Constitutional Nationalism and Legal Exclusion: Equality, Identity Politics and Democracy in Nepal* (New Delhi: Oxford University Press, 2013).

Malik, Ikram Ali. *Muslim League Session 1940 and the Lahore Resolution 1940: Documents* (Islamabad: National Institute of Historical and Cultural Research, 1990).

Malloy, Tove H. *National Minority Rights in Europe* (Oxford: Oxford University Press, 2005).

Malloy, Tove H. ed. *Minority Issues in Europe: Rights, Concepts, Policy* (Berlin: Frank & Timme GmbH, 2013).

Malloy, Tove H., Alexander Osipov, and Balazs Vizi. eds. *Managing Diversity Through Non-Territorial Autonomy: Accessing Advantages, Deficiencies, and Risks* (Oxford: Oxford University Press, 2015).

Mamdani, Mahmood. *Citizen and Subject: Contemporary Africa and the Legacy of Late Colonialism* (Princeton: Princeton University Press, 1996).

Mann, Michael. *The Dark Side of Democracy: Explaining Ethnic Cleansing* (Cambridge: Cambridge University Press, 2005).

Marsh, Christopher. *Unparalleled Reforms: China's Rise, Russia's Fall, and the Interdependence of Transition* (Lanham: Lexington Books, 2005).

Martin, Terry. *The Affirmative Action Empire: Nations and Nationalism in the Soviet Union, 1923–1939* (Ithaca: Cornell University Press, 2001).

McCauley, Martin. *Afghanistan and Central Asia: A Modern History* (London: Pearson, 2002).

McCrudden, Christopher and Brendan O'Leary. *Courts and Consociations: Human Rights versus Power Sharing* (Oxford: Oxford University Press, 2013).

McGarry, John and Brendan O'Leary. eds. *The Politics of Ethnic Conflict Resolution* (London: Routledge, 1993).

McLean, Iain, Guy Lodge, and Jim Gallagher. *Scotland's Choices: The Referendum and What Happens Afterwards* (Edinburgh: Edinburgh University Press, 2013).

Mill, John Stuart. *Considerations on Representative Government* (London: Parker, Son and Bourn, 1861).

Modeen, Tore, and Allan Rosas. eds. *Indirect Public Administration in the Fields of Education and Pensions* (Åbo: Åbo Academy Press, 1990).

Modeen, Tore. *The International Protection of Minorities in Europe* (Åbo: Åbo Akademi, 1969).

Mukomel, Vladimir. *Natsional'nye men'shinstva. Pravovye osnovy i praktika obespecheniia prav lits, prinadlezhashchikh k natsional'nym men'shinstvam, v sub'ektakh Iuga Rossiiskoi Federatsii* [National Minorities. Legal Fundamentals and Practices of Securing the Rights of Persons Belonging to National Minorities in the Subjects of the Russian Federation] (Moscow: CEPRI, 2003).

Mullard, Saul. *Opening the Hidden Land: State Formation and the Construction of Sikkimese History* (Leiden: Brill, 2011).

Mylonas, Harris. *The Politics of Nation-Building: Making Co-Nationals, Refugees, and Minorities* (Cambridge: Cambridge University Press, 2012).

Myntti, Kristian. *Minoriteters och urfolks politiska rättigheter* [Political Rights of Minorities and Indigenous Peoples] (Rovaniemi: Lapplands universitet, 1998).

Nag, Kingshuk. *Battleground Telengana: Chronicle of an Agitation* (New Delhi: Harper Collins, 2012).

Nimni, Ephraim. ed. *National Cultural Autonomy and its Contemporary Critics* (London: Routledge, 2005).

Nimni, Ephraim, Alexander Osipov, and David J. Smith. eds. *The Challenge of Non-Territorial Autonomy. Theory and Practice* (Oxford: Peter Lang, 2013).

Noorani, A. G. *India–China Boundary Problem 1846–1947: History and Diplomacy* (New Delhi: Oxford University Press, 2011).

Nootens, Geneviève. *Désenclaver la démocratie, Des Huguenot à la paix des braves* (Montréal: Québec Amérique, 2004).

Norman, Wayne. *Negotiating Nationalism: Nation-Building, Federalism, and Secession in the Multinational State* (Oxford: Oxford University Press, 2006).

Novotorzhskiy, G. *What is a Rule of Law State?* (Paris: 1914).

Novotorzhskiy, G. *Natsionalniy vopros, avtonomiya i federatsiya* [The National Question, Autonomy and Federation] (Moscow: Cooperative Association of USSR "Revolutionary flag", 1906).

Novotorzhskiy, G. *The Significance of the Right to Land for the Working Class* (still in print), http://http.www.epubbooks.ru/books.php?author=%CD%EE%E2%EE%F2%EE%F0%E6%F1%EA%E8%E9,%20%C3.

Novotorzhskiy, G. *The Socialisation of Land* (Publishing House of V. Raspopov, 1906).

O'Leary, Brendan and Joanne McEvoy. eds. *Power-Sharing in Deeply Divided Places* (Philadelphia: University of Pennsylvania Press, 2013).

Orton, Anna. *India's Borderland Disputes: China, Pakistan, Bangladesh, Nepal* (New Delhi: Epitome Books, 2010).

Osipov, Alexander. *Natsional'no-kul'turnaia avtonomiia: idei, resheniia, instituty* [National-Cultural Autonomy: Ideas, Decisions, Institutions] (St. Petersburg: Tsentr nezavisimykh sotsiologicheskikh issledovanii, 2004).

Pain, Emil. *Etnopoliticheskii mayatnik. Dinamika i mekhanizmy etnopoliticheskikh protsessov v postsovetskoi Rossii* [Ethnopolitical Pendulum. Dynamics and Mechanisms of Ethnopolitical Processes in Post-Soviet Russia] (Moscow: Institut sotsiologii RAN, 2004).

Parekh, Bhikhu. *Rethinking Multiculturalism, Cultural Diversity and Political Theory.* (Basingstoke: Macmillan, 2000).

Pateman, Carole. *The Sexual Contract* (Stanford: Stanford University Press, 1988).

Pentassuglia, Gaetano. *Minorities in International Law* (Strasbourg/Flensburg: Council of Europe and ECMI, 2002).

Pereira, Faustina. *The Fractured Scales: The Search for a Uniform Personal Code* (Calcutta: Stree Publishers, 2002).

Phuntso, Karma. *The History of Bhutan* (New Delhi: Random House Press, 2013).

Pimenova, E. *Yedinstvo gosudarstvo i avtonomiya* [The Unity of the State and Autonomy] (St Petersburg: Azbuka, 1906).

Pineda, Baron L. *Shipwrecked Identities, Navigating Race in Nicaragua's Mosquito Coast* (New Jersey: Rutgers University Press, 2006).

Pobes, Coro Rubio. *La identidad vasca en el siglo XIX* [The Basque Identity in XIXth Century] (Madrid: Biblioteca nueva, 2003).

Ponnambalam, Satchi. *Sri Lanka: The National Question and the Tamil Liberation Struggle* (London: Zed Books and Tamil Information Centre, 1983).

Potier, Tim. *Conflict in Nagorno-Karabakh, Abkhazia and South Ossetia. A Legal Appraisal* (The Hague: Kluwer International Law, 2001).

Protsyk, Oleh and Benedikt Harzl. eds. *Managing Ethnic Diversity in Russia* (Abingdon/New York: Routledge, 2012).

Ra'anan, Uri, Maria Mesner, Keith Armes, and Kate Martin. eds. *State and Nation in Multi-Ethnic Societies: The Breakup of the Multinational State* (Manchester/New York: Manchester University Press, 1991).

Raghavan, V. R. *The Naxal Threat: Causes, State Responses and Consequences* (New Delhi: Vij Books, 2011).

von Rauch, Georg. *Geschichte der baltischen Staaten* [The History of the Baltic States] (München: Deutscher Taschenbuch Verlag, 1990).

Rawls, John. *A Theory of Justice* (Oxford: Oxford University Press, 1971/1973).

Raza, Rafi. ed. *Pakistan in Perspective 1977–1997* (Karachi: Oxford University Press, 1997).

Reiterer, Albert F. *Cyprus: Case Study about a Failure of Ethno-National Understanding* (Frankfurt am Main/New York, NY: Lang, 2003).

Renner, Karl. *Das Selbstbestimmungsrecht der Nationen in besonderer Anwendung auf Österreich* [The Right of Nations to Self-Determination especially in Austria] (Leipzig/Vienna: Deuticke, 1918).

Renner, Karl (under the pen name Rudolf Springer). *Der Kampf der österreichischen Nationen um den Staat* [The Struggle of the Austrian Nations for the State] (Vienna/Leipzig: Deuticke, 1902).

Renner, Karl. *Staat und Nation* [The State and the Nation] (Wien: Dietl, 1899).

Roshwald, Aviel. *Ethnic Nationalism and the Fall of Empires: Central Europe, Russia & the Middle East 1914–1923* (London: Routledge, 2001).

Rossiter, Clinton. ed. *The Federalist Papers* (New York: The New American Library, 1961).

Rothschild, Joseph. *Ethnopolitics: A Conceptual Framework* (New York: Columbia University Press, 1981).

Ruiz-Vieytez, Eduardo. *The History of Legal Protection of Minorities in Europe (XIIth–XXth Centuries)* (Derby: University of Derby, 1999).

Russell, Jane. *Communal Politics under the Donoughmore Constitution 1931–1947* (Colombo: Thisara Prakasakayo, 1982).

Sahlins, Peter. *Boundaries: The Making of France and Spain in the Pyrenees* (Berkeley/Los Angeles: University of California Press, 1989).

Said, Edward. *Orientalism* (London: Penguin Books, 1978).

Samad, Yunas. *A Nation in Turmoil: Nationalism and Ethnicity in Pakistan 1937–1958* (New Delhi: Sage, 1995).

Sarvanamuttu, Paikiasothy. *Democratization of the Peace Process: Sri Lanka* (Colombo: Centre for Policy Alternatives, 2005).

Sathe, S. P. *Judicial Activism in India: Transgressing Borders and Enforcing Limits* (New Delhi: Oxford University Press, 2002).

Sautman, Barry and June Teufel Dreyer. eds. *Contemporary Tibet: Politics, Development and Society in a Disputed Region* (New York: M. E. Sharpe Inc., 2006).

Saveliev, Victor. *Nationalno-kulturnaya avtonomiya kak forma ethnokulturnogo samoopredeleniya narodov Rossii* [National-Cultural Autonomy as a Form Self-Determination for Peoples of Russia] (Moscow: RAGS, 2008).

Schneider, Anne L. and Helen Ingram. *Policy Design for Democracy* (Lawrence: University Press of Kansas, 1997).

Schrijver, Frans. *Regionalism after Regionalisation: Spain, France and the United Kingdom* (Amsterdam: Amsterdam University Press, 2006).

Schwarzmantel, John. *Citizenship and Identity: Towards a New Republic* (London: Routledge, 2003).

Science and Technique of Democracy. 'The Participation of Minorities in Public Life' (Strasbourg: Council of Europe, 2011).

Scott, James C. *Domination and the Arts of Resistance: Hidden Transcripts* (New Haven, CT: Yale University Press, 1990).

Seymour, Michel. *De la tolerance à la reconnaissance* [From Tolerance to Recognition] (Montreal: Boréal, 2008).

Sharma, Pitamber. *Unraveling the Mosaic: Spatial Aspects of Ethnicity in Nepal* (Kathmandu: Himal Books, 2008).

Sieghart, Paul. *Sri Lanka: A Mounting Tragedy of Errors* [Report of a Mission to Sri Lanka in January 1984 on behalf of the International Commission of Jurists and its British Section] (Dorchester: Justice, 1984).

Singh, Jaswant. *Jinnah: India–Pakistan Independence* (New Delhi: Rupa, 2009).

Singh, R. A. *Military Governance in Pakistan* (New Delhi: Raj Publications, 2007).

Singh, K. S. ed. *Tribal Movements in India* (Delhi: Manohar Publishers, 1982, reprinted in 2006).
Singh, Marendra Prasad and Veena Kukreja. *Federalism in South Asia* (New Delhi: Routledge, 2014).
Sisson, Richard and Leo E. Rose. *War and Secession: Pakistan, India and the Creation of Bangladesh* (Berkeley: University of California Press, 1991).
Skurbaty, Zelim A. ed. *Beyond a One-Dimensional State: An Emerging Right to Autonomy?* (Leiden/Boston: Martinus Nijhoff Publishers, 2005).
Smith, Anthony D. *Nationalism and Modernism. A Critical Survey of Recent Theories of Nations and Nationalism (*London/New York: Routledge, 1998).
Smith, Anthony D. *The Ethnic Origins of Nations* (New York: Blackwell, 1986).
Smith, David J. and John Hiden. *Ethnic Diversity and the Nation State: National Cultural Autonomy Revisited* (London/New York: Routledge, 2012).
Smith, David J. and Karl Cordell. eds. *Cultural Autonomy in Contemporary Europe* (London: Routledge, 2008).
Sokolovskiy, V. V. *Ktrakiy uchebnik russkovo gosudarsvennovo pravo* [Short Textbook of Russian State Law] (Odessa: Economic Typography, 1890).
Spiro, Peter J. *Beyond Citizenship: American Identity after Globalization* (Oxford: Oxford University Press, 2007).
van der Stoel, Max. *Peace and Stability through Human and Minority Rights: Speeches by the OSCE High Commissioner on National Minorities* (Baden-Baden: Nomos Verlagsgesellschaft, 1999).
Sugar, Peter F. *Southeastern Europe under Ottoman Rule, 1354–1804* (Seattle: University of Washington Press, 1977).
Suksi, Markku. *Sub-State Governance through Territorial Autonomy: A Comparative Study in Constitutional Law of Powers, Procedures and Institutions* (Berlin/Heidelberg : Springer-Verlag, 2011).
Suksi, Markku. *On the Constitutional Features of Estonia* (Åbo: Åbo Akademi, 1999).
Suksi, Markuu. ed. *Autonomy, Applications and Implications* (The Hague: Kluwer Law International, 1998).
Sundarayya, Sri Putchalapalli. *Telengana People's Struggle and its Lessons* (New Delhi: Foundation Books, 1972).
Suny, Ronald Grigor. *The Making of the Georgian Nation* (Bloomington/Indianapolis: Indiana University Press, 1994).
Suny, Ronald. *The Revenge of the Past: Nationalism, Revolution, and the Collapse of the Soviet Union* (Stanford: Stanford University Press, 1993).
Tarr, Alan, Robert Williams, and Josef Marko. eds. *Federalism, Sub-National Constitutions and Minority Rights* (Westport: Praeger, 2004).
Taylor, Rupert. ed. *Consociational Theory, McGarry and O'Leary and the Northern Ireland Conflict* (London: Routledge, 2009).
Tillin, Louise. *Remapping India: New States and their Political Origins* (London: Hurst, 2013).
Tishkov, Valery. *Ethnicity, Nationalism and Conflict in and after the Soviet Union. The Mind Aflame* (London: Sage, 1997).
de Tocqueville, Alexis. *Democracy in America*, translated by Harvey C. Mansfield and Delba Winthrop (Chicago: University of Chicago Press, 2000).
Todorov, Tzvetan. *The Conquest of America and the Question of the Other* (Norman: University of Oklahoma Press, 1999).
Tolz, Vera. *Russia: Inventing the Nation* (London: Arnold, 2001).

Tully, James. *Strange Multiplicity: Constitutionalism in the Age of Diversity* (Cambridge: Cambridge University Press, 1995).

Upreti, Bhuwan Chandra. *Nepal: Transition to Democratic Republican State* (New Delhi: Kalpaz Publications, 2010).

Vaidik, Ved Pratap. *Ethnic Crisis in Sri Lanka: India's Options* (New Delhi: National Publishing House, 1980).

Venice Commission. *The Participation of Minorities in Public Life* (Strasbourg: Council of Europe Publishing, 2008).

Veronensis, Severinus de Monzambano (pen name of Samuel von Pufendorf). *De Statu Imperii Germanici ad Laelium fratrem, Dominum Trezolani, liber unus* [About the State of the Empire, to Laelius, the Brother of Germanicus, the Lord, Trezolani, One Book] (Genevae: P. Columesium, 1667).

Verstichel, Annelies, André Alen, Bruno de Witte, and Paul Lemmens. eds. *The Framework Convention for the Protection of National Minorities: A Useful Pan-European Instrument?* (Antwerp: Intersentia, 2008).

Walker, R. B. J. *Inside/Outside: International Relations as Political Theory* (Cambridge: Cambridge University Press, 1993).

van Walt van Praag, Michael. *The Status of Tibet: History, Rights, and Prospects in International Law* (Boulder: Westview Press, 1987).

Walzer, Michael. *Arguing About War* (New Haven, CT: Yale University Press, 2004).

Weber, Eugen. *Peasants Into Frenchmen: The Modernization of Rural France, 1880–1914* (Palo Alto: Stanford University Press, 1976).

Welhengama, Gnanapala and Nirmala Pillay. *The Rise of Tamil Separatism in Sri Lanka: From Communalism to Secession* (London: Routledge, 2014).

Weller, Marc. ed. *Asymmetric Autonomy as a Tool of Ethnic Conflict Settlement* (Philadelphia: University of Pennsylvania Press, 2009).

Weller, Marc and Stefan Wolff. eds. *Autonomy, Self-Governance and Conflict Resolution: Innovative Approaches to Institutional Design in Divided Societies* (London: Routledge, 2005).

Wheare, Kenneth C. *Federal Government* (New York: Oxford University Press, 1964).

Whelpton, John. *A History of Nepal* (Cambridge: Cambridge University Press, 2005).

White, George W. *Nation, State, and Territory: Origins, Evolutions, and Relationships* (Lanham, MD: Rowman & Littlefield, 2007).

Wilson, A Jeyaratnam. *Sri Lankan Tamil Nationalism: Its Origin and Development in the 19th and 20th centuries* (New Delhi: Penguin, 2000).

Woelk, Jens, Francesco Palermo, and Joseph Marko. eds. *Tolerance Through Law: Self-Governance and Group Rights in South Tyrol* (Leiden/Boston: Martinus Nijhoff Publishers, 2008).

Wright, Sue. ed. *Language, Democracy and Devolution in Catalonia* (Clevedon: Multilingual Matters, 1999).

Yurdusev, Nuri A. *Ottoman Diplomacy, Conventional or Unconventional?* (Basingstoke: Palgrave Macmillan, 2004).

Zamindar, V. Fazila-Yacoobali. *The Long Partition and the Making of Modern South Asia: Refugees, Boundaries and Histories* (New York: Columbia University Press, 2007).

Zhang, Qianfan. *The Constitution of China: A Contextual Analysis* (Oxford/Portland: Hart, 2012).

Zorin, Vladimir. *Dnevnik ne dlia sebia—Kn.2: Strasti Okhotnogo riada* [A Diary for Myself; Book 2—Passions of Okhotny Ryad] (Moscow: Violanta, 1999).

Zorin, Vladimir. 'Federalizm—nashe istoricheskoe budushchee' [Federalism is our Historic Future]. *Budushchee federalizma v Rossii: Rossiia i Respublika Bashkortostan. Materialy mezhregional'noi nauchno-prakticheskoi konferentsii* [The Future of Federalism in Russia: Russia and the Republic of Bashkortostan. Proceedings of the Inter-regional Scientific—Practical Conference] (Ufa: Institut povysheniia kvalifikatsii pri Administratsii Prezidenta Respubliki Bashkortostan, 2002).

ARTICLES AND CHAPTERS

Acton, John Emerich Edward Dalberg. 'Nationality'. *Home and Foreign Review*, vol. 1 (1862): pp. 1–25.

Agurto, Jorge. 'Peru'. In *The Indigenous World 2014*, edited by Cæcilie Mikkelsen (Copenhagen: IWGIA, 2014), pp. 164–5.

Ahmad, Raza. 'The Endemic Crisis of Federalism in Pakistan'. *The Lahore Journal of Economics*, vol. 15 (2010): p. 15.

Aidarov, Aleksandr and Wolfgang Drechsler. 'The Law and Economics of the Estonian Law on Cultural Autonomy for National Minorities and of Russian National Cultural Autonomy in Estonia'. *Halduskultuur—Administrative Culture*, vol. 12, no. 1 (2011): pp. 43–61.

Aikio-Puoskari, Ulla. *Rapport om den samiska undervisningen i grundskolorna i Norden: En nordisk jämförelse med utgångspunkt i undervisningens grundförutsättningar* [Report on the Sami Teaching in Primary Schools in the Nordic Countries: A Nordic Comparison based on the Fundamental Conditions of Instruction] (Enare: Samiskt Parlamentariskt Råd/Sametinget, 2011).

Akhtar, Aasim Sajjad. 'Balochistan versus Pakistan'. *Economic and Political Weekly*, vol. XLII, nos 45–6 (2007): pp. 73–9.

Alavi, Hamza. 'Nationhood and Nationalities in Pakistan'. *Economic and Political Weekly*, vol. 24, no. 27 (1989): pp. 1527–34.

Alenius, Kari. 'The Birth of Cultural Autonomy in Estonia: How, Why and for Whom?'. *Journal of Baltic Studies*, vol. 38, no. 4 (2007): pp. 445–62.

Anaya, James S. 'Indigenous Peoples' Participatory Rights in Relation to Decisions about Natural Resource Extraction'. *Arizona Journal of International and Comparative Law*, vol. 22, no. 1 (2005): pp. 7–8.

Anaya, James. 'International Human Rights and Indigenous Peoples: The Move Towards the Multicultural State'. *Arizona Journal of International and Comparative Law*, vol. 21, no. 1 (2004): p. 26.

Andeva, Marina. 'The NTA Model in Development or in Revision? The Case of the Republic of Macedonia', accessed August 2014, http://ecpr.eu/Filestore/PaperProposal/2508d467-48d2-48f9-ae89-57bf8d6f4d28.pdf.

Andreescu, Gabriel. 'Cultural and Territorial Autonomy and the Issue of Hungarian Identity'. *Hungarian Studies*, vol. 21, nos 1-2 (2007): pp. 61–84.

Andreescu, Gabriel. 'Universal Thought, Eastern Facts: Scrutinizing National Minority Rights in Romania'. In *Can Liberal Pluralism be Exported? Western Political Theory and Ethnic Relations in Eastern Europe*, edited by Will Kymlicka and Magda Opalski (Oxford: Oxford University Press, 2001), pp. 270–82.

Antkowiak, Tom M. 'Resources, and Rhetoric: Indigenous Peoples and the Inter-American Court'. *University of Pennsylvania Journal of International Law*, vol 35, no. 1 (2014): pp. 113–87.

Arraiza, Jose Maria. 'Squaring Indigenous Circles: The Making of Nicaragua's Indigenous Communal Property Regime'. *International Journal on Minority and Group Rights*, vol. 69, no. 19 (2012): p. 72.

Bahcheli, Tozun and Sid Noel. 'Power Sharing for Cyprus (Again)? European Union Accession and the Prospects for Reunification'. In *From Power Sharing to Democracy Post-Conflict Institutions in Ethnically Divided Societies*, edited by Sid Noel (Montreal/Kingston: McGill-Queen's University Press, 2005), pp. 215–38.

Barkey, Karen. 'Islam and Toleration: Studying the Ottoman Imperial Model'. *International Journal of Politics, Culture, and Society*, vol. 19 (2005): pp. 5–19.

Bauböck, Rainer. 'Territorial or Cultural Autonomy for National Minorities?'. *IWE-Working Paper Series*, no. 22 (2011).

Bauböck, Rainer. 'Autonomy, Power-Sharing and Common Citizenship: Principles for Accommodating National Minorities in Europe'. In *European Integration and the Nationalities Question*, edited by John McGarry and Michael Keating (London: Routledge, 2006), pp. 85–102.

Bauböck, Rainer. 'Territorial or Cultural Autonomy for National Minorities?'. In *The Politcs of Belonging: Nationalism, Liberalism and Pluralism*, edited by Alain Dieckhoff (Lanham, MD: Lexington Books, 2004), pp. 221–58.

Baumann, Robert F. 'Subject Nationalities in the Military Service of Imperial Russia: The Case of the Baskirs'. *Slavic Review*, vol. 46, nos 3–4 (1987): pp. 489–502.

Baxi, Upendra. 'The Rule of Law in India: Theory and Practice'. In *Asian Discourses on the Rule of Law*, edited by Randall Peerenboom (London: Routledge, 2004), p. 334.

Benton, Lauren. 'Constitutions and Empires'. *Law and Social Inquiry*, vol. 31, no. 1 (2006): pp. 177–98.

Berg, Holger. 'Ingerisoomlased võivad saavutada kultuurautonoomia sügiseks' [Ingrian Finns Can Achieve Cultural Autonomy in Autumn]. *Eesti Päevaleht* (2003), accessed 20 June 2012, http://www.epl.ee/news/eesti/ingerisoomlased-voivad-saavutada-kultuurautonoomia-sugiseks.d?id=50959337.

Bermeo, Nancy. 'The Import of Institutions'. *Journal of Democracy*, vol. 13, no. 2 (2002): pp. 96–110.

Besson, Samantha. 'Deliberative Demoi-cracy in the European Union: Towards the Deterritorialisation of Democracy'. In *Deliberative Democracy and its Discontents*, edited by Samantha Besson and Jose Luis Marti (Aldershot: Ashgate, 2006), pp. 181–214.

Bexell, Magdalena, Tallberg Jonas, and Uhlin Anders. 'Democracy in Global Governance: The Promises and Pitfalls of Transnational Actors'. *Global Governance*, vol. 16 (2010): pp. 81–101.

Bickerton, James. 'Seeking New Autonomies: State Rescaling, Reterritorialization and Minority Identities in Atlantic Canada'. In *Political Autonomy and Divided Societies: Imagining Democratic Alternatives in Complex Settings*, edited by Alain-G. Gagnon and Michael Keating (Basingstoke: Palgrave Macmillan, 2012), pp. 98–117.

Bieber, Florian. 'Power Sharing after Yugoslavia: Functionality and Dysfunctionality of Power-Sharing Institutions in Post-War Bosnia, Macedonia, and Kosovo'. In *From Power Sharing to Democracy Post-Conflict Institutions in Ethnically Divided Societies*, edited by Sid Noel (Montreal/Kingston: McGill-Queen's University Press, 2005), pp. 85–103.

Blaser, Mario, Ravi de Costa, Deborah McGregor, and William D. Coleman. 'Reconfiguring the Web of Life: Indigenous peoples, Relationality, and Globalisation'. In *Indigenous Peoples and Autonomy, Insights for a Global Age*, edited by Mario Blaser,

Ravi de Costa, Deborah McGregor, and William D. Coleman (Vancouver: UCB Press, 2010), p. 17.

Bohman James. 'From Demos to Demoi: Democracy across Borders'. *Ratio Juris*, vol. 18, no. 3 (2005): pp. 293–314.

Bollen, Kenneth A. and Pamela Paxton. 'Subjective Measures of Liberal Democracy'. *Comparative Political Studies*, vol. 33, no. 1 (2000): pp. 58–86.

Boltjes, Miek. 'The Implementation Challenge in Intrastate Peace Processes: An Analysis'. In *Implementing Negotiated Agreements: The Real Challenge to Intrastate Peace*, edited by Miek Boltjes (The Hague: TMC Asser Press, 2007), pp. 6–8.

Bonner, Michelle and Matt James. 'The Three R's of Seeking Transitional Justice: Reparation, Responsibility, and Reframing in Canada and Argentina'. *The International Indigenous Policy Journal*, vol. 2, no. 3 (2011): pp. 1–29.

Bourdieu, Pierre. 'A Paradoxical Foundation of Ethics'. In *Practical Reason. On the Theory of Action* (Stanford, CA: Stanford University Press, 1998), pp. 141–5.

Bourdieu Pierre, Loic J. D. Wacquant, and Samar Farage. 'Rethinking the State: Genesis and Structure of the Bureaucratic Field'. *Sociological Theory*, vol. 12, no. 1 (1994): pp. 1–18.

Bourdieu, Pierre. 'The Field of Cultural Production, or the Economic World Reversed'. In *The Field of Cultural Production: Essays on Art and Literature*, edited and introduced by Randal Johnson (New York: Columbia University Press, 1993), pp. 29–73.

Bourdieu, Pierre. 'The Production of Belief: Contribution to an Economy of Symbolic Goods'. In *The Field of Cultural Production: Essays on Art and Literature*, edited and introduced by Randal Johnson (New York: Columbia University Press, 1993), p. 80.

Bowring, Bill. 'Austro-Marxism's Last Laugh?: The Struggle for Recognition of National-Cultural Autonomy for Rossians and Russians'. *Europe-Asia Studies*, vol. 54, no. 2 (2002): pp. 229–50.

Bowring, Bill. 'Minorities Protection in Russia: Is There a "Communist Legacy"?'. In *Institutional Legacies of Communism: Change and Continuities in Minority Protection*, edited by Karl Cordell, Timofey Agarin, and Alexander Osipov (Abingdon: Routledge, 2013), pp. 45–58.

Bowring, Bill. 'Russian Legislation in the Area of Minority Rights'. In *Managing Ethnic Diversity in Russia*, edited by Oleh Protsyk and Benedikt Harzl (Abingdon: Routledge, 2012), pp. 15–36.

Bowring, Bill. 'The Russian Constitutional System: Complexity and Asymmetry'. In *Asymmetric Autonomy and the Settlement of Ethnic Conflicts*, edited by Marc Weller and Katherine Nobbs (Philadelphia: University of Pennsylvania Press, 2010), pp. 48–74.

Bowring, Bill. 'The Tatars of the Russian Federation and National-Cultural Autonomy: A Contradiction in Terms?'. In *Cultural Autonomy in Contemporary Europe*, edited by David J. Smith and Karl Cordell (London/New York: Routledge, 2008), pp. 417–35.

Bowring, Bill. 'Burial and Resurrection: Karl Renner's Controversial Influence on the "National Question" in Russia'. In *National Cultural Autonomy and its Contemporary Critics*, edited by Ephraim Nimni (London: Routledge, 2005), pp. 191–206.

Bowring, Bill. 'The Crimean Autonomy: Innovation or Anomaly?'. In *Autonomy, Self-Governance and Conflict Resolution: Innovative Approaches to Institutional Design in Divided Societies*, edited by Marc Weller and Stefan Wolff (Abingdon: Routledge, 2005), pp. 75–97.

Brahm Levey, Geoffrey. 'National Cultural Autonomy and Liberal Nationalism'. In *National-Cultural Autonomy and its Contemporary Critics*, edited by Ephraim Nimni (London/New York: Routledge, 2005), pp. 150–65.

Braude, Benjamin. 'The Foundation Myths of the Millet System'. In *Christians and Jews in the Ottoman Empire: The Functioning of a Plural Society*, edited by Benjamin Braude and Bernard Lewis (New York: Holmes and Meier, 1982): pp. 69–87.

Brilmayer, Lea. 'Secession and Self-Determination: A Territorial Interpretation'. *Yale Journal of International Law*, vol. 16 (1991): pp. 179–80.

Brown, Graham K. 'Federalism, Regional Autonomy and Conflict: Introduction and Overview'. *Ethnopolitics*, vol. 1, no. 8 (2009): pp. 1–4.

Brubaker, Rogers. 'Religion and Nationalism: Four Approaches'. *Nations and Nationalism*, vol. 18, no. 1 (2012): pp. 2–20.

Brubaker, Rogers. 'Ethnicity without Groups'. *Archives Européennes de Sociologie*, vol. XLIII, no. 2 (2002): pp. 163–89.

Brunner, Georg and Herbert Küpper. 'European Options of Autonomy: A Typology of Autonomy Models of Minority Self-Governance'. In *Minority Governance in Europe*, edited by Kinga Gál (Budapest: Local Government and Public Service Reform Initiative of the Open Society Institute, 2002), pp. 13–36.

Bührmann, Andrea. 'Gender—A Central Dimension of Diversity'. In *Routledge Handbook of Diversity Studies*, edited by Steven Vertovec (Abingdon: Routledge, 2014), pp. 23–33.

Capotorti, Francesco. 'The Protection of Minorities under Multilateral Agreements on Human Rights'. *The Italian Yearbook of International Law*, vol. 2 (1976): p. 14.

Castellino, Joshua. 'International Legal Responses to Uprisings in the Middle East'. *City: Analysis of Urban Trends, Culture, Theory, Policy, Action*, vol. 18, no. 2 (2014): pp. 167–74.

Castellino, Joshua. 'Territorial Integrity and the "Right" to Self-Determination: An Examination of the Conceptual Tools'. *Brooklyn Journal of International Law*, vol. 33, no. 2 (2008): pp. 503–68.

Cheneval, Francis and Frank Schimmelfennig. 'The Case for Demoicracy in the European Union'. *Journal of Common Market Studies*, vol. 51, no. 2 (2013): pp. 334–50.

Choudhry, Sujit and Nathan Hume, 'Federalism, Secession and Devolution: From Classical to Post-Conflict Federalism'. In *Research Handbook on Comparative Constitutional Law*, edited by Tom Ginsburg and Rosalind Dixon (Cheltenham: Edward Elgar, 2011), pp. 363–72.

Choudhry, Sujit. 'Bridging Comparative Politics and Comparative Constitutional Law: Constitutional Design for Divided Societies'. In *Constitutional Design for Divided Societies: Integration or Accommodation?*, edited by Sujit Choudhry (Oxford: Oxford University Press, 2008), pp. 5–6.

Choudhry, Sujit. 'Does the World Need More Canada? The Politics of the Canadian Model in Constitutional Politics and Political Theory'. In *Constitutional Design for Divided Societies: Integration or Accommodation?*, edited by Sujit Choudhry (Oxford: Oxford University Press, 2008), p. 158.

Clarance, William. 'Woolf and Bandaranaike: The Ironies of Federalism in Sri Lanka'. *Political Quarterly*, vol. 72, no. 4 (2002): p. 482.

Coakley, John. 'Approaches to the Resolution of Ethnic Conflict: The Strategy of Non–Territorial Autonomy'. *International Political Science Review*, vol. 15, no. 3 (1994): pp. 297–314.

Coakley, John. 'National Territories and Cultural Frontiers: Conflicts of Principle in the Formation of States in Europe'. *West European Politics*, vol. 5, no. 4 (1982): pp. 34–49.

Codagnone, Cristiano and Vassily Filippov. 'Equity, Exit and National Identity in a Multinational Federation: the "Multicultural Constitutional Patriotism" Project in Russia'. *Journal of Ethnic and Migration Studies*, vol. 26, no. 2 (2000): pp. 263–88.

Cohen, Anthony P. 'Nationalism and Social Identity: Who Owns the Interest of Scotland?'. *Scottish Affairs*, no. 18 (1997): pp. 95–107.
Connor, Walker. 'Homelands in a World of States'. In *Understanding Nationalism*, edited by Montserrat Guibernau and John Hutchinson (Oxford: Blackwell, 2001), pp. 53–73.
Connor, Walker. 'Nation-Building or Nation-Destroying?'. *World Politics*, vol. 24, no. 3 (1972): pp. 319–55.
Cooper, Frederick. 'Empire Multiplied'. *Comparative Studies in Society and History*, vol. 46, no. 2 (2004): pp. 247–72.
Cornell, Svante E. 'Autonomy as a Source of Conflict: Caucasian Conflicts in Theoretical Perspective'. *World Politics*, vol. 54 (2002): pp. 245–76.
de Costa, Ravi. 'Afterword'. In *Indigenous Peoples and Autonomy, Insights for a Global Age*, edited by Mario Blaser, Ravi de Costa, Deborah McGregor, and William D. Coleman (Vancouver: UCB Press, 2010), p. 241.
Coughlan, Reed. 'Cyprus: From Corporate Autonomy to the Search for Territorial Federalism'. In *Autonomy and Ethnicity: Negotiating Competing Claims in Multi-Ethnic States*, edited by Yash Ghai (Cambridge/New York: Cambridge University Press, 2000), pp. 219–41.
Coyle, Michael. 'Negotiating Indigenous Peoples' Exit from Colonialism: The Case for an Integrative Approach'. *Canadian Journal of Law and Jurisprudence*, vol. 27 (2014): p. 286.
Coyle, Michael. 'Transcending Colonialism? Power and the Resolution of Indigenous Treaty Claims in Canada and New Zealand'. *NZULR*, vol. 24 (2011): p. 596.
Cox, Kevin, Murray Low, and Jenny Robinson. 'Political Geography: Traditions and Turns'. In *Handbook of Political Geography*, edited by Kevin Cox, Murray Low, and Jenny Robinson (London: Sage, 2008), pp. 1–14.
Darwin, John. 'Empire and Ethnicity'. *Nations and Nationalism*, vol. 16, no. 3 (2010): pp. 383–401.
Daskalovski, Zhidas. 'Macedonia'. In *Nations in Transit 2007: Democratization from Central Europe to Eurasia*, edited by Jeannette Goehring (New York: Rowman & Littlefield, 2007), pp. 445–70.
Davidson, Keith. 'Language and Identity in Switzerland'. *English Today*, no. 26 (2010): pp. 15–17.
Davies, Margaret. 'Legal Pluralism'. In *The Oxford Handbook of Empirical Legal Research*, edited by Peter Cane and Herbert M. Kritzer (Oxford: Oxford University Press, 2010), pp. 805–27.
Davis, Michael C. 'Establishing a Workable Autonomy in Tibet'. *Human Rights Quarterly*, no. 30 (2008): pp. 227–58.
Decker, Christopher D. 'Enhancing Minority Governance in Romania: Report on the Presentation on Cultural Autonomy to the Romanian Government'. *European Centre for Minority Issues Report*, no. 53 (2005), accessed 13 September 2010, http://www/ecmi.de/download/Report_53.pdf.
Decker, Christopher. 'Contemporary Forms of Cultural Autonomy in Eastern Europe: Recurrent Problems and Prospects for Improving the Functioning of Elected Bodies of Cultural Autonomy'. In *The Participation of Minorities in Public Life* (Strasbourg: Council of Europe Publishing, 2008), pp. 89–90.
Decker, Christopher D. 'The Use of Cultural Autonomy to Prevent Conflict and Meet the Copenhagen Criteria: The Case of Romania'. In *Cultural Autonomy in Contemporary Europe*, edited by David J. Smith and Karl Cordell (London: Routledge, 2008), pp. 101–14.

Delledonne, Giacomo. 'Speaking in Name of the Constituent Power: The Spanish Constitutional Court and the New Catalan *Estatut*'. *Perspectives on Federalism*, no. 3 (2011), accessed June 2015, http://www.academia.edu/523782/Speaking_in_Name_of_the_Constituent_Power_the_Spanish_Constitutional_Court_and_the_New_Catalan_Estatut.

Deng, Francis M. 'Ethnicity: An African Predicament'. *The Brookings Review*, vol. 15, no. 3 (1997): p. 28.

Dharmalingam, Visvanather. 'Tamil Demands at Thimpu'. *Tamil Times* (September 1985).

Dimitrova-Grajzl, Valentina. 'The Great Divide Revisited: Ottoman and Habsburg Legacies on Transition'. *Kyklos*, vol. 60, no. 4 (2007): pp. 539–58.

Dinstein, Yoram. 'Autonomy'. In *Models of Autonomy*, edited by Yoram Dinstein (Tel Aviv: Tel Aviv University Press, 1981), p. 219.

Dobos, Balázs. 'The Development and Functioning of Cultural Autonomy in Hungary'. *Ethnopolitics*, vol. 6, no. 3 (2007): pp. 451–69.

Drobizheva, Leokadia. 'Zavoyevaniya demokratii i ethnonatsionalnye problemy' [Achievements of Democracy and Russia's Ethnonational Problems]. *Obshestvennye Nauki i sobremennost*, no. 2 (2005): pp. 16–28.

D'Souza, Paul. 'Conflict of Kashmir and the Problem of Disappearance'. *Economic and Political Weekly*, vol. L, no. 5 (2015).

Edrisinha, Rohan. 'The Federal Debate in Sri Lanka'. In *Varieties of Federal Governments: Major Contemporary Models*, edited by Rekha Saxena (New Delhi: Foundation Books/Cambridge University Press, 2011), pp. 447–64.

Eide, Asbjørn et al. 'Cultural Autonomy: Concept, Content, History and Role in the World Order'. In *Autonomy: Applications and Implications*, edited by Markku Suksi (The Hague: Kluwer Law International, 1998), pp. 251–76.

Eiler, Ferenc and Nóra Kovács. 'Minority Self-Governments in Hungary'. In *Minority Governance in Europe*, edited by Kinga Gál (Budapest: Local Government and Public Service Reform Initiative of the Open Society Institute, 2002), pp. 173–97.

Engels, Bettina. 'Contentious Politics of Scale: The Global Food Price Crisis and Local Protest in Burkina Faso'. *Social Movement Studies*, vol. 14, no. 2 (2015): pp. 180–94.

Erk, Jan. 'From Nationalists to Internationalists and Back'. *Public Administration*, vol. 92, no. 2 (2014): pp. 518–24.

Erk, Jan. 'The Risks of Scholarly Insulation: When Political Science Forgets Law and History'. *Comparative European Politics*, vol. 11, no. 4 (2013): pp. 530–49.

Erk, Jan and Lawrence Anderson. 'The Paradox of Federalism: Does Self-Rule Accommodate or Exacerbate Ethnic Divisions?'. *Regional and Federal Studies*, vol. 19, no. 2 (2009): pp. 191–202.

European Commission for Democracy through Law (Venice Commission), Opinion on the Act on the Rights of Nationalities in Hungary. Adopted by the Venice Commission at its 91st Plenary Session (Venice, 15–16 June 2012). (Strasbourg: Venice Commission, 19 June 2012) accessed 27 November 2012, http://www.venice.coe.int/docs/2012/CDL-AD(2012)011-e.pdf.

Evans, Mary. 'Getting Real: Contextualising Gender'. In *Sage Handbook of Gender and Women's Studies*, edited by Kathy Davis, Mary Evans, and Judith Lorber (London: Sage, 2006), pp. 474–8.

Falk, Richard. 'Revisiting Westphalia, Discovering Post-Westphalia'. *The Journal of Ethics*, vol. 6, no. 4 (2002), pp. 311–52.

Fearon, James D. 'Commitment Problems and the Spread of Ethnic Conflict'. In *The International Spread of Ethnic Conflict: Fear, Diffusion, and Escalation*, edited by David

A. Lake and Donald S. Rothchild (Princeton: Princeton University Press, 1998), pp. 107–26.

Feit, Harvey. 'Governmental Rationalities and Indigenous Co-Governance: James Bay Cree Co-Existence, from Mercantilist Partnerships to Neoliberal Mechanisms'. In *Unsettled Legitimacy: Political Community, Power, and Authority in a Global Era*, edited by Steven Berstein and William D. Coleman (Vancouver: UBC Press, 2010), pp. 97–128.

Feit, Harvey A. 'Neoliberal Governance and James Bay Cree Governance'. In *Indigenous Peoples and Autonomy, Insights for a Global Age*, edited by Mario Blaser, Ravi de Costa, Deborah McGregor, and William D. Coleman (Vancouver: UCB Press, 2010), p. 60.

Finley-Brook, Mary and Karl Offen. 'Bounding the Commons: Land Demarcation in Northeastern Nicaragua'. *Bulletin of Latin American Research*, vol. 28, no. 3 (2009): p. 345.

Fleischhauer, Ingeborg. 'The Nationalities Policy of the Tsars Reconsidered—The Case of the Russian Germans'. *The Journal of Modern History*, vol. 53, no. 1 (1981): pp. D1065–D1090.

Fomichenko, Michael. 'Natsional'no-kul'turnaia avtonomiia kak forma samoopredeleniia narodov v Rossii' [National-Cultural Autonomy as a Form of Self-Determination of Peoples in Russia]. *Natsional'nye interesy*, vol. 8, no. 3 (2005): pp. 35–41.

Friend, Celeste. 'Social Contract Theory'. *Internet Encyclopaedia of Philosophy*, 2004, accessed 2 February 2015, http://www.iep.utm.edu/soc-cont/.

Fukuyama, Francis. 'The End of History?'. *The National Interest*, no. 16 (1989): pp. 3–18.

Gates, Scott and Kaare Strøm. 'Power-Sharing, Agency and Civil Conflict—Power-Sharing Agreements, Negotiations and Peace Processes'. *CSCW Policy Brief*, no. 1 (2007): pp. 1–15.

Gellner, David N. 'Caste, Ethnicity and Inequality in Nepal'. *Economic and Political Weekly*, vol. XLII, no. 20 (2007): pp. 1823–8.

Ghai, Yash. 'Ethnic Identity, Participation and Social Justice: A Constitution for New Nepal?'. *International Journal on Minority and Group Rights*, vol. 18, no. 3 (2011), pp. 309–34.

Ghai, Yash. 'Autonomy as a Participatory Right in the Modern Democratic State. Public Participation, Autonomy and Minorities'. In *Political Autonomy and Divided Societies: Imagining Democratic Alternatives in Complex Settings?*, edited by Zelim A. Skubarty (Leiden/Boston: Martinus Nijhoff Publishers, 2005), pp. 3–45.

Ghai, Yash. 'Ethnicity and Autonomy: A Framework for Analysis'. In *Autonomy and Ethnicity: Negotiating Competing Claims in Multi-Ethnic States*, edited by Yash Ghai (Cambridge/New York: Cambridge University Press, 2000), p. 8.

Ghai, Yash. 'Introduction: Nature and Origins of Autonomy'. In *Practising Self-Government: A Comparative Study of Autonomous Regions*, edited by Yash Ghai and Sophia Woodman (Cambridge: Cambridge University Press, 2013), pp. 9–10

Ghai, Yash and Jill Cotterell. 'Federalism and Political Inclusion: Choices for Nepal'. In *Varieties of Federal Governance: Major Contemporary Models*, edited by Rekha Saxena (New Dehli: Foundation Books/Cambridge University Press, 2011), pp. 282–312.

Ghai, Yash and Sophia Woodman. 'Unused Powers: Autonomy Legislation in the PRC'. *Pacific Affairs*, no. 2 (2009): pp. 29–46.

Giuliano, Elise and Dmitry Gorenburg. 'The Unexpectedly Underwhelming Role of Ethnicity in Russian Politics, 1991–2011'. *Demokratizatsiya. The Journal of Post-Soviet Democratization*, vol. 20 (2012): pp. 175–88.

Grigsby, William. 'Caribbean Coast: Multilingual, Multicultural and...Finally Autonomous?'. *Envio*, no. 266 (2003).

Guglielmetti, Chiara and Sonja Avlijaš. 'Regionalization and Regional Development in Serbia'. In *Regional Dynamics in Central and Eastern Europe: New Approaches to Decentralization*, edited by Francesco Palermo and Sara Parolari (Leiden: Martinus Nijhoff Publishers, 2013), p. 204.

Guruswamy, Menaka. 'Integration of the Army and New Constitutionalism in Nepal'. *Economic and Political Weekly*, vol. XLV, no. 9 (2010): pp. 28–31.

Gustafson, Bret. 'Manipulating Cartographies: Plurinationalism, Autonomy, and Indigenous Resurgence in Bolivia'. *Anthropological Quarterly*, vol. 82 (2009): pp. 985–1016.

Habermas, Jürgen. 'Legitimationsprobleme im modernen Staat'. In *Legitimationsprobleme politischer Systeme*, edited by Peter Graf Kielmansegg (Opladen: Verlag für Sozialwissenschaften, 1976), pp. 39–42.

Hanf, Theodor. 'Konfliktminderung durch Kulturautonomie. Karl Renners Beitrag zur Frage der Konfliktregelung in multi-ethnischen Staaten' [Conflict Mitigation through Cultural Autonomy. Karl Renner's Contribution to the Question of Conflict Management in Multi-Ethnic States]. In *Staat und Nation in multi-ethnischen Gesellschaften*, edited by Erich Fröschl, Maria Mesner, and Uri Ra'anan (Vienna: Passagen Verlag, 1991), pp. 61–90.

Harris, Gerard Leslie. 'A Revolution in Tudor History?: Medieval Government and Statecraft'. *Past and Present*, vol. 25, no. 1 (1963): pp. 9–20.

Hassan, Sajjad M. 'Understanding the Breakdown in Northeast India: Explorations in State–Society Relations'. *Working Paper*, no. 07–83 (2007).

Hechter, Michael and William Brustein. 'Regional Modes of Production and Patterns of State Formation in Western Europe'. *American Journal of Sociology*, vol. 85, no. 5 (1980): pp. 1061–94.

Heinrich, Mario. 'Regionale Selbstverwaltung, Chancen und Probleme: Bemühungen des Europarats um eine Europäische Charta der regionalen Demokratie' [Local Self-Government, Opportunities and Problems: Europe's Efforts to Establish a European Charter of Regional Democracy]. In *Volksgruppen und regionale Selbstverwaltung in Europa*, edited by Anna Gamper and Christoph Pan (Vienna/Baden-Baden: facultas. wuv and Nomos, 2008), p. 69.

Heintze, Hans Joachim. 'On the Legal Understanding of Autonomy'. In *Autonomy: Applications and Implications*, edited by Markku Suksi (The Hague/Boston: Kluwer Law International, 1998), pp. 7–32.

Henrard, Kristin. 'Minorities and Socio-Economic Participation: The Two Pillars of Minority Protection Revisited'. *International Journal on Minority and Group Rights*, vol. 16, no. 4 (2009): pp. 549–76.

Henrard, Kristin. '"Participation", "Representation" and "Autonomy" in the Lund Recommendations and their Reflections in the Supervision of the FCNM and Several Human Rights Conventions'. *International Journal on Minority and Group Rights*, vol. 12 (2005): p. 141.

Hernández-Díaz, Jorge. 'The Construction of Post-Liberal Citizenships: Claims of Municipal Autonomy and Indigenous Demands in Mexico'. *Latin American Research Review*, vol. 45 (2010): p. 138.

Hiden, John and David Smith. 'Looking beyond the Nation State: A Baltic Vision for National Minorities between the Wars'. *Journal of Contemporary History*, vol. 41 (2006): pp. 387–99.

Hiskey, Jonathan T. and Gary L. Goodman. 'The Participation Paradox of Indigenous Autonomy in Mexico'. *Latin American Politics and Society*, vol. 53, no 2 (2011): p. 62.

Hobsbawm, Eric. 'Mass-Producing Traditions: Europe, 1870–1914'. In *Inventing Traditions*, edited by Eric Hobsbawm and Terence Ranger (Cambridge: Cambridge University Press, 1983), pp. 263–307.

Hooker, Juliet. 'Beloved Enemies': Race and Official Mestizo Nationalism in Nicaragua'. *Latin American Research Review*, vol. 40, no. 3 (2005): pp. 38–9.

Idiaquez, M. M. 'Ethnic Communities of the Pacific and North-Central Nicaragua'. *Envio*, no. 136 (1992), accessed 5 March 2015, http://www.envio.org.ni/articulo/2557.

Inalcik, Halil. 'Centralisation and Decentralisation in Ottoman Administration'. In *Studies in Eighteenth Century Islamic History*, edited by Thomas Naff and Roger Owen (Carbondale/Edwardsville: Southern Illinois University Press, 1977), pp. 27–52.

Isa, Gomez F. 'Cultural Diversity, Legal Pluralism, and Human Rights from an Indigenous Perspective: The Approach by the Colombian Constitutional Court and the Inter-American Court of Human Rights'. *Human Rights Quarterly*, vol. 36, no. 4 (2014): p. 738.

Jacobs, Dirk and Marc Swyngedouw. 'Territorial and Non-Territorial Federalism in Belgium: Reform of the Brussels Capital Region, 2001'. *Regional and Federal Studies*, vol. 13, no. 2 (2003): pp. 127–30.

Jackson-Preece, Jennifer. 'Minority Rights Enforcement in Europe: A Difficult Balancing Act'. *International Journal of Peace Studies*, vol. 3, no. 2 (1998): pp. 35–55.

Kaikobad, Kaiyan Homi. 'Some Observations on the Doctrine of Continuity and Finality of Boundaries'. *British Yearbook of International Law*, vol. 49 (1983): pp. 119–27.

Kann, Robert A. 'Karl Renner (December 14, 1870–December 31, 1950)'. *Journal of Modern History*, vol. 23, no. 3 (1951): p. 244.

Kaufman, Eric. 'Dominant Ethnicity and Dominant Nationhood. Empirical and Normative Aspects'. In *Dominant Nationalism, Dominant Ethnicity. Identity, Federalism and Democracy*, edited by Andre Lecours and Geneviève Nootens (Brussels: PIE/Peter Lang, 2009), pp. 35–56.

Keating, Michael. 'Rival Nationalisms in a Plurinational State. Spain, Catalonia, and the Basque Country'. In *Constitutional Design for Divided Societies. Integration or Accommodation?*, edited by Sujit Choudhry (Oxford: Oxford University Press, 2008), p. 317.

Keating, Michael. 'Europe, the State and the Nation'. In *European Integration and the Nationalities Question*, edited by John McGarry and Michael Keating (London: Routledge, 2006), pp. 23–34.

Keating, Michael. 'Territory, State and Nation in the European Union. How Relevant is Renner?'. In *National Cultural Autonomy and its Contemporary Critics*, edited by Ephraim Nimni (London: Routledge, 2005), pp. 181–90.

Keating, Michael. 'Plurinational Democracy in a Post-Sovereign Order'. *Queen's Papers on Europeanisation*, no. 1 (2002): p. 1.

Keating, Michael. 'So Many Nations, So Few States: Territory and Nationalism in the Global Era'. In *Multinational Democracies*, edited by Alain-G. Gagnon and James Tully (Cambridge: Cambridge University Press, 2001), pp. 30–64.

Keating, Michael. 'Regional Autonomy in the Changing State Order: A Framework of Analysis'. *Regional Politics and Policy*, vol. 2, no. 3 (1992): pp. 45–61.

Keerawella, Gamini and Rohan Samarajiva. 'Sri Lanka in 1994: A Mandate for Peace'. *Asian Survey*, vol. 35, no. 2 (1995): p. 156.

Kelleher, Shane. 'Minority Veto Rights in Power Sharing Systems: Lessons from Macedonia, Northern Ireland and Belgium'. *Adalah's Newsletter*, May 2005.

Kettley, Carmen, James Sullivan, and Jessie Fyfe. 'Self-Determination Disputes and Complex Power Sharing Arrangements: A Background Paper for Debate'. *Cambridge Centre of International Studies Working Paper* (2001), pp. 4–5.

Keyder, Cağlar. 'The Ottoman Empire'. In *After Empire: Multiethnic Societies and Nation-Building. The Soviet Union and Russian, Ottoman and Habsburg Empires*, edited by Karen Barkey and Mark von Hagen (Boulder, Colorado: Westview, 1997), pp. 30–44.

Khanal, Khrisna. 'Federalizing the Nepali State: Challenges and Opportunities'. In *South Asia: Envisioning a Regional Future*, edited by Smruti P. Pattanaik (New Delhi: Pentagon Security International, 2011), p. 141.

Khazanov, Anatoly M. 'Ethnic Nationalism in the Russian Federation'. *Daedelus* no. 1 (1997): p. 126.

Korhecz, Tamás. 'Non-Territorial Autonomy in Practice: The Hungarian National Council in Serbia'. In *Autonomies in Europe: Solutions and Challenges*, edited by Zoltán Kantór (Budapest: L'Harmattan, 2014), pp. 151–63.

Kössler, Karl. 'Beyond Majoritarian Autonomy? Legislative and Executive Power-Sharing in European Regions'. In *Law, Territory and Conflict Resolution*, edited by Francesco Palermo, Enrico Milano, and Matteo Nicolini (Leiden/Boston: Martinus Nijhoff Publishers, forthcoming).

Kössler, Karl. 'Constitutions and Secession: From "Perpetual Union" to a Right to Separate?'. In *Qualified Autonomy versus Secession*, edited by Annegret Eppler, Charlie Jeffery, and Stefan August Lütgenau (Innsbruck: StudienVerlag, forthcoming).

Kovats, Martin. 'The Political Significance of the First National Gypsy Minority Self Government in Hungary'. *Contemporary Politics*, vol. 6 (2000): pp. 247–62.

Kovats, Martin. 'The Good, the Bad and the Ugly: Three Faces of "Dialogue"—the Development of Roma Politics in Hungary'. *Contemporary Politics*, vol. 3 (1997): pp. 55–71.

Krasner, Stephen D. 'Rethinking the Sovereign State Model'. *Review of International Studies*, vol. 27 (1996): p. 17.

Krizsán, Andrea. 'The Hungarian Minority Protection System: A Flexible Approach to the Adjudication of Ethnic Claims'. *Journal of Ethnic and Migration Studies*, vol. 26 (2000): pp. 247–62.

Kumar, Krishan. 'Nation-States as Empires, Empires as Nation-States: Two Principles, One Practice?'. *Theory and Society*, vol. 39 (2010): pp. 119–43.

Kumar, Satish. 'Problems of Federal Politics in Pakistan'. In *Society and Politics in Pakistan*, edited by Pandav Nayak (New Delhi: South Asian Publisher, 1984), pp. 22–30.

Kymlicka, Will. 'The Rise and Fall of Multiculturalism?: New Debates on Inclusion and Accommodation in Diverse Societies'. In *The Multiculturalism Backlash*, edited by Steven Vertovec and Susanne Wessendorf (London/New York: Routledge, 2010), pp. 97–112.

Kymlicka, Will. 'National Cultural Autonomy and International Minority Rights Norms'. In *Cultural Autonomy in Contemporary Europe*, edited by David J. Smith and K. Cordell (London: Routledge, 2008), pp. 43–57.

Kymlicka, Will. 'National Cultural Autonomy and International Minority Rights Norms'. *Ethnopolitics*, vol. 6, no. 3 (2007): pp. 379–93.

Kymlicka, Will. 'The Evolving Basis of European Norms of Minority Rights: Rights to Culture, Participation and Autonomy'. In *European Integration and the Nationalities*

Question, edited by John McGarry and Michael Keating (London: Routledge, 2006), pp. 35–63.

Kymlicka, Will. 'Renner and the Accommodation of Sub-State Nationalisms'. In *National Cultural Autonomy and its Contemporary Critics*, edited by Ephraim Nimni (London: Routledge, 2005), pp. 137–49.

Kymlicka, Will. 'Western Political Theory and Ethnic Relations in Eastern Europe'. In *Can Liberal Pluralism be Exported? Western Political Theory and Ethnic Relations in Eastern Europe*, edited by Will Kymlicka and Magda Opalski (Oxford: Oxford University Press, 2001), pp. 13–106.

Kymlicka, Will. 'Nation-Building and Minority Rights: Comparing West and East'. *Journal of Ethnic and Migration Studies*, vol. 26 (2000): pp. 183–212.

Kymlicka, Will. 'Two Models of Pluralism and Tolerance'. *Analyse & Kritik*, vol. 14 (1992): pp. 33–56.

Kymlicka, Will and Christine Straehle. 'Cosmopolitanism, Nation-States, and Minority Nationalism: A Critical Review of Recent Literature'. *European Journal of Philosophy*, vol. 7, no. 1 (1999): pp. 65–88.

Lacina, Bethany. 'The Problem of Political Stability in Northeast India: Local Ethnic Autocracy and the Rule of Law'. *Asian Survey* XLIX (2009): pp. 998–1020.

Lagerspetz, Mikko. 'Cultural Autonomy of National Minorities in Estonia: The Erosion of a Promise'. *Journal of Baltic Studies*, vol. 45, no. 4 (2014): pp. 457–75.

Lagerspetz, Mikko, and Voigt, Henri. 'Estonia'. In *Handbook of Political Change in Eastern Europe*, edited by Sten Berglund et al. (Cheltenham, UK/Northampton, MA: Edward Elgar, 2013), pp. 51–84.

Lary, Diana. 'Orientalism and Occidentalism'. *Journal of the Canadian Historical Association*, vol. 17, no. 2 (2006): pp. 3–15.

Lecours, Andre and Geneviève Nootens. 'Understanding Majority Nationalism'. In *Contemporary Majority Nationalism,* edited by Alain-G. Gagnon, Andre Lecours, and Geneviève Nootens (Montreal/Kingston: McGill-Queen's University Press, 2011), pp. 3–18.

Legare, Andre and Markku Suksi. 'Rethinking the Forms of Autonomy at the Dawn of the 21st Century'. *International Journal on Minority and Group Rights*, vol. 15, nos 2–3 (2008): pp. 143–55.

Lell, Helga Maria. 'The Concept of Citizenship: Multicultural Challenges and Latin American Constitutional Democracy'. *Birkbeck Law Review*, vol. 87, no. 2 (2004): p. 110.

Lenin, V. I. 'Centralisation and Autonomy', accessed 28 March 2011, http://www.marxists.org/archive/lenin/works/1913/crnq/6.htm#v20pp72-045.

Lenin, V. I. 'On the Establishment of the U.S.S.R.', accessed 28 March 2011, http://www.marxists.org/archive/lenin/works/1922/sep/26.htm.

Lenin, V. I. 'Original version of the article "The Immediate Tasks of the Soviet Government"', accessed 11 November 2014, https://www.marxists.org/archive/lenin/works/1918/mar/23b.htm.

Lenin, V. I. '"Our Foreign and Domestic Position and Party Tasks", Speech Delivered To The Moscow Gubernia Conference Of The R.C.P.(B.)', accessed 11 November 2014, https://www.marxists.org/archive/lenin/works/1920/nov/21.htm.

Lenin, V. I. 'Peace Without Annexations and the Independence of Poland as Slogans of the Day in Russia', *Sotsial-Demokrat*, no. 51 (1916), accessed 11 November 2014, https://www.marxists.org/archive/lenin/works/1916/feb/29.htm.

Lenin, V. I. 'Resolution on the National Question', *Collected Works* (Moscow: Progress Publishers, 1917, 1964), pp. 302–3, Supplement to *Soldatskaya Pravda*, no. 13 (1917): p. 302.
Lenin, V. I. 'The Discussion on Self-Determination Summed Up', accessed 28 March 2011, http://www.marxists.org/archive/lenin/works/1916/jul/x01.htm.
Lenin, V. I. 'The Tasks of the Revolution'. *Rabochy Put*, nos 20 and 21 (1917), accessed 3 June 2014, http://www.marxists.org/archive/lenin/works/1917/oct/09.htm.
Lenin, V. I. 'The Question of Nationalities or "Autonomisation"', accessed 28 March 2011, http://www.marxists.org/archive/lenin/works/1922/dec/testamnt/autonomy.htm.
Lijphart, Arend. 'Self-Determination versus Pre-Determination of Ethnic Minorities'. In *Power-Sharing Systems*, edited by Will Kymlicka (Oxford: Oxford University Press, 1995), p. 275.
Linz, Juan and Alfred Stepan. 'Toward Consolidated Democracies'. *Journal of Democracy*, vol. 7, no. 2 (1996): pp. 14–33.
Lipset, Seymour Martin. 'The Revolt against Modernity'. In *Mobilization, Center-Periphery Structures and National Building*, edited by Per Torsvik (Bergen: Universitets Forlaget, 1981), p. 451.
Lupea, Ioana. 'Acceptance or Lack of Tolerance towards Minorities in Romanian Public Administration'. *Accept Pluralism Policy Brief Issue*, no. 14 (2012), accessed 28 November 2012, http://cadmus.eui.eu/bitstream/handle/1814/24379/ACCEPT_PLURALISM_PB_2012_14_Romania.pdf?sequence=1.
Mahajan, Gurpreet. 'Federal Accommodation and Ethnocultural Identities in India'. In *Federalism in Asia*, edited by Baogang He, Brian Gallidan, and Takashi Inoguchi (Cheltenham: Edward Elgar, 2007), pp. 82–100.
Malik, Maleiha. 'Minorities and Law: Past and Present'. *Current Legal Problems*, vol. 67, no. 1 (2014): pp. 67–98.
Malloy, Tove H. 'The Lund Recommendations and Non-Territorial Arrangements: Progressive De-Territorialization of Minority Politics'. *International Journal on Minority and Group Rights*, vol. 16, no. 4 (2009): pp. 665–79.
Malloy, Tove H. 'Social Cohesion Estonian Style: Minority Integration through Constitutionalized Hegemony and Fictive Pluralism'. In *Minority Integration in Central Eastern Europe. Between Ethnic Diversity and Equality*, edited by Timofey Agarin and Malte Brosig (Amsterdam/New York: Rodopi, 2009), p. 245.
Malloy, Tove H. 'Towards a New Paradigm of Minority Law-Making: A Rejoinder to Palermo and Woelk's Law of Diversity'. In *European Yearbook of Minority Issues*, vol. 4 (Leiden/Boston: Martinus Nijhoff Publishers, 2006), pp. 5–27.
Mancini, Susannna. 'Rethinking the Boundaries of Democratic Secession: Liberalism, Nationalism and the Right of Minorities to Self-Determination'. *International Journal of Constitutional Law*, vol. 6, nos. 3–4 (2008): pp. 553–84.
Marasinghe, M. L. 'Ethnic Politics and Constitutional Reform: The Indo-Sri Lanka Accord'. *International and Comparative Law Quarterly*, vol. 37 (1988): pp. 551–87.
Marin, X. Arbos. 'The Federal Option and Constitutional Management of Diversity in Spain'. In *The Ways of Federalism in Western Countries and the Horizons of Territorial Autonomy in Spain*, edited by Alberto López-Basaguren and Leire Escajedo San Epifanio (Berlin: Springer, 2014), pp. 375–99.
Marko, Joseph. 'Five Years After: Continuing Reflections on the Thematic Commentary on Effective Participation. The Interplay between Equality and Participation'. In *Minorities, their Rights, and the Monitoring of the European Framework Convention for the Protection of National Minorities: Essays in Honour of Rainer Hofmann*, edited

by Tove H. Malloy and Ugo Caruso (Leiden/Boston: Martinus Nijhoff Publishers, 2013), p. 98.

Marko, Joseph. 'Effective Participation of National Minorities in Public Affairs in Light of National Case Law'. *International Journal on Minority and Group Rights*, vol.16, no. 4 (2009): pp. 621–42.

Marko, Joseph. 'The Referendum on Decentralization in Macedonia in 2004: A Litmus Test for Macedonia's Interethnic Relations'. In *European Yearbook for Minority Issues* (Leiden/Boston: Martinus Nijhoff Publishers, 2004/2005), pp. 695–721.

Marko, Joseph. 'The Referendum on Decentralization in Macedonia in 2004: A Litmus Test for Macedonia's Interethnic Relations'. *European Yearbook of Minority*, vol. 4, no. 2 (2004): pp. 695–721.

Matin, Nilufar, Mohammad S. Islam, Musingo T. E. Mbuvi, Bernard O. Odit, Paul O. Ongugo, and Mohammad A. Syed. 'Group Inequality and Environmental Sustainability: Insights from Bangladesh and Kenyan Forest Commons'. *Sustainability*, vol. 6, no. 3 (2014): pp. 1462–88.

McGarry, John, Michael Keating, and Margaret Moore. 'Introduction: European Integration and the Nationalities Question'. In *European Integration and the Nationalities Question*, edited by John McGarry and Michael Keating (London/ New York: Routledge, 2006), pp. 1–20.

McGarry, John and Margaret Moore. 'Karl Renner, Power Sharing and Non-Territorial Autonomy'. In *National Cultural Autonomy and its Contemporary Critics*, edited by Ephraim Nimni (London/New York: Routledge, 2005), pp. 74–94.

McGarry, John and Brendan O'Leary. 'Must Pluri-national Federations Fail?'. *Ethnopolitics*, vol. 8 (March 2009): pp. 5–25.

McGarry, John and Brendan O'Leary. 'Consociation and its Critics: Northern Ireland after the Belfast Agreement'. In *Constitutional Design for Divided Societies: Integration or Accommodation?*, edited by Sujit Choudhry (Oxford: Oxford University Press, 2008), p. 399.

McGarry, John and Brendan O'Leary. 'Federation and Managing Nations'. In *Multinational Federations*, edited by Michael Burgess and John Pinder (London/ New York: Routledge, 2007), pp. 189–91.

McGarry, John and Brendan O'Leary. 'Consociational Theory, Northern Ireland's Conflict, and its Agreement: What Critics of Consociation Can Learn from Northern Ireland'. *Government and Opposition*, vol. 41 (2006): pp. 249–77.

McGarry, John and Brendan O'Leary. 'Federation as a Method of Ethnic Conflict Regulation'. In *From Power Sharing to Democracy Post-Conflict Institutions in Ethnically Divided Societies*, edited by Sid Noel (Montreal/Kingston: McGill-Queen's University Press, 2005), pp. 263–96.

McGarry, John and Brendan O'Leary. 'Introduction: The Macro-Political Regulation of Ethnic Conflict'. In *The Politics of Ethnic Conflict Regulation: Case Studies of Protracted Ethnic Conflicts*, edited by John McGarry and Brendan O'Leary (London/ New York: Routledge, 1993), pp. 1–47.

McGoldrick, Dominic. 'Canadian Indians, Cultural Rights and the Human Rights Committee'. *The International and Comparative Law Quarterly*, vol. 40, no. 3 (1991): pp. 658–69.

Meringer, Eric Rodrigo. 'Accommodating Mestizaje on Nicaragua's Rio Coco, Miskitu Activism before the Sandinista's Revolution'. *AlterNative: An International Journal of Indigenous Peoples*, vol. 10, no. 3 (2014): p. 204.

Middleton, Townsend and Sara Shneiderman. 'Reservations, Federalism and the Politics of Recognition in Nepal'. *Economic and Political Weekly*, vol. XLIII, no. 19 (2008): pp. 39–45.

Mill, John Stuart. 'Considerations of Representative Government'. In *Utilitarism, on Liberty and Considerations on Representative Government*, edited by H. B. Acton (London: J. M. Dent & Sons, 1862/1976), pp. 187–428.

Miller, David. 'Nationality in Divided Societies'. In *Multinational Democracies*, edited by Alain-G. Gagnon and James Tully (Cambridge/New York: Cambridge University Press, 2001), p. 314.

Mongia, Radhika. 'Historicizing State Sovereignty: Inequality and the Form of Equivalence'. *Comparative Studies in Society and History*, vol. 49, no. 2 (2007): pp. 384–411.

Mukherjee, Bumba. 'Why Political Power-Sharing Agreements Lead to Enduring Peaceful Resolution of Some Civil Wars, but not Others?'. *International Studies Quarterly*, no. 50 (2006): pp. 479–504.

Müller, Jan-Werner and Kim Lane Scheppele. 'Constitutional Patriotism: An Introduction'. *International Journal of Constitutional Law*, vol. 6, no. 1 (2007), pp. 67–71.

Musaev, Vadim. 'Kul'turnaya avtonomiya kak sredstvo razresheniya natsional'nyh problem: istoriya i perspektivy' [Cultural Autonomy as a Means of Resolving National Problems: History and Prospects]. In *Perekrestok kul'tur: mezhdisciplinarnye issledovaniya v oblasti gumanitarnyh nauk* (Moscow: Logos, 2004), pp. 83–107.

Myntti, Kristian. 'The Sami Cultural Autonomies in the Nordic Countries'. In *Minority Governance in Europe*, edited by Kinga Gál (Budapest: Local Government and Public Service Reform Initiative of the Open Society Institute, 2002), pp. 153–70.

Neumann, Franz L. 'Federalism and Freedom: A Critique'. In *Federalism: Mature and Emergent*, edited by Arthur W. Macmahon (Garden City: Doubleday, 1955), pp. 44–57.

Nicolaïdis, Kalypso. 'European Demoicracy and its Crisis'. *Journal of Common Market Studies*, vol. 51, no. 2 (2013): pp. 351–69.

Niemiec, Christopher P. and Richard M. Ryan. 'Autonomy, Competence, and Relatedness in the Classroom. Applying Self-Determination Theory to Educational Practice'. *Theory and Research in Education*, vol. 7, no. 2 (2009): pp. 133–44.

Nimni, Ephraim. 'Democratic Theory and the Autonomy of Non-Christian Religious Courts in the UK'. In *New Multicultural Identities in Europe*, edited by Erkan Toğuşlu, Johan Leman, and İsmail Sezgin (Leuven: University of Leuven Press, 2014), pp. 195–211.

Nimni, Ephraim. 'Cultural Minority Self-Governance'. In *Political Participation of Minorities: A Commentary on International Standards and Practice*, edited by Marc Weller and Katherine Nobbs (New York: Oxford University Press, 2010). pp. 634–60.

Nimni, Ephraim. 'Nationalism, Ethnicity and Self-Determination: A Paradigm Shift?'. *Studies in Ethnicity and Nationalism*, vol. 9, no. 2 (2009): pp. 319–32.

Nimni, Ephraim. 'Nationalist Multiculturalism in Late Imperial Austria as a Critique of Contemporary Liberalism: The Case of Bauer and Renner'. *Journal of Political Ideologies*, vol. 4, no. 3 (1999): pp. 289–314.

Noorani, A. G. 'The Challenge of Power-Sharing in Sri Lanka'. *Economic and Political Weekly*, vol. XXX, no. 12 (1995): pp. 622–5.

Nordquist, Kjell-Åke. 'Autonomy as a Conflict-Solving Mechanism: An Overview'. In *Autonomy: Applications and Implications*, edited by Markku Suksi (The Hague: Kluwer Law International, 1998), pp. 69–71.

Oberst, Robert C. 'Federalism and Ethnic Conflict in Sri Lanka'. *Publius*, vol. 18 (1988): pp. 175–93.

Oberst, Robert C. 'Policies of Ethnic Preferences in Sri Lanka'. In *Ethnic Preference and Public Policy in Developing States*, edited by Neil Nevitte and Charles H. Kennedy (Boulder: Lynne Rienner, 1996), pp. 135–54.

Oeter, Stefan. 'Minderheiten im institutionellen Staatsaufbau' [Minorities in the Institutional Structure of the State]. In *Das Minderheitenrecht europäischer Staaten* [Minority Law of European States], Teil 2, edited by Jochen Abr. Frowein, Rainer Hofmann, and Stefan Oeter (Berlin: Springer, 1994), p. 494.

O'Halloran, Patrick J. 'Post-Conflict Reconstruction: Constitutional and Transitional Power-Sharing Arrangements in Bosnia and Kosovo'. In *From Power Sharing to Democracy Post-Conflict Institutions in Ethnically Divided Societies*, edited by Sid Noel (Montreal/Kingston: McGill-Queen's University Press, 2005), pp. 104–19.

O'Leary, Brendan. 'The Logics of Power-Sharing, Consociation and Pluralist Federations'. In *Settling Self-Determination Disputes: Complex Power-Sharing in Theory and Practice*, edited by Barbara Metzger, Marc Weller, and Niall Johnson (Leiden: Martinus Nijhoff Publishers, 2008), pp. 47–55.

O'Leary, Brendan. 'Debating Consociational Politics: Normative and Explanatory Arguments'. In *From Power Sharing to Democracy Post-Conflict Institutions in Ethnically Divided Societies*, edited by Sid Noel (Montreal/Kingston: McGill-Queen's University Press, 2005), pp. 3–43.

O'Leary, Brendan. 'The Limits to Coercive Consociationalism in Northern Ireland'. *Political Studies*, no. 37 (1989): pp. 562–87.

O'Leary, Brendan and John McGarry. 'Territorial Pluralism: Its Forms, Flaws and Virtues'. In *Federalism, Plurinationality and Democratic Constitutionalism: Theory and Cases*, edited by Ferran Requejo and Miquel Caminal (New York: Routledge, 2012), pp. 17–50.

Osco, Marcelo Francesco. 'Ayllu: Decolonial Critical Thinking and (AN)other Autonomy'. *Indigenous Peoples and Autonomy, Insights for a Global Age*, edited by Mario Blaser, Ravi de Costa, Deborah McGregor, and William D. Coleman (Vancouver: UCB Press, 2010), p. 30.

Osiander, Andreas. 'Sovereignty, International Relations, and the Westphalian Myth'. *International Organization*, vol. 55, no. 2 (2001): pp. 251–87.

Osipov, Alexander. 'Changing the Angle: Does the Notion of Non-Territorial Autonomy Stand on Solid Ground?'. *ECMI Issue Brief*, no. 29 (2013).

Osipov, Alexander. 'National-Cultural Autonomy in Russia: A Matter of Legal Regulation or the Symbolic Construction of an Ethnic Mosaic?'. In *Managing Ethnic Diversity in Russia*, edited by Benedikt Harzl and Oleh Protsyk (New York: Routledge, 2012), pp. 62–84.

Osipov, Alexander. 'Non-Territorial Autonomy and International Law'. *International Community Law Review* 13 (2011): pp. 393–411.

Osipov, Alexander. 'National Cultural Autonomy in Russia: A Case of Symbolic Law'. *Review of Central and East European Law*, vol. 35, no. 1 (2010): pp. 27–57.

Oversloot, Hans. 'The Homogeneity of Russia, or the Remains of an Empire (Federalism and Regionalism)'. In *Managing Ethnic Diversity in Russia*, edited by Oleh Protsyk and Benedikt Harzl (Abingdon/New York: Routledge, 2012).

Packer, John. 'Reflections on Implementation Mechanisms of Selected Autonomy, Self-Rule and Similar Arrangements'. In *Implementing Negotiated Agreements: The Real*

Challenge to Intrastate Peace, edited by Miek Boltjes (The Hague: TMC Asser Press, 2007), p. 71.

Packer, John. 'The Origin and Nature of the Lund Recommendations on the Effective Participation of National Minorities in Public Life'. *The Helsinki Monitor*, vol. 29, no. 4 (2000): pp. 41–2.

Packer, John. 'Problems in Defining Minorities'. In *Minority and Group Rights in the New Millennium*, edited by Deirdre Fottrell and Bill Bowring (The Hague: Kluwer International Law, 1999), p. 49.

Packer, John. 'On the Definition of Minorities'. In *The Protection of Ethnic and Linguistic Minorities in Europe*, edited by John Packer and Kristian Myntti (Åbo: Institute for Human Rights, 1995), pp. 23–65.

Pajvančić, Marijana. 'The Basic Principle of the Constitutional State. The Constitution of Serbia'. *Facta Universitatis. Law and Politics Series*, no. 8 (2010): pp. 43–64.

Palermo, Francesco. 'Addressing Contemporary Stalemate in the Advancement of Minority Rights: The Commentary on Language Rights of Persons Belonging to National Minorities'. In *Minorities, their Rights, and the Monitoring of the European Framework Convention for the Protection of National Minorities. Essays in Honour of Rainer Hofmann*, edited by Tove H. Malloy and Ugo Caruso (Leiden/Boston: Martinus Nijhoff Publishers, 2013), pp. 121–40.

Palermo, Francesco. 'Concluding Remarks: New Regionalism in Central, Eastern and South-Eastern Europe: Traditional Models and Beyond'. In *Regional Dynamics in Central and Eastern Europe*, edited by Francesco Palermo and Sara Parolari (Leiden/Boston: Martinus Nijhoff Publishers, 2013), pp. 241–3.

Palermo, Francesco. 'Central, Eastern and South-Eastern Europe and Territorial Autonomy: Are They Really Incompatible?'. In *Political Autonomy and Divided Societies. Comparative Territorial Politics*, edited by Alain–G. Gagnon and Michael Keating (Basingstoke: Palgrave Macmillan, 2012), p. 82.

Palermo, Francesco. 'The "New Nomos" of Cross-Border Cooperation'. In *Globalization, Technologies and Legal Revolution. The Impact of Global Changes on Territorial and Cultural Diversities, on Supranational Integration and Constitutional Theory. Liber Amicorum in Memory of Sergio Ortino*, edited by Francesco Palermo, Giovanni Poggeschi, Günther Rautz, and Jens Woelk (Baden-Baden: Nomos, 2012), pp. 71–90.

Palermo, Francesco. 'At the Heart of Participation and of its Dilemmas. Minorities in the Executive Structures'. In *Political Participation of Minorities. A Commentary on International Standards and Practice*, edited by Marc Weller (Oxford: Oxford University Press, 2010), pp. 434–52.

Palermo, Francesco. 'When the Lund Recommendations are Ignored. Effective Participation of National Minorities through Territorial Autonomy'. *International Journal on Minority and Group Rights*, vol. 16, no. 4 (2009): pp. 653–63.

Palermo, Francesco. '"Bridges" in Self-Determination Disputes? External Relations of Sub-National Entities and Minority Groups'. In *Settling Self-Determination Disputes. Complex Power-Sharing in Theory and Practice*, edited by Marc Weller and Barbara Metzger (Leiden/Boston: Martinus Nijhoff Publishers, 2008), pp. 667–88.

Palermo, Francesco. 'Linguistic Diversity within the Integrated Constitutional Space'. *European Diversity and Autonomy Papers*, no. 2 (2006), accessed February 2015, http://www.eurac.edu/documents/edap/2006_edap02.pdf.

Palermo, Francesco. 'The Use of Minority Languages: Recent Developments in EC Law and Judgments of the ECJ'. In *Maastricht Journal of European and Comparative Law*, vol. 8, no. 3 (2001): pp. 299–318.

Palermo, Francesco and Jens Woelk. 'From Minority Protection to a Law of Diversity? Reflections on the Evolution of Minority Rights'. In *European Yearbook of Minority Issues* (Leiden/Boston: Martinus Nijhoff Publishers, 2005), pp. 5–13.

Pap, András László. 'Minority Rights and Diaspora-Claims: Collision, Interdependence and Loss of Orientation'. In *Beyond Sovereignty: From Status Law to Transnational Citizenship*, edited by Osamu Ieda and Balázs Majtényi (Sapporo: Hokkaido University Slavic Research Center, 2006), pp. 243–54.

Parekh, Bhikhu. 'The Cultural Particularity of Liberal Democracy'. In *Prospects for Democracy,* edited by David Held (Cambridge: Polity Press, 1993), pp. 156–75.

Peach, Ian. 'The Power of a Single Feather: Meech Lake, Indigenous Resistance and the Evolution of Indigenous Politics in Canada'. *Review of Constitutional Studies*, vol. 16, no. 1 (2011): p. 1.

Peake, Gordon. 'Power Sharing in a Police Car: The Intractable Difficulty of Police Reform in Kosovo and Macedonia'. In *From Power Sharing to Democracy Post-Conflict Institutions in Ethnically Divided Societies*, edited by Sid Noel (Montreal/Kingston: McGill-Queen's University Press, 2005), pp. 120–214.

Pedrini, Seraina, Andre Bächtiger, and Marco R. Steenbergen. 'Deliberative Inclusion of Minorities: Patterns of Reciprocity among Linguistic Groups in Switzerland'. *European Political Science Review*, no. 5 (2013): pp. 483–512.

Pereira, Faustina. 'The Chittagong Hill Tracts Peace Accord and the Long Road to Peace: A Case Study'. In *International Law and Indigenous Peoples*, edited by Joshua Castellino and Niamh Walsh (Leiden: Martinus Nijhoff Publishers, 2005), pp. 293–302.

Perreault, Tom and Barbara Green. 'Reworking the Spaces of Indigeneity: The Bolivian Ayllu and Lowland Autonomy Movements Compared'. *Environment & Planning D: Society and Space*, vol. 31 (2013): pp. 43–60.

Pervez, A. 'Fallout of Continued Use of AFSPA', *Economic and Political Weekly*, vol. XLVI, no. 9 (2011).

Pfabigan, Alfred. 'The Political Feasibility of Austro-Marxist Proposals for the Solution of the Nationality Problem of the Danubian Monarchy'. In *State and Nation in Multi-Ethnic Societies: The Breakup of the Multinational State*, edited by Uri Ra'anan, Maria Mesner, Keith Armes, and Kate Martin (Manchester/New York: Manchester University Press, 1991), pp. 53–63.

Philpott, Daniel. 'The Religious Roots of Modern International Relations'. *World Politics*, vol. 52 (2000): pp. 211–12.

Pierré-Caps, Stéphane. 'The Principle of Personal Autonomy: A Solution for the Future?'. In *The Politics of Belonging. Nationalism, Liberalism, and Pluralism*, edited by Alain Dieckhoff (Lanham: Lexington Books, 2004), pp. 259–82.

Pierson, Paul. 'Increasing Returns, Path Dependence, and the Study of Politics'. *American Political Science Review*, vol. 94, no. 2 (2000): pp. 251–67.

Poggeschi, Giovanni. 'Federalism in Russia: Ethnic and Asymmetrical'. In *Asymmetries in Constitutional Law. Recent Developments in Federal and Regional Systems*, edited by Francesco Palermo, Carolin Zwilling, and Karl Kössler (Bolzano/Bozen: Quaderni dell'Accademia Europea di Bolzano, 2009), pp. 97–116.

Potier, Tim. 'Regionally Non-Dominant Titular Peoples: The Next Phase in Minority Rights?'. *JEMIE* Paper, no. 6 (2001): 3, accessed August 2014, http://www.ecmi.de/jemie/download/JEMIE06Potier11-07-01.pdf.

Poulter, Sebastian. 'Limits of Pluralism'. In *Discrimination: The Limits of Law*, edited by Bob Hepple and Erika M. Szyszczak (London: Mansell, 1992), pp. 183–215.

Pradhan, Rajendra and Ava Shreshta. 'Ethnic and Caste Diversity: Implications for Development'. *NMR Working Paper Series*, no. 4 (2005): pp. 1–23.

Premratane, E. 'Sri Lanka: From a Unitary to a Federal State' (Paper presented at Euro Region Summer University, Institute of Federalism, University of Fribourg, Switzerland, September 2003), p. 9.

Prina, Federica. 'Homogenisation and the "New Russian Citizen": A Road to Stability or Ethnic Tension?'. *Journal on Ethnopolitics and Minority Issues in Europe*, vol. 10, no. 1 (2011): pp. 59–93.

Quer, Giovanni M. 'De-Territorializing Minority Rights in Europe: A Look Eastward'. *Journal on Ethnopolitics and Minority Issues in Europe*, vol. 12, no. 1 (2013): pp. 76–98.

Ra'anan, Uri. 'Nation and State: Order out of Chaos'. In *State and Nation in Multi-Ethnic Societies*, edited by Uri Ra'anan, Maria Mesner, Keith Armes, and Kate Martin (Manchester/New York: Manchester University Press, 1991), pp. 3–32.

Radhuber, Isabella. 'Indigenous Struggles for a Plurinational State: An Analysis of Indigenous Rights and Competences in Bolivia'. *Journal of Latin American Geography*, vol. 11, no. 2 (2012): pp. 167–90.

Ram, Melanie. 'Romania: From Laggard to Leader?'. In *Minority Rights in Central and Eastern Europe*, edited by Bernd Rechel (London/New York: Routledge, 2009), pp. 180–94.

Ramani, Srinivasan. 'Moment for Peace and Constitution Building in Nepal'. *Economic and Political Weekly*, vol. XLVI, no. 41 (2011): pp. 22–5.

Ratner, Steven R. 'Drawing a Better Line: Uti Possidetis and the Borders of New States'. *American Journal of International Law*, vol. 90 (1996): pp. 590–624.

Rehman, Javaid. 'The Concept of Autonomy and Minority Rights in Europe'. In *Minority Rights in the 'New Europe'*, edited by Peter Cumper and Steven Wheatley (The Hague: Martinus Nijhoff Publishers, 1999), pp. 217–31.

Renan, Ernest. 'What is a Nation?'. In *Nation and Narration*, edited by Homi Bhabha (London/New York: Routledge, 1990), p. 19.

Renner, Karl. 'State and Nation'. In *National-Cultural Autonomy and its Contemporary Critics*, edited by Ephraim Nimni (London/New York: Routledge, 2005), pp. 15–47.

Requejo, Ferran. 'Value Pluralism and Multinational Federalism'. In *The Conditions of Diversity in Multinational Democracies*, edited by Alain-G. Gagnon, Montserrat Guibernau, and Francois Rocher (Montréal, Québec: The Institute for Research on Public Policy, 2004), pp. 15–40.

Requejo, Ferran. 'European Citizenship in Plurinational States: Some Limits of Traditional Democratic Theories: Rawls and Habermas'. In *European Citizenship, Multiculturalism and the State*, edited by Ulrich Preuss and Ferran Requejo (Baden-Baden: Nomos, 1998), pp. 29–49.

Reynolds, Susan. 'Empires: A Program of Comparative History'. *Historical Research*, vol. 79, no. 204 (2006): pp. 151–65.

Ripiloski, Sasho and Stevo Pendarovski. 'Macedonia and the Ohrid Framework Agreement: Framed Past, Elusive Future'. *Perceptions*, vol. 18, no. 2 (2013): pp. 135–61.

Roach, Steven. 'Minority Rights and an Emergent International Right to Autonomy: A Historical and Normative Assessment'. *International Journal on Minority and Group Rights*, vol. 11 (2004): pp. 411–32.

Romero Bonifaz, Carlos. 'Los Ejes de la Constitución Política del Estado Plurinacional de Bolivia' [The Axes of the Political Constitution of the Plurinational State of Bolivia]. In *Miradas. Nuevo Texto Constitucional*, edited by Vicepresidencia del Estado Plurinacional, Universidad Mayor de San Andrés e Instituto Internacional para la

Democracia y la Asistencia Electoral (La Paz: Instituto Internacional de Integración del Convenio Andrés Bello, 2010), pp. 19–36.

Roshwald, Aviel. 'Between Balkanisation and Banalisation: Dilemmas of Ethno-Cultural Diversity'. In *Cultural Autonomy in Contemporary Europe*, edited by David J. Smith and Karl Cordell (London: Routledge, 2008), pp. 29–42.

Roshwald, Aviel. 'Between Balkanization and Banalization: Dilemmas of Ethno-Cultural Diversity', *Ethnopolitics* vol. 6, no. 3 (2007): pp. 365–78.

Roudometof, Viktor. 'From Rum Millet to Greek Nation: Enlightenment, Secularization, and National Identity in Ottoman Balkan Society, 1453–1821'. *Journal of Modern Greek Studies*, vol. 16, no. 1 (1998): 11–48.

Ruiz, Esteban Arlucea. 'The Qualitative Development of the Spanish System of Autonomous Communities: Changes to the Statutes of Autonomy'. In *The Ways of Federalism in Western Countries and the Horizons of Territorial Autonomy in Spain*, edited by Alberto López Basaguren and Leire Escajedo San Epifanio (Berlin: Springer, 2014), pp. 575–86.

Sabaratnam, Lakshmanan. 'The Boundaries of the State and the State of Ethnic Boundaries: Sinhala–Tamil Relations in Sri Lankan History'. *Ethnic and Racial Studies*, vol. 10 (1987): pp. 291–315.

Samaraweera, Vijaya. 'The Muslim Revivalist Movement, 1880–1915'. In *Collective Identities, Nationalism and Protest in Sri Lanka*, edited by Michael Roberts (Colombo: Marga Institute, 1979), pp. 261–3.

Samoilenko, Olga. 'Formy samoopredeleniia ravnopravnykh narodov Rossiiskoi Federatsii' [Forms of Self-Determination of Russia's Equal Peoples]. *Pravo i politika*, vol. 9, no. 11 (2008): pp. 2633–8.

van de Sandt, Joris. 'Communal Resource Tenure and the Quest for Indigenous Autonomy on State Law and Ethnic Reorganisation in two Colombian *Resguardos*'. *Journal of Legal Pluralism* vol. 48 (2003): p. 125.

Satyendra, Nadesan. 'Thimpu Declaration: The Path of Reason'. *Tamil Times*, vol. 6, no. 4 (1987).

Schamiloglu, Uli. 'The Formation of a Tatar Historical Consciousness: Sihabäddin Märcani and the Image of the Golden Horde'. *Central Asian Survey*, vol. 9, no. 2 (1990): pp. 39–49.

Schilling-Vacaflor, Almut. 'Bolivia's New Constitution: Towards Participatory Democracy and Political Pluralism?'. *European Review of Latin American and Caribbean Studies*, vol. 90 (2011): pp. 3–22.

Schilling-Vacaflor, Almut. 'Indigenous Identities and Politico-Juridical Demands of CSUTCB and CONAMAQ in the Constitutional Change Process of Bolivia'. *T'inkazos, La Paz*, vol. 11 (2008): pp. 23–4.

Schmitter, Philippe C. and Terry Lyn Karl. 'Conceptual Travels of Transitologists and Consolidologists: How Far to the East Should they Attempt to Go?'. *Slavic Review*, vol. 53, no. 1 (1994): pp. 173–85.

Schöpflin, George. 'Hungary and the EU'. In *Beyond Sovereignty: From Status Law to Transnational Citizenship*, edited by Osamu Ieda (Sapporo: Hokkaido University Slavic Research Center, 2006): pp. 215–24.

Schröder, Peter. 'The Constitution of the Holy Roman Empire after 1648: Samuel Pufendorf's Assessment in his Monzambano'. *The Historical Journal*, vol. 42, no. 4 (1999): pp. 961–83.

Sen, Arup K. 'Kashmir: A State of Exception'. *Economic and Political Weekly*, vol. L, no. 8 (2015).

Sériot, Patrick. 'Ethnos et demos: la construction discursive de l'identité collective' [Ethnos and Demos: the Discursive Construction of Collective Identity]. *Langage et société*, no. 9 (1997): pp. 39–51.

Shatilov, Alexei. 'Avtonomiya—poniatiye, soderzhaniye, vidy' [Autonomy—The Notion, Meaning, Types]. *Pravo i Zhizn'*, no. 38 (2001): pp. 75–84.

Shaw, M. N. 'The Heritage of States: The Principle of Uti Possidetis Juris Today'. *British Yearbook of International Law*, vol. 67 (1996): pp. 97–101.

Shaw, Stanford J. 'Ottoman Empire'. In *The Oxford Encyclopedia of the Islamic World. Vol. 4*, edited by John L. Esposito (Oxford: Oxford University Press, 2009), pp. 280–95.

Simpson, Leanne. 'Anticolonial Strategies for the Recovery and Maintenance of Indigenous Knowledge'. *American Indian Quarterly*, vol. 283, no. 4 (2004): pp. 373–84.

Skubarty, Zelim A. 'Introduction'. In *Beyond a One-Dimensional State: An Emerging Right to Autonomy?*, edited by Zelim A. Skubarty (Leiden/Boston: Martinus Nijhoff Publishers, 2005), pp. xxxi–lviii.

Smith, David J. 'Minority Territorial and Non-Territorial Autonomy in Europe: Theoretical Perspectives and Practical Challenges'. In *Autonomies in Europe: Solutions and Challenges*, edited by Zoltán Kantór (Budapest: L'Harmattan, 2014), pp. 15–23.

Smith, J. David. 'Narva Region within the Estonian Republic: from Autonomism to Accommodation?'. *Regional and Federal Studies*, vol. 12, no. 2 (2002): pp. 89–110.

Smith, David. J. 'Cultural Autonomy in Estonia. A Relevant Paradigm for the Post-Soviet Era?' ESRC, 'One Europe or Several?'. *Working Paper 19* (2001).

Soleinik, N. N. 'Pereyaslavskaya Rada 1654 goda: Sovremennoye politico-pravovoye issledovaniye' [The Pereyaslavakaya Rada of 1654: Contemporary Political and Legal Research]. *Vedomosti of Belgorod State University*, vol. 28, no. 22 (165) (2013): pp. 207–10.

Soruco Sologuren, Ximena. 'Estado plurinacional-pueblo, una construcción inédita en Bolivia' [The People's Plurinational State, an Unprecedented Construction in Bolivia]. *OSAL*, Año X, no. 26 (2009), accessed 3 June 2015, http://bibliotecavirtual.clacso.org.ar/clacso/revista/20100316123037/04sologu.pdf.

Stansiulis, Daiva. 'Relational Positionalities of Nationalisms, Racisms, and Feminisms'. In *Between Woman and Nation: Nationalisms, Transnational Feminisms, and the State*, edited by Caren Kaplan, Norma Alarcon, and Minoo Moallem (Durham NC: Duke University Press, 1999): pp. 182–213.

State, Bogdan. 'Immigrant Integration on Åland—An Exploratory Study'. *Åland Peace Institute Report*, no. 2 (2007), accessed February 2015, http://www.peace.ax/en/publications/report-series.

Stavenhagen, Rodolfo. 'Politics, Identity, and Mexico's Indigenous Rights Movement (review)'. *Human Rights Quarterly*, vol 33, no. 4 (2011): pp. 1169–76.

Stepanov, Valerii. 'Natsional'no-kul'turnaia avtonomiia v Rossii kak ideia i pravovaia norma' [National-Cultural Autonomy in Russia as an Idea and a Legal Norm]. In *Pravovye aspekty etnicheskih otnoshenii v Rossii* [Legal Aspects of Ethnic Relations in Russia] (Moscow: Delovaia Stolitsa, 2004), pp. 91–117.

Stern, Sarah A. 'The Permeable Boundaries of Ottoman Jewry'. In *Boundaries and Belonging: States and Societies in the Struggle to Shape Identities and Local Practices*, edited by Joel Migdal (Cambridge: Cambridge University Press, 2004), pp. 49–70.

Stjepanovic, Dejan. 'Regions and Territorial Autonomy in Southeastern Europe'. In *Political Autonomy and Divided Societies: Imagining Democratic Alternatives in Complex Settings*, edited by Alain-G. Gagnon and Michael Keating (London: Palgrave and Macmillan, 2012), pp. 185–99.

Stratham, Paul. 'Understanding Anti-Asylum Rhetoric: Restrictive Politics or Racist Publics?'. *The Political Quarterly*, vol. 74, Supplement s1 (2003): p. 165.

Strauss, Gerald. 'Holy Roman Empire Revisited'. *Central European History*, vol. 11, no. 3 (1978): pp. 290–301.

Stroschein, Sherill. 'Territory and the Hungarian Status Law: Time for New Assumptions?'. In *Beyond Sovereignty: From Status Law to Transnational Citizenship*, edited by Osamu Ieda (Sapporo: Hokkaido University Slavic Research Center, 2006), pp. 53–70.

Stuligross, David. 'Autonomous Councils in Northeast India: Theory and Practice'. *Alternatives*, vol. 24 (1999): pp. 497–526.

Suberu, Rotimi and Larry Diamond. 'Institutional Design, Ethnic Conflict Management, and Democracy in Nigeria'. In *The Architecture of Democracy. Constitutional Design, Conflict Management and Democracy*, edited by Andrew Reynolds (Oxford/New York: Oxford University Press: 2002), p. 406.

Suksi, Markku. 'Territorial Autonomy: The Åland Islands in Comparison with Other Sub-State Entities'. In *Autonomies in Europe: Solutions and Challenges*, edited by Zoltán Kantór (Budapest: L'Harmattan, 2014), pp. 37–58.

Suksi, Markku. 'Två språk i kommunalförvaltningen—möjligheter enligt kommunallagstiftningen' [Two Languages in Local Government—Opportunities under Municipal Legislation]. *Tidskrift, utgiven av Juridiska Föreningen i Finland*, no. 5 (2012): pp. 517–37.

Suksi, Markku. 'Functional Autonomy'. In *International Journal on Minority and Group Rights*, vol. 15 (2008): pp. 195–225.

Suksi, Markku. 'Personal Autonomy as Institutional Form—Focus on Europe Against the Background of Article 27 of the ICCPR'. *International Journal on Minority and Group Rights*, vol. 15, nos 2–3 (2008): pp. 157–78.

Suksi, Markku. 'The Constitutional Development of the Baltic Countries'. In *Human Rights in the Baltic States*, edited by Taina Dahlgren (Helsinki: The Finnish Helsinki Committee and the Ministry of Foreign Affairs, 1993), pp. 47–136.

Sunstein, Cass R. 'Constitutionalism and Secession'. *University of Chicago Law Review*, vol. 58, no. 2 (1991): p. 633.

Suny, Ronald Grigor. 'The Empire Strikes Out: Imperial Russia, "National" Identity, and Theories of Empire'. In A State of Nations: Empire and Nation-Making in the Soviet Union, 1917–1953 (Oxford: Oxford University Press, 2001), first delivered as a paper for the University of Chicago Conference, Empire and Nations: The Soviet Union and the Non-Russian Peoples, 24–6 October 1997, pp. 21–2, accessed 1 June 2014, http://www.dartmouth.edu/~crn/crn_papers/Suny4.pdf.

Swenden, Wilfried. 'Personality versus Territoriality: Belgium and the Framework Convention for the Protection of National Minorities'. In *European Yearbook for Minority Issues* (Leiden/Boston: Martinus Nijhoff Publishers, 2002/2003), pp. 331–56.

Talbot, Ian. 'The Punjabization of Pakistan: Myth or Reality'. In *Pakistan: Nationalism without a Nation*, edited by Christophe Jaffrolot (New Delhi: Manohar, 2002), pp. 54–65.

Taras, Ray. 'Conclusion: From Matrioshka Nationalism to National Interests'. In *New States, New Politics: Building the Post-Soviet Nations*, edited by Ian Bremmer and Ray Taras (Cambridge: Cambridge University Press, 1997): pp. 685–707.

Taras, Ray. 'Conclusion: Making Sense of Matrioshka Nationalism'. In *Nations and Politics in the Soviet Successor States*, edited by Ian Bremmer and Ray Taras (Cambridge: Cambridge University Press, 1993).

Tarr, G. Alan. 'Creating Federalism in Russia'. *South Texas Law Review*, no. 40 (1999): pp. 689–713.

Tas, Latif. 'The Myth of the Ottoman Millet System: Its Treatment of Kurds and a Discussion of Territorial and Non-Territorial Autonomy'. *International Journal on Minority and Group Rights*, vol. 21, no. 4 (2014): pp. 497–526.

Tawhida, Ahmed. 'A Critical Appraisal of EU Governance for the Protection of Minority Rights'. *International Journal on Minority and Group Rights*, vol. 17 (2010): p. 281.

Taylor, Charles. 'Cross-Purposes: The Liberal-Communitarian Debate'. In *Debates in Contemporary Political Philosophy*, edited by Derek Matravers and Jon Pike (London: Routledge, 2003): pp. 195–212.

Teschke, Benno. 'Theorizing the Westphalian System of States: International Relations from Absolutism to Capitalism'. *European Journal of International Relations*, vol. 8, no. 1 (2002): pp. 5–48.

Thornberry, Patrick. 'The Democratic or Internal Aspect of Self-Determination with Some Remarks on Federalism'. In *Modern Law of Self-Determination*, edited by Christian Tomuschat (Dordrecht/Boston: Martinus Nijhoff Publishers, 1993), p. 118.

Tiebout, Charles M. 'A Pure Theory of Local Expenditures'. *Journal of Political Economy*, vol. 64, no. 5 (1956): pp. 416–24.

Tierney, Stephen. 'Beyond the Ontological Question: Liberal Nationalism and the Task of Constitution-Building'. *European Law Journal*, vol. 14, no. 1 (2008): p. 136.

Tishkov, Valery. *Zabyt o natsii. Post-natsionalisticheskoye ponimaniye natsionalism* [Forget about the Nation. A Post-Nationalist Understanding of Nationalism]. *Voprosii Philosophii* (1998): pp. 3–26.

Tishkov, Valery. 'O natsii i natsionalisme' [On the Nation and Nationalism]. *Svobodnaya Mysl*, no. 3 (1996).

Tkacik, Michael. 'Characteristics of Forms of Autonomy'. *International Journal on Minority and Group Rights*, vol. 15 (2008): p. 371.

Toggenburg, Gabriel N. 'The Dark and the Bright Side of the Moon: Looking at Linguistic Diversity through the Telescope of the Common Market'. In *Globalization, Technologies and Legal Revolution. The Impact of Global Changes on Territorial and Cultural Diversities, on Supranational Integration and Constitutional Theory. Liber Amicorum in Memory of Sergio Ortino*, edited by Francesco Palermo et al. (Baden-Baden: Nomos, 2012), pp. 275–315.

Tomovska, Ivana. 'Post-Conflict Developments and Decentralization in Macedonia'. In *European Yearbook for Minority Issues* (Leiden/Boston: Martinus Nijhoff Publishers, 2008), pp. 146–7.

Toniatti, Roberto. 'Minorities and Protected Minorities: Constitutional Models Compared'. In *Citizenship and Rights in Multicultural Societies*, edited by Tiziano Bonazzi and Michael Dunne (Keele: Keele University Press, 1995), pp. 45–81.

Torode, Nicky. 'National Cultural Autonomy in the Russian Federation: Implementation and Impact'. *International Journal on Minority and Group Rights*, vol. 15, nos 2–3 (2008): pp. 179–93.

Tree, Erich Fox. 'Global Linguistics, Mayan Languages, and the Cultivation of Autonomy'. In *Indigenous Peoples and Autonomy, Insights for a Global Age*, edited by Mario Blaser, Ravi de Costa, Deborah McGregor, and William D. Coleman (Vancouver: UCB Press, 2010), p. 91.

Ulmann, Walter. 'This Realm of England is an Empire'. *Journal of Ecclesiastical History*, vol. 30 (1971): pp. 175–203.

Van Cott, Donna Lee. 'Building Inclusive Democracies: Indigenous Peoples and Ethnic Minorities in Latin America'. *Democratization*, vol. 12, no. 5 (2005): pp. 825–42.

Van Cott, Donna Lee. 'Indigenous Struggles'. *Latin American Research Review*, vol. 38, no. 2 (2003): p. 221.

Van Parijs, Philippe. 'Must Europe Be Belgian? On Democratic Citizenship in Multilingual Polities'. In *The Demands of Citizenship*, edited by Catriona McKinnon and Iain Hampsher-Monk (London/New York: Continuum, Bloomsbury Publishing, 2000), pp. 235–53.

de Varennes, Fernand. 'The Challenges of Globalization for State Sovereignty: International Law, Autonomy and Minority Rights'. *Globalization, Technologies and Legal Revolution. The Impact of Global Changes on Territorial and Cultural Diversities, on Supranational Integration and Constitutional Theory. Liber Amicorum in Memory of Sergio Ortino*, edited by Francesco Palermo et al. (Baden-Baden: Nomos, 2012), pp. 113–37.

Verkhovskiy, Alexander. 'The Ethnopolitics of the Federal Authorities and the Activisation of Russian Nationalism', accessed 2 June 2014, pp. 19–33, http://carnegieendowment.org/files/ProEtContra_62_19-33.pdf.

Visi, Balázs. 'Hungary: A Model with Lasting Problems'. In *Minority Rights in Central and Eastern Europe*, edited by Bernd Rechel (London/New York: Routledge, 2009), pp. 119–34.

Vogt, Roland. 'Belgium: A Nation State without a National Identity?'. In *European National Identities: Elements, Transitions, Conflicts*, edited by Roland Vogt, Wayne Cristaudo, and Andreas Leutzsch (New Brunswick, New Jersey: Transaction Publishers, 2014), pp. 13–29.

Volpi, Frederic. 'Language, Practice and the Possibility of a Transnational Liberal-Democratic Ethos'. *Global Society*, vol. 16, no. 1 (2002): pp. 89–101.

Walker, Neil. 'Late Sovereignty in the European Union'. In *Sovereignty in Transition*, edited by Neil Walker (Oxford: Hart, 2003), pp. 3–32.

Walsh, Niamh. 'Minority Self-Government in Hungary: Legislation and Practice'. *Journal on Ethnopolitics and Minority Issues in Europe* (2000), accessed 21 November 2013, http://www.ecmi.de/fileadmin/doc/JEMIE04Walsh30-07-01.pdf.

Watts, Ronald L. 'Multinational Federations in Comparative Perspective'. In *Multinational Federations*, edited by Michael Burgess and John Pinder (London/New York: Routledge, 2007), p. 232.

Weiler, Joseph. 'Editorial'. *European Journal of International Law*, vol. 23, no. 4 (2012): p. 911.

Weller, Marc. 'Introduction'. In *Asymmetric Autonomy and the Settlement of Ethnic Conflicts*, edited by Marc Weller and Katherine Nobbs (Philadelphia: University of Pennsylvania Press, 2010), pp. 2–7.

Wiberg, Matti. 'Political Autonomy: Ambiguities and Clarifications'. In *Autonomy: Applications and Implications*, edited by Markku Suksi (The Hague: Kluwer Law International, 1998), p. 43.

Wickramasinghe, Nira. 'Producing the Present: History as Heritage in Post-War Patriotic Sri Lanka'. *Economic and Political Weekly*, vol. XLVIII, no. 43 (2013): pp. 1–29.

Wilkinson, Steven I. 'Conditionality, Consociationalism, and the European Union'. In *From Power Sharing to Democracy Post-Conflict Institutions in Ethnically Divided Societies*, edited by Sid Noel (Montreal/Kingston: McGill-Queen's University Press, 2005), pp. 239–63.

Williams, Rowan. 'Civil and Religious Law in England: A Religious Perspective'. *Ecclesiastical Law Journal*, vol. 10 (2008): pp. 262–82.

Wimmer, Andreas and Yuval Feinstein. 'The Rise of the Nation-State across the World, 1816 to 2001'. *American Sociological Review*, vol. 75, no. 5 (2010): pp. 764–90.

Woelk, Jens. 'Bosnia-Herzegovina: Trying to Build a Federal State on Paradoxes'. In *Constitutional Dynamics in Federal Systems: Sub-National Perspectives*, edited by Michael Burgess and G. Alan Tarr (Montreal/Kingston: McGill-Queen's University Press, 2012), p. 119.

Woelk, Jens. 'Minderheitenschutz durch territoriale Autonomie: "Reservate" oder nachhaltige Intergrationsprozesse?' [Minority Protection through Territorial Autonomy: 'Reserved' or Sustainable Integration Processes?]. In *Jahrbuch des Föderalismus 2002. Föderalismus, Subsidiarität und Regionen in Europa*, edited by Europäisches Zentrum für Föderalismusforschung (Baden-Baden: Nomos, 2002), pp. 117–37.

Wolff, Jonas. 'The New Constitutions and the Transformation of Democracy in Bolivia and Ecuador'. In *New Constitutionalism in Latin America: Promises and Practices*, edited by Detlef Nolte and Almut Schilling-Vacaflor (Farnham: Ashgate, 2012), pp. 183–202.

Wolff, Stefan. 'Complex Power-Sharing and the Centrality of Territorial Self-Governance in Contemporary Conflict Settlements'. *Ethnopolitics*, vol. 8, no. 1 (March 2009): pp. 27–45.

Wolff, Stefan. 'Between Stability and Collapse: Internal and External Dynamics of Post-Agreement Institution Building in Northern Ireland'. In *From Power Sharing to Democracy Post-Conflict Institutions in Ethnically Divided Societies*, edited by Sid Noel (Montreal/Kingston: McGill-Queen's University Press, 2005), pp. 44–66.

Wolff, Stefan and Marc Weller. 'Self-Determination and Autonomy: A Conceptual Introduction'. In *Autonomy, Self-Governance, and Conflict Resolution: Innovative Approaches to Institutional Design in Divided Societies*, edited by Marc Weller and Stefan Wolff (London: Routledge, 2005), pp. 1–25.

Wong, Mabel. 'Reclaiming Identity: Rethinking Non-Territorial Autonomy'. *Journal on Ethnopolitics and Minority Issues in Europe*, vol. 12, no. 1 (2013): pp. 56–75.

Woodman, Sophia and Yash Ghai. 'Comparative Perspectives on Institutional Frameworks for Autonomy'. In *Practising Self-Government: A Comparative Study of Autonomous Regions*, edited by Yash Ghai and Sophia Woodman (Cambridge: Cambridge University Press, 2013), p. 452.

Wydra, Doris. 'The Crimea Conundrum: The Tug of War between Russia and Ukraine on the Questions of Autonomy and Self-Determination'. *International Journal on Minority and Group Rights*, vol. 10, no. 2 (2004): pp. 111–30.

Xanthaki, Alexandra. 'Normative Directions'. In *Indigenous Peoples' Access to Justice*, edited by Wilthon Littlechild and Elsa Stamatopoulou (New York: Institute for the Study of Human Rights, Columbia University, 2014), pp. 21–40.

Xanthaki, Alexandra. 'Multiculturalism and International Law: Discussing Universal Standards'. *Human Rights Quarterly*, no. 1 (2010): pp. 21–48.

Yanov, Aleksandr. 'The Collapse of the Putin "Triads" ', *Novaya Gazeta*, no. 19, 20 February 2013, accessed 11 November 2014, http://www.novayagazeta.ru/comments/56546.html.

Yeğen, Mesut. 'The Kurdish Question in Turkish State Discourse'. *Journal of Contemporary History*, vol. 34 (2009): p. 557.

Young, Iris Marion. 'Hybrid Democracy: Iroquois Federalism and the Postcolonial project'. In *Political Theory and the Rights of Indigenous Peoples*, edited by Duncan Ivison, Paul Patton, and Will Sanders (Cambridge: Cambridge University Press, 2000), p. 254.

Zahar, Marie-Joëlle. 'Power Sharing in Lebanon: Foreign Protectors, Domestic Peace, and Democratic Failure'. In *Sustainable Peace: Power and Democracy after Civil Wars*, edited by Philip G. Roeder and Donald Rothchild (Ithaka: Cornell University Press, 2005), pp. 219–40.

Zhang, Yongyin. 'System, Empire and State in Chinese International Relations'. *Review of International Studies*, special issue, vol. 27 (2001): pp. 43–63.

Zorin, Vladimir Yu. 'Razmyshleniya o natsionalino-kulturnoi avtonomii' [Considerations on National-Cultural Autonomy]. *Zhisn' Natsional'nostei*, no. 3 (2010): pp. 58–64.

Zorin, Vladimir. 'Etnopoliticheskii faktor v razvitii rossiiskogo federalizma: opyt zakonotvorchestva' [Ethnopolitical Factor in the Development of Russian Federalism: the Experience of Law-Making]. *Etnopanorama*, 1, no. 2 (1999): pp. 13–18.

Zumbansen, Peer. 'Carving Out Typologies and Accounting for Differences Across Systems: Towards a Methodology of Transnational Constitutionalism'. In *The Oxford Handbook of Comparative Constitutional Law*, edited by Michael Rosenfeld and András Sajó (Oxford: Oxford University Press, 2012), p. 84.

OTHER SOURCES

Aalen, Lovise and Magnus Hatlebakk. 'Ethnic and Fiscal Federation in Nepal', 2008, accessed 17 October 2014, http://www.cmi.no/publications/publication/?3082=ethnic-and-fiscal-federalism-in-nepal.

Ali, S., K. M. Panikker, and H. N. Kunzru, *Report of the States Reorganization Committee* (New Delhi: Government of India, 1955).

Amnesty International, 'Maze of Injustice, A Summary of Amnesty International's Findings'. *Amnesty International*, accessed 5 March 2015, http://www.amnestyusa.org/our-work/issues/women-s-rights/violence-against-women/maze-of-injustice.

Amnesty International India, 'Briefing: The Armed Forces Special Powers Act: A Renewed Debate in India on Human Rights and National Security', *Amnesty International India* (2013).

Anaya, James. 'The Situation of Indigenous Peoples in the United States of America', UN Doc A/HRC/21/47/Add.1 (2012).

Asian Centre for Human Rights. '*The Maladministration of Indigenous and Tribal Peoples of India*'. ACHRF 33/2004, (4 August 2004).

Barère de Vieuzac, Bertrand. 'Rapport du Comité de salut public sur les idiomes'. *Report of the Committee of Public Health on Languages* (1794), accessed 12 December 2014, http://www.tlfq.ulaval.ca/axl/francophonie/barere-rapport.htm.

Capotorti, Francesco. 'Study on the Rights of Persons Belonging to Ethnic, Religious and Linguistic Minorities', UN Doc. E/CN.4/Sub.2/384/Rev.1.

Chakma, Suhas. 'Guns and Talks in India's Wretched of the Earth', *Kashmir Times*, Index: Review/42/2004, accessed 13 October 2004.

Choudhry, Sujit. 'Rethinking Comparative Constitutional Law: Multinational Democracies, Constitutional Amendment, and Secession', paper presented at the annual meeting of the Law and Society Association, Berlin, 25 July 2007, p. 1.

Dechênes, Jules. 'Proposal Concerning a Definition of the Term "Minority"', UN Doc. E/CN.4/Sub.2/1985/31.

'Derzhava. Dostoinstvo. Dostatok. Interv'iu s predsedatelem Komiteta Gosudarstvennoi Dumy Rossiiskoi Federatsii po delam natsional'nostei V. Iu. Zorinym' [Country. Dignity. Wealth. Interview with the Chair of the Nationalities Committee of the State

Duma of the Russian Federation V. Iu. Zorin], *Zhizn' Natsional'nostei*, no. 6 (1996), pp. 12–16.

Elections Nunavut, 'Voter Information', accessed 8 June 2015, http://www.elections.nu.ca/apps/authoring/dspPage.aspx?page=qualify.

Human Rights Watch, 'India: Getting Away with Murder: 50 Years of the Armed Forces Special Powers Act', *Human Rights Watch* (2008).

Human Rights Watch. 'Sri Lanka'. In *World Report on Human Rights 2014* (New York: Human Rights Watch, 2014), accessed 24 October 2014, http://www.hrw.org/world-report/2014/country-chapters/sri-lanka.

Magyar Nemzeti Tanács, 'Beszámoló a Magyar Nemzeti Tanács kétéves tevékenységéről 2010. június 30.–2012. Június 30' [Report on the Activities of the Hungarian National Council, 30 June 2010–June 30, 2012], *Magyar Nemzeti Tanács: Subotica* (2012): pp. 122–78.

Minster, Christopher. 'Spain's American Colonies and the Encomienda System', accessed 3 March 2015, http://latinamericanhistory.about.com/od/theconquestofperu/p/Spain-S-American-Colonies-And-The-Encomienda-System.htm.

Phanjoubam, Pradip. 'Surrogate Wars, Surrogate Governments'. *Outlook Magazine*, 27 May 2003.

Phanjoubam, Pradip. 'The Fourteen Spokes of a Revolution'. *Outlook Magazine*, 20 October 2003.

Rajapakse, Mahinda. 'Mahinda Chinthana: Victory for Sri Lanka Presidential Election', 2005, accessed 16 October 2014, http://www.president.gov.lk/pdfs/MahindaChinthanaEnglish.pdf

'Report submitted by Nepal to United Nations Human Rights Committee under Article 40 of the Covenant', UN. Doc. CCPR/C/74/Add.2 (18 May 1994) para 1.

Salinas de Dosch, Ana Lucia. 'Understanding Latin America Indigenous Movements: From Marginalisation to Self-Determination and Autonomy?'. Paper delivered in 3d International Seminar & Workshop on Latin American and Asian Studies (LASA III), Institute of Occidental Studies, Universiti Kebangsaan Malaysia, 17–18 October 2012.

Secretariat of the Convention on Biological Diversity. 'Recognising and Supporting Territories and Areas Conserved by Indigenous Peoples and Local Communities, Global Overview and National Case Studies'. *CBD Technical Series*, no. 64 (2012): p. 30, accessed 2 March 2014, http://www.cbd.int/doc/publications/cbd-ts-64-en.pdf.

Waseem, Mohammad. 'Federalism in Pakistan', 2010, p. 5, accessed 16 October 2014, http://www.forumfed.org/pubs/Waseem-Fed-Overview.pdf.

'An Empty Verdict', *Economic and Political Weekly*, vol. XLIX, no. 47, 22 November 2014.

'Education Partnership in Nova Scotia', *Aboriginal Affairs and Northern Development Canada*, 09 September 2011, accessed 5 March 2015, https://www.aadnc-aandc.gc.ca/eng/1312900494134/1312900618854.

'Nipissing First Nation Passes First Ontario Aboriginal Constitution', CBCNEWS, 21 January 2014, accessed 5 March 2015, http://www.cbc.ca/news/canada/sudbury/nipissing-first-nation-passes-first-ontario-aboriginal-constitution-1.2505488.

'The Government of Canada Recognizes the Inherent Right of Self-Government as an Existing Aboriginal Right under Section 35 of the *Constitution Act, 1982*', *Aboriginal Affairs and Northern Development Canada*, accessed 3 March 2015, http://www.aadnc-aandc.gc.ca.

Index